Y0-BRN-905

Romania and Transylvania in the 20th Century

Ildikó Lipcsey

Corvinus Publishing

Buffalo -Toronto

2006

Preliminary translation:
András Dani and
Thomas Szappanos

Final translation by
Peter Csermely

Art: Marta Buda

MAJOR   PATRONS:

George De Kova Foundation
Illyés Foundation

ISBN: 1-882785-15-0
ISBN: 1-882785-16-9 (Paper)

Library of Congress Control Number:
2005932693

Printed in the United States

Table of Contents

PREFACE   5

I. THE GREAT NATIONAL DREAM COMES TRUE   22

II. THE COMMUNIST TAKEOVER: 1945-1948   84

III. THE GHEORGHIU-DEJ ERA   118

IV. THE CEAUSESCU -ERA: 1965-1989   145

V. TRANSITION ATTEMPTS   191

VI. THE REALITIES OF ROMANIAN INTERNAL POLITICS   225

VII. ON THE WAITING LIST: 1997   237

VIII. ON THE THRESHOLD OF NEW ELECTIONS: 1999   259

APPENDIX A – THE ROMANIAN INTELLIGENCE SERVICE   278

APPENDIX B - SABIN GHERMAN ARTICLE   299

APPENDIX C – ADRIAN SEVERIN ARTICLE   304

BIOGRAPHICAL ENDNOTES   308

GEOGRAPHIC PLACE NAMES   326

BIBLIOGRAPHY   328

About the Author

Ildikó Lipcsey was born January 27th, 1945 in Óbudavár in (then) Zala County to Transylvanian parents.

1963 Senior matriculation in the Ilona Zrinyi Grammar School of Miskolc.
1970 Bachelor degree at the ELTE University (History and Romanian studies).
1972 Masters degree (Philosophy).
1989 PhD (candidate).
1970-1992 Expert on Romania in the Institute of History of the Hungarian Academy of Sciences. From 1982, Head of the Documentation and Information Section.
1992-2001 -- Member of the Bureau of National Security.
1982-1992 -- Lecturer, in Hungary and abroad, on the subject of the history of East-Central Europe in the 19th and 20th century. In charge of special historical studies at the ELTE. Lectures at other places of higher learning.
1996 -- Editor in Chief of the *Erdélyi Magyarság* monthly at the request of the Writers Association and the Foundation of Transylvanian Hungarians. Organizer of various conferences.
2002 -- President of the Transylvanian Federation.
Published about 1,500 mostly historical and ethnographical articles and essays.

List of published books

Erdélyi autonómiák. (Autonomies in Transylvania) Bp, Akad. Nyomda, 1990.
Páskándi, Géza: *Háttérvázlat* (Background scetches). Bp., Ungvár, Primor-Intermix, 1994.
A Magyar Népi Szövetség az önfeladás útján. (The Hungarian Peoples Union on the Road to Self-destruction) Bp. Possum, 1998.
Nicolae Iorga és az erdélyi magyarok. (Nicolae Iorga and the Transylvanian Hungarians) Bp. Possum, 1998.
A CASBI. A magyar vagyonok államosítása Romániában. (The Nationalisation of Hungarian assets in Romania) Possum 2002.
Magyar 56 a Kárpát-medencében. The Hungarian 56 (Revolution) in the Carpathian Basin) 1996.
Magyar-román kapcsolatok. (Hungarian-Romanian Relations) 1956-58. Bp. 2004.
Nemzedéksirató. (Lament for a generation) Bp. Kráter, 2004.
Romania and Transylvania in the 20th Century. Corvinus USA, 2006.

Preface

Background

Romania lies in the Lower Danube basin, in South-Eastern Europe. Situated between East, South and Central Europe, transitional is the most outstanding characteristic feature of the country's geography, history, economy, society, culture and civilization. Its territory covers 237,500 square kilometers with a population of 22,760,449 and a boundary of 3152.9 km. in length. The country, which can be considered the catchment basin of the Danube River, is not homogenous either from a geographic or historical point of view. It comprises several distinct areas: the Eastern Carpathians, the Southern Carpathians, the Banate Mountains, the Transylvanian Erzgebirge (Ore Mountain), the Transylvanian Basin, the Plain of the Tisza River, the Sub-Carpathians, the Romanian Plain, the Mountains of Oltenia and Géta, the Moldova Mountains and Dobrudja. Its moderate continental climate is often affected by fronts arriving from the Atlantic Ocean and the Mediterranean Sea. Oak, beech and pine forests cover its hills and mountains, and the rich flora of Alps, woods, steppes, ponds, marshlands, rivers and the sea can also be found there. The country's natural resources are extraordinarily abundant. [1]

From historical point of view, it consists of three main areas: the Eastern-European Moldova and the Southern European or Balkan Wallachia (Hung: Havasalföld) united in 1859, and Transylvania, that represented a Central European model of development, annexed in 1920. [2] Romania had laid claims to territories of each of its neighbors, namely, Hungary, the Ukraine, Russia, the Republic of Moldova, the rump Yugoslavia and Bulgaria. This claim is based on a 13th century theory, widely spread in the Roman Catholic Romanian community - its proportion was more than fifty percent of the population in the 19th century - and kept alive in the Latin-German-Hungarian cultural circles. Ideologically, it is based on the theory of Daco-Roman or Daco-Romanian Continuity. This theory gives foundation to Romanian territorial claims not only to Moldova, which was occupied by Russia and Austria, but also on Eastern Hungary and Transylvania. (Transylvania incorporates the so-called historic Erdély [Transylvania] and Bánát as well as Arad, Bihar, Szatmár and Máramaros counties.)

Regarding the geographical distribution of the Romanian community, it can best be described as quite dispersed. Data relating to it were gathered, at the end of the 19th century, from (inexact) Balkan, Russian, Austrian, Hungarian and Romanian statistical surveys. Accordingly, the number of Romanians living

---

[1] Bulla, Béla - Mendel, Tibor - Kocsis, Károly: The geography of the Carpathian Basin (A Kárpát-medence földrajza). Budapest, Lucidus Publishing, 1999.

[2] Borsi, Kálmán Béla: Together or on separate paths. The intertwined history of the Kossuth emigration and Romanian national aspirations (Együtt vagy külön utakon. A Kossuth-emigráció és a román nemzeti törekvések kapcsolatának története). Magveto Publishing, Budapest, 1984.

outside of Romania (that is, outside the Kingdom of Hungary) in the 1880's was estimated as follows:

Bukovina and Vienna	circa 200,000
Bessarabia	c. 1,000,000
Bulgaria	c. 50,000
Serbia	c. 150,000
Albania	c. 200,000
Epirus	c. 250,000
Macedonia	c. 350,000
Greece	c. 30,000

The population of Romania, including minorities:

1864	4,093,452
1878	4,485,696
1918	7,250,000

The number of Romanians living in Hungary also followed a rising trend:[3]

1900	2,798,559, 16.6% of the population
1910	2,948,186, 16.1% of the population

Ethnic changes in Transylvania

While during the 13th century, Romanian family names were found only in six out of 1,000 settlement, by the 15th century, 100,000 of Transylvania's half a million population were of Romanian origin. At the end of the 1600's, their numbers grew to almost one-third, 200,000 of the 700,000 inhabitants.[4]

In the 17th century, in the wake of wars - Hungarians and Szeklers (Székely) were subject to military service - and epidemics, Transylvania's population decreased by half. The decline affected primarily the Hungarian community, as its number diminished by 40 percent, while the Romanian community increased by 150 percent. This demographic explosion took place at the turn of the 17th and 18th centuries. The estimated number of emigrants from the Romanian Grand Duchy can be put at 350,000.[5]

This represents a several hundred percent increase. Therefore, the attractions of the more developed living conditions and more moderate seigniorial burdens, and as a result of invitation, the number of Romanian inhabitants gradually exceeded that of both the Hungarians and the Germans (Saxons and Schwabians).

---

[3] Katus, László: Hungarians and other nationalities reflected in the census. 1850-1910 (Magyarok, nemzetiségek a népszámlálás tükrében. 1850-1910). History (História). 1982, issue 4-5. pp. 18-21.

[4] History of Transylvania, vol. I (Erdély története, I. köt.). Akadémiai Publishing, Budapest, 1987. pp. 341-346.

[5] Ibid, vol. II. pp. 809, 978.

According to data developed by the academician Domokos Kosáry, the ethnic division in Transylvania in the 18th century appeared as follows:[6]

	Hungarian Szekler	Saxon	Romanian	Total
1730	195,000	110,000	420,000	725,000
1761	271,000	120,000	547,000	983,000
1794	350,000	150,000	800,000	1,300,000

Between the end of the 18th and the middle of the 19th century, the population of Transylvania increased by one third, from 1.5 to above 2 million. The estimates are supplanted by the more reliable data obtained in the population censuses of 1786, 1787 and 1850-1851.

The ethnic and national division of the Grand Duchy's population according to contemporary church statistics, estimates and the population census of 1850-1851.

	Romanian %	Hungarian %	German %	Gypsy %	Jewish %	Total population
1766*	58.9 52	27.5 41	13.6			953,886
			6.5			1,453,742
1773	63.5	24.2	12.3			1,066,017
1786	30.5	49.7	18.2	0.7	0.2	1,664,545
1794	50	33	12.5	4.3	0.1	1,458,559
1844	60.1	28.6	10	0.8	0.2	2,143,310
1850-1851	59.5	25.9	9.4	3.8	0.8	2,062,379

Denominational distribution of Transylvania's population, 1850 to 1910.[7]

Denomination	1850	1880	1900	1910
Roman Catholic	219,536	263,816	331,199	375,325
Greek Catholic	664,154	575,866	691,896	749,404
Greek Orthodox	621,852	662,936	748,928	792,864
Protestant	196,356	199,551	222,346	229,028
Unitarian	45,112	55,068	64,494	67,749
Jewish	15,606	29,993	53,065	64,074
	11,692			

---

[6] Kosáry, Domokos: The Influx of the Vlahs (Az oláhok beözönlése). Hungarian Review (Magyar Szemle), October, 1940. pp. 246-253.
[7] Transylvanian-Hungarian Yearbook, 1918-1929 (Erdélyi Magyar Évkönyv. 1918-1929). Juventus Publishing, Cluj Napoca (Kolozsvár), 1930. pp. 1-7.

| Other | 893 | 423 | 366 | 611 |

The ethnic-national distribution of historic Transylvania's population, as based on the combined population censuses of 1850/51 and 1930 (according to the pre-1848 regional division):[8]

Ethnicity	The counties and the vicinity of Fogaras		The Szekler regions		The Saxon regions	
	1850/51	1930	1850/51	1930	1850/51	1930
Romanian	781,791	1,203,046	54,246	102,167	207,810	320,650
Hungarian	159,396	319,613	303,975	440,243	25,063	68,288
German	46,166	56,887	1,163	2,399	141,425	177,738
Jewish	10,644	45,229	1,042	10,370	165	9,725
Gypsy	41,117	41,750	10,027	11,657	25,244	16,025
Other	6,935	9,638	2,464	1,724	1,544	4,492
Total	1,049,049	1,676,163	372,912	568,560	401,251	596,918

Thus, the overall totals are:

Ethnicity	Transylvania, including the Partium	
	1850-51	1930
Romanian	1,043,847	1,625,863
Hungarian	488,434	828,144
German	191,754	237,024
Jewish	11,851	65,324
Gypsy	76,383	69,432
Other	10,953	15,854
Total population	1,823,222	2,841,222

Two opposing concepts:

1. Transylvanism

Károly Kós expressed the essence of the concept in one sentence, "the Transylvania issue can and should be solved by Transylvanians and in a traditionally Transylvanian manner. In other words, the solution is autonomy."[9] The pitfall of the Transylvania issue lies in the fact that - in a country of 102,000

---

[8] The 1850 Transylvanian Census (Az 1850 évi erdélyi népszámlálás). Budapest, Central Statistical Bureau, 1989. pp. 14-16;
  Katus, László: The nationalities of Transylvania in 1910 (Erdély népei 1910-ben). History (História), 1986, issue 2. pp. 24-27.
[9] Kós, Károly - Pál, Árpád - Zágoni, István: The shouted word (Kiáltó szó). Cluj Napoca, 1920. pp. 9-13.

sq. kilometers, the population of which was 5.5 million in 1920 and today is 7.5 million (70-71 % Romanian, 22 % Hungarian and 4 % German), (1) no Romanian state existed before 1920, and (2) a Romanian majority developed gradually over the centuries (circa 1300, Romanian names were found in only 6 of the 1,000 settlements; under reign of King Matthias (the end of the 15th c.), some 100,000 out of Transylvania's half a million inhabitants were Romanians; by the end of the 17th century, over a span of 25 years, the number of Romanian citizens grew by 650%.)

The question, which concerned many people, was whether it was proper, in 1848, to restore the Union with Hungary. And the question has not been raised only by Romanians, but also by Hungarians, especially those who were born in the region. The pro-Unionists claim: Transylvania has always been a part of the Hungarian Crown. Autonomist state, however, that history and culture have followed a separate path and they emphasize the different character and soul of the Transylvanian people. In connection with this concept, we are going to present a short historical summary regarding: 1) changes to Transylvania's status; 2) definition of county, Szekler and Romanian self-government; 3) some proposals of Transylvania's autonomy.

The relationship of Hungary and Transylvania

Miklós Mester writes in his famous monograph,[10] published in 1936 – for which Iuliu Maniu signed, as Gyula (the Hungarian form of Julius) Maniu, his letter of thanks for a complimentary copy written in Hungarian – that, in the era of the voivodes, "Transylvanian administration represented a typical medieval autonomy." The Voivode of Transylvania governed the country, but his authority was limited only to the seven royal counties. His powers extended to the Szekler and Saxon municipalities only in military issues and only when required for the defense of the country.

1. In the time of the Principality, when Hungary was divided into three parts, the Hungarian kings transferred the court to Transylvania. Transylvania embodied Hungarian sovereignty and statehood. The Diet elected the Prince, who had his own army and conducted independent foreign policy; laws were enacted in Hungarian and Latin. Transylvania's independence was, however, circumscribed, as it had to pay an annual tribute of 10-40,000 gold florins to the Ottoman Empire.

2. The Diploma Leopoldium, issued in 1691, stated that Transylvania was an autonomous but non-sovereign state. As kings of Hungary, the Habsburgs held the title of Prince. Transylvania had its own Diet, and the King appointed the governor on its recommendation to head the government, but the Transylvanian Chancery was located in Vienna. The Diet's administrative independence gradually diminished: foreign policy, defense and finance, the

---

[10] Mester, Miklós: Autonomous Transylvania and Romanian national aspirations at the National Assembly of 1863-1864, Nagyszeben (Az autonóm Erdély és a román nemzeti törekvések az 1863-1864. évi nagyszebeni országgyulésen). Budapest, 1936. p. 156.

three areas embodying independence, were gradually taken away. The commander of the occupying Austrian army assumed the office of Governor, and the Diet became irrelevant.

3. The Unionist Movement can be clearly followed from 1790 onwards. Prince Ferenc Rákóczi II considered the confederation of Hungary and Transylvania almost a century earlier. In the course of the 1834-35 and 1837-38 Diets, Transylvanians took a stand for the Union because they expected the region to be included in secular and economic developments and, at the same time, render the Romanian population, in majority in Transylvania, into a minority in Hungary.

4. Transylvania's independence ended with the enactment of the Union in 1848. The tragic conflicts that followed between Hungarians and Romanians are well known. Although the treaty on national minorities, signed by Kossuth and Balcescu in July 1849, was too late, it could have served as a starting point. Both continued to work on their confederation plans - in exile - and their points of view even converged. Kossuth accepted, in the end, the idea of a personal union between Hungary and Transylvania.

5. After defeat of the 1848-49 War of Independence, Transylvania was governed directly from Vienna. As a sign of diminishing Austrian absolutism, Transylvania's "autonomy" was re-instituted by the October Diploma of 1860. The Duna Confederation plan, attributed to Kossuth, surfaced in 1862. During the 1863-64 Diet, held in Szeben (now Sibiu), Romanians of Transylvania demanded autonomy for Transylvania, but then and later, their vision of autonomy was contrary to the union of Hungary and Transylvania.

6. In the 1905 resolution of the Romanian National Party of Transylvania (Erdélyi Román Nemzeti Párt), issued in Szeben, the autonomy was replaced by the demand for establishing administrative regions along the language boundaries and acknowledging the Romanians' claim as a state-founding people. Further demands, formulated during 1910-14: Romanian language administration and judicial jurisdiction in the regions inhabited by Romanians, autonomy for their Church, 3 new episcopates, the appointment of Romanian administrative officials, Lord Lieutenants (sheriffs) and state secretaries. As well as, reallocation of parliamentary seats according to ethnic ratios, creation of 50 Romanian ridings, 3 state secondary schools (high schools).[11]

7. At the December 1, 1918 meeting of the National Assembly at Alba Iulia (Gyulafehérvár), 1,228 (sic) Transylvanian-Romanians declared the union of Transylvania and Romania, preceding the peace negotiations.[12] They referred to Wilson's doctrine of self-determination, as did the 50,000 (mostly Hungarian, some Romanians and Saxons) representatives of the opposition

---

[11] Szász, Zoltán: The Hungarian-Romanian treaty dialogues of Tisza, 1910-1914 (A Tisza-féle magyar-román paktumtárgyalások, 1910-1914). Hungarian-Romanian linguistic studies. Lóránd Eötvös University of Liberal Arts and Sciences (ELTE), Romanian Faculty. Budapest, 1984. pp. 440-455.

[12] Marea Adunare nationala. Bucuresti, Editura Academiei. 1972.

National Assembly in Cluj Napoca (Kolozsvár), but who voted, on December 22, 1918 in favor of Transylvania joining Hungary.[13] The Alba Iulia Resolution, drafted by the Transylvanian Romanians, promised full national (ethnic) freedom for the people of Transylvania, and territorial self-government until the convocation of the constituent National Assembly. What was omitted from the Resolution was that the final decision on the self-government of Transylvania would be made with the inclusion of Hungarians and Germans.

The Resolution, decreed by the Transylvanian Romanians on December 1, 1918 declared the transfer of 26 counties of Hungary to Romania. The Romanian King, in Bucharest, gave his royal assent on December 11.

A Governing Council (cabinet-council) of 12 Transylvanian Romanian politicians, headed by Maniu, was appointed to govern Eastern Hungary, i.e. Transylvania and the Partium. Bucharest, by taking control over foreign policy, defense, finance, postal service, customs and railways, limited the council's administrative power from the beginning. In reality, dual power and administration was established. After the Károlyi government demobilized the combat-ready Szekler division in Hungary, the Royal Romanian Army acted like an occupying force in Transylvania. A state of martial law was imposed, censorship was introduced, as well as a ban on public meetings, forced military recruiting, internment and corporal punishment (caning).[14]

The Governing Council's decree 1 of January 23, 1919 declared the official language to be Romanian, but it also assured the free use of other languages in all spheres of life, including place names. This was true, but only until the official list of Romanian place names could be compiled. It also promised that Hungarian institutions would remain intact. This was observed for the first few months, but shortly after, in the same year, the Hungarian University of Kolozsvár, with 50 buildings, was taken over without compensation. Many other Hungarian institutions - schools and theaters - shared the same fate.

8. From the Trianon Treaty of June 4, 1920 - with the exception of the four years following the Second Vienna Resolution (August 30, 1940) - Transylvania has been a part of Romania.

County, Szekler and Saxon autonomous administration in Transylvania

From the 13th century on, social autonomy characterized Transylvania's internal life instead of centralized power, an important factor for future events. The self-administering bodies were as follows: 1. Hungarian comitats (counties) of the nobles; 2. the Szekler seats; 3. the Saxon seats. (The institution of the mediaeval Romanian "kenézség" - the leaders of armed troops or groups - gradually modified and disappeared.) Each of the three self-governing bodies had legislative, executive and administrative rights and enjoyed autonomy in religious,

---

[13] Raffay, Erno: Transylvania in 1918-1919 (Erdély 1918-1919-ben). JATE Publishing, Szeged, 1988. pp. 158-162.

[14] Ibid, p. 199.

cultural and defense issues. The members of the three communities held collective rights and responsibilities. The communities had their own national assemblies, and their organizational structures developed along similar lines.

The institution of comitat (royal county) administration was established in the 13-14th centuries. Passing and executing local laws, judicial matter and collecting tithes fell under its jurisdiction. During the period of the Grand Duchy, the self-governing powers of the Hungarian comitats developed further in the areas of local administration (maintaining law and order, roads, constructions and control over where taxes - the thirtieth - were collected), financial administration (tax collection, coinage, control of state monopolies) and defense (mobilizing the noble and commoner militias). Laws governing local administration were in effect between 1691 and 1848. Austrian autocracy nullified them in 1849, to be re-instituted by the October Diploma. The terms of the Compromise of 1867 introduced the comitat system in Transylvania to the detriment of the counties' self-governing power.

The system of Szekler seats (*sedes* in Latin; the seats of Maros, Udvarhely, Csík, Gyergyó, Kászon, Sepsi, Kézdi, Orbai and Aranyos) was formed in the 14th century. Administrative rules were laid down by statutes and local regulations. Each member of the community took part in their drafting and the resulting rules enjoyed a high degree of respect. The first Szekler book of laws, compiled in 1555, consisted of 88 paragraphs, covering civil, property, criminal and trade, as well as military and local administrative laws. The Captain of Udvarhely convened the Szekler's annual National Assembly. Szekler autonomy began to decay during the time of Prince Gábor Bethlen - due in part to the introduction of serfdom. Empress Maria Theresa's new tax law and the organization of border-guards - compulsory military service - were all introduced at a cost to Szekler independence.

From 1359, the Saxon Universitas (community) enjoyed the right of electing their own officials. Autonomy extended to both their cities and Church. From 1690, Saxon paid a token tax after 2,000 dwellings. After 1651, their legal independence suffered minor setbacks against centralized powers. It was permitted for non-Saxons to buy property in Saxon cities, a situation not previously allowed. However, the laws were enforceable on each and every member of the Saxon community until 1848.[15]

Some autonomy concepts

The idea of autonomy has always been present in Transylvania, from the 14th to the 20th century, if under the surface. The latter date saw the birth of Transylvanism, the sense of place, the concept of a Transylvanian existence. Its supporters claimed that Transylvania has always been a separate unit geographically, historically and culturally, and its uniqueness should be preserved in the future. Between 1920 and the end of the 1930s, Transylvanism for the

---

[15] Hungarian National Archives (Magyar Országos Levéltár /hereafter MOL/). Section K, K63-1939-27/4. pp. 22-26.

Saxons and Schwabians meant a minority ideology and literary movement. For the Romanians, it meant mostly the latter, as their loyalty to the Romanian nation was stronger than to that of Transylvanism.

1. The following plan was drafted in the first few months of the Romanian occupation, by Elemér Gyárfás, a leading Hungarian personality in Transylvania, and its leading idea was as follows:

> [...] The major interest of the three nations of Transylvania - Hungarians, Romanians and Saxons - are: to maintain law and order, the safety of people and properties, the freedom of religion and the liberty of conscience, secure cultural and economic development, to protect freedom and democracy, and to form close and indissoluble union and alliance for the future benefit of Transylvania.
>
> [...] The question of what territories should belong to Transylvania is considered a foreign political issue.
>
> [...] The three nations will form a Governing Council of 24: 10 Romanian, 10 Hungarian and 4 Saxon members.
>
> [...] The members of the Governing Council will fill the positions of Ministers and Under-Secretaries - of the 12 ministries, five controlled by Romanian and Hungarian politicians, respectively, and 2 by Saxon representatives.
>
> [...] All laws and regulations in effect before October 31, 1918 in Transylvania will remain effective fully and unchanged, with the single exception that those rights, functions and offices which were up to now under the authority of the King and the Hungarian government will be transferred to the Governing Council until such time as changed.
>
> [...] Within 15 days of its founding, Governing Council will convoke the National Assembly of Transylvania to meet no later than 3 months later. In addition to elected representatives, the bishops of the churches in Transylvania and one secular member of each see may attend with full voting rights.
>
> [...] The Governing Council will present legislation, for National Assembly approval, on the following subjects:
>
> a) The organization of the legislative bodies of Transylvania, the coat-of-arms and national colors of the country, the use of insignia of the three nations;
>
> b) Universal suffrage;
>
> c) Agrarian reform;
>
> d) The modification of the 1868 Act, concerning the equal rights of nationalities, in correspondence with the rights and dignity of the three nations forming the union;
>
> e) Realigning county borders as closely as possible with the language of the inhabitants ... and to harmonize jurisdictional and election districts.
>
> [...] Transylvanian citizens are those who:
>
> a) were born or held public office in Transylvania before October 31, 1918;

b) were had citizenship legally conferred on them;

c) are descendants of those covered under points a) and b); on the territory of Transylvania only Transylvanian citizens are allowed to hold public office, to exercise political rights, to own real estate, to be members of legally formed entities and social associations, and to be members or officials of managerial and supervisory committees of public companies.[16]

2. As early as 1918, Oszkár Jászi correctly saw that it was impossible to form homogenous nation states on the territory of the Austro-Hungarian Empire. Therefore, the Monarchy, and only the Monarchy, had to be transformed into a federal state. Transylvania would become a part of Hungary, where the national minorities would enjoy canton-like autonomy.[17]

3. The idea of Transylvanian autonomy and federation (confederation) can be found in other sources, as well. In his plan, drafted in 1918, Charles Seymor, an adviser of US President Wilson, envisaged Transylvania as an independent state joining a confederacy consisting of Hungary, Austria, Serbia-Croatia-Slovenia, Transylvania, Bohemia and Poland-Ruthenia.[18]

The signing of the Trianon Treaty on June 4, 1920 put an end to all hopeful transition plans. As a result, the state-creating Hungarian nation became a national minority in Transylvania. However, Hungarians merely changed citizenship, not their motherland. As a reaction, they temporarily withdrew into political passivity.

4. Three years later, on January 23, 1921 in a political pamphlet, *The Shouted Word* (Kiáltó Szó), Károly Kós, István Zágoni and Árpád Pál put forward the terms for a short-term and long-term program: 1. The enforcement in Romania of the Alba Iulia Resolution and the international treaty on national minorities (both assured the use of Hungarian language in public administration and judicial jurisdiction, as well as cultural and religious autonomy and proportional representation in the government); 2. The transition of Transylvania into a federal state within the scope of the United States of Europe (Európai Egyesült Államok).[19]

Lawyer and journalist István Zágoni answered the question, "What does the Hungarian nation in Transylvania demand?" by saying: national autonomy for itself and every other nation in Transylvania. He was content to let the democratically elected National Assembly of Cluj Napoca (Kolozsvár), guide the future of the Hungarian nation. National autonomy should extend to: 1. The protection and growth of national assets, i.e., economic independence; 2. The exclusive right to education in the mother-tongue - with

---

[16] Lipcsey, Ildikó: Transylvania, 1918-1920 (Erdély 1918-1920). Manuscript, p. 8. The memorandum was forwarded to Maniu.

[17] Jászi, Oszkár: The dissolution of the Habsburg monarchy (A Habsburg Monarchia felbomlása). Budapest, Gondolat Publisher, 1983.

[18] Ádám, Magda: An American's plan for Central Europe in 1918 (Egy amerikai terve Közép-Európára. 1918-ban). History (História), 1987, issue 4. pp. 16-20.

[19] Kós - Pál - Zágoni: The shouted ... op.cit. p. 47.

a minimum threshold of 20 students; 3. Maintaining law and order, i.e., an independent police force and army.

5. Anti-Hungarian Romanian policy diminished under the government of Iulius Maniu (1928-1932). Hungarian politicians and legal experts had also worked out a framework of "Szekler public autonomy" on the basis of the Alba Iulia Resolution.

6. Between the two wars, several Transylvanian, Hungarian, French and British plans were drafted on the transformation of the region, from federalization to the formation of alliances. All had one prime target: to try and avoid the outbreak of another world war as a result of the unfavorable peace treaty. At the end of the 1930s, as a result of revived secret diplomatic activities, Otto Habsburg drafted one, and Churchill, during the war, made efforts to redraw the borders of the region, with new strategic alliances.[20]

7. During World War II, Endre Bajcsy-Zsilinszky wrote a political pamphlet on the federative reorganization of Hungary. In his plan, Slovakia would join Hungary as an associated country, while Voivodina (northern areas of present day Serbia and Croatia), Transcarpathia or Ruthenia (now part of the Ukraine) and Transylvania would be autonomous regions within the alliance. Collective rights would be assured for ethnic minorities living in this Hungarian federation. The national assembly of Transylvania would be made up of the representatives of the two Romanian, one Hungarian and one Saxon canton, based on numerical parity with the population distribution. These cantons would send representatives to the Hungarian Parliament to conduct common policy. "The Switzerland of the East," i.e., Transylvania as envisaged by Jászi and Bajcsy-Zsilinszky, would have almost total independence in public administration, within the Hungarian state -- a plan almost identical to the one drafted by Kossuth in exile.[21]

8. Between 1944 and 1946, this plan received support from many sides. The Soviet Union seemed to support it when it hinted that the form of government for Romania-Hungary under Soviet military control, in effect in Northern Transylvania since November 14, 1944 would be extended to all of Transylvania. In 1944, a working group led by Litvinov, elaborated another plan in Moscow. The plan thought it feasible to have an independent Transylvania between Hungary and Romania, naturally, as part of the Soviet sphere of influence and the bridgehead of Soviet policy in the Balkans. This was also incorporated in several American analyses, underlining that the Soviet plans included an autonomous or independent Transylvania.[22]

---

[20] Habsburg, Otto: Yalta and its aftermath. Selected articles and studies (Jalta és ami utána következett. Válogatott cikkek, tanulmányok). Munich, Újváry "GRIFF" Publisher, 1978. p. 13.

[21] Bajcsy-Zsilinszky, Endre: Transylvania. Past and future. Geneva, 1944.

[22] Tofik, Iszlamov: Russian foreign policy regarding Transylvania during the Second World War (Erdély a szovjet külpolitikában a második világháború alatt). Our Past (Múltunk). 1994, issue 1-2, pp. 29-32.

9. In 1945, Transylvanian social democrats, encouraged by the Soviet military command in the autumn of 1944, prepared the following plan for an autonomous Transylvania:[23]

Transylvania, as an independent state, will be a federative republic, called "The Federal Republic of Transylvania." Three nations of equal rights constitute the federation - Romanian, Hungarian and German. The constitution must enshrine equal rights for all three nationalities. Thus, every minority enjoys freedom and control over its affairs. The three groups, or rather their constitutional representatives, will convene to deal exclusively with central governing issues.

Transylvania has had its own parliament for centuries. Parliament is to be maintained in the Federal Republic of Transylvania. The territory of the Republic is identical with historic Transylvania. The Head of State is the President. The Federal Council is the central body of public administration. The President of the Federal Republic of Transylvania is also the head of the Federal Council, in other words, the head of state and the head of government is the same person. The seat of the Federal Council is Cluj Napoca.

The National Assembly will elect the President of the Federal Republic of Transylvania, as well as the members of the Federal Council. The Constitution of the Federal Republic of Transylvania must state that the three languages - Romanian, Hungarian and German – have equal status in official use. A statute regulates the use of languages in detail. The Languages Act of Transylvania, passed by the 1863-1864 Diet of Sibiu (Nagyszeben) and assented by Emperor Franz Joseph I, will be accepted almost verbatim.

A separate statute governs the public administration and legislative division of independent Transylvania. Here again, the decisions of the 1863-1864 Transylvanian Diet can be taken as guidelines. The Transylvanian legislative system is, in many ways, similar to that of the cantons in Switzerland. The objective is to provide legal protection for ethnic minorities. The new International Security Organization as a whole, and its members separately, guarantee the neutrality of the Transylvanian Federal Republic. Therefore, the citizens are not subject to compulsory military service. An armed Militia will maintain law and order within the boundaries of the country.

The national colors of independent Transylvania will be blue and gold. Every member nationality is free to use its own flag beside the Republic's flag.

Today, intellectuals and politicians are again reconsidering the issues of Transylvania's independence and the formation of an independent and sovereign Transylvanian state. They state that neither the annexation of Transylvania to one

---

[23] New Hungarian Central Archives. Files of the Foreign Policy Bureau of the Hungarian Social Democratic Party (Új Magyar Központi Levéltár. MSZDP Külpolitikai Osztályának iratai.). 283. Fond, 12/82 o.e.

country or another, nor its division, nor an exchange of population is a feasible solution. Neither a united Europe, nor any kind of European integration can be established without solving the Transylvania issue, as it represents a potential powder keg.

2. Dacian-Romanian Continuity:
The theoretical basis of Romanian irredentism[24]

The Dacian-Romanian continuity theory is held to mean that (1) during the Roman occupation, Dacian natives were Romanized and the present Romanian nation is the amalgamation of the two nations, and (2) after the Roman withdrawal, this nation remained in place and, during the migration period, it absorbed other tribes and nations.

But what are the provable historical facts, based on archeological and linguistic research, and medieval written record?

After the unification of the Dacian tribes, the Dacian king, Burebista, intended to conquer the Greek towns at the mouth of River Dnieper. His troops advancing towards present day Bulgaria, Serbia and Slovakia, and raids in the Balkans, towards Macedonia, forced Rome to respond. The wars of Decebal (Decebalus in Latin), between 101 and 106, against the Dacians resulted in the conquest of the Dacian kingdom. This had disastrous consequences for the Dacian people; its ruling class effectively disappeared through mass suicide or Roman slaughter. After the campaign, the majority of the 10,000 gladiators in Rome's circuses were Dacians. Adult males were conscripted and sent to remote provinces.

To resettle the uninhabited lands, Rome settled Romanized barbarian tribes and pensioned soldiers among who were found Greeks, Celts, Illyrians, Germans, Thracian-Dacians, Semites, Africans as well as Romans. The Dacian themselves can be considered a fragmentary minority in the Roman province of Dacia. Roman science and culture left no traces on them, and no assimilation of language took place because the new settlers were bilingual.

In 271, due to the attacks of the Goths, Emperor Marcus Aurelius was forced to withdraw from remote, and difficult to defend, Dacia. He resettled the Roman population in the Balkans. Consequently, in Dacia and in Transylvania as well, the conditions for a Roman way of life ceased to exist. Of 265 Dacian archeological sites excavated, only one was established after 271 AD - villages became depopulated. The fact that burials ceased points to the fact that the former inhabitants left the area. No medieval records mention former Roman towns, settlements or their inhabitants. Therefore, no traces of Roman ancestors can be found in Transylvania for almost a thousand years, between 271 - 896. According

---

[24] Roesler, Robert: Dacian-Roman Continuity (A dákóromán kontinuitásról): Romanische Studien. 1871;
Tamás, Lajos: Romains, Romans et Roumains dans l' histoire de la Dacie Trajane. Budapest, 1936.

to the archeological findings - graves - Germanic, Turkic, Slav and Cumanian peoples left more traces.[25]

On the other hand, linguistic research has provided definite proof regarding the birth of the Romanian nation and their original home.

Between the 4th and 13th centuries, the ancestors of the Romanians lived in the Western region of the Balkans, together with Albanians. Under centuries of Roman rule, not only town-dwellers but also the Thracian-Illyrian shepherds were Latinized.

Animal husbandry goes with migratory way of life, a search for new pastures - the Romanian world 'vlach' also denotes an occupation – and the ancestors of the Romanians slowly moved up the Balkans and reached the lower Danube in the 10th-11th centuries. South of the Carpathians, they came under the rule of the Pechenegs and the Cumanians. Some splinter groups were left behind and their descendants can still be found on the Balkan Peninsula, in Macedonia, Greece and Albania.[26]

Romanians first appeared in Transylvania in the 12th century. They were first mentioned in written records in 1210 and 1222. They found an advanced public administration and a highly organized Hungarian state. During the 300 years of the medieval Hungarian Kingdom, mention is made of only a few Romanian families. The Várad census of 1210-1230 recorded 389 names, none of them of Romanian origin. The regions that became depopulated, after the Mongol invasion of Hungary in 1241, drew the mountain dwelling Romanians. In a census done at the end of the 13th century, Romanian names were recorded in three out of 511 settlements. The first of their settlements, in Cluj (Kolozs) County, was established in 1332. According to a document from 1293, the king gathered and settled a few thousand Romanians as highland border guards on a royal land grant of 36,000 hectares. Their communities were led by Cumanian-Turk *kenézes*, to whom the king granted lands. Later, in the course of time, the majority of the *kenéz* merged into the Hungarian nobility.[27]

The first Romanian villages in Transylvania, other than the royal estate and the Szekler lands, were established in the 14th century. No place names or body of water of Romanian origin - which would indicate a continuity of Romanians - can be found in Transylvania. Those were taken over from the Hungarian language, such as river names already known in Roman times: Temes, Körös, Szamos, Maros, now called Timis, Krisul, Somes, Mures.

The two Romanian principalities - Moldova and Muntenia (Havasalföld) – were established in the 14th century in the Trans-Carpathian regions. Their sovereigns managed to establish a strong central power, supported by their armies and the middle classes, namely small boyars, free peasants and the emerging bourgeoisie of towns, against the power of the big boyars. Their development was

---

[25] History of Transylvania, vol. I. pp. 11-112.

[26] Vékony, Gábor: Dacians, Romans, Romanians (Dákok, rómaiak, románok). Budapest, Akadémiai Publishing, 1989. pp. 24-26.

[27] History of Transylvania, vol. I. p. 345.

interrupted by the Ottoman occupation in the 16th century, which lasted until the 1877-78 Russo-Turkish war.

The Romanian state can be dated from the union of the Voivodeships of Moldova and Muntenia in 1859. The country took its first steps on the path of modernization and the European ways of development under the rule of Prince Alexandru Ioan Cuza (1859-1866). However, the people did not embrace the top-down initiatives. Translating the Belgian Constitution (and adopting it as the principality's constitution), as well as adapting the French Penal Code and Civil Code, trade and exchange acts to Romanian circumstances, in addition to the "Europeanization" of public finances and transport, proved to be vain attempts.[28] The beginning of the 20th century found a medieval Romania. Renowned Russian-Jewish sociologist Dobrogeanu-Gherea - born Solomon Katz - said: "the Romanian boyar has recently changed his caftan and turban to top hat and tails, but the new, European garb covers a Balkan character." As to the country's economic state, Dobrogeanu-Gherea called it semi-feudal, semi-capitalist, where 73 % of the population worked in agriculture (in 1914) and only 6 % in industry. Beside the system of large estates (latifundia), a Romanian twist appeared - the Jewish leasehold system – which became a source of anti-Semitism.[29]

At the beginning of the 20th century, workers and the middle class still represented quite a thin segment. Only 18% of the population was urbanized. Therefore, this society can be considered lopsided, whose ruling class was alien - mainly Greek - as a consequence of the Fanariota-era (in the 18th and 19th centuries, princes and their courtiers descended from the Fanar district of Constantinople).

The young Romanian state, formed with the guarantees of the Great Powers of the time (led by King Ferdinand of the German Hohenzollern-Sigmaringen family) - balancing between Russia and the Austro-Hungarian Monarchy - finally signed a secret military treaty with the Monarchy in 1883. Germany also joined the treaty, which guaranteed mutual assistance and support in case of any outside attack. Thereby, Romania actually joined the Central Powers. This explains why, though Romania supported Romanian cultural institutions and schools in Transylvania, it did not accept open irredentism.[30]

On a parallel track, though, the Cultural League was established in 1882. Its stated aim was to declare that *every Romanian, living inside or outside the country, belongs to one cultural unit* paving the way for *a program of uniting every Romanian in one country*. Romanian national strategy thereby drafted the objective, recently revived, that Romanians should be united in one country, "from the Tisza to the Dniester." The Cultural League was financed out of the Romanian national budget and it established branch offices in every important

---

[28] Pászka, Imre: Romanian thought, 1866-1945 (Román eszmetörténet. 1866-1945). Budapest, Aetas, Századvég Publisher, 1994. p. 323

[29] Dobrogeanu-Gherea, Constantin: Neoiobagia. Bucuresti, 1910.

[30] Aradi, Nóra: The Liga Culturala and Transylvanian Romanian national aspirations (A Liga Culturala és az erdély román nemzeti törekvések). Budapest, Sárközy Publishing, 1939.

university town across Western Europe. These branch offices served as the means of flooding the world with propaganda material justifying Romanian national objectives. Of particular success was the effort of linking the *Dacian-Romanian origin* and *brotherhood*. The ideological-propaganda activity of the Cultural League complemented the work of a Romanian organization in Transylvania, named ASTRA, which was formed to support Romanians economically and financially, and to acquire Hungarian lands and properties for transfer to Transylvanian Romanian.[31]

Romanian irredentism targeted Transylvania. When Romanians state their claim of <u>historical right</u> to Transylvania, they make no reference to ethnic or numerical majority. Rather, they base it on the false claim that they are the original inhabitants who remained in the region after the withdrawal of the Romans, and were continuously present from the 3rd century until the arrival of the Hungarians who founded a nation. Therefore, Transylvania - in their opinion - belongs to Romania on the basis of historical continuity of inhabitation.

Transylvanian Romanians during the Dualism

The 1867 Compromise ended Transylvania's separation when the Union was established. The issue of ethnic minorities provided food for thought for many politicians: Ferenc Deák and Lajos Mocsáry sought the solution in the system of public administration based on self-governments, while József Eötvös leaned toward the concept of confederation. The 1868 Act on Nationalities stated that every citizen of the country formed one nation in the political sense - the united and indivisible Hungarian nation - and every citizen of the country, regardless of ethnic origin, had equal rights. The official language was Hungarian, however, in the internal operation and communication of lower level administrations, jurisdictions and municipalities, the languages of national minorities were allowed. The same referred to religious life. The state ensured instruction in the mother tongues at the elementary and secondary school levels, and provided every opportunity for ethnic minorities to establish linguistic, scientific, cultural, economic, industrial and trade institutions. Therefore, on this level, the Act guaranteed collective rights, but it did not accept ethnic minorities as political units.[32]

In the time of Dualism, the Hungarian Empire gradually centralized its authority and consequently, independent political life in Transylvania declined. The Hungarian Cultural Association in Transylvania (Erdélyi Magyar Kulturális Egyesület) represented a certain level of individuality. The separation of the

---

[31] Szász, Zoltán: Romanian associations in Hungary, 1867-1918 (Román egyesületek a magyar államban, 1867-1918). History (História). 1993, issue 2. pp. 19-20.

[32] Hévizi, Józsa: Various types of autonomy in Hungary and Europe (Autonómia-típusok Magyarországon és Európában). Budapest, Püski Publishing, 2001. pp. 197-201.

Saxons ended, although Saxon citizenry enjoyed a certain favored position in the Dual Monarchy.[33]

Transylvanian Romanians chose political inactivity to protect them against Dualism, but at the same time took every opportunity to influence international public opinion and draw attention to Romania. An important change in the policy pursued by the Transylvanian Romanians took place in 1905. A change occurred in the Romanian National Party (Román Nemzeti Párt) resulting in the ascension of the activist (militant) wing. The Party's program, drafted in 1905 in Szeben, dropped the concept of Transylvanian autonomy. It was replaced by the endorsement of the state-founding character of the Romanian people, assurance of its ethnic and constitutional rights through the institutions of public administration, universal and secret ballot, and the adjustment of administrative borders in accordance with language boundaries.[34]

The 1907 "Lex Apponyi" (legislation introduced by Count Albert Apponyi, Minister of Public Education, 1906-10) caused massive protest since, although the new on School Act decreed an increase in the salaries of teachers in public and church schools, but at the same time placed emphasis on the Hungarian character of the state. The law declared that the language of instruction was Hungarian where half of the pupils were Hungarian, and teaching Hungarian was also compulsory whenever their population was in excess of 20%. In spite of all this, 40% of the country's population did not speak Hungarian. Between 1910-14, Tisza's (Count István Tisza, Prime Minister, 1903-05 and 1913-17) point of view changed, as did that of the Romanians. In 1910, their demands were for the free use of the Romanian language in public administration, the appointment of Romanian civil servants, 50 Romanian electoral districts, 3 new bishoprics, the revision of the Apponyi Act, 3 Romanian secondary schools, national colors, etc. In return, they were ready to accept the fact of the Compromise. In 1912, the scope of their demands expanded to church autonomy, administration and judiciary in the Romanian language and a proportionate share in parliamentary seats. In 1913, they asked for Romanian high-sheriffs and Under-Secretaries. Tisza promised one Romanian state secondary school, 30 electoral districts and the review of the Apponyi Act.[35]

After World War I, a new chapter began in the history of Transylvania. A race began between the Central Powers and the Entente to win over Romania and, naturally, Transylvania was the stake. In early October 1914, during the of Russian-Romanian talks, the Russia promised Transylvania and South Bukovina in return for Romania's neutrality. Transylvania found itself on the merry-go-round of international politics.[36]

---

[33] Ibid, pp. 24-25.

[34] Jordáky, Lajos: The birth of the Romanian National Party (A Román Nemzeti Párt megalakulása). Budapest, Akadémiai Publishing, 1974. Treatises from the Sphere of the Historical Sciences. New series. p. 72.

[35] Bíró, Sándor: In minority and majority. /Romanians and Hungarians, 1867-1940/ (Kisebbségben és többségben. /Románok és magyarok 1867-1940/). Bern, European Protestant Hungarian University, 1989. p. 82.

[36] Pászka: Romanian ... op.cit. pp. 7-32, 33-75, 111.

I. The great National Dream comes true

In a study written in 1891, Alexandru Averescu - commander of the Romanian army in 1916 and subsequently Prime Minister - worked out the detailed plan of a Romanian attack on Hungary. He, as well as Iorga, waited for the favorable historic moment: whenever Hungary broke away from Austria, or the Austro-Hungarian Monarchy was attacked, Romania would join the anti-Hungarian side.

The favorable moment for the unification of all Romanian areas came during World War I. In accordance, the Cultural League changed its name to the Alliance for All-Romanian Political Unity (Szövetség az Összes Román Politikai Egységéért). At the Crown Council meeting on August 3, 1914 the leaders of Romania voted for neutrality. This, in spite of the signed treaty with the Central Powers and despite the secret treaty worked out in 1883. Also, in face of the Transylvanian Romanian politicians who made contact with their brethren in the Trans-Carpathians region (Regát) and encouraged them to occupy Transylvania. This meant that 30% of men were mobilized, new divisions were formed and special attention was paid to the technical equipment of the army.

The Entente had previously promised that Romania's territorial claims against Transylvania would be supported. While a race began between the Central Powers and the Entente to win Romania's favor (it meant numerous favorable trade and economic contracts for the country), Romania took a wait-and-see position. The progress of war determined whether Romania would enter the conflict and on which side.

1915 brought success to the Central Powers. The fortunes of war took an unfavorable turn in the summer of 1916: the Brusilov-offensive drove the Austro-Hungarian army back. Romania finally came to a crossroads and, considering its interests, the choice was obvious.

In a secret agreement signed in Bucharest on August 17, 1916 the Entente agreed that Romania would carve out large areas from the Monarchy (roughly, the river Prut would be the eastern and the River Tisza the western border of Romania; more precisely: the town of Vásárosnamény would be annexed, the border would run 16 km. East of Debrecen and the border would run along the River Tisza to the village of Algyo where it would make a 3km. arc to the junction of rivers Tisza and Danube, and from that point the Danube would be the border). In return, Romania was obligated to attack the Austro-Hungarian Monarchy. According to the agreement, Romanian claim will only be met if Romania does not sign a separate peace treaty.[37]

The relatively large, 400,000-strong, Romanian army that attacked Transylvania was halted after a fortnight and driven back by October. On December 6, 1916, four months after the Entente-Romanian secret agreement was signed, Mackensen's troops took Bucharest. Romania signed the separate peace treaty with the Central Powers on May 7, 1918 and this act meant that, in regard

---

[37] Ormos, Mária: From Padua to Trianon, 1818-1920 (Padovától Trianonig, 1818-1920). Budapest, Kossuth Publishing, 1983. pp. 14-15.

of the secret agreement of August 17, 1916 the Entente would not support Romania's territorial claims. Under the terms of the separate peace treaty, the Romanian army would be reduced to 10 divisions, the country's economic activity would be put under strict control and, with the exclusion of Bessarabia, Romania could not lay any territorial claim to any territories, including Transylvania.

In spite of developments, beginning in the summer of 1916, the Austro-Hungarian Monarchy began to look for a way to sign a separate peace treaty. The future Little Entente launched a massive propaganda campaign in favor of secession from the Monarchy, and the union of the Southern Slav, Czech and Slovak regions, as well as the union of areas inhabited by Romanians in Transylvania to the Kingdom of Romania. Their efforts enjoyed strong support by France and Russia.

The outcome of the war, and the peace that followed, was determined by the entry of the United State of America. In his address to Congress, on January 8, 1918 President Wilson formulated his ideas on peace, the dismemberment of the Austro-Hungarian Monarchy and the rights of ethnic minorities to self-government. Under these circumstances, the German successes on the Western front in March to May carried no importance. At their meeting in Rome on May 8, 1918 the leaders of the nations of the Austro-Hungarian Monarchy declared that they did not wish to continue living within the bounds of the Monarchy. In his statement of May 29, President Wilson found it acceptable.

Austrian Emperor Karl I, also as Hungarian King Károly IV, issued a proclamation on October 16, 1918 transforming of the Monarchy into a federation, while leaving Hungary's territory intact. President Wilson's reply to the proclamation was made public on October 16, in which he rejected the proposal of a federal state. This gave the nations of the Monarchy the final impetus for their secession.

On the same day, October 18, a Romanian MP addressed the Hungarian Parliament for the last time. Alexandru Vaida-Voevod described the terms of the Arad resolution of October 12, which stated, among other things: "concerning the World War situation, the political establishment of the Romanian nation of Hungary and Transylvania states that the war has justified the centuries old Romanian demand for full national independence. Based on the natural right that every nation should have the right to decide its political status, a right which has been acknowledged by the governments of both the Monarchy and Hungary, the Romanian nation wishes to exercise this right and demands the to decide, freely, by itself and without any influence, its own institutional, positional and regulatory situation. The Romanian nation in Hungary and Transylvania does not recognize the authority of this Parliament and government to represent the Romanian nation in Hungary and Transylvania. It rejects another nation's right to act as the representative of the interests of the Romanian nation in Hungary and Transylvania, as these interests can only be represented by members delegated by its own National Assembly."[38]

---

[38] History of Transylvania, vol. III. p. 1702.

The Romanians also rejected Oszkár Jászi's proposal for a plebiscite to decide the future of Transylvania. On October 31, headed by Iuliu Maniu, the Military Committee of the Romanian National Council was established in Vienna - its task, to transport 50,000 Romanian soldiers home via Serbia.

Thus, the nations declared their intentions to secede. In spite of this, Mihály Károlyi (head of the Hungarian National Council and later President of the First Republic) demobilized the Hungarian army, and after the declaration of the Civil Revolution, he issued a statement of neutrality. The Romanian National Council launched preparations for convening the Grand National Assembly and the organization of the Romanian national militia.

The demobilization of the army and the declaration of neutrality left Hungary's borders defenseless, allowing the ethnic minorities to proceed with their legitimate - or ostensibly legitimate - territorial takeovers. The establishment of the line of demarcation thus opened the way for the Romanian army to march into Transylvania and to advance as far as the River Maros. On November 8, the Romanian National Council called upon the Hungarian government to transfer control of 26 counties to Romania.

The 'territory rescue' talks between the Hungarian delegation, headed by Oszkár Jászi - who was called 'the friend of national minorities', even by the Romanians - and the representatives of the Romanian National Council, took place on November 12-15. It clarified the two sides' stands once and for all. The essence of Jászi's proposal was based on Wilson's right of self-determination for each of the three nations of Transylvania, i.e., for Romanians, Hungarian and Saxons alike. According to his memoirs, Jászi's proposal included the following points:

1. Romanian rule wherever Romanians are a majority;
2. A Romanian delegate is to be present in the Hungarian government to discuss every issue of common concern;
3. Former acts and laws remain in force as a transition but new ones can only be passed with the assent of the Romanian authority;
4. With the exception of the high sheriffs and government commissioners, all members of the administration remain in office; former officials are to receive adequate legal protection and no one can be dismissed without proper disciplinary procedure;
5. National minorities are mutually to be afforded the protection of Act of 1868 paragraph 44;
6. The Romanian National Council guarantees the protection of individuals and property;
7. The provisional Romanian authority cannot make use of the military forces of the Kingdom of Romania;
8. The Hungarian government and the Romanian Council are to set up a joint committee to transition the new order;
9. Contentious issues to be settled by a five-member court made up of two members delegated by the Hungarian and the Romanian Councils respectively, and one by the Hungarian government; the five members are to jointly elect a president;

10. This agreement to be in force until the peace talks. Thereafter, nothing will limit the freedom of the parties;
11. The observance of the agreement is to be guaranteed by the honor of the two nations.

On their way home from Vienna, on a special train provided by the Hungarian government, Iuliu Maniu expressed their stand far more succinctly: "secession for good."[39]

The Romanian National Council, meeting in Arad, made its answer public on November 14, in which it rejected Jászi's and the Hungarian government's proposal. On November 20, Ferdinand, King of Romania, ordered the mobilization of the Romanian army. (The establishment of Czechoslovakia was declared on October 28 in Prague and on October 30 in Túrócszentmárton [now Martin, Slovak Republic]; on October 29, Croatia announced its secession, which was followed by the establishment of a Serbian-Croatian-Slovenian state.)

At the session of the Grand National Assembly held at Alba Julia (Gyulafehérvár) on December 1, 1918 the representatives of the Romanians in Transylvania wished to establish, with the aid of the Romanian army of occupation, a *fait accompli* before the peace talks. The members of the elected Governing Council, consisting of Transylvanian Romanians, held ministerial rank. The aim was to ensure a kind of autonomy for Transylvania, but the decisions were made without the participation of Hungarians and Saxons. They also disregarded the resolutions of the opposition National Assembly meeting in Cluj Napoca (Kolozsvár), where the participants, also referring to the right of self-determination, declared that Transylvania wished to remain a part of Hungary.

Certain Hungarian sources were later fond of quoting Maniu's address: "Our aim is to achieve national unity, and in this regard we want to ensure the sanctity of the freedom of every nation and person. We will not eliminate the national character of any of the nations living together, and every person may choose his language and religion, both in his private life and in his relation to the state."

In addition to the election of the 150-member Grand National Council and the selection of the members of the Governing Council (cabinet), the discussion of Vasile Goldis' proposal and the wording of the Alba Iulia Resolutions were undoubtedly the most important events regarding ethnic policy between the two world wars. Goldis proposed complete autonomy for all of Transylvania. This, however, was omitted from the final text. The paragraph covering minorities, No. III/1, stated: "Complete national liberty for the coexisting nations. Every nation has the right to education and government in its own language, its own administration staffed by its own elected people. Every nation is to be represented in the legislative bodies and administration in proportion to its population."[40]

---

[39] Cites: Kós-Pál-Zágoni: The shouted ... op.cit. p. 27.
[40] Cites the Alba Iulia Resolutions: Mikó, Imre: Twenty two years. The political history of the Transylvanian Hungarians from December 1, 1918 to August 30, 1940 (Huszonkét év. Az erdélyi magyarság politikai története 1918. December 1-tol 1940 Augusztus 30-ig). Budapest, 1941.

It must be pointed out that the Alba Iulia Resolutions - though enacted in Romania on December 11 – can not be considered as the result of a referendum, since it was declared 1) by a handful, and 2) only in the name of Romanian citizens, i.e., the main ethnic minorities, the Hungarians and Saxons, were not represented.

On December 16, the Hungarian National Council in Transylvania issued its proclamation entitled "Hungarian self-government for Transylvania," which included a message to the world: "Hungarians living in Transylvania recognize every nation's right to its own administration, but does not agree that that right, which they are ready to acknowledge and are valid for every other nation, should be taken away from them. Transylvanian Hungarians wish to realize the right of national self-government, and they have no wish to rule over any others. However, they don't acknowledge any other people's right to exercise the right of self-government by violating the Hungarians' own right to it. On this basis, the Transylvanian Hungarians do not accept any other factors to determine their destiny, only their own elected (self-governing) body, i.e., the Hungarian Governing Council in Transylvania."[41]

On the same day, Colonel Vyx informed the Hungarian government that, under the pretext that the Romanian population was in danger, he had to evacuate the towns of Satu Mare (Szatmár), Carei (Nagykároly), Cluj Napoca (Kolozsvár) and Arad. West of that line a neutral zone was marked, running from Vásárosnamény, through Debrecen, Békéscsaba, Gyula and Hódmezovásárhely to Szeged.[42]

The representatives of Transylvanian Hungarians convened a protest meeting on December 22 in Cluj Napoca. Romanian General Mosoiu sent word to the Hungarian Council that if it did not ban the meeting, he would shell the town. In spite of the threat, the meeting took place. Representatives of 50,000 people of 28 counties took part in the meeting in the assembly hall of the Craftsmen Union's headquarters. On December 23, Vyx demanded the evacuation of further territories West of Cluj Napoca. The Hungarians felt deceived. They understood that that instead of the promised British and French troops, the army of the former national minority occupied the region, whose advance reached its peak in August 1919 when the Romanian army marched into Budapest.[43]

In the morning hours of December 24, the XIIIth Romanian Royal Infantry Brigade, under the command of General Gherescu, marched into Cluj Napoca. Mayor Gusztáv Heller, standing under the statue of King Matthias in the town's main square, received them with the following speech: "The Hungarians have laid down their arms. But we do not repudiate our national selfhood, because the rights of self-determination apply to us as well, and you must not demand this from us. We have surrendered. Our only weapon is justice - what our people attributed to the person whose statue stands behind us. It is thus that we will appear before the

---

[41] Ibid.

[42] Ormos-Jászi: The dissolution … op.cit. p. 115.

[43] Lipcsey, Ildikó: 133 Days. The first Romanian occupation of Budapest (133 nap. Budapest elso román megszállása). Budapest, manuscript.

26

court of justice of Europe." The destiny of Transylvania was sealed by the occupation of its capital.

In actuality, dual power developed in Transylvania after the Hungarian government dismissed the combat-ready Szekler division. The Romanian army coming from Trans-Carpathia (Regát, the old Kingdom of Romania) acted as an occupying force. It imposed martial law, censorship, a ban on meetings, forced recruiting, internment and flogging. The administration of foreign affairs, defense, finance, post, customs and railways were taken out of the grasp of the Romanian Governing Council's authority. The Act on the equal use of language was also repealed.

At the Paris peace talks, and subsequent peace treaties, the laws of war came uppermost instead of Wilson's right of self-determination; strategic principles instead of ethnic principles when borders were drawn. The defeated powers were penalized and decisions were made in their absence. The map of Europe was significantly redrawn.[44]

For Germany: the Saar basin was put under international control, the left bank of the Rhine became a demilitarized zone and France annexed Alsace-Lorraine. A part of Upper Silesia was annexed to Czechoslovakia, the other to Poland, together with some areas of East Prussia. Former German colonies were divided among the powers of the Triple Entente.

For Austria: Vienna, the center of an empire with a population of 52 million became the capital of a country of 5.6 million inhabitants. Czechoslovakia, created on the northern frontier of Hungary, laid claim to the cities of Miskolc and Salgótarján and wanted to draw the border at the town of Vác and, in order to establish a corridor to Yugoslavia, laid claim to territories around the Ferto Lake. Czechoslovakia, by the way, was not a country consisting of two nations of equal rights. The Czechs acted as much of an occupation force in Slovakia as the Romanian troops of the Regát in Transylvania. In Yugoslavia, the Croatian people were greatly disappointed, because instead of their federative ideas, a unified Southern Slav country was established under Serb rule, through the artificially fabricated union of nations of different regions and civilizations.[45] Comparing the state of the two major losers, Germany and Hungary, 3 out of every 20 German and 7 out of every 20 Hungarian citizens found themselves in a foreign country. More precisely: Hungary lost two-thirds of both its territory and population. Total losses amounted to 223,745 sq. km. (71.52 %) in territory and 13,281,000 persons (63.56 %) in population.[46]

Hungary's area of 283,000 sq. km. decreased to 93,000 sq. km. Its population of 18,264,533 decreased to 7,600,000; whereas Romania's territory and population increased threefold.

[44] Rehák, László: Minorities in Yugoslavia (A kisebbségek Jugoszláviában). Novi Sad (Újvidék), Forum Publishing, 1967. p. 76.
[45] Ibid, p. 105.
[46] Chronology of Hungarian History, vol. III (Magyar történeti kronológia, III. köt.). Budapest, Akadémiai Publishing, 1982. p. 873.

	Territory	Population
1914	137,903 km^2	7,234,919 [47]
1920	304,244 km^2	16,262,127 [48]
Increase	166,340 km^2	9,027,258

Detailed survey of territories and their population annexed to Romania.

From Hungary - Transylvania	57,818 km^2	2,686,833 people
Máramaros, Szatmár and Ugocsa	18,592 km^2	466,956 people
Kôrös region	17,086 km^2	1,145,113 people
Bánát	17,980 km^2	910,393 people
From Bessarabia	44,422 km^2	2,555,070 people
From Bukovina	10,442 km^2	811,742 people

It appears that the "Big Four" drew the borders of the new Europe as casually as if it were a small African colony at stake, said Endre Bajcsy-Zsilinszky. It was due to this carelessness, irresponsibility, serving only the interests of the major powers, that the peace carried the seed of another war at the very moment of its creation.[49]

The first Averescu government: March 13, 1920 - December 1921

Ion C.C. Bratinau's liberals were at the helm at the close of the First Word War; he was also the person who represented the country at the peace talks. In May 1919, Bratinau promised equal rights for religious and ethnic minorities, as well as the decentralization of administrations. However, Bratinau was not put all his cards on the table. During the Paris Peace talks, when asked in a letter how Romania intended to ensure the rights of national minorities, he gave the following answer: "Romania ensures unlimited development in language, education and church issues, but it will never tolerate any foreign intrusion into its practice of legislation."[50]

In September 1919, Bratinau came into conflict with the Entente over several issues: he demanded the entire Bánát for Romania, delayed withdrawal of Romanian troops from Hungary and protested the minority agreement and the signing of the peace treaty with Austria, claiming that it infringed on the rights of the sovereign state. Following his resignation in December 1919, Alexandru Vaida-Voevod, one of the prominent leaders of the Romanian National Party,

---

[47] Enciclopedia romane, vol. III. 1904. In 1904, it estimates the population of Romania at 6 million, including the minorities. The Dictionar statistic data is from 10 years later.

[48] Halmos, Dénes: International treaties (Nemzetközi szerzodések). Budapest, 1983.

[49] Bajcsy-Zsilinszky, Endre: Our place and fate in Europe (Helyünk és sorsunk Európában). Budapest, 1941. p. 129.

[50] Viorel, Tilea: The workings of Romanian diplomacy: November 1919 - March 1920 (Románia diplomáciai muködése 1919 november-1920 március). Lugos, Hungarian Minority (Magyar Kisebbség), 1926; Viitorul, 1919, octombrie-noiembrie.

formed a government. It enjoyed only a brief tenure because, although the he represented his country effectively to the victorious governments, as a diplomat and as a politician he was hampered by intrigues within his own party's members from the Regat. For tactical reasons, after concluding an agreement with the leaders of his National Liberal Party, the popular General Averescu formed a short-lived government. Since his party could not be considered a serious political entity, he made efforts to increase its numbers with conservatives, liberals, former members of the Romanian National Party and anti-Semitic elements. Averescu dissolved the all-powerful Governing Council of Transylvania, as well as the councils charged with the temporary management of affairs in Bukovina and Bessarabia. His name hallmarked the first budget and financial reforms.

Preparations for agrarian reform in Romania were begun in 1920. Fundamental differences begin to appear – naturally, the historical circumstances were also different - between the implementation of agrarian reforms in Transylvania and Romania. Romania was a typical agrarian country where 73% of the population worked in agriculture and only 6 % industry. Only 18% were urban dwellers. The infrastructure was rather undeveloped. Some 800,000 people suffered from syphilis, tuberculosis and other diseases symptomatic of low levels of civilization. Illiteracy was of the same order. The fact that Transylvania accounted for 50% of the country's light and 80% of heavy industrial capacity clearly shows the differences in levels of development between Transylvania and the Regat.

Expropriated lands totaled 2 million hectares in Romania (i.e., The Regat, approx. 5 million acres).[51] In Transylvania - the area of which was smaller than that of Moldova and Muntenia (137,903 km^2) together - no limit was set. Thus, 2,494,585 catastral acres (1 c.a.= 1.42 acres) were expropriated by 1925, which was later increased to 3,200,000 c.a.[52]

The Averescu Government signed the Trianon Peace Treaty on June 4, 1920. The same year, the State Secretariat for Ethnic Minorities was established. However, its existence didn't change the fact that the majority of the Romanian wielders of power openly espoused the idea that "Romania belongs to Romanians"[53] and minorities should be dislodged from all spheres of life. Many protested when Hungarians and Jews demanded representation in Parliament.[54]

General Averescu overstepped himself when he handed in a proposal for the nationalization of the Resita Co., which was in the hand of the Liberals. The Liberal Party demanded different reforms and, as the founder of Greater Rumania - as it proclaimed itself - it wanted absolute power in political and economic life. After the short-lived government of conservative Take Ionescu - from December 1921 to January 17, 1922 - the highly respected Ion Constantin C. Bratianu

---

[51] Official Gazette (Hivatalos Közlöny). 1921, July 14 and 23.
[52] Móricz, Miklós: The fate of Transylvania (Az erdélyi föld sorsa). Budapest, Hungarian Men's Association (Erdélyi Férfiak Egyesülete). 1932. p. 83.
[53] Dezbateri parlamentare. Deputariilor (Parliamentary Diary. House of Representatives.) Bucharest, 1920, August 19.
[54] Ibid, 1920, July 4.

became Prime Minister of Romania. This brought to an end the two year transition without, of course, eliminating the differences in the types of development of the three main regions: Transylvania represented the Central European, Moldova the East-Central European and Muntenia the Balkan way of life.

The rise and fall of the National Liberal Party:
January 1922 - March 1926

It can be stated that the manipulation of the parties began with the ethnic minority issue as early as the 1922 elections. It manifested itself, among other things, that in the race for votes, every party - there was no difference between the Liberals, the Peasant Party or any others - could promise anything: the honoring of treaties in force, cultural and religious autonomy, or even a National Minorities Act.

The Liberals did not forget the ethnic minorities, either. The Bratianu's government's program of 1922, in addition to free market and austerity, included - though neglecting details - the settlement of the ethnic minority issue.[55] In a speech delivered in Arad, Vintila Bratianu held out the prospect of measures that would guarantee economic and social development.[56] Vaida-Voevod, expelled from the Transylvanian National Party, criticized the Liberal Party by saying that through the nationalization of companies it became a majority shareholder of firms originally, Hungarian or of other nationalities, thus able to label them as patriotic firms.[57] The editorial of *Eastern News* (Keleti Ujság) rightly observed, "The Rumanian parties' infighting is vehement. But we must not find ourselves in a situation where, during and after their fight, all parties vent their rage on us."[58]

As a result of the February election, the Liberals took 309 of the 387 parliamentary seats. Their landslide victory spelled serious defeat for the National Party. In his letter to the King, Maniu wrote, "Election Day has turned into a day of mourning and despair in Transylvania, and has brought disgrace on the nation and caused a European scandal."[59]

The indignation expressed by the Conservative opposition to the Liberals, led by Marghiloman, was interesting from the Hungarian point of view, as well: "There is only one representative of the two million Hungarians in the Chamber. The Szeklerland (Terra Siculorum), where the Romanian population consists of 1%, can not send a single representative. The Liberals have achieved victory by resorting to tricks and unfair means not befitting a civilized country."[60]

Both the Romanian parties and the Hungarians of Transylvania had to accept that the Liberals wanted to achieve total control. The program presented by

---

[55] Eastern Journal (Keleti Újság). 1922, February 21.

[56] Ibid, 1922, February 22.

[57] Ibid, 1922, February 22.

[58] Ibid, 1922, February 14.

[59] Cites: Szász, Zsombor: The path of Romanian political life (A román politikai élet útja). Hungarian Review (Magyar Szemle). 1930, August. p. 288.

[60] Le Progres. 1922, March 13.

Vintila Bratianu stated the following: "Romanian labor, initiatives in all areas ... and all opportunities for earning money should be preserved for Romanians who, due to unfavorable historic circumstances, were hampered in economic and financial development." The Party, consisting of Boyars, industrial and financial middle class and top army officers, also vouched to lead Rumania on the road of modern capitalist development.[61]

The government, disregarding the reality of the situation in the country - initiated large-scale industrialization program, as would happen during the 50's and 70-80's - and was of the opinion that foreign capital was unnecessary. As part of this program, direct tax was higher by 205 million Leis in Transylvania, a total increase of 22.2% vs. a 1.9% decrease in the Romanian Kingdom (i.e. the Regat); overall tax increases amounted to 72% in Transylvania compared to the 31.3% national average. Sales taxes grew by 24.6% in Transylvania, while it dropped by 11% in the Regat. The minorities alone had to suffer these grievances.[62]

The 1925 Public Administration Act dissolved the old administrative regions and divided the country into 71 counties. It encountered massive opposition, even among Romanians in Transylvania. According to the 1926 Voting Act, the governing party had to achieve a minimum of 40% of the votes and the remaining 50% would be distributed between parties achieving at least 2%.

The victory of the National Liberal Party of the Regat was not universally welcomed, because it meant that they exercised control throughout the country. Liberals took over every high position in the State, political and economic life and the army. The Romanians in Transylvania had thought that they would replace the Hungarians in positions of power in Transylvania and not their brothers from the Regat. The Liberal era also brought the Regat's customs with it: corruption, baksheesh (petty bribery), uncertainty and Balkan attitudes. The so-called "Parliamentary Democracy" of Romania was characterized not only by the multi-party system, but also by censorship, martial law and centralization.[63]

The new Romanian constitution: 1923

During 1922-1923, during the debates on drafting the new Constitution, confrontations of opinions and counter-opinions on the minority issue were an everyday. The draft spoke exclusively of Romanian citizens, to whom all Romanian laws applied, international treaties guaranteeing free use of their language and religion, therefore - as the reasoning in both chambers of the Parliament went - there was no need for a separate law dealing with them. Moreover, Angelescu, one of the prominent figures of Romanian cultural policy between the two World Wars, stated that as a result of appropriate Romanian state policy, Hungarians would not remain Hungarian for long. To this end, he indeed did everything in his power to make it come true. The first draft of the

---

[61] Cites: Mikó: Twenty two years. ... op.cit.
[62] Ibid.
[63] Bucharest, 1922, October 17.

31

Constitution declared, "that all Romanians, regardless of their origin, language or denomination, are entitled to all the rights of freedom assured by the Constitution and the law." At the request of several representatives of the ethnic minorities, Iorga took the floor on December 16th, 1922 and asked that the text be changed to read: "all Romanian citizens."[64] Nevertheless, some MP's were of the opinion that the Hungarians enjoyed the same rights as the Romanians - their lamentations offended the patriotic feeling of the Romanians.[65]

Others were of the opinion that - although national minorities constituted an immense burden for Romania - as long as they were engaged in nurturing their language and culture, there was no reason to fear them. But the moment that they start demanding privileges and territorial claims, they represented a great threat, because these are not compatible with national sovereignty.[66] Satisfying their demand for autonomy would create a state within a state. There were some voices supporting the minorities, as well. For example, Ioan Lupas reminded the House that the Alba Iulia Resolutions are binding on both sides.[67] Therefore, the Constitution has to recognize the minorities, and furthermore, must guarantee the development of their churches and cultural institutions. Iorga also expounded in the same vein because he very much wanted to take over the government with the support of the minorities. "The Alba Iulia Resolutions contain noble ideas, which, if not in their present form, but in essence, must be included in the Constitution. First of all, the autonomy of the Churches and schools should be recognized. I reject the idea of territorial autonomy because the Hungarian and Saxon live in scattered, small groups, and it is impossible to accomplish. I recognize the minorities' right to use their own language."[68]

Unlike the Czechoslovak, Polish and Yugoslav Constitutions, the Romanian Constitution did not incorporate laws for the protection of ethnic minorities. It only spoke about "Romanian citizens" to whom the laws of the country applied regardless of their national origin, language and religion. Most importantly, new Constitution stated that Romania was a "united and indivisible country."[69] Vintila Bratianu also thought that this was the most important principle in the new Constitution. However, it did settle the citizenship status of Romanian-born Jews, which international public opinion had demanded for almost a century, and was one of the major conditions for signing the Peace Treaty with Romania![70]

---

[64] Parliamentary Diary. Senate (Dezbateri parlamentare. Senatul.). Bucharest, 1922, December 16.

[65] Ibid, 1923, March 18.

[66] Parliamentary Diary. House of Representatives. (Dezbateri parlamentare. Deput.) Bucharest, 1923, April 24.

[67] Ibid, 1923, April 21.

[68] Eastern Journal (Keleti Újság). 1923. April 22; Neamul Romanesc. 1924, January 29.

[69] Balogh, Arthur - Szego, Imre: Romania's new constitution (Románia új alkotmánya). Cluj Napoca, Concordia Publishing, 1923.

[70] Bitoleanu, Ion: Din istoria Romaniei moderne. 1922-1926. Bucharest, 1981. pp. 90-92.

The second Averescu government

In the run up to the elections of 1926, Gheorge Tatrescu, national minority expert of the Liberal Party inquired about the Hungarians' complaints. In its memorandum, the National Hungarian Party (Országos Magyar Párt, henceforth OMP) basically demanded political, economic and cultural stability for the Hungarian community. In February 1926, the OMP and the Liberals formed a coalition for local elections and OMP candidates won in 30 out of 49 towns in Transylvania.

After the election which, according to the Romanian National Peasant Party (Román Nemzeti Paraszt Párt) was again characterized by terror, Stefan Pop Cicio declared the following in Parliament: when the Hungarians ruled the country we went to vote between the bayonets of the gendarmes, but we were free to vote for the Romanian National Party (Román Nemzeti Párt). But not for the first time in Romanian history, voters of the Romanian opposition were prevented from going to the polls.[71] Although Averescu was the Prime Minister, in reality, the Liberals were pulling the strings, as in 1920-21. This was true for the minority policy, as well. At the beginning of the 1927 school year, Angelescu launched another attack against Hungarian schools. He decreed that Szekler settlements must erect public school buildings at their own expense. However, due to lack of financial resources, the existing parochial schools were turned into public schools – where instruction in the Romanian language became compulsory. In October, another decree stated that teachers of minority origin were not allowed to teach the Romanian language. In response, Iorga, in December 1926, again called attention to the government's minority policies on the floor of Parliament, pointing out that "the Hungarian minority is a historical fact in Romania, whose cultural institutions and schools should be protected..."[72]

Iorga spent a considerable time, August-September of 1927, in Transylvania. His visit can be seen as a kind of campaign tour, visiting big cities one after the other, including Sibiu (Nagyszeben) and Brasov (Brassó) as well. In a memorable and far-reaching lecture at the University of Cluj Napoca (Kolozsvár) on December 10, he summarized and spoke highly about the history of Hungarians in Transylvania. He stressed the unique development of the region, for which it deserved special consideration. He corrected his former opinion that Romanians lived under oppression in Transylvania for a thousand years. "The statement, that the nation suffered from terrible oppression in past centuries, should be erased from Romanian books... We must not think of the Hungarian kings as having been surrounded by cannibals who assaulted the poor Romanian people with unbridled fury. If it had been so, we should properly have asked ourselves: why did we let it happen? The truth is that, in this sense, no one lived in slavery here who refused to be a slave."[73]

---

[71] Dimineata, 1926, July 9.
[72] Bács County Diary (Bácsmegyei Napló). 1927, April 15.
[73] Eastern Journal (Keleti Újság). 1926, September 12.

The last days of the Liberals: 1928

The fall of the Liberals made their political opponents, at home and abroad, as well as diplomats and journalists accredited in Bucharest, to take stock of the situation. They all agreed that the parliamentary and constitutional appearance camouflaged a dictatorship. A staff members of the Hungarian Embassy in Bucharest wrote, on November 6, 1928, the following to the Foreign Minister in connection with the fall of the Liberals: "The greater the power the Liberals seized, the worse they administered it. They labored under the curse of a dictatorial majority, because the silenced public opinion was unable to warn them of their severe excesses, and the logical consequences of their profligacy. The Romanian character, made up of a mix of Latin hysteria and Slav Byzantinism, is unable to exercise impartial criticism, in any case... The ecstasy of victory, which has started to dampen in the rest of the world, continues to exert its influence on the Romanians, who actually contributed the least to that victory. Their rapture has degenerated into a power trip in their case... With their continuously assertion of sovereignty, they committed severe violations of civil rights against foreign properties, and it was under this slogan that they shamelessly broke their solemnly taken obligations... Under the pretext of nationalization, they commit the gravest deprivation of civil rights and recent laws threaten foreign properties... They thoughtlessly banish their King, they take advantage of the discord within the Royal Family and they openly proclaim that the Dynasty would only remain on the throne as long as it serves their interest..."[74]

Corruption and the squandering of the national wealth also contributed to the stagnation of industry and trade and the diminishing of means of payment. The policy of self-imposed seclusion led to bankruptcy, the country was in desperate need of foreign loans. International financial circles were in accord, stating that Romania first had to meet its former financial obligations, to pay its pre-war debts towards Germany, to settle the so-called Optant-case and the national minority issue. While Romanian officials went from door to door in France and Germany, looking for loans, the National Peasant Party (Nemzeti Paraszt Párt, hereafter NPP), making the most of its foreign influence, blocked the Liberals from acquiring further loans. On December 22, 1927 Maniu stated in Parliament that the opposition would not incur the debts of the Liberal Party.

In January 1928, the opposition organized mass meetings nationwide "to overthrow the government." In this context, Vaida-Voevod declared that the illegal measures of the government revolutionized the masses. Although the authorities made every effort to hamper it - they simply blocked the roads - the NPP held its congress on January 29. Several promises were made, primarily about putting an end to "Balkan" circumstances and unlawful acts. Vaida-Voevod repeated his famous statement - "Transylvania must belong to Transylvanians" – and, by way of illustration, he noted that Bucharest sent several persons to be prefects in Transylvania who were formerly imprisoned in the Regat.[75] Pop Cicio

---

[74] MOL, Ministry of Foreign Affairs, K. 63. 1928/27 31 file.
[75] Ibid.

considered it noteworthy that, in the opinion of the Romanian peasants in Transylvania, their life was better under Hungarian rule than under the Liberals.

The NPP issued the following communiqué in the spring of 1928: the Party's MP's and Senators would not take part in the work of the Parliament; the government was deemed to be an enemy of the country; every means are justified in the fight against the government; the "illegitimate government" should not take out more loans, and should not be allowed to add further burdens onto the population.

On June 27, the news of the breakdown of the loan talks spread like wildfire in Bucharest, although the government had been reporting success for weeks. Britain was held to be primarily responsible for the inability to stabilize the Lei. International power-relations and the interests of some European powers had a great impact on the sate of internal development of the country. The ever-increasing influence of France in Romania had filled Britain with apprehension for some time. Independent-minded and ambitious Mary, the Queen of Romania, would have liked to be rid of the aggressive guardianship of the Bratianus. To this end, she nurtured good relations not only with the NPP but with the British Embassy as well.

Finally, the council of ministers forced Bratianu, who clung to power by tooth and nail, to resign on November 3. In addition to the mass campaign and the failure of loan negotiations, the opposition contributed to the fall of the Liberals, even though the government was inclined to meet the fundamental demands such as the control of the National Bank and the State Railways and to begin Hungarian-Romanian talks on the Optant-case.

The years of searching: From passivity to the establishment of the National Hungarian Party

With the Trianon Treaty (June 4, 1920), the founders of the Hungarian nation become a national minority in Romania. Their status was circumscribed in two documents: the Alba Iulia Resolutions of December 1, 1918 and the Minority Convention (Kisebbségi Egyezmény) signed in 1919 and guaranteed international overview. Both documents would have assured 1) the proportionate representation of minorities in the government, 2) self-government in education, culture and religion, and 3) the national autonomy of the Szeklers and Saxons. The League of Nations, headquartered in Geneva, was responsible to investigate and provide legal remedies for the complaints of the minorities.

In the years between the two world wars, regardless of the party in power, efforts continued to assimilate the minorities, or to induce them to move by changing their traditional ethnic circumstances through forced resettlement (Romanian settlers in Hungarian areas). The discriminative measures and laws had an impact on all layers of society. However, a significant shift occurred in their situation in the years before and after World War Two. After 1945-47, 1) international protection for national minorities ceased with the end of the League of Nations, 2) with the elimination of the multi-party system, the situation changed whereby the Romanian opposition - especially during the campaign -

would at least listen to certain minority complaints, and finally 3) the centuries old and independent political, social, economic and denominational institutions and schools were gradually closed.

Minorities could submit their complaints in the form of petitions to the Council of the League of Nations. The petition would be seen first by the Secretary-General who decided on its merit and would then pass it on to the Council. However, the issue was put on the agenda only if a council member acknowledged the fact of injustice. Issues were not dealt with if they were submitted by countries that were not members of the Council, or if a minority turned directly to the League of Nations. Thus, if a member of the Council acknowledged that a minority suffered an injustice, the member contacted the country concerned and expected a response in three weeks. (Generally, the countries affected made every effort to stifle the issue.) If an answer arrived, then it was passed to the *ad hoc* Triple Committee, together with the petition, for investigation. The report was sent to the Council that submitted the issue to an open session. The representative of both the country and the minority could take part in the session; however, the latter only had observer status. In addition to the League of Nations, national minorities could turn to the Permanent International Court of The Hague, but only in case of disagreement between the country responsible for protecting the minority and a councilor of the Council.

Sixty-four petitions of the violation of the rights of Hungarian minorities were submitted to Geneva from Hungary and the successor states - only 8 reached the Triple Committee.[76] The following is a sample of complaints from Romania: the difference in magnitude and compensation for expropriations in Transylvania and The Regat during the land reform; 23,460 senior and 119,155 minor Hungarian officials were discriminated against during the change in regime; 112 Hungarians were sent to forced labor; 385 hectares were taken from the Unitarian Church and 9 pastors were caned. Several complaints were submitted regarding cultural issues, the closure of schools and the destruction of paintings and statues. Maniu precisely defined the status of the Hungarians: international protection and guarantees are futile, none of the great powers will go to war in defense of minority rights in any country, that is, none of the Great Powers will fight for the rights of the Hungarians.

Hungarians were not the only ones who suffered injustice of this kind. Between 1921 and 1936, 852 minority complaints were submitted and 381 were rejected. On top of it, the deficiency of the procedure was that a minority individual was not able to submit a complaint, either to his country or to international institutions, as a legal entity.[77] Despite its imperfections, the League of Nations, designated to protect minorities, did, to some extent, curb the brutality

---

[76] The Fate of the Romanian, Czechoslovakian and Yugoslavian Minorities before the League of Nations, 1930-1937 (A romániai, csehszlovákiai, jugoszláviai kisebbség sorsa a Népszövetség elott. 1930-1937). Budapest, Political Science Academy, manuscript, 1938.

[77] Mikó, Imre: The plaints of the Romanian-Hungarian minorities presented to the League of Nations (A romániai magyar kisebbség panaszai a Nemzetek Szövetsége elott). Credit (Hitel). 1936, issue 3. pp. 203-216.

of anti-minority policies. Regrettably, the Great Powers did not learn the lesson, and failed to establish an improved system of minority protection after World War II, allowing any country to claim that criticizing its minority policy was an intrusion into its internal affairs.

After two years of passivity,[78] when Hungarians voluntarily gave up a number of positions, primarily those officials who were unwilling to swear a loyalty oath to the Romanian state, some 200,000 people immigrated to Hungary. Political activism started when the Hungarian People's Party (Magyar Néppárt) was formed with the participation of 3,000-4,000 Hungarians in Huedin (Bánffyhunyad) on Sunday, June 6, 1921.[79] The leaders of the party stated that self-government should be assured for all nations and denominations in Transylvania and to achieve this, they demanded the implementation of the Alba Iualia Resolutions. The establishment of the People's Party, led by the intelligentsia and supported by middle and small landholders, gave an impetus to Hungarian political movement. One of the prominent leaders of the People's Party, polyhistor Károly Kós, indicated in his pamphlet *Shouted Word*, that the ultimate goal was "national autonomy."[80]

The ideal of legalizing the national struggle inspired those who established the Hungarian Alliance in Cluj Napoca on January 9, 1921.[81]

On January 28-29, 1922, the leaders of Hungarians in Transylvania unanimously declared in Cluj Napoca that it was absolutely essential to take part in the elections, and action must be taken to achieve this aim. Accordingly, the Executive Committee of the Hungarian Alliance, supported by other factions, must take a lead in preparations for the elections. During the talks conducted with the leaders of the Szekler counties, the parties agreed to the notion of a unified Hungarian party and that the Hungarian Alliance should control the campaign. Hungarian politicians visited the areas inhabited by Hungarians, and made efforts to make contact with the representatives of the Saxons as well. On March 6-7, 1922, during the election preparations, the Hungarians wished to field some 50 candidates, but most of them were not accepted onto the rolls. In cities populated almost entirely by Hungarians, Tirgu Mures and Cluj Napoca, several thousand people were simply left off the voters lists. (The Romanian National Party [Román Nemzeti Párt] suffered a similar fate. Citing technical reasons, 24 candidates were erased from the rolls.)

The National Hungarian Party (Országos Magyar Párt, NHP from now on) was established on December 22, 1922. Between 1923 and 1938, it was the leading force in the struggle of Transylvanian Hungarians both in the Romanian House of Representatives and the Senate, most succinctly and accurately expressed as "a policy of airing grievances." At the same time, the 23-member executive committee was elected, and the establishment of the party delegates was relegated to the counties.

---

[78] Eastern Journal (Keleti Újság). 1921, May 26.
[79] Opposition (Ellenzék). 1921, May 31.
[80] Kós-Pál-Zágoni: The shouted ... op.cit.
[81] Mikó: Twenty two years.... op.cit. p. 24.

The *Organizational Statutes* and *Rules of Procedure of the Romanian National Hungarian Party* were elaborated and adopted at the inaugural meeting. The Organizational Statute of the NHP included the following statements regarding its members, structure, officials and departments:[82]

The National Hungarian Party's structure was as follows:

1.   Village, town and local branch, established on the basis of neighborhoods, if possible (one neighborhood organization consists of 10-20 local families);
2.   District branch;
3.   County and municipal branch;
4.   National General Assembly and Central Party leadership.

The General Assembly was the main representative and decision-making body of the NHP. Its authority extended over the operation and program of the party, election of the central bodies and control of all bodies in charge of party administration. The county and municipal branches delegated members to the National Assembly.

The National Assembly was empowered to elaborate and modify the Party's organizational statutes and to elect, for a four-year term, the President, four Vice-presidents, two controllers, and the members of the Executive and Disciplinary Committees.

The Executive Committee consisted of fifty members, elected by the General Assembly, as well as *ex-officio* Executive Committee members. *Ex-officio* members were defined as: central officials, the party's Senators and MP's, members of the Presidential Council, members of the Hungarian Episcopacy, presidents of the county and municipal branches, or their deputies. The Executive Committee had complete authority between Assemblies and was responsible for all the political, economic, financial and administrative, etc. issues of the Party. The Executive Committee elected 8-member Presidential Council.

The authority of the Presidential Council extended over the preparation of the issues to be discussed at the meetings of the Executive Committee and the execution of the resolutions. Empowered by the Executive Committee, the Presidential Council managed all the tasks of the Committee and was obliged to report on its activities at each session of the Executive Committee.

The Senators and MP's of the Hungarian Party formed the "Parliamentary Group," headed by the Party President, or his Deputy.

In order to examine the living conditions of the Hungarian minority, and to be able to offer adequate recommendations and proposals in line with the interest of the Hungarian nation, the following Advisory Departments were established within the party: Legal, Economical, Public education Social, Press, Minority and historical and Hungarian house building.

The program of the NHP set the following targets:

1.   On the basis of the Alba Iulia Resolutions and international agreements, it asked for the enactment of the legal entity status - collective rights - of national minorities into the constitution. Furthermore, national autonomy, in

---

[82] Ibid, p. 42.

which every nation governs itself, in its own language, and has control over its own administration and judicial jurisdiction, as well.

2. The reestablishment of municipal and village autonomy was one of the fundamental demands, as well as the decentralization of public administration and an extension of its jurisdiction, and the prevention of illegal activities by civil servants.

3. The politicians who compiled the NHP's program considered it fundamental, in a constitutional state, to ensure the independence of judges and the strict separation of legislative, judicial and administrative authority; that the legislative function can not be usurped by the government or other authority through the use of "Decree"-s. In addition, the NHP demanded the reestablishment of trial by jury and the abolition of the secret police and martial law.

4. In religion and public education, on the basis of legal continuity, the constitutional acknowledgement of the rights of the legally recognized denominations and the existing self-government bodies and their right for establishing and operating educational institutions from elementary school to university, as well as the return of school buildings, were demanded.

5. Of great importance to peasants and landowners, the revision of the agrarian reform, the exemption of church, school and foundation lands, in general, from the reform as well as full compensation for expropriated properties.

6. Also included among the demands, the right to strike, labor insurance, lifting the measures limiting free industrial and market activities, the introduction of a progressive tax system and the calculation of a just and tax-free subsistence wage.

7. Stated: "We demand to arrange military service on the basis of the militia system, a maximum three-month active service - done in the soldier's own recruiting district - and the use of mother tongue as the service language."

8. Finally, the program felt it necessary to make mention of the need for lifting of regulations limiting the protection of individual freedoms, the right of public meeting and assembly and the assurance of the freedom of the press.

Assault against Hungarian institutions

By early 1922, Hungarians categorized their complaints. Among the list of economic complaints was the liquidation of medium and large estates, the exclusion of Hungarians from land distribution, the replacement of Hungarian management with Romanian officials at companies, plants, banks, trust companies and shops. As early as 1920-22, news kept surfacing of the closing of Hungarian schools; state, as well as church run schools. The Romanian government knew full well the reason for depriving Catholic, Protestant and Unitarian schools of their existence: education in these institutions was an important factor in maintaining national identity. The real assault against

Hungarian education was launched in 1923. In November and December of that year, two important decrees were issued:[83]

1. Romanian curriculum was introduced into church run schools.
2. The admission of students of other denominations was banned. It was particularly prejudicial to Jewish citizens, who were brought up in the Hungarian culture. The aim was obvious, to separate the nearly 180,000 Transylvanian Jews from the Hungarians.

The Act of July 24, 1924 decreed that:

1. The children of citizens of Romanian origin, who had forgotten their mother tongue, had to be enrolled in Romanian schools. The practice of name investigation started at this time. Those who had Romanian names, or had names easily Romanized, automatically had to attend Romanian schools.
2. The so-called "cultural zone" was established. It meant that Romanian teachers who went to teach in the entirely Hungarian populated counties of Csík, Udvarhely, Háromszék, Marostorda and Aranyostorda received 50% higher salary, 10 hectares of land, as well as other benefits.

The Matriculation Act of 1924 decreed that examination of subjects learned in Hungarian had to be taken in Romanian in front of a panel. Although he was a Romanian, Professor Iorga stated that it was educational massacre.[84] According to statistics in his possession, 70% of the minority students were unable to pass the exams. The Matriculation Act was followed by the Private Education Act of April 1925. It reduced the standing of church run schools to private institutions, thereby revoking their right to issue graduation certificates.

In 1923, the NHP (National Hungarian Party: *Országos Magyar Párt*), lacking representation in Parliament, tried to break out of its isolation and started to look for allies in its fight for minority rights. These efforts "resulted" in a secret agreement between the Hungarian Party and the Romanian People's Party (Néppárt), which became known as the "Ciucea Pact." Former premier, General Averescu and his People's Party were also searching for allies. He offered an opportunity for the Hungarian Party to present its demands and have them acknowledged by at least a segment of the Romanian leadership. Under the terms of the pact, the NHP, representing the Hungarians, accepted the People's Party's program and was willing to form an alliance with it in Parliament. In return, the leaders of the People's Party promised to meet the wishes of the Hungarians. They were:[85]

1. Minorities should not be left off the electoral rolls, i.e., they should be allowed to exercise their right to vote.
2. The autonomy of Hungarian churches should be assured by, and incorporated into, law. The legal and property situation of the closed churches is to be

---

[83] Ibid.

[84] Neamul Romanesc, 1925, July 22.

[85] Gyárfás, Elemér: The first attempt: The Averescu Pact's precedents, reasons for the alliance, textual revisions, consequences, dissolution and conclusions (Az elso kísérlet: az Averescu-paktum elozményei, megkötésének indokai, szövegek módosításai, következményei, felbomlása és tanúsága). Hungarian Minority (Magyar Kisebbség). 1937, issue 2-3. pp. 357-358.

settled. Acknowledge the right of churches to self-taxation, and ascertain the state subsidy for the salaries of clergymen and teachers. Accept the right of minorities to establish a full range of educational establishments and that they are to be treated equal with Romanian ones.

3. All discriminative measures against Hungarian denominational schools should be terminated. Return all school buildings and equipment to the churches, villages and institutions.

4. The licenses of Hungarian social and charity organizations, theaters and the Transylvanian Hungarian Public Educational Association (EMKE, Erdélyi Magyar Közmuvelodési Egyesület) should be restored. Diplomas earned at foreign universities should be accredited.

5. Romanian citizens of Hungarian language should be able to communicate with the authorities in their mother tongue - both written and spoken. Repeal the decree prohibiting the use of Hungarian - even among themselves - by office workers. In areas where at least 25% of the population is Hungarian, officials of Hungarian nationality or, at least, Hungarian-speaking clerks should be employed in public administration. These settlements' names should be displayed in the minority language alongside that of the State. In areas inhabited mainly by Hungarians, settlement names should remain Hungarian. Acts and decrees should be issued in Hungarian, as well. A minority department should be set up in the Ministry of the Interior, headed by a Hungarian-born official, and similar departments should be organized in the Ministry of Public Education and Religious Affairs.

6. Judicial procedures should be conducted in the language of the parties concerned. Hungarian lawyers must be allowed to argue cases in Hungarian.

7. The agrarian laws must be revised. Guarantee the use of mother tongue in trade, business and private life, including trade-signs, advertisements and bookkeeping.

8. The status of public servants who refused to take the loyalty oath should be rectified and they should be allowed to return to their positions. Confiscated flats and homes should be returned. And finally: "allow the use of the red, white and green Hungarian national colors be displayed in a properly compatible manner with the symbols of the Romanian State."

After the 1926 elections, a sizable Hungarian group - 15 MPs and 12 senators - entered the Romanian Parliament. At its meeting, held in Gheorgheni (Gyergyószentmiklós) in October, 1926, the NHP came to the following decision: the National Hungarian Party would not ally itself with any Romanian party and would, henceforth, enter general elections independently. The meeting was an important milestone in the life of both the Party and the Transylvanian Hungarian minority, as it created an opening towards the Hungarian masses and an invitation to the so-called reformers into the party hierarchy.

In 1927, members of the former Hungarian People's Party and the reformers' group re-established, for a one-year duration, the Hungarian People's Party. It is worth noting that, in August 1927, the Party had publicly sought suggestions for the creation of a minority law. In response, that Gyula Tornya, a lawyer, drafted his proposal, revised by Dr. Géza Deutsek, secretary of the

Hungarian People's Party, who also consulted with the representatives of the Saxon minority. The central point of the essay was that Romania was a country inhabited by several nations and constitutional autonomy, guaranteed by international agreements, should be granted to its minorities. In its details, the essay-proposal contained the following, among others:[86]

1. Within the Romanian State, in addition to the "national entity" of the Romanian majority, there exist Hungarian, Saxon, Ukrainian, Polish and Turkish "national entities" - national minorities - as well.
2. These minorities desire to form autonomous communities of *constitutional* character in order to meet their national, cultural and other needs.
3. The elected Supreme Council would represent the minorities, and an Executive Committee, elected by county and township bodies, would operate alongside it.
4. In order to maintain autonomy, minorities must be able to rely on the financial sources provided by companies, foundations, donations, fees and other funds raised.
5. The minorities assert their right to raise their national colors on national holidays.
6. Every citizen should have the right to state to which minority he or she wished to belong.
7. Equality with the majority, as well as with every majority group, was the stated goal.

Separate chapters were dedicated to the issues of citizenship rights, the freedom of worship, of meeting and assembly, including the status of independent cultural, economic, industrial, trade, social and athletic training institutions, choral societies, museums, hospitals, casinos and libraries, which would obtain state subsidies in proportion to the given minority's contributing to the state budget. The chapter on the use of language is remarkable, stating: "the languages of the national entities living in the Romanian state to be recognized as native languages, and as such, to be freely used without any prejudice, in private and public domains." In other words, the languages of the national minorities should be accepted as official languages.

Where any national minority reaches 20% of the population, records and decrees must necessarily be published in all the languages in use. The plan made the one-fifth proportion a condition of the language of education. In addition, in settlements of a Romanian majority, where 20 school children of minority origin are registered, if five parents ask for the formation of a special class for them, it must be provided. The paper included a demand, in addition to denominational schools, for state, vocational, commercial, agrarian schools and teachers' training colleges. Likewise, the revived People's Party also worked out a draft plan in which it demanded, among other things, administrative, judicial and fiscal autonomy for Transylvania (Bánát and Máramaros).

---

[86] Tornya, Gyula: The framework of the National Minorities Law (A népkisebbségi törvény tervezete). Published by the Transylvanian-Hungarian People's Party, Cluj Napoca (Kolozsvár), Lyceum Press, 1928.

National Peasants' Party governments:
November 10, 1928 - April 30, 1931

The reason for the popularity of the Transylvanian National Party, as opposed to the Liberals, was that, during the age of Dualism, it was the leading force in the struggle of Romanians in Transylvania.[87] Its main support was based on the intelligentsia of peasant origin, town-dwellers, clergymen and village teachers, i.e., the new Romanian middle class of Transylvania. The party operated along the lines of Maniu's ideas as part of the legislative process in Parliamentary opposition. Maniu considered the Party as the representative of the Transylvanian Romanians' interests and its cooperation with any other party was subjected to this principle. It was a great disappointment to the Transylvanian Romanians that the Romanians of the Regat pushed them into the background after 1920. This also influenced the party's search for allies. From 1924, Maniu conducted talks on a union with the Ion Mihalache lead Peasants' Party, established in 1918, which also garnered the support of intellectuals and well-off peasants. They achieved their goal in 1926. Mihalache played a significant role in working out the agrarian reform in 1921 and maintained close relations with the Peasants' Party of Bukovina and, from 1922 on, with the People's Party of Bukovina. Its leader was Constantin Stere who, in 1907, demanded the radical distribution of large estates and then, in 1920, thought trend of the future in Europe was the emergence of agrarian states. The party, after expanding its leadership with Virgil Madgearu, Pantelimon Halippa and Grigore Iunian, gradually grew into national scope and, by 1928, became the second strongest party in the country. Their demands focused mainly on agrarian issues: the division of large estates, community autonomy, church autonomy, supplying equipment for and protecting peasant farms from capitalist exploitation, affordable credit, and the establishment of cooperatives. However, they also recognized intolerability of social distinctions. They criticized centralization, the gradual limiting of democracy and held that radical social change was possible. It was no accident that one of the conditions of the Romanian National Party was the exclusion of the radical demands from the joint party's program.

As a result of the merger, the National Peasants' Party was formed, once again under the leadership of Iuliu Maniu. His program, as his government's program, extended to various areas. It demanded - while in opposition, and promised when in power - a balanced budget, free elections, a constitutional parliamentary system, restoration of democratic rights, austerity, an end to corruption and the review of the land reforms. While the Liberals bandied about vast industrialization schemes, the Peasants' Party emphasized the agrarian character of the country, and demanded the common use of pastures and woods, the provision of loans and credit for cooperatives, a labor code similar those in developed countries, decentralization, the end of self-imposed economic

---

[87] Re: The National Agrarian Party: Scurtu, Ioan: Din viata politica Romaniei, 1926-1947. Bucurest, Editura Stiintifica si Enciclopedica, 1983.

seclusion, the free influx of foreign loans, assurances for the operation of trade unions, compliance with the peace treaties. Finally, the program visualized something that no government had done before: a Minority Act that would eliminate the minorities' "reason to run to the League of Nations in Geneva." In short, it promised everything that a Party in opposition could.[88]

Following its victory in the 1928 elections, Maniu's party won an overwhelming majority in the parliament: 349 Peasants' Party and 13 Liberal MPs. However, numerous problems arose. First, the Great Depression brought to the surface those difficulties that the country had not been able to overcome previously, partly due to the Liberals' economic policies and partly due to the country's circumstances. They included, among other things, the reorganization of finances, the unfavorable price of wheat resulting from the agrarian crisis, and widespread corruption. At the same time, due to the resistance of the Liberal Party, Maniu's government was unable to significantly introduce its new administration system, because its decentralization plan was deemed too close to regionalism. This draft act, however, would have met the demands for autonomy of the Romanians in Transylvania and Bessarabia. On the other hand, it managed to strengthen the scope of the Interior Ministry's authority and that of prefects appointed to head county administrations; the same development took place with the gendarmerie. An Act was passed regulating the relationship between employer and employee. Martial law was lifted, and by seizing some key political positions – the economy was still controlled by the Liberals – the government managed to mitigate, somewhat, the situation characterized earlier as "Bucharest manages Transylvania as a colony, which serves the capital with all its resources." Instead of agrarian reform, an act on the buying and selling of land was passed.[89]

In the elections, the Hungarian Party received 172,699 votes, and so, during the Maniu government, 13 MP's and 6 Senators won seats in Parliament. Along the representatives of the Hungarian middle class, craftsmen, small holders and the Hungarian-oriented Jews were also represented in Parliament. The Hungarian Party - as during the elections in May 1990 - made its voice heard not only on minority but also on national issues. Its representatives took an active role in talks concerning the establishment of stability, and acts on labor relations and industrial chambers.

Maniu made a pledge shortly after forming his government, stating that the minority issue will be solved in the interest of "the spiritual unity of the country," and he regarded the Alba Iulia Resolutions as the starting point.[90] Gyula Tornyai, member of the re-established Hungarian People's Party, worked out a draft for the national minority bill and, concurrently, the same task was given to Pop Ghita by the Romanian National Peasants' Party. Pop Ghita stated that instruction in a

---

[88] Szász, Zsombor: Romanian political life, part 1 (A román politikai élet. 1. rész). Hungarian Review (Magyar Szemle). 1931, July. p. 292.

[89] Jancsó, Benedek: The Romanian Agrarian Party (A Román Parasztpárt). Hungarian Review (Magyar Szemle), 1928, May-June. pp. 140-145.

[90] Szász: Romanian Political ... op.cit.

44

minority language should not consist of a few hours of lessons but "all subjects should be taught in the mother tongue, and the minorities have a right not only in elementary, but also in secondary schools, even university education."[91] He also thought it right to employ civil servants that spoke the language of the minority living in a given area. His contribution to the issue greatly enraged some Romanian circles. The media of the right, the newspaper *Universul*, lamented on the shameful rejection of national policy.

The Hungarian Party expressed its trust in the government by ceasing to send petitions to the League of Nations, and stated that it considered the minority issue an internal one and expected a Romanian solution to it. In return, in a memorandum, the Party compiled the most pressing demands, which were partly met. They were as follows:
1. Report on state subsidies to schools;
2. The acknowledgement of the public status of church schools;
3. The opening of closed schools;
4. The acknowledgement of parents' right to send their children to the school of their choice;
5. The revision of the curriculum; and
6. The repeal of the matriculation statute declaring that subjects learnt in Hungarian must pass examinations in Romanian.

In 1929, for example, Hungarian schools received significant aid of 25 million lei. The 26% tax levied on theater tickets was reduced to 13%. In 1929, finally after 10 years, it was decreed that civil servants who refused to swear allegiance to the Romanian State and had not assumed other citizenship, were finally granted pension. In the 1930 local administration elections, the Hungarians won 25% of the county councilor posts and 28.8% of the city alderman posts. However, in the wake of the worsening economic situation - generally argued with poor grasp of the language - more and more officials and civil servants were dismissed. We have no reason to doubt that Maniu, who was Transylvania and once a minority member, felt more tolerance and sympathy towards the issues of minorities. Under the circumstances, when the majority of the parties found even the Alba Iulia Resolution too much, it was no wonder that he could not sell a minority law. Hungarians and the Saxons were disappointed that the new administrative reform did not change the situation in the use of mother tongues. It was the Maniu government that decreed the establishment of Romanian language kindergartens in the Szekler counties. The practice of the "cultural zone," "origin research" and "name analysis" remained unchanged.

Facing Maniu, Ciato Ludovic thought that minorities were in more favorable situation in Romania than in the Austro-Hungarian Monarchy, but the Germans and Hungarians should be treated tactfully in order not to make them feel "homeless in their homeland."[92] Iorga's colleague, Ion Sin-Ciorgiu was of the opinion that the Alba Iulia Resolutions were hastily conceived, and carried autonomist tendencies that threatened the existence of the Romanian State. In

---

[91] Ibid.
[92] Ciato, Ludovic: Problema minoritara in Romania-Mare. Cluj, Tip. Lyceum, 1924. p. 28.

opposition, he could not agree to anything other than cultural autonomy, controlled by the Romanian State.[93]

The autonomy of Transylvania and the Banate, announced in January of 1928 by the Hungarian Peoples Party, was as alien to the Romanian intelligentsia of Transylvania as autonomy for the Szekler Land. Cornea Toma, former prefect of Sighisoara, was among the few who intended to begin a similar process. His thesis contained his vision of dividing Transylvania into cantons, similar to Switzerland.[94]

A speech by István Bethlen (Hungarian Prime Minister at the time) in 1927 was the beginning of revisionist propaganda. From that moment, the phraseology of pro-minority politicians started to weaken on solidarity and understanding. Members of both houses of the Romanian Parliament protested against the change in Hungary's foreign policy. Nevertheless, in the period of 1930-32, various attempts to settle the two countries' relations through peace treaties, compromise or confederation - see the efforts of Briand, Laval, Tardieu - made themselves felt.[95] Maniu's address to the Geneva disarmament congress, in February 1930, submitted a concrete plan for closer co-operation of Romania, Hungary, Czechoslovakia and Austria.[96] The accumulation of economic burdens and political intrigues continued to hinder the work of Maniu's government. The question of the restoration of monarchy led to a break in the Peasant Party itself. Maniu opposed the return of King Charles because he clearly saw the King's leaning towards dictatorship and intentions to dissolve all the parties. Between June 1930 and April 1931, Peasant Party governments were taking turns in power. The crisis was obvious: Maniu and his government had to resign. Their paper, the Cluj Napoca-based *Patria,* interpreted this as, "A collective drama of the Transylvanian spirit."

Minority issues during the Iorga government

Iorga and his government of experts began to execute their program at the deepest point of the economic crisis. The question was whether they have a comprehensive and effective plan? And if so, could it be realized for the benefit of both the country and the minorities? In addition to stabilizing the economic situation, the government promised to solve the minority issue "and support those whom the logic of a relentless history has made our fellow citizens and who, by way of their own work-ethic must be our partners."[97] In other words, a plan that

[93] Sin-Giorgiu, Ion: Problema minoritara in Romania. Bucharest, Editura, independenta, 1932.

[94] Cornea, Toma: The Minority Question (A kisebbségi kérdés). Political dissertation. Cluj Napoca, Studium Publishing, 1928.

[95] Re: The plans for cooperation: Ormos, Mária: France and eastern security, 1931-1936 (Franciaország és a keleti biztonság, 1931-1936). Budapest, Akadémiai Publishing, 1969.

[96] Ránki, György: Economics and Foreign Policy (Gazdaság és külpolitika). Budapest, Magveto Publishing, 1981.

[97] Eastern Journal (Keleti Újság). 1931, April 22.

would offer a solution for the minority issue. While the government continued its traditional Francophone orientation, it stated that it would accept any offered help and make efforts to establish good relations with its neighbors.

Minority expert Elemér Jakabffy, who represented Hungarians in Romania at international forums, wrote about this expectation in his article "Iorga fever." "Political life today is somewhat similar in which doctors surround the patient and only recognize the symptoms, without understanding the illness. Our public life, without a doubt, is suffering from Iorga-fever and political doctors have not established the nature of the fever. Iorga is that political figure from whom we have more statements in print than from a dozen former ministers and statesmen put together. It is obvious that, in case of a politician who has made so many statements, it is difficult to ascertain which statement is the basis and compass of his political beliefs."[98]

While introducing his government, Iorga pointed out the fact that the country is not homogenous ethnically, and it had to be taken into account. One of his first stringent measures was the dissolution of Parliament. Levying taxes on wealth resulted in government officials and teachers going without pay for months. He stated that self-imposed national seclusion was damaging, and considered it as the main obstacle in solving the economic problems. He promised that the department of Hungarian language and literature would be established at the Bucharest University.[99]

He made similar promises to the Saxons in Sibiu (Nagyszeben). The first step towards solving the minority issue was the appointment, by the King at the end of April, of a Minister for Transylvania, Prof. Emil Hatigeanu. Then, a few days later, Iorga called Árpád Bitay and Rudolf Brandsch to his office - with whom he had contacts going back to the 1920s - and appointed them to head the newly established Minority Sub-ministry.

The office, theoretically, had the following tasks - its mandate was only to advise, collect data and provide expert opinion:
1. to draft an act that would guarantee the coexistence of the Romanians and minority nations;
2. to study the issues concerning the minorities;
3. to set up a committee of minority experts;
4. to advise the ministries that were involved in the preparation of laws affecting the minorities;
5. to select delegates to international congresses dealing with minority issues; and
6. to compile monthly report on minority situations, both inside the country and abroad. Iorga also set up an interim committee charged with examining the national composition of the country's population.

About Rudolf Brandsch's activities, Iorga stated not less than that he was working on the basic principles of cultural autonomy for the national minorities', because "providing cultural autonomy for the numerous national minorities with

---

[98] Ibid, 1931, May 1.
[99] MOL, K. 63. 31/27/7.t. 238 file.

centuries of culture who live in the Romanian state, does not threaten the unity of the country."[100] It was extremely humiliating that, due to failing the language exams, hundreds of Hungarian railway men were dismissed just before their retirement. They were also excluded when state and church aid was distributed. They were hindered in the free use of their mother tongue; the government failed to solve the problems of the Transylvanian Museum Association (Erdélyi Múzeum Egyesület), the EMKE and the agricultural school of Algyó. Aside from a few exceptions, the balance tipped to language and cultural complaints; the number of social issues significantly declined. Iorga, as many times previously, promised a resolution to legitimate complaints.

But in reality, new Matriculation Act was more disadvantageous for the minorities than Angelescu's one, which stated, "With the exclusion of national subjects, the students are obliged to sit for both written and oral exams in all other subjects exclusively in the language of the school."[101] As modified by Iorga, "at the same time, students are allowed to use the school's language of instruction, as well." But "at the same time" meant less than "exclusively."[102] Iorga reassured the concerned that after the student had answered a question in Romanian, he could also repeat it in his mother tongue.[103] In another proposal, Iorga held out the possibility for the national minorities to establish colleges, moreover, one of its sections promised state subsidy for the institutions, but due to the vehement resistance of the House of Representatives, it was not passed.[104] However, he did succeed in passing into law the accreditation of university diplomas obtained in Hungary before 1926, and only Romanian matriculation subjects required a supplementary examination.

It is typical of Romanian thinking that even these cautious reforms, promises by Iorga and were considered excessive. According to one of the representatives, the problem was not that the minorities did not enjoy the same rights as the Romanians but that re-Romanization of Transylvania had not been completed. Therefore, he asked for a state subsidy for the re-Romanization of "Hungarized" Romanians. There was no clear agreement between the Prime Minister and the opposition on the issue of Transylvanian regionalism, either. The new Public Administration Act, which dissolved county, municipal and village administrative bodies, and replaced them with Prefectures and introduced total centralization, brought about great resistance. This forced Vaida-Voevod to quit Parliament, saying that he did not want to be an accomplice to the illegal acts of the government. In October, Goldis issued a statement on the situation in Transylvania, in which he emphasized that the Transylvanians should carry out public administration in Transylvania.

---

[100] Neamul Romanesc. 1931, September 20.
[101] Hungarian Minority (Magyar Kisebbség). 1931, July 1.
[102] Parliamentary Diary. House of Representatives (Dezbateri parlamentare. Deput.). Bucharest, 1931, July 25.
[103] Ibid, 1931, June 30.
[104] Eastern Journal (Keleti Újság). 1931, July 1.

Shortly after New Year, the first act of the Government was to again reduce pensions. In February, there were vigorous arguments about the Conversion Law, which shifted a portion of the agricultural debts to the government. The Liberals rose in opposition, Argentoinau wanted to raise the monies needed by taxing assets and property. The French loans were delayed; instead, they recommended the cooperation of the Danubian states. It appeared that Romanian-Hungarian economic cooperation might come to the foreground.

New elections were called in May – the authorities tried, again, to keep the opposition isolated. As for the National Hungarian Party, it won 10 seats in the House of Representatives and 2 in the Senate. (1922: 3 MPs, 3 senators; 1923: 26 MPs and 3 senators; 1926: 14 MPs and 12 senators; 1927: 8 MPs and 1 senator; 1928: 16 MPs and 6 senators.)

Reviewing Iorga's initiatives made in the interest of minorities, it seems that the 1920-1932 period was a series of partial results and failures. On the other, hand it became clear that his readiness to help extended, as he stated it several times, that "everything should be granted in the cultural sphere, but only in the cultural sphere." He considered it an inalienable right of every human being, and those who disallowed it from the minorities could not be reckoned a public-spirited. He promised cultural equality, or, as he termed it, "autonomy," on the occasion of a government debate in 1923, while he was the Prime Minister, and later when he retired from political activity. It was his deep-seated conviction that political independence, or "autonomy," even in a limited form and in however limited an area, carried within itself the possibility of secession or even the restoration of the Habsburg Monarchy. His fears of these possibilities dictated his feelings about:
1.   The establishment of the Hungarian state;
2.   The autonomy of Transylvania; and
3.   The union of the nations in the Danube Basin.

Discounting his election speeches, or his statements to the foreign press, we must credit Iorga for his various flamboyant, if not very effective, acts supporting Hungarian cultural and scientific efforts. They must be taken as positive steps, if for no other reason than he was among the few who placed a value on cultural values. Their safeguarding, safekeeping was as much his concern as the politicians and writers of the minorities. "I am an honest believer in the Romanian-Hungarian spiritual cooperation, and of the point of view that the cultural and spiritual life of the masses of Hungarians living in Romania must be empowered by the widest rights of freedom.."

This aid was depleted when it came to the invitation and maintenance of Hungarian teachers invited to the summer university organized under him, the translation and publishing of anthologies, and the cost of inviting Hungarian theatre companies to perform in Bucharest. By his own admission, he was familiar with the written archival records of Hungary's history but also, through his Hungarian-speaking wife, the classics of Hungarian literature. All this was consistent with the history-falsifying Iorga, whose activities between the World Wars have been criticized by scores of Romanian historians.

From the closing of the Minority Sub-ministry to the
Minority Statute: 1932-1937

The time of the 'government of experts' passed after thirteen months. For a relatively short period, from June 6, 1932 until November 1933, Maniu shared power with Vaida-Voevod in a government of the National Peasant Party. Although it was not Maniu who deposed Iorga from power, the latter's disappointment was so boundless that he drew a very unflattering portrait of Maniu in his memoirs. According to him Maniu, in his starched collar similar to the Hungarian noblemen, was a remnant of the Austro-Hungarian Monarchy, just to introduce "the dictatorship of a handful of Transylvanian politicians who are short of competence and width of intellectual horizon, proud of their social origins, as opposed to their compatriots from the Regat of gypsy and Fanariot descent."[105]

Maniu and his party won 63% of the parliamentary seats during the election in December, and he repeated his well-known promises: decentralization and state subsidies for agriculture. Shortly afterwards, Maniu and the King came into conflict on personal issues and he had to depart. It is worth reading radical Lupu's opinion; he who left the Maniu-Michalache united National Peasant Party and established his independent Peasant Party in 1927. Lupu states the truth when he says that the King decided that he would rule the country instead of - or even opposed to - the governments. "Why did the parliamentary majority come into conflict with Maniu and reconciled with Vaida-Voevod? What explosion blew Maniu and Michalache out of the government in three days? They say that it is a party issue. It is not; changing the leader of the country is of great interest for the nation. The Fanariot era was reviving - the time when the Voivode summoned the Grand Logofat to his chamber, dismissed him and appointed another. This strange process has been going for two and half a years in Romania, irreconcilable with the constitutional government practices of a modern state. European monarchs, by contrast, were able to preserve their thrones only if they observe constitutional practices."[106]

Maniu left but the Peasant Party remained in government, with Vaida-Voevod at its head. He, as an accomplished Transylvanian Romanian politician, did not really believed in the rapprochement of nations in Central Europe and, in order to counterbalance Hungarian revisionist policy, visited several foreign countries in May 1933, aside from attempting to improve his country's economic situation and floating foreign loans. Nevertheless, he too was unable to maneuver between his party and the king's circle for long.

---

[105] Nicolae, Iorga: Cinci ani de restauratie. Valenii-de-Munte, 1932. p. 12.
[106] Szász, Zsombor: The second Agrarian Party government (A második parasztpárti kormány). Hungarian Review (Magyar Szemle), 1934, March. pp. 239-240.

Right-wing tendencies in the last Liberal governments

On November 14, 1933 the Liberals formed the government again. Prime Minister Duca began his work with firm resolution and a strong-handed policy. His major target was to avoid the danger of German occupation, while maintaining the unconditional observation of the peace treaties, and to demolish the extreme right in the country. At its meeting on December 9, the Cabinet disbanded the Iron Guard. In the following election, Duca won more than 50% of the votes. The fact that the Liberals won more votes in the Szeklerland than the Hungarian Party indicates the fairness of the voting. On December 29, Iron Guards assassinated Duca at the railway station of Sinaija. It was followed by a series of shocking murders – the last victims of which was Iorga - and marked the beginning of country's drift to the right. The Liberal Angelescu followed Duca as head of government - he of bad reminiscences for Hungarians - and immediately proclaimed martial law.

He was followed a few days later, on January 3, 1934 by Tatarescu, who represented the young Liberals gathered around the Credit Bank who conformed to the King's policy. For several years, the situation seemed to come to a lull in the highest governing circles of Romania. Following the return of the King, governments changed one another with Titulescu shaping the country's foreign policy and the Liberals governing in the spirit of Duca's heritage, i.e., aligned with Great Britain and France, as well as nursing close relations with the Little Entente - government orders, the establishment of new industries, the increase of state control, the reduction of customs fees, the cancellation of 50-70% of the debts and lifting the barriers against foreign capital were uppermost in the plans. The result was a record output of the Romanian economy in 1938. However, under the Tatarescu-government, certain measures were also aimed to reduce the authority of Parliament. Its minority policy, following the trend of the age, was dominated by the unfortunate and tragic antagonism of revisionism and anti-revisionism - the dismissal of minority employees grew to serious proportions, e.g.- the Act on the protection of national labor force, passed on July 16, 1934 stated that 80% of company employees had to be of Romanian origin, and teachers were forced to pass strict language exams.

In February 1934, the daily, *Corentul*, conducted an inquiry and directed seven questions to 160,000 public personalities and asked for support and proposals to stop the threat of minorities' gaining ground.[107] The questions were as follows:

1. Do you think that, under the present circumstances, the native Romanian element is in an overwhelmingly inferior situation vis-à-vis the national minorities?
2. Do you believe that a policy serving the future of the nation can prevail if the society's elite does not consist of the members of the majority nation?
3. If it is so, what do you propose for solution?

---

[107] Szász, Zsombor: Numerus Valachicus. Hungarian Review (Magyar Szemle), 1935, May. pp. 94-104.

    ☞ In the short run?

    ☞ In the long-term?

4. Don't you think that it would be the duty of the Romanian State to protect the scattered intellectual elements of the majority nation by administrative measures?

5. What are the most urgently demanded measures today?

6. Do you think that the various levels of current public education meet the demands of the Romanian nation?

7. What other public educational organizations would you propose, while selecting among the above-mentioned levels, in order to guarantee intellectual and moral discipline in the continuing interests of the Romanian State?

The majority of answers indicated that the most feared threat was the "expansion" of the minorities. Almost all the responses agreed that the introduction of a 75-80% *numerus clausus* (ed., reverse affirmative action) was necessary. Moreover, Gheorghe Bratianu proposed to repatriate certain minority groups, including the Romanians in Macedonia. Professor Juga of the Cluj University claimed it was catastrophic that the Hungarians' proportion was still around 80% in public offices, the post office, the railways and banks of Transylvania. He demanded urgent state measures to rectify it. It is no coincidence that the experts of that time had a predilection to quote various statistics and tables about the proportion of minorities and majorities in factories, law offices and banks run by minority owners.

When Sabin Manuila, like many of his compatriots, spoke about the threats of national minorities, they referred first of all to Jews. The Romanian *numerus clausus* also aimed "to re-Romanize the Szeklers and the Hungarians of Rimetea (Torockó)," a pioneer of such an idea was none other than Nicolae Iorga, as early as the beginning of the 20th century. He introduced such 'proofs' as, "Slowly but surely we have to reclaim the Szeklers whose faces, songs, houses and dances are like ours."[108] It is almost certainly his legacy that the official Romanian policy accepted this idea in 1935-37 and a 15-year plan was worked out, in May 1935, to re-Romanize the Szeklers. In an interview given to the *Universul*, Gociman Aurel stated that 300,000 of the 550,000 Szeklers in Transylvania were originally Romanians, and who should and could be re-Romanized through intensive linguistic instruction and by moving Szekler civil servants to Romanian territories. (Naturally, this theory is wholly unscientific.)

In July 1935, a new party, the National Christian Party (Nemzeti Keresztény Párt) was established by the merger of Transylvanian writer-politician Octavian Goga's National Agrarian Party (Nemzeti Agrárpárt) and the anti-Semitic Professor Ioan Cuza's Christian National Defense League (Keresztény Nemzeti Védelmi Liga) of Iasi. The fundamental party principle - which two professors of the Cluj University, Silviu Dragomir and Ion Lupas, also joined - was 'Romania belongs to Romanians'. Minorities, examined in detail, were divided into three categories:

---

[108] Neamul Romanesc, 1927. decembrie 13.

1. The German (Saxon) minority that has adapted itself to Romanian circumstances and which has the right to hold offices in proportion to its number.
2. The revisionist minorities controlled from abroad: the Hungarians, the Bulgarians and the Ukrainians, on whom the *numerus clausus* should be enforced.
3. The Jews, who should be completely excluded from the political, economic and artistic life of the country.

Under the name of 'Numerus Valachicus', an anti-Semitic and anti-minority direction developed into a movement under Alexandru Vaida-Voevod. In a pamphlet, "Call to the Country," issued on May 12, 1935 he stated, among other things,[109] 'Numerus Valachicus' doesn't lay claim to anything illegal, it only demands what is due to the Romanian citizens living on Romanian land. 'Numerus Valachicus' stands for Romanian truth, and every good Romanian, whether educated, a peasant or a worker, male or female, young or old, has to vote for it. The entire Romanian nation awaits the dawn of its day of truth. 'Numerus Valachicus' is identical with creative nationalism, which is destined to uniting the various generations of all social classes in to one community by organizing fraternal societies under the principles of law and order, prestige, labor and unselfishness, in the spirit of the slogan "for the Nation and the King, for the Motherland and Justice." 'Numerus Valachicus' is the thunderbolt that smashes corruption and the embezzlement of public monies, breaks the chains of international capitalism, which exploits the energy of the nation. Moreover, 'Numerus Valachicus' will establish cartels for the workers, liberate the peasants from serf hood, institute schools, put an end to the financial elite for the glory of the nation and God, and establish press and literature on the basis of pure, national, morality and Christian principles. It will naturally not tolerate anything which is hostile to the Romanian nation and race; it will put an end to looseness, corruption and exploit the extraordinary wealth of the Romanian land; it will end the insufferable situation that based on the Alba Iulia Resolutions, minority treaties, the League of Nations, the constitution, democracy and France, the natural rights of the Romanians in their homeland are ignored. 'Numerus Valachicus' will, of course, solve the Jewish issue, which has become chronic, especially in the Northeastern part of the country and is one of the severe threats to the interests of the Romanians, because "we Romanians are the real owners of Great Romania." This slogan was repeated several times, for emphasis, in the pamphlet by Vaida-Voevod.

These movements naturally extended over the entire country and also influenced official policy towards national minorities. In July 1934, an Act was passed making it compulsory that the staffs of economic, industrial and trade companies, as well as at private ventures, be staffed by at least 80% Romanians, and special committees were set up to oversee its observance.

This was still not enough for the leader of the Iron Guard, Corneliu Codreanu. At the Third Congress of the Anti-revisionist League, he demanded

---

[109] Vaida-Voevod, Alexandru: Chemarea catre tara. Bucuresti, 1935. pp. 7-11.

that all minority public servants should be removed from within 100 km of the borders. From 1935, greater attention was paid to Romanian spelling of geographical names. Iorga himself found it too severe a measure, stating that, during the Dualism, Romanian papers in Transylvania were allowed to spell geographical names in Romanian. The tax burden in the Hungarian-inhabited regions increased further. In 1934-35, in the Romanian populated Buzau County it was 22.5%, in Hungarian populated Csík, 121.6%.

Angelescu again raised his voice in the nation's educational policy. He stated that re-Romanization should begin in kindergarten. In the 1934-35 academic year, according to official Romanian sources, 175,000 of the 261,000 school age Hungarian children were educated in Romanian schools. From 1934 on, minority teachers had to pass compulsory aptitude tests. In 1938, this measure was rendered stricter by limiting applicants for Romanian literature and language teacher tests only to Romanians. For minority teachers, finding posts at state schools and secondary schools became more difficult from 1936 on; the act was only modified in the 1938-39 school year when name analysis was no longer the deciding factor on which school children could attend.

Changes in internal politics were indicated by several new phenomena. In addition to the right wing, peasant parties came to dominate political life. In 1932, Grigore Iunian established a new Party, the Radical Peasant Party (Radikális Parasztpárt). Its primary goal was to try to prevent the Iron Guard from seizing power. In 1935, the youth wing of the party took a firm stand on the retention of the parliamentary system, the dissolution of the Senate, the enlarged role of parliamentary committees and local autonomy, central subsidies for peasants' domestic industry, the expansion of industrial production utilizing domestic raw materials, and the observation of peace treaties. From 1934 on, Radulescu-Motru thought the 'Peasant State' best fitted the psyche of the Romanian nation. In his book, 'The Ideology of the Romanian State',[110] he saw reality thus, "As the Romanian state developed under peculiar and adverse circumstances, first under Turkish, then European powers, we have always lived in a provisional state ... The real Romanian state ... is the exact opposite of the Romanian state described in the Constitution. This has been often noted by many people. It comes as no surprise to anybody, this contradiction between the Constitution and political reality. Yet you can not build a people's future on lies. The Romanian state is the creation of the European big powers, the creature of obsolete European mentality. Their aim was to create a democratic and civil state but both ideas are foreign to the national traditions of the Romanian people. The Romanian state must return to its real base - the peasantry."

Michalache drafted the new program of the National Peasant Party. He aimed it as "centered upon a united, cooperative and national peasant state," stressing the need to raise the level of the villages to that of the towns, and where the state must manage out the exchange of agricultural and industrial products.

---

[110] Szász, Zsombor: The new Constitution and the minorities (Az új alkotmány és a kisebbségek). Hungarian Minority (Magyar Kisebbség). 1938, May. p. 69.

Michalache also emphasized that, because 70-80% of the Romanian citizens worked in agriculture, the Romanian State was of a peasant character.

Then, he laid out how the Party planned to address the minority issue:

1. "...the National Peasant Party is of the opinion that, beyond racial differences, the majority and minority nations have to sincerely unite in the love and defense of the homeland;

2. To achieve this goal, the National Peasant Party - having faith in the principle of political and civic freedom and equality, and disregarding differences among races, denominations and languages – is of the firm opinion that the basis of dealing with the minorities are international treaties of which Romania is a signatory.

3. The National Peasant Party's considers it a duty to respect the use of minority languages in church services and education, in line with international treaties. To this aim, and to improve the financial situation of minority clergy and teachers, the Party is ready to provide state financial aid to facilitate their social and cultural situation.

4. In order to train those people who wish to embark in public administration in regions inhabited by minorities, the Party is ready to set up minority language and literature departments in Romanian-language state secondary (high) schools to promote cultural and intellectual rapprochement of the races. Similarly, it will take look after the training of minority teachers, both women and men.

5. The Party will pay special attention to the issue of re-Romanizing citizens who became denationalized."[111]

The split in the Liberal Party became evident in the 1937 election. Constantin C. Bratianu, who entered the campaign with a traditional program, wanted to remain in opposition. Tatarescu - the head of the Romanian delegation at the peace talks in 1946 - joined forces with the noticeably right-leaning Vaida-Voevod of the National Peasant Party, the leader of the Romanian Front (Frontul Romanesc), the minority German Party, and Iorga. Maniu, who, at this time still thought the King's dictatorship far more dangerous than that of the Iron Guard, signed an election pact with the latter, on the condition of preserving democracy and continuing the British-French orientation. Fifty-six parties entered the election in December of 1937 - none of them achieved the 40% necessary to form the government (the right wing received a total of 25%).[112]

To the surprise of the whole country, the King asked the National Christian Party, led by Goga - which reached 10% of the popular vote - to form the government. The Monarch justified his decision by saying, "It is obvious that public opinion in the country is tending towards nationalism. That is why I asked the National Christian Party to form a government because it is more nationalistic than the others." In his press communiqué, Octavian Goga, a friend of the

---

[111] Szász, Zsombor: Constitutional revisions in Romania (Alkotmányrevizió Romániában). Hungarian Review (Magyar Szemle). 1935, October. p. 164.

[112] Szász, Zsombor: The new Romanian nation (Az új román állam). Hungarian Review (Magyar Szemle). 1938, April. p. 372.

prominent Hungarian poet, Endre Ady, and translator of Imre Madách' drama, "The Tragedy of Man," extended it by stating "What is happening here is nothing but the Romanian race's effort to be master in its own land..." This consisted of Goga's immediate issuing of discriminatory measures against Jews.[113]

Goga viewed his coming to power as a wave of protest against oppressive and foreign elements and the victory of the national idea. Romania for Romanians" - he voiced, like many of his contemporaries. The forebears of the Iron Guardsmen, as well as the Guardsmen themselves, held the conviction that, "We want a Romania free of Jews and Hungarians!" This was nothing new, either, but it was the first time that the persecution of Jews became part of the government's program. In a radio speech, Goga envisaged the following urgent measures that needed to be addressed:[114]

1. "We have suspended the publication of papers *Adevarul*, *Dimineata* and *Lupta*. I will take similar measures against others, including those obscene publications, which the go against the traditional Romanian spirit.
2. I have canceled the free railway passes of more than 120 Jewish journalists.
3. I have under consideration the canceling of Jews' permits for selling alcohol in the villages and re-issuing them to disabled war veterans instead.
4. I have begun a study into the revision of citizenship of those Jews, who flooded into Romania by the hundreds of thousands following the war, in order to amass wealth by corruption and fraud. The removal of these people requires detailed measures to be taken.
5. Similarly under study is the urgent appointment of government commissioners to foreign companies in order to ensure the enforcement of the act protecting the Romanian labor force.
6. Also under study is the Romanization of all companies operating with domestic capital and receiving benefits from the State, while only employing foreigners to the exclusion of Romanians.
7. Goga also decreed that only over-40 year-old Christian women were allowed to work in Jewish households."

Due to British and French protests, the anti-Semitic measures were withdrawn after three weeks.[115] At his government's directive, the British ambassador - though in the most diplomatic words - warned the Romanian Foreign Secretary to observe the minority treaty. In early February, in the League of Nations in Geneva, the issue of anti-Semitism in Romania was also raised but the Romanians justified the measures by claiming that without them the chances of the far more anti-Semitic Iron Guard would increase to a dangerous extent.[116]

It was primarily France that intervened on behalf of the Romanian Jews. The French ambassador was not satisfied with verbal warning, but he handed written notes to Goga. He stressed that, if Romania did not change its anti-Semitic policies, it was putting its foreign loans in jeopardy. As the Romanian

---

[113] MOL, Ministry of Internal Affairs, K. 149. VII. reserv. 190. File 4057.
[114] MOL, K.63. 1938-27/1
[115] MOL, K.63. 1938-27/4
[116] MOL, K.63. 1938-27/7

government failed to respond to either the first or the second note of the Congres Jui Mondial (World Jewish Congress) in Geneva, the protest was put on the agenda of the Council's meeting on May 8-14, 1938.[117] The Romanian delegation, in an attempt to have the petitions withdrawn, offered to have all discriminatory measures against the Jews lifted. The representatives of Congres Jui Mondial took 'a wait and see attitude' but did not withdraw the petitions. At the end of the year, well-informed diplomats in Bucharest reported that Romania was considering some sort of plan for the solution of the Jewish issue in Central Europe. Their deportation was under consideration, and in this Romania expected the assistance of Poland and Hungary, as well.

Royal dictatorship - an attempt to avoid an extreme Right-wing threat

In the absurd situation, when only 39 out of the 387 seat legislation belonged to the governing party, nothing could be done except to hold a general election. The hopes of the Iron Guard, that they could double their support in the upcoming election, filled the Romanian political parties with fear. Thus, with their support, the King - and the parties, as well - thought that introduction of a direct, royal dictatorship was the only feasible alternative.

Several former ministers took posts in the new government, headed by church prelate Miron Cristea. Martial law was again proclaimed, power was assumed by the new prefects. The new assembly convened in accordance with the wishes of the King, i.e., executive power - the King's - grew; he appointing the members of the government and it was accountable to him; between parliamentary sessions, the King ruled by decree and was not obliged to seek parliamentary assent to sign political and military agreements; age of suffrage was raised from 21 to 30; MP terms went from 4 to 6 years and that of Senators from 4 to 9 years. The constitutional assurance of human rights became illusory. The Court of Appeals was authorized to override the constitutionality of laws; constitutional laws could only be modified at the initiative of the King.[118]

Several sections of the Constitution dealt with national minorities. The Orthodox Romanian Church was declared the dominant Church and the Greek Catholic Church enjoyed preference over the rest. The Orthodox Patriarch, the country's Archbishops, as well as every Orthodox Romanian and Greek Catholic Diocesan Bishop were deemed to hold Senate seats. For the rest of denominations, one bishop of each church, if he represented more than 200,000 believers, was allowed a seat. As a result, only the Calvinist bishop held Senate membership by law, the Unitarians none. None of the three Catholic bishops, representing more than 500,000 Hungarian believers, held a Senate seat because the Archbishop of Bucharest represented the Catholic Church. It was also stated that Romanian majority considerations should be observed in filling public offices.

---

[117] MOL, K.63. 1938-27/4
[118] Eastern Journal, Legal guide (Keleti Újság, Jogi kalauz). 1938, February 28.

The constitution did not invalidate the Act on the Protection of National Labor, and none of the measures or laws humiliating the minorities were modified. Forced conversion from the Roman Catholic religion to the Greek Catholic Church continued. The constitution limited both the freedom of assembly and the use of languages. As an example, invitation cards of Hungarian associations, family notifications, obituaries and engagement could not publicized in Hungarian. Any Hungarian folk song, no matter how innocuous, was forbidden.

Romania renewed its diplomatic activity between March and September 1938. Steps were taken to strengthen the country's borders. A day after of Anschluss (Austria's occupation by Germany), on March 13, participants at the meeting held in the Royal Palace were certain that German expansion would not stop at Austria. After Czechoslovakia, Romania was sure to be the next target, whose crude oil supply was of the greatest interest to Germany. In response, the bolstering of defenses of the Western borders of the country was launched on April 19. On May 22, Romanian Secretary of State Petrescu-Comnen summoned German ambassador Fabricius to his office and informed him: if an armed conflict broke out between Germany and Czechoslovakia, it would lead to a Europe-wide war. In this case, Romania would not be neutral to the fate of Czechoslovakia. He asked Fabricius to intercede with his government in the interest of avoiding a catastrophe.

Changes in Hungarian-Romanian relations at the end of the 1920's
Plans for cooperation in Central-Europe and Szekler autonomy

The relations of Hungary to its neighbors, including Romania, were based on the fundamental principle of 'everything returned', while Romania took a stand of 'not an inch'. During 1921, Czechoslovakia, the Serbo-Croatian-Slovenian Kingdom and Romania concluded an agreement - the establishment of the Little Entente - which envisaged not only mutual assistance in case of a Hungarian attack against any of the parties but also the coordination of their policy on issues in connection with Hungary. For example, united, they wanted to force extremely high war damage reparations. The amount was not defined in 1922, but the total state assets of Hungary were segregated for its coverage. When the question of loan for Hungary was raised, the Romanian, Czechoslovak and Yugoslav parties, under the pretext of overseeing the utilization of the loan, strove to be included in the committee supervising Hungarian disarmament. (It is worth noting that the Romanian military occupation of Hungary resulted in 700 civilian casualties and damages of 9 billion Crowns - the Hungarian currency of the time.) In response to the 1928 declaration of peaceful [border] revision by Hungary, and the support expressed by conservative British politician Lord Rothermere, as well as the Hungarian-Italian alliance, forced the Little Entente to further reinforce their anti-Hungarian military alliance during their Bucharest conference in June 1928.

The same year, when Transylvanian Iuliu Maniu was in government, the possibility and necessity of cooperation in Central-Europe, in the form of various confederation plans, came into prominence in international politics. On the other hand, in Romania, this issue was raised as the autonomy of the German and Szekler minorities, and became the central topic of the studies by the experts of minority issues.

As early as in the beginning of the 1920's, C. A. Macartney, as opposed to his French contemporaries, was convinced that the Paris Treaty was a wrong decision and carried the seeds of another war. Besides, it was natural that the French, British and Germans, while eager to establish their own political and economic spheres of interest, were intent in assuring that the peace and security of Europe enjoyed a priority.

Aristide Briand, honorary president of the Pan-European Union, was of the opinion that the new peace alliance would be permanent, the starting point being the Pan-European Union itself, to which he would link the Danube States, and could not exclude Germany's joining. His aim was to increase French influence and extend economic cooperation, as well. At this stage, Britain's opposition became apparent. In May 1931, Germany declared its vision of a German-Austrian customs union. This idea activated both its Western opponents: France and Britain. Benes' July 1931 confederation proposal of Austria, Czechoslovakia and Hungary, supported by Britain, was openly aimed against Germany. As mentioned before, Maniu had ideas of his own, as early as 1930, about a kind of Danubian system of alliance.

At the Geneva disarmament conference in February 1932, André Tardieu took a stand on the side of the cultural autonomy of the minorities. Romanian Gafencu conducted talks in Hungary on the realization of the Tardieu-plan, as Budapest hosted the Central-European Economic Conference in early February 1932, attended by delegations from Austria, Czechoslovakia, Hungary, Poland, Romania and Yugoslavia.

When István Bethlen (Prime Minister of Hungary, 1921-1931) met Romanian King Carol II in Timisoara (Temesvár) in January 1932 and the idea of a personal union and the Romanian-Hungarian confederation, originally proposed in 1919-1920, were discussed again. On November 18 of the same year, university professors, army officers and clergymen established the Transylvanian Committee of Anti-Revisionist Movement. Its founding document envisaged the repeated occupation of Budapest by Romanian forces in case of any action threatening the territorial integrity of Romania.

Fundamentally, the 1930's mark the beginning of a duality in Romanian politics. On the one hand, the expressions of official attempts to promote friendly relations, while on the other, what the stated government line did not dare voice - the claim for seizing new territories, the call for further anti-Hungarian measures and hardening of Romanian foreign policy towards Hungary - were beginning to be heard in certain official and unofficial circles of society. It is also a tradition in Romanian diplomacy - derived from the substance of the Little Entente - that Bucharest and Prague (and perhaps Belgrade) coordinate their politics.

Gábor Tusa finished his study, entitled *Szekler Religious and Educational Autonomy*, on Christmas 1929. The essence of his theory was that: one, human rights, ensured by the Constitution, were the natural and inalienable rights of man; two, cultural autonomy is established by the minority and the State only acknowledges it; and three, the assurance of territorial autonomy is the responsibility of the State.[119] The rights given to the Szeklers and Saxons referred only to education and religious issues and are included in the sphere of cultural autonomy, guaranteed by the 11th point of the minority agreement. The analytical clarification of concepts also provided Tusa the opportunity to point out that cultural autonomy, too, has not been realized in Romania.

The above-mentioned 11th point was also the starting point of József Papp's study entitled *Transylvanian Szekler religious and educational self-government* [120]. The point states: "Romania assents to the establishment of religious and educational self-governments in the Szekler and Saxon communities in Transylvania, under the control of the Romanian state." According to Papp, not one step was taken by the Romanian State toward this target. In fact, several rights were annulled, such as the establishment of the cultural zone, the confiscation of private properties, the establishment of state schools at the expense of the villages. He recalled that minority cultural autonomy in Estonia, introduced in 1925 - enshrined in the Estonian constitution - considered the interested parties as pseudo-legal entities. Papp tried, primarily, to define the concept of 'local self-government'. He wrote: "it means the relegation of certain state tasks and rights, i.e., public power, to local self-government bodies to be carried out by the interested parties." In actual fact, it means that the drafting of rules, the organization and the budgeting responsibilities would be vested in local bodies. Papp published the following detailed program: 1) Szekler autonomy should be realized, which is simply personal cultural autonomy, for every citizen over the age of 18; 2) the self-governing body that is to be established should be considered a state administrative agency; 3) its sphere includes the operation, management and supervision of schools; 4) it has the right to make the rules and collect taxes; 5) its financial base will be provided by state subsidies and its own resources; 6) the state has a supervisory role over this self-government system.

Arthur Balogh published his study, *Szekler religious and educational self-government*, in a Transylvanian Scientific Pamphlets (Erdélyi Tudományos Füzetek), the publication of the Transylvanian Museum Society.[121] Balogh, who represented Transylvanian-Hungarians at international minority conferences, stated explicitly: "we may only speak about the rights of minorities, if the minority gains collective rights." He felt that the least a national minority might demand was cultural autonomy, but the target of a minority was "to take certain areas of public activities and rights out of state jurisdiction and vest them in the minority, as a pseudo-legal entity, which has its own minority self-government."

---

[119] Tusa, Gábor: Szekler religious and educational autonomy (A székely vallási és tanügyi autonómia). Cluj Napoca, Miverva Press, 1930.

[120] Papp, József: Transylvanian Szekler religious and educational self-government (Az erdélyi székelyek vallási és tanügyi önkormányzat). Lugos, 1931.

[121] Balogh, Arthur: Szekler religious and educational self-government (A székely vallási és iskolai önkormányzat). Cluj Napoca-Kolozsvár, Miverva Press, 1932.

Incidentally, Balogh defined the Szekler and Saxon communities to mean the totality belonging to these minorities.

Dénes Molnár of Tirgu Secuiesc (Kézdivásárhely) forwarded his contribution to József Papp's study on June 22, 1931, the second month of the Iorga government. According to his analysis, Szekler and Saxon religious and school self-government meant the following: one, the maintenance of minority schools had to be covered by the state budget (as opposed to the 10 billion budget deficit of the 1933 Liberal government that was shifted to the inhabitants of Transylvania in the form of taxes); and two, this principle should cover the Regat and Moldova, since Szeklers lived there in significant number. Molnár felt two steps to be necessary: the office of self-government to be extended to the entire Hungarian population of Romania and also the shifting of every central administrative task to local bodies in the Szekler counties, not only in the Church and educational areas.

The National Hungarian Party (OMP) took seriously Iorga's promise for settling the minority issue. After the Party passed a resolution on July 24, 1931, it asked Árpád Paál, one of the authors of *The Shouted Word* (Kiáltó Szó), to prepare a study.[122] The *Law proposal for the self-determination of public education of Szekler communities,* his draft of 125 paragraphs, Paál wrote the following: the Szekler community is the entirety of the Romanian citizens who have lived in the Szeklerland and its vicinity (Csík, Háromszék, Udvarhely, Marosszék, Aranyosszék counties) as natives (having resided there for one generation before December 9, 1919), of Hungarian mother tongue and were also registered in the general census. The authority of the Szekler community's self-government would extend to manage church and educational issues in given areas, under the supervision of the State.

A general census to occur on the basis of questionnaires distributed to each household. "The Szekler community provides personnel and assets for the management of Church and educational tasks on its home grounds." Home grounds meant the Churches and schools, the estate of the institutions and its personnel, were under community protection in order that they may support their educational institutions themselves.

The middle level agency of the Szekler community area covers the public arena. Its task is to operate secondary (high) schools, vocational schools, orphanages, and to supervise elementary education. In addition, it is to directly supervise and manage common property. It is to submit proposals to the central Szekler board regarding the donations offered by the communities for public education and welfare purposes. Representatives were to be elected by the following ratios: 10 after 10-20,000 citizens and 20 for over 20,000. The manager of the community area was to be responsible for the financial-economic activities of mines, forests, as well as industrial and trade companies.

---

[122] Paál, Árpád: Law proposal for the self-determination of public education of Szekler communities (Törvénytervezet a székely közületek közmuvelodési önkormányzatához). Cluj Napoca, 1932.

The council of community areas was to elect the central body, the Grand Council of Szekler Communities: the Members of the Parliament, the Control Commission, to appoint officials representing the community members according to the following numbers: 2 officials in cases of less than 10,000 members, 4 after 10-20,000 members, 6 officials in the Central Board for over 20,000 members. The task of the Central Board was to manage welfare and public educational issues at the highest level of authority of self-government, including the determination of the number of institutions of higher (university), technical and vocational education, and the appointment of tutors and teachers. The planned seat of the Grand Council of Szekler Communities to be in Orodheiu Secuiesc (Székelyudvarhely). The sphere of authority of the Szekler Communities would not encroach on the controls of the State and the Churches, but its office was to maintain close relations with the Ministries in charge of public education and Church affairs. At its General Assembly on July 6, 1933, the NHP included Szekler autonomy in its program, based on Paál's draft bill.

In his study, entitled *Szekler Community Self-government*, written in 1934, Imre Mikó listed his objections against both the Alba Iulia Resolutions, as well as the [international] treaties on minorities. As well, he also presented his own ideas. He considered it a serious fault that self-government had not been granted to the entire Hungarian population in Transylvania, that it only extended to cultural, religious and educational fields, even though the minority agreement signed with the Ruthenians in Czechoslovakia included political self-government, too, and the agreement did not refer to Szeklers in either Moldova or Bukovina. Imre Mikó also reminded us that a resolution was passed at the 9th Minority Congress in Bern, on September 16-19, 1933, that 'on the territory of those countries where a minority people have settled in a closed community, the development of said people, from the view of the state, autonomy, the complete cultural, administrative and political self-determination is the most reasonable solution.'[123]

The formation of Hungarian-Romanian relations: 1936 – 1940

During 1936-37, certain events between the Little Entente and Hungary influenced their relationship. Poland volunteered several times to mediate between Hungary and Romania. On February 7, 1937, when László Bárdossy again assumed the post of ambassador in Bucharest, he called on Foreign Minister Mihai Antonescu posed the question, "What is Romania's stand on Hungary achieving military parity?"[124] As the Italians stipulated that the Italian-Romanian treaty hinged on Hungary and Romania settling their affairs – and the rapidly improving Hungarian-Yugoslav relationship was looked at with envy by both Czechoslovakia and Romania – in June of 1937, the Romanian ambassador to Hungary received instruction to convey that the Romanian government supports Hungary's achieving military equality, but only if a mutual non-

---

[123] Mikó, Imre: Szekler community self-government (A székely közületi önkormányzat). Hungarian Minority (Magyar Kisebbség). 1934, July-August.
[124] MOL, K. 63. 1938. 27/7 file.

aggression pact is also signed. This coincided with the Romanian king's visit to Warsaw and was meant to impress on the Poles that relations were returning to normal.[125]

The Hungarian reply was that this could only happen if it was *preceded* by a serious gesture by the Romanians regarding the minority issue. The Romanians, on the other hand, were adamant - in spite of all the Polish and Italian arguments - that the non-aggression treaty must precede the minority statute. At the end of November, 1937 Antonescu summoned ambassador Bárdossy and informed him that bilateral talks can be resumed after the Romanian elections.[126]

The elections over, Romania began to build up its forces on its western frontier. Oradea (Nagyvárad) was teeming with soldiers by December 29. A report, forwarded to the Hungarian Interior Ministry on January 15, 1938 notes that in the area North and South of the Körös River, a chain of 30 fortifications were established, each having concrete walls of 2 to 5 meters thick, set 150 meters apart and connected by trenches. Each fort had dual access - camouflaged by sod. This conflicted with the oft-repeated statement of peaceful Romanian intentions. Rather, it illuminated a fear of a possible Hungarian attack.

The shaping of Hungarian-Romanian relations after 1938

In response to international events during 1938, Romania seemingly softened from its previous stand and looked to be taking concrete steps in the question of the Hungarians of Romania. On the eve of the Anschluss, Romanian diplomats - through Turkish and Polish intermediaries - let it be known that the government was ready to issue a new minority law in the interest of improved Hungarian-Romanian relations. It is interesting to note the comments of the Polish ambassador to Romania made to Bárdossy, in which he said that in the interest of settling the Hungarian-Romanian affairs, his government urged him to go to extreme measures.[127] According to him, the German threat to both countries should force closer cooperation, said cooperation to be sealed by a personal union between the two under the crown of Romanian King Carol II.[128] The Romanian side, also exerting pressure through Italy, tried to moderate Hungary's demands by voicing that it was the government's wish come to an agreement. The sticking point was Hungary's demand to retain an oversight role over the execution of minority affairs.

Hungarian politicians were of the opinion that Romanian politicians were deeply divided. Titulescu, along with Comnen, wished to continue the policies of the past towards the Hungarian minority and Hungary; the other side came to the

---

[125] Ibid.
[126] Ibid.
[127] MOL, K. 63. 11/1938-27/6 file.
[128] Ibid.

conclusion that Hungarian-Romanian raprochement was beneficial to both sides - especially since they increasingly saw the Little Entente as impotent.[129]

On March 12, 1938 in view of the Anschluss, Tatarescu summoned ambassador Bárdossy and informed him that the Little Entente intended to continue the talks with Hungary begun the previous year.[130] At a meeting in Sinaia (Szinaja) on May 14, 1938 the representatives of Hungary and the Little Entente met.[131] The Romanian minority statute was proclaimed. With it, the king tried to reassure the West that his intention was to defuse the minority issue, to lay it to rest.[132]

The statute assigned accountability to the Prime Minister's office and assigned chief councillor status to the Minorities Section of the Ministry of Education. The Section's activities were detailed in an enacting writ in August, 1938. Its activities encompassed all areas of the minority question but was restricted to a fact finding, oversight capacity. It could make recommendations to the Prime Minister who would then pass those along to the relevant Ministries.

The Cabinet records contain the following 28 points:[133]

1. Romanian citizens have the right, without differentiation based on language, race or religion, to establish schools, institutions, cultural and denominational associations;
2. The state will implement subsidies from the national budget to the supporters of these schools.
3. An appropriate portion of the 14% municipal tax will be turned towards minority private schools.
4. Their right to publicly exist is to be clarified.
5. Those person legally responsible for a childs education are solely entitled to determine a child's nationality and school.
6. Minority Sunday schools and youth organizations have a right to function, within the law and their bylaws.
7. Minority high school religious teachers may be appointed and installed, but must take an examination based on their theological diploma.
8. High school matriculation examinations must be taken before teachers who are conversant with the students' native tongue who may take the examination in their native language.
9. Civilian authorities must respect the rights of the religious representatives of the historical minorities.
10. Secular authorities do not have the right to interfere in the matter of religious services.
11. The Pastors' stipends from government grants, under the terms of the Education Act, is to be in the same proportion.

---

[129] Ibid.
[130] Campus, Eliza: Din politica externa a Romaniei. 1928-1940. Bucuresti, Editura Militara, 1980.
[131] Calafeteanu, Ion: Diplomatia romaneasca in sud-estul Europei. 1938-1940. Bucuresti, Editura politica, 1980.
[132] Mikó, Imre: The Minority Statute (A kisebbségi statutum). Credit (Hitel). 1938, May.
[133] Monitorul Oficial. 1938. August, issue 4, p. 178.

12. A Romanian citizen's racial origin, linguistic or religious affiliation can not present a barrier to holding a state, county or municipal office.
13. A minority representative on a municipal council may express himself in his native language but the minutes of those meetings must be kept in Romanian.
14. Those minority citizens who still are not conversant in the state language, may present their petition in their native language, accompanied by a notarized Romanian translation.
15. Official written exchanges will be in the language of the state.
16. Administrators in minority settlements are responsible to know the language of the local minority.
17. In settlements mainly populated by a minority, judges and assistant judges are to be named from among them.
18. In newspapers, journals and gazettes, the place name where it is published may appear in the minority language.
19. Family names may be retained and written in the original.
20. Those state or municipal employees, who possess Romanian school diplomas or certificates are free from further Romanian language examinations.
21. Those minority employees working in public schools, part of the elementary or high school teaching staff, have a right to the 50% railway discount.
22. In the judicial system, minority citizens may present their case in their native tongue if not represented by legal cousel.
23. Citizens of the historical minorities may be represented in the affected areas:
    - Chambers of commerce and trade;
    - Economic chambers; and
    - Labor organizations.
24. Minority banks and financial institutions may develop unimpeded as similar sized Romanian institutions.
25. Commercial signage must be displayed in Romanian. The minorities may present them in their own language, as well.
26. In Romania, only the Romanian flags may be displayed. The government may grant permission for certain associations, and in certain locations, to display their own flags or unique symbols.
27. The situation of the Transylvanian Association, the Szekler National Museum of Sfântu Gheorghe (Sepsiszentgyörgy) and the Teleki Library of Tirgu Mures (Marosvásárhely) must be amicably resolved.
28. The Transylvanian Hungarian Economic Association's continued activity is to be ensured.

The fundamental weakness of the declaration was that the Cabinet tried to address the minority problem through decree, not through legal and constitutional methods. Moreover, certain objections arose regarding some of the points.[134]

Point 1: Classifying minority schools as private schools should have ensured them the same rights as public schools.

---

[134] MOL, K.63. 1938-27/4 file.

Points 2-3 only state vague generalities regarding state support. Apart from teaching in the mother tongue(s), the state refused to sanction the same rights as in point 5, where it defines who has the right to define the student's ethnicity.

Point 7 maintains the prejudicial point of equivalency testing.

According to point 8, students must take their examinations before their own teachers; the state can only appoint an examination supervisor.

Point 9 does not ensure the autonomy of the churches, especially as the decree of May 13, 1938 states that funds for this purpose from church sources must be remitted to the state.

Point 12 does not ensure proportional representation in state offices.

Point 13 states that where the minority population reaches 10%, minutes of meetings must be kept in the minority's language.

In spite of point 14, the authorities still refused to accept petitions in the Hungarian language. It must be noted that the intent of point 16 is that the officials in minority settlements must be chosen from the minorities, similar to the selection of the judges and assistant judges, not appointed from above. These two points to be observed in large settlements and towns, also.

Point 19, where family names are to be reinstated to their original form.

Regarding point 20, the previous ruling must be withdrawn whereby half of company directors must be Romanians. Re point 20, signs other than business signs must be able to be displayed in Hungarian.

And finally, point 27, the resolution of the situation of the cited Hungarian institutions need concrete proposals not generalities.

What was omitted from the statute: the resolution of the citizenship rights of those omitted from the voting rolls; alteration of the intention of public administrative districts whereby the Szekler townships in Romanian counties are to be realigned; the apportioning of the old Saxon university funds according to the previous statutes to what was rightfully the Hungarian minority's portion; the right of freedom of association and of assembly; the status of pensions, in line with the old Monarchy pensions; rescinding the rules regarding the definition and application of the cultural zones; the return of the Catholic schools and other significant Catholic assets; settlement of the Concordats; the acceptance of monks as of legal standing (pseudo-legal entities); the settlement of the Szekler community properties; an end to the prohibition of public, theatrical and art lovers meetings; cessation on the limits on the purchase and ownership of agricultural lands by the minorities; rescinding the suspension of the agricultural colleges of Csombor and Tirgu Secuiesc (Kézdivásárhely); the return of the school building of the Roman Catholics in Ditro and other Unitarian institutions and freedom for their existence; and finally, the creation of Szekler educational and school autonomy.

Apart from the Hungarian papers, hardly any news surfaced about the creation of the new Chief Commissioner's office and the statute. The secretary of the diplomatic corps of Bucharest put it down to censorship, forbidding newspapers to report it.[135] The silence surrounding the statute reinforced the

---

[135] Ibid.

feeling in Transylvanian Hungarian circles that it was meant as 'window dressing'.

If the minority statute did not cause a stir in the Romanian press, the Hungarian – Little Entente conference in Bled certainly did. On August 27, Maniu commented on it to the foreign press. "Hungary bulldozed the Little Entente's foreign policy and reaped complete victory at the Bled conference. The Little Entente acceded to Hungary's demand for equality in rearmament and in return received nothing. A non-aggression pact is not the equal of this concession, as Hungary has already obligated itself in several international treaties not to start armed aggression against her neighbors. The Little Entente lost vis-à-vis Hungary and conceded the revision of the Peace Pact ..."[136]

The Munich Pact shocked the Romanian public. That is the only explanation why, in certain influential Romanian circles, the thought of a possible Hungarian-Romanian border adjustment arose. According to Romanian reasoning, this was a possibility in the Hungarian populated areas of Oradea (Nagyvárad) and Arad. The Romanian ambassador in Budapest made a similar comment in the presence of his Polish colleague.[137]

Both sides were kept in active speculation by the Czechoslovak – Hungarian talks held in Komárom between October 9-13, 1938, the offered autonomy for the Hungarian populated areas, the nearness of the territorial revisions and their impact on Hungarian – Romanian relations and the Transylvanian question. The Hungarian ambassador in London reported that the Romanian ambassador expressed his hopes thus: "the solution to the Hungarian – Czechoslovak territorial question will drag on, until the major power will decide among themselves." To this, he added, "while the return of the Hungarian populated areas of Czechoslovakia to Hungary will not be difficult, the problem of the Hungarian minorities living elsewhere can only conceivably be resolved by their resettlement.[138] At this time, both the Polish and Italian diplomatic circles hoped to resolve Hungarian – Romanian relations by having non-officials - men of stature - from both sides sit down at the table. Polish diplomats mentioned the names of Stephen Bethlen and Tatarescu.[139]

The Hungarian People's Union's impact on Hungarian-Romanian Relations to the Second Vienna Resolution

Shortly after the introduction of the Minority Statute, Romania was divided into 10 administrative provinces. The creators of the law aimed to ensure a Romanian majority in each province. Thus, Háromszék and Brasov counties were attached to Buceg with its center in Bucharest, and Lower-Fehér, Torda-Aranyos, Maros-Torda, Fogaras, Greater and Lesser Kukullo, Szeben, Csik and Udvarhely were melted into Maros province, administered from Alba Iulia.

---

[136] MOL, K.63. 1938-27/7 file.
[137] Ibid.
[138] Ibid.
[139] Ibid.

A decree was published on December 16, 1938 creating the National Rebirth Front as the sole political organization. According to the executive instruction's 6th point, minorities that become part of the organization may create sub-groups where they may exercise all those rights afforded to them by the laws in effect. The law was aimed in part to serve the King's notions and partly as shocked reaction to the Vienna Resolution.[140]

Three facts spoke on the side of Hungarian cooperation: the Romanian Germans quickly joined the Front; civil servants, churchmen, small businessmen and anyone with any official contact with the State were obligated to do so; and finally, the Hungarian People's Union was obligated to take the place of the Hungarian Alliance and the National Hungarian Party. On February 11, 1939 the HPU held its founding meeting in Cluj Napoca where Nicholas Bánffy stated the goals as: the unified representation, safeguarding and promoting the interests of Hungarians living in Romania in cultural, economic and social areas. Due to the grass roots organization, the Hungarian masses found a place in the Union. Every representative of Transylvanian Hungarians was present from the NHP to the organizers of the Tirgu Mures meeting. Contemporaries, as well as following generations, debated whether it was worth for the Hungarians to join the Front. Those siding with joining, raised as their main arguments that, 1) the royal dictatorship severely limited the activities of the opposition and minority parties, and 2) the magnitude of the mobilization of the Hungarians created an unprecedented success. The structure was based on the Szekler 'tens' or the Saxon 'neighborhood' organizations. A neighborhood consisted of 5 to 12 families, represented by a corporal (ed.: leader of ten), 10-20 'tens' or neighborhoods made a 'supreme ten' with the supremes making up a district. As an example, in Cluj Napoca the neighborhood organizations represented 140,000 people.

The 15 representatives of the Hungarians received positions in the upper echelon of the Front leadership, the Directory and Council. The Hungarian People's Union had barely begun to draft its rules and by-laws when Tiso announced the creation of an independent Slovak Republic. The following day, March 15, 1939 the German army marched into Czech-Moravia and the Hungarian forces began to take control of Transcarpathia. The posting of 5 Hungarian divisions on the Hungarian-Romanian border created panic in Romania, followed by a flurry of military orders, mobilization and a mass call-up. The events of Oradea were reported in detail.[141] Here, draft notices went out on March 17 and the workers, and their families, occupied on the construction of border fortifications were sent back to their homes in the Regat. The troops manning the fortifications and the gendarmerie were increased. For Hungarians, it was the beginning of random identification checks and house searches. On the night of the 21st, the local detachment vacated its entire barracks and packed up the headquarters' documents. They requisitioned food, vehicles and horses from the border villages. The Regat and Bessarabian units were also mobilized and

---

[140] MOL, K.63. 1940-27/1 file.
[141] MOL, K.63. 1939-27/7. I. file.

brought to strength by call-ups, alongside the Transylvanian units. The mobilized army was concentrated along the Satu Mare-Sighetu-Marmatiei (Szatmár-Máramarossziget) and the Satu Mare-Oradea (Szatmár-Nagyvárad) lines. According to reports, the 'panic-like withdrawal' took place between March 17 and 22.

The call-up around Cluj Napoca took place after the signing of the German-Romanian economic agreement, as demanded by Germany. Here, it affected the Hungarians of officer rank of the former Austro-Hungarian army. At the meeting of the grand council of the NRF – attended by the leaders of the HPU – Calinescu stated that volunteers outnumbered draftees by four to one, hinting that they are ready to protect the country's borders.

In March, England announced a guarantee of Romania's borders. Popular Hungarian opinion reflected that since the British guarantee, Romania further withdrew from détente with Hungary and remedying the Transylvanian Hungarians' complaints. This opinion was noted on June 3, 1939 by Utassy, military attaché in London.[142] After taking possession of Transcarpathia, the Hungarian government suggested an agreement to address the minorities. It was rejected by Romania. Representing the HPU, Nicholas Bánffy and Paul Szász forwarded a memorandum to King Karl II, detailing the most recent Hungarian grievances. The newest affront was that, during the mobilization, Hungarian homes, radios and establishments were requisitioned by the army.

Ambassador to Britain, Barcza, received confirmation from the British Minister of War for his sense that since the guarantee extended to Romania, the need to address the minority question has receded into the background. Bárdossy, the Hungarian ambassador in Bucharest, held several interesting discussions during the course of the year with the Romanian Minister of the Exterior, Gafencu, regarding the minority question and the relations of the two countries. Gafencu did not deny that the HPU memorandum contained valid grievances. (The Hungarians optimistically joined the Front on the basis of promises made to them.) He stated that the Romanian government has not yet had the time to devote to the Hungarian suggestions regarding the minority agreement. He also stressed that, through the leaders of the HPU, they can make themselves heard while the Hungarian government could not. He alluded to Budapest putting Belgrade ahead of Bucharest. In spite of it, Yugoslavia wanted nothing to do with any minority agreement, instead suggesting a reopening of the Bled conference.

The subsequent meaningful talks between Bárdossy and Gafencu took place on June 26. Gafencu raised in rebuke that Count Stephen Csáky, Hungarian Minister of the Exterior, only offered the minority agreement to later take advantage in London and Paris of its rejection, saying; „The Romanians are not willing to create cordial relations."[143] Bárdossy countered that the Romanian government does not take decisive steps against local transgressions. „The Hungarian government is not the one that has a need for the minority agreement. In signing an agreement of this kind, we hoped - he added - that the

---

[142] Ibid.
[143] Ibid.

69

Transylvanian authorities will finally understand that the Romanian government not only promises, but directly takes responsibility for, the respecting of the rights of the minorities."[144] The HPU's point of view was that the positive regulations towards the Hungarian minority were, once again, meant for foreign consumption, assigning a propaganda role to them. As an example, the 20 million Leu that the government assigned in the budget to the Hungarian denominational schools in the school year 1939-40. And again, the omission in the 1939 law of the 'name analysis' regarding public school attendance. The HPU petitioned the Prime Minister to exempt the non-Romanian citizens of Hungarian origin from paying the so-called foreign duties. He raised objection to the mass relocation of Hungarian civil servant from Transylvania to the Regat, Bessarabia and Dobrudja.

The HPU came to an agreement with the government during the elections of June, 1939. Under its terms, they could count on 12 representative and 5 senatorial seats (according to the new Election and Governance Act, Brasov and Háromszék counties, as well as a portion of Bucegi province, could not sent representatives to Parliament). The HPU nominees received 16,000 more votes than in 1937, securing 9 representative and 6 senatorial mandates. This time around, Hungarian experts were voted in, not politicians and lawyers. The Hungarian representatives listened to the Throne Speech where the King agrees to ensure, with legal assurances, the minorities' economic, spiritual and cultural development and that the government will wholeheartedly carry it out. Their reply: „Enact into law the minority statute."

On the day Calinescu was assassinated by the Iron Guard, September 21, the HPU was poised to present a nearly 100 page memorandum. It consisted of several chapters, the first of which was a list of decrees and laws that local authorities circumvented. The second was a 19 point list of government assurances made at the January 17 agreement; the fourth listed government actions contravening the agreement. The fourth itemized the affronts suffered since joining the NRF.

During the Hungarian-Romanian economic talks held in Sinaia (Szinaja) on August 17, 1939 another border incident took place at Geszt. According to the Romanian version, a Hungarian border patrol of 10 violated the border and attacked 2 people on the Romanian side; one was shot dead, the other injured. The report notes that since May, this is the 15th incident of its kind.[145] The Hungarian military advocate's finding was that 3 Romanian border police strayed onto Hungarian territory (picking apples) and fired on the Hungarian patrol attempting to disarm them. The Romanian side was forced to accept the inquiry's findings.

It was suggested by Yugoslavia that it would be expedient if Hungary and Romania both reduced their military readiness and presence on their mutual border. At the same time, they offered the Yugoslavia government's assisstance. On September 28, Gafencu announced the acceptance of the reduction proposal

---

[144] Ibid.
[145] Ibid.

and said that the Romanian government was willing to gradually reduce the currently over staffed units to 30-35% of their numbers through demobilization, already begun. The Hungarian side announced that the proportion of troops allowed on R & R would be increased from 30 to 50%.[146]

The German-Russian 'Friendship and Border Agreement' signed on September 29, 1939 – the Molotov-Ribbentrop Pact – placed the Bassarabian and Bukuvina question on the agenda. Romania was clear that the Soviet Union would, sooner or later, suggest the alteration of the Romanian-Russian border. The majority hoped that, by ceding these areas, Soviet support may be garnered in other directions, i.e., the claims against Bulgaria and Hungary.[147]

On December 11, Gafencu reinstated before Bárdossy that Romania is willing to cede Bessarabia, to cede Dobrudja but not Transylvania, the cradle of the Romanian people - that territory, if need be, will be defended to the last drop of blood.[148] Few Romanian politicians thought as Prime Minister Argentoianu whose foreign policy notions played a large part in his November downfall. He began with the obvious that Romania was unable to carry on a three front battle with her neighbors over territorial claims. Therefore, he was wiling to entertain a compromise, where he partially satisfied their territorial claims: for the Soviets East Bessarabia, for Bulgaria South Dobrudja, and for Hungary the handing over of the Hungarian occupied areas along the border.[149]

After the downfall of Argetoianu, the King asked Tatarescu to form a government. He made promises to enact the minority laws. At the same time, he asked the minority leaders for their cooperation. Nicholas Bánffy recounted in his memoirs, dated January 6, 1940 the minority politics since the agreement between the government and the HPU.[150] First he counted the gains. One, they did not impede the growth of the HPU's associated groups. Two, denominational teachers received government aid. Three, the citizenship status of almost 80,000 people was settled. Four, they ratified the Reformed bishopric of Királyhágómellék. Bánffy felt the need to stress that in spite of the noted benevolent government actions and deeds, the lot of the Hungarian minority could not be said to have improved. In fact, in some respects, it got worse. What followed was a list of the most burning complaints. One, several thousand government employees were let go – without a pension – under the excuse of being unfamiliar with the Romanian language. Two, the pension cases of Hungarians take long months and the pension office holds back a significant portion. Three, the transfer of Hungarian public servants out of Transylvania continued. Four, in Hungarian populated areas, their numbers in public offices is not representative. Five, to be allowed to start heritage language classes with 20 students (as opposed to 60). High school students should be allowed to take their examinations in the language of the school's instruction. The unfair

---

[146] MOL, K.63. 1939-27/7. II. file.
[147] MOL, K.63. 1939-27/7. I. file.
[148] MOL, K.63. 1939-27/7. II. file.
[149] Ibid.
[150] MOL, K 63. 1940-27/1 file.

differentiation of denominational schools should cease. Six, the Ministry of Nationality Education pensioned all teachers over 60 but has not, for years, held exams for new teachers. Seven, high school teachers should also receive government funding. Eight, the Reformed and Unitarian priest, as well. Nine, come to an agreement on the contentious issues between the Catholic Church and the government. Ten, rescind the National Labor Law, which made employment difficult for Hungarian workers. Eleven, minority craftsmen should be able to get a license and a master's certificate (guild membership). Twelve, admit Hungarians to the Chambers of Commerce of agricultural-, economic-, and industrial-workers. Thirteen, allow free use of the Hungarian language in everyday use, public administration and the justice system. Remove the signs forbidding the use of the Hungarian language. Fourteen, ensure the appointment of Hungarian mayors and deputy mayors. Fifteen, punish those official who abused their powers. Sixteen, permit the HPU to hold its meetings. Seventeen, clarify the situation of the Private Assets of Csik.

An earlier memorandum made recommendations regarding the inclusion of the minorities in the public service.[151]

1. Of the three representatives of communities, a number proportional to their ratio should be set aside; one, if the Hungarian population makes up 30%, two, if 60% and all three if it reaches 90%;
2. In towns that are not county seats, one of the 5 representatives after every 20%;
3. In county seats, of the 7 representatives, one after every 15%; and
4. In chartered municipalities, out of the 12 representatives, one after every 10%.

Significant political changes took place in Romania during the summer: on June 21, the King's decree abolished the Front and created his National Party, one that the Hungarians refused to join. German successes on the battlefield resulted in the sudden prominence of German sympathizing political circles. On June 26, Molotov's ultimatum gave Romania 24 hours to withdraw fro Bessarabia and Northern Bukovina. Romania had no choice but to comply. On July 29, general mobilization was ordered – paralleling the Hungarian army's arrival at the end of July on Romania's border – and the government was assumed by the German sympathizer, Gigurtu. He and Foreign Minister Manoilescu met with Hitler in Berchtesgaden on July 26, two weeks after Hungarian Prime Minister Paul Teleki and Foreign Minister Stephen Csáky, and continued on to Rome. Arriving back home, Manoilescu made a statement to the press that Romania will satisfy Hungary's revisionist claims with a population exchange. This was the stance taken by Romania at the August 16 conference at Turnu-Severin, headed by Pop Valer. However, unable to get the two sides to agree, Germany and Italy were invited to arbitrate over the disputed territories.[152] On August 30, at 2:50 PM in

---

[151] Ibid.
[152] Hóry, András: Behind the scenes. The events preceding the Second World War, how and what really happened (A kuliszák mögött. A második világháború elozményei, ami és ahogy a valóságban történ). Vienna, 1965.

the Belvedere Palace, when the Central Powers read out their decision that Cluj Napoca is also returned to Hungary, Manoilescu fainted.
With the Second Vienna Resolution, 43,591 sq. km. and 2,195,546 people were returned to Hungary, representing 42% of Transylvania's area and 43% of its population. In fact, it meant that Szolnok-Doboka, Szilágy, Beszterce, Naszód and Csik counties in their entirety, Maros-Torda, Udvarhely and Háromszék counties in almost their entirety and except for the Eastern portion of Cluj (Kolozs) county, the so-called 'Northern Transylvania' was returned to Hungary.[153]

The distibution of nationalities in Norther Transylvania in 1941:[154]

Nationality	By nationality	%	By language	%
Hungarian	1,380,506	53.6	1,343,695	52.1
German	44,688	1.7	44,508	1.8
Romanian	1,029,470	39.9	1,069,211	41.5
Jewish	75,241	3.0		

Distribution by county:

County	Hungarian	Romanian
Beszterce-Naszód	10.01	71.2
Bihar	71.2	25.1
Csik	87.1	12.2
Háromszék	95.0	4.2
Kolozs	30.7	66.9
Máramaros	49.0	51.0
Maros-Torda	56.2	36.5
Szatmár	62.3	34.9
Szilágy	34.5	61.8
Szolnok-Doboka	22.5	73.2
Udvarhely	98.3	0.7

Distribution in the main towns:

	Hungarian %	Romanian %	Jewish %
Kolozsvár	88.1	9.1	0.8
Marosvásárhely	94.5	3.9	0.4
Nagyvárad	92.0	5.2	1.4
Szatmár	92.2	4.6	2.4

[153] Ibid.
[154] The 1941 census. Budapest, Central Statistical Bureau, 1978.

Hungarians in Southern Transylvania

While Northern Transylvanian Hungarians rejoiced in the return to the mother country, in Southern Transylvania, which remained a part of Romania, they went from second-class citizens to third class. During September-October of 1940, Romanian authorities tried, directly or indirectly, to encourage the resettlement of Hungarians to Northern Transylvania. They directed the factories and industrial concerns to compile lists of Hungarians. At banks and companies, Iron Guards appeared almost immediately to review the workers' national affiliation. Another means of detrimental differentiation was the military draft or call-up for labor, from which the authorities were pleased to supply certificates of exemption – if the person renounced Romanian citizenship, left former life and home behind and moved to Northern Transylvania.[155]

General Ion Antonescu (1882-1946), head of the government, received a delegation of the leaders of the organizations that were left behind in Southern Transylvania, Elmer Gyárfás, Paul Szász and Adam Teleki. To them he stated, "… while he remains at his post, the life and property of the Southern Transylvanian Hungarians is safe." At the same time, he hinted that because of the anti-Romanian activities in Northern Transylvania, he could barely restrain the Iron Guard from taking revenge on the Southern Transylvanian Hungarians.[156] Gyárfás and Szász requested action on the following matters:

1. Settling the situation of the Hungarian press, as only the 6 O'clock News (6 Órai Újság) was allowed to publish.
2. The return of the Alba Julia Secondary School and College properties.
3. Withdrawing the ban on the use of Hungarian language over the telephone. Gyárfás, at the same time, made an appeal to Hungarian diplomats to convey to the Hungarian government to take steps and prevent the expulsion of Romanians from Northern Transylvania and the violent actions committed against them.

At this time – directly after the Second Vienna Resolution – one Hungarian memorandum followed another, cataloguing the affronts received by Hungarians in Southern Transylvania, matched by Romanian ones listing similar complaints of Romanians in Northern Transylvania. After dividing Transylvania, the Axis powers involved did not abrogate their responsibility and submitted several written proposals regarding how to normalize relations in a mutually acceptable fashion, addressing, among other things, the anti-minority sentiments and territorial claims.

In the summer of 1941, the Axis powers sent a special delegation of one German and one Italian envoy to Northern and Southern Transylvania. The delegation finished its inquiry by the end of November and submitted its findings to their governments. In it, a peaceful resolution was highly recommended.[157]

---

[155] MOL, K.63. 1940-27/4 file.
[156] MOL, K.63. 1940-27/7, 1/2 file.
[157] MOL, K.63. 1940-27/7. III. file.

In June 1941 a confidential order of the Romanian authorities forbade the use of Hungarian in the towns and villages of Southern Transylvania, in both public and private. Although the order was withdrawn, the language of use with the authorities remained unchanged. The use of Hungarian was forbidden in telephone conversations, calling at home and abroad. Although the discriminatory distinction placed on Hungarian language mail was lifted on September 24, 1941 the Romanian postal service ignored it. The introduction of the need for travel permits was equivocal with shackling the Hungarians to their place of birth. The issuing of permits depended on the local gendarmes who often refused, whether to visit the sick or attend school. Permits were also needed for travel within a 20 km. zone of the Hungarian-Romanian border.

The June 7, 1942 food and produce requisitions of the Ministry of Public Supplies exclusively affected the Hungarians. Hungarians serving in the Romanian armed forces had the same general complaints: they were ordered to do the most menial tasks, exposed to the most drastic means of punishment, lacking adequate clothing, quartered in the worst places, without adequate medical services, lacking basic hygienic facilities and were continually persecuted for the use of their Hungarian language.[158]

Hungarian nationals were assigned to serve in penal battalions with common criminals and Iron Guardists. Later, those serving in support or labor units were reassigned to active battalions and sent to the front lines, sometime with marginal training, mostly with none. The intent was to raise the ratio of Hungarians in the front line units to 20%.[159]

Draft into labor battalions became more frequent after 1942. Hungarians drafted into Romanian labor battalions had the following complaints: they were assigned to the most physically demanding tasks (railway or tunnel building), subjected to severe punishment, like caning, housed in unheated billets giving no protection from the weather, and treatment equal to that meted out to the Russian prisoners of war. While Romanian labor draftees served 2-3 months, Hungarian nationals were expected to serve 9-10 months in one stretch. Hungarians 50 years of age and above were drafted without any regard to their health. Hungarians were denied leave. The exception was 8 days at Christmas to replace their worn out clothes; others enjoyed leaves of 30-45 days.[160]

Call-ups for labor continued during August of 1943. By fall, there were hardly any men under 50 - the main support of families - not serving in one of the labor camps. Many did not return from the short leave of absence, preferring to desert. The two governments exchanged several notes during 1943-44 regarding the equalization of the terms of Romanian and Hungarian labor service. Thus, the Hungarian government accepted the proposal that labor battalions be treated as military units and their national composition reflect the composition of the total population. On the other hand, it did not accept that the period of the call-up not exceed 6 months – something not honored in Romania, either.

---

[158] Monitorul Oficial. 1942, September 10.594.648 ordinance
[159] Monitorul Oficial. 108.608/1942 ordinance.
[160] Monitorul Oficial. 221.453/1942 ordinance.

The Hungarian consul in Romania reported from two labor camps in February of 1944.[161] In the Brad-Deva sector's two camps, each held 6 companies. Of the 2,500 labor-draftees stationed in Brad, 1,000 were Hungarian. The labor encampment of Livezeny held 2,200 Hungarians, who maintained a 32 km. sector of the Livezeny-Bambest railroad. Leaves were especially difficult to obtain here as the Romanian National Railway insisted on keeping the Hungarian laborers. Many were not allowed to go home after 10 months, sometimes more, of service. Similar complaints were voiced by the Romanian foreign representatives, according to who 63,000 Northern Transylvanian Romanians were drafted for labor service during June of 1944.[162]

Romanian dictatorship seemed unaffected by the possibility of retribution against the Romanians of Northern Transylvania. In 1941, they raised the specter of population exchanges, followed in June of the same year by defining new military zones in the larger, Hungarian populated, towns of Southern Transylvania. While residency permits were rubber stamped in May of 1940 and 1941, on August 5, 1941 a proclamation stated: residency permits for Hungarians and Jews fell under different restrictions. The penalty for failure to obtain a permit was eviction. In 1942, as a result of tightening the laws applied to military zones, these areas were de-Hungarianized (ed.: ethnically cleansed).

The dismissal of Hungarians continued in 1942-43.[163] Hungarian owned companies were not being registered; craftsmen could obtain neither commercial licenses nor work permits. Earlier, farmers were severely affected by the commandeering of wheat in 1941 and of cattle in November 1942. The discriminative tax of 1941-42 was levied only in the counties of Hunedoara (Hunyad) and Cluj (Temes) and only on self-employed Hungarians but from April 1943, it was extended to all of Southern Transylvania, to all professions, from lawyers to the corner flower vendor. In the fiscal year starting April 1, 1942 the tax levied on Hungarian self-employed workers rose to 4 to 30 times the previous year's level. From the second half of 1942 on, directed by a secret regulation, almost every chamber of industry and commerce in Southern Transylvania refused to issue licenses to Hungarians. At the same time, chambers of labor refused to issue or renew employer's work permits and insurance policies, and to register apprentice contracts.

Claiming military necessity, countless Hungarian properties were expropriated - without compensation. Not only were craftsmen and merchants prevented from receiving licenses, credit and goods, but the entire Hungarian population of Southern Transylvania often suffered from discrimination. In 1943, in places and on occasions, they were restricted in, or excluded from, the distribution of food rationing cards. Several memoranda contained complaints by Hungarian public servants who had been transferred to the Regat (pre-1920 Romania). The problem was not only that they were replaced with Romanian

---

[161] New Hungarian National Archives (Új Magyar Központi Levéltár). External Affairs material: Romania. 15/pol.-1944.
[162] Ibid, 126/pol. - 1944.
[163] MOL, K.63. 1940-27/7. II. file.

clerks and had no chance of return to Transylvania, but also that, under the new circumstances, they chose an uncertain existence rather than suffer the hatred towards Hungarians. Despite the fact that in 155 villages in Southern Transylvania the proportion of Hungarians exceeded 50%, Romanian officials were appointed who did not know the local language and customs. The same situation existed in the cities. Hungarians life became intolerable in the military regions and border zones (the latter a 10 - 30 km. deep corridor along the frontier).

Many teachers of denominational schools fled Southern Transylvania as early as October-November, 1940. Their place had to be assumed by the clergymen - without proper teacher's certificates. As the authorities continued to refuse to issue temporary permits, the danger of closing threatened 26 Calvinist and 2 Roman Catholic church schools. Pursuant to the Act on Private Education, certified teachers in middle school had to have two, in high school six, qualifying examinations. The authorities made every effort to defer the qualifying examinations. On the January, 1943 exam, 25 Roman Catholic and Calvinist secondary school teachers were turned away under the pretense that only those of Romanian origin were allowed to take them.

Further curtailments were introduced in 1943. Thus, in May 1943, the Ministry of Public Education ordered the church schools authorities - under penalty of closure - to strictly observe that part of the Act on Private Education in which, schools with only one teacher should employ only men and those with a larger staff should have a majority of males. In September 1943, the government suspended teaching - for an undetermined period - in the Bethlen College Secondary School of Aiud (Nagyenyed) and in the College for Girls and the Trade School, both of Brasov.[164]

In the same year, certain steps were taken to resume talks between Hungary and Romania. Deputy Prime Minister Mihai Antonescu (1904-1946), later Minister of Foreign Affairs - no relation to Ion Antonescu - stated several times, in the presence of the Hungarian envoy to Bucharest, that he always wished to foster good neighborly relations with Hungary and was ready to solve the problems, not the least of which was the Slavic danger threatening both nations. However, he was also naturally of the opinion that the two countries should, "with mutual understanding, through bilateral talks," revise the Vienna Resolution, i.e., that Northern Transylvania should be returned to Romania.[165]

After the Romanian government repeated its proposal for talks three times, the Hungarian side felt it had to accept. After all, they accepted the fact of a Slav threat, that it would ease the lot of Hungarians in Southern Transylvania since Hungary accepted the concern about the Slavic danger, and felt that talks would help to ease the lot of the Hungarians in Southern Transylvania. As well, it was felt that such talks were presumed to be in the interest of the Axis Powers. Nicholas Bánffy held secret discussions with several Romanian politicians in the summer of 1943. His mission did not bear fruit. The Transylvanian issue - as

---

[164] Ibid.
[165] Ibid.

proposed by Maniu - could not be excluded from the agenda of either official or informal Hungarian-Romanian talks.[166]

Romanian-Hungarian rapprochement: 1944

On his 70th birthday, Juliu Maniu gave a reception in the morning of January 8, 1944, in his flat at 10 Str. Sfintilor (Saints' Street). The occasion turned out to be one of the preparatory talks on pulling out of the war. Maniu was in possession of a letter from [President of pre- and postwar Czechoslovakia] Benes, reporting on the Stalin-Molotov-Benes talks held in December 1943. In it Benes asked Moscow - among other things – to severely punish Hungary and to completely satisfy Romania's territorial demands. Representatives of the various parties were present at the reception, including those of the main rival, the Liberal Party. Angelescu's greeting took on special meaning, indicating both confidence in Maniu and the role he was designed to play: "You are the only person who can maneuver our boat through the troubled sea of events..." In his reply, Maniu emphasized that he made obeisance to neither the National Peasant Party, nor King Karl II, nor Marshall Antonescu's dictatorship, and that he was always zealous backer of a responsible and democratic government elected by the people. He also stressed - referring to the promises of Western governments on the matter - that Romania would never relinquish an inch of Romanian land, especially Transylvania.[167]

A member of the Hungarian diplomatic corps, Tibor Forrai, had an illuminating meeting with Maniu in early 1944. Maniu hated three things consistently: the Germans, the Liberals and King Karl II and his circle. His hatred was so implacable that he was willing, occasionally, to entertain a compromise the Hungarians, or dangle the hope either of an autonomous Transylvania or a central-European confederation. Maniu was completely certain of a German defeat and the victory of the British-American-Soviet alliance. He didn't consider either Romania's or Hungary's prospects promising, but felt that Hungary's position was worse. The rapprochement and reconciliation of the two nations was impossible without a solution to the Transylvanian issue - stated Maniu - and he did not leave any doubt that the 'solution' of the Transylvanian issue could be nothing else but the restoration of the August 30, 1940 frontiers. (At the same time, Maniu 'wrote off' Bessarabia and Bukovina as a loss.) He stressed several times that the two nations [Romanian and Hungarian] should come to an agreement in order to sue for a separate peace. "It would be of great importance for Hungary to find ways of making peace with all its nationalities ... in order to take its rightful place in the post-war central European confederation."[168]

---

[166] Bánffy, Miklós: Memoirs (Emlékirat). Manuscript. Budapest, Károli Gáspár Reformed University (Károli Gáspár Református Egyetem), Ráday Archives.
[167] New Hungarian National Archives (Új Magyar Központi Levéltár). External Affairs material: Romania. 6/pol.-1944.
[168] Ibid, 18/pol. - 1944.

In early March, Maniu showed Benes' letter to senior Romanian politicians visiting Arad. This is worthy of note in order to understand why Maniu, and after 1945 Petru Groza, emphasized the importance of the Romanian minority policy "based on the principle of absolute equality." "Romania will not only regain its lost territories, but also may hope to be compensated by the West for the possible loss of Bessarabia and Bukovina. Democratic government and the complete emancipation of minorities are the necessary preconditions of this. Furthermore, Romania must stand ready to make its armed forces immediately available whenever requested by the Allied forces, and be ready to carry out its commands without hesitation." Simply put, Romania regained Transylvania, with Soviet support, only in return for meeting the above-mentioned conditions. On the basis of what transpired at the Teheran Conference, Maniu took the re-annexation of Northern Transylvania as a *fait accompli*, except for some minor border adjustments in Bihar and Szatmár counties to the benefit Hungary.

Following the German occupation of Hungary (March 19, 1944), anti-German feeling began to intensify both in Northern and Southern Transylvania. The local anti-war forces of Northern Transylvania and Hungary were in constant contact from 1943 on; the representatives of the Independent Smallholders' Party, the Peasant Party and the leftist Peace Party regularly visited Cluj Napoca. True to Transylvanian traditions - or in modern political terms, on a popular front basis - Social Democrats as well as the representatives of the rural Transylvanian Youth (Erdélyi Fiatalok), the conservative Transylvanian Party (Erdélyi Párt) and the Hungarian denominations also took part in the meetings.

In comparison, Southern Transylvanians were more decisively anti-German and took a more determined stand in pulling out of the war. The reason for this was that, for example, Paul Szász had accurate information about the Romanian plans on breaking away. The Hungarian consuls in Arad and Brasov were also well informed that anti-German Romanian opposition had taken certain overtures towards the Hungarians. The Hungarians in Southern Transylvania, who suffered in labor camps and endured all kinds of persecution, counted on a German defeat, and were aware of its consequences for Transylvania. They pointed out that Hungarians in Transylvanian would be well advised to make positive gestures towards the Romanians. It was Bishop Aaron Márton who called attention to this. Later, in 1946, when the Hungarian minority was in extreme peril, he collected and signed a petition in which, together with the senior officials of the Hungarian churches and institutions, protested against another Trianon. In his petition to Paris, he stated that Hungarians in Transylvania did not want to live any longer under Romanian rule. For his action, he was jailed from 1949 to 1955 and was freed only after Vatican intervention. His elevation to beatification and sainthood is in progress.

Referring to an anonymous secret source, the Hungarian consul in Brasov reported on a conference called by ex-Prime Minister Tatarescu in Bucharest on January 15, 1944.[169] The fact that 500 people participated indicates its importance. The representatives of Bukovina, Bessarabia and Moldova took the

---

[169] Ibid, 11/pol. - 1944.

floor in the morning and those of Muntenia, Oltenia, Banat and Transylvania in the afternoon. Parts of the meeting went on behind closed doors, but of the open sessions the Hungarian diplomat sent the following report:

1. Agreement was reached with Antonescu that he will step aside in favor of Tatarescu at the appropriate time, meaning that civilian rule will once again replace the military;
2. Tatarescu was commissioned to establish contacts with the British;
3. The objective is to regain Northern Transylvania, and, if possible, to save Bessarabia and Bukovina; and
4. Concurrently, Romania and Turkey are to take steps against Germany with all civilian and military means.

What attracted notice was that neither Maniu, Mihaleche, nor Dinu Bratianu took part in the crucial Bucharest conference. They met in Brasov, even though they were following the same notion. Following the conference, Romanian representatives opened negotiations with Soviet delegates in Istanbul. Their position was that when the advancing Soviet Army reached Romania's borders, it would yield its Eastern province (including part of Moldova and even Dobrudja) without resistance, on condition that the Soviet Union would give, in return, all of Transylvania and Hungarian territory to the Tisza River, as well as Sub-Carpathia.[170]

Romania's withdrawal from the war

Romanian and Hungarian representatives began, almost simultaneously in the summer of 1943, putting out feelers in Geneva, Cairo, Stockholm and Lisbon about the possibility of pulling out of the war. Even the possibility of a concerted withdrawal was raised. As mentioned previously, Nicholas Bánffy arrived in Romania during the second half of July 1943 to conduct secret talks. His trip bore no fruit because the reason for Hungarian-Romanian hostility, the issue of Transylvania, remained unsolved. The same state of affairs was present at the meeting arranged by the Polish secret service between the two countries and western diplomats.

Prince Barbu Stirbey, traveling through Turkey, arrived in Moscow in early March, to present the request of the Romanian government for a separate peace.[171] The Soviet conditions, forwarded by Prince Stirbey to Maniu, contained the following: (implying that negotiations would be conducted in Ankara not between the Romanian government, but between the Opposition (Maniu) and the Soviets) following the pull out, the Romanian Army, under Soviet command, would wage war against the Germans; the Soviet Union demands compensation from Romania (the Romanian party hoped to satisfy this by handing over oil shares); the Soviets insisted on the borders of June 1940, but would not oppose the transfer of Northern Transylvania to Romania. Maniu, who at this time thought a Hungarian attack against Southern Transylvania a possibility, accepted

---

[170] Ibid, 26/pol. - 1944.
[171] Ibid, 24/pol. - 1944.

the terms and only asked that the final decision on territorial issues be left to the peace talks. All this, while hoping Romania can regain Bukovina.

Several events took place in April of 1944 which put pressure on the politicians to come to a decision: the Soviet forces crossed the line of the River Prut; the Allied governments suggested that Romania obtain a truce from the Soviet Union; and the Soviets expressed a strong wish that the Romanian Communist Party be involved in the peace preparations.

On April 12, Soviet Foreign Minister Molotov informed Romania of the following: joint military operations can only be undertaken after an unconditional surrender; the Soviet-Romanian border will remain as of the June 26, 1940 decision, which awarded Bessarabia and Northern Bukovina to the Soviet Union; as compensation, the Soviet Union agrees to the nullification of the Vienna Resolution and Romania will receive all, or substantially all, of Transylvania; the amount of reparations to be paid by Romania is to be decided; and Soviet prisoners of war are to be permitted to return home. As Molotov stated, the Soviet Union will honor Romania's national sovereignty and inviolability but all roads and transportation means must be made available, until the end of the conflict, to the Soviet Union and its allies.

Hungarian foreign agencies were extremely well informed of the secret Romanian talks. Diplomatic sources were aware of the mission of Romanian politician, Visoianu, and his tasks: all of Bessarabia and Northern Bukovina is to be handed over to the Soviets; the return of Northern Transylvania; Romania will only reparations only to the Soviet Union; the British should not expect an immediate changing of sides; but the Soviet Union should.[172]

Events took a rapid turn. One of the last reports of Hungarian diplomats dated August 19, 1944 - actually two documents of the same date – contains a wealth of information.[173] The first covers the visit of Mihai Antonescu to the Führer's headquarters where he promises Ribbentrop to suspend talks with the Allies. On his return home, he immediately contacted Romanian diplomats in neutral countries and instructed them to the opposite. Regarding the situation of the Romanian and Soviet armies, the latter were already at Iasi but - in light of the negotiations Gafencu was holding in Geneva with the Soviet representatives - the attack was postponed. In the meantime, Visoianu and Stirbey were in Cairo, attempting to convince the Allies to suspend the bombing raids on Romania.

The second report of August 19 details the preparations made for the overthrow of Antonescu.[174] The civil Romanian politicians, opponents of the military regime, feared that the German-leaning Iron Guard would gather its remaining strength and grab power. This urged the opposition parties to take the decisive step, the breaking away planned for August 26.

That it happened on August 23 can be attributed to General Antonescu, who decided, in the morning of that day, to give the order: Romania would continue

---

[172] Ibid, 136/pol. - 1944.
[173] Ibid, 153/pol. - 1944.
[174] Ibid, 154/pol. - 1944.

the war against the Soviet Union, on Germany's side.[175] Secondly, on August 20, the Soviet armies advanced, without opposition, towards the Romanian capital from the direction of Iasi.[176]

This was a setback to the Romanian notion that the withdrawal would be preceded by American and British paratrooper landings. Also, that it would may be possible to avoid turning the country into a theatre of Soviet military operations[177], and ultimately, to avoid the intervention of Soviet power into the workings of the country. Even in 1943, Stalin did not hide his intention that he only intended to support the introduction of local communist regimes in Central Europe until the Red Army could take permanent control.

King Mihai addressed the nation by radio on August 23 and announced that all resources will be spent on regaining Northern Transylvania.

Thirteen days later, in the early morning hours of September 10 to 11, the leaders of the delegation to the Soviet - Romanian truce talks received the text of the terms for the suspension of hostilities.[178] This was found to be more onerous than what was agreed in the spring of 1944 in Cairo and several delegates voiced their displeasure, including the communist Lucretiu Patrascanu. They were most offended that the country was not treated as one that took part in the war (as a co-belligerent).[179] They also raised the problem of Soviet forces stationed on Romanian soil. To this point, Molotov stressed: Romania must accept the fact that it lost the war - although this was left out of the final draft – and Soviet troops will remain in Romania 'until it's necessary'.

On September 12, the Romanian delegation - Patrascanu, Prince Stirbey, Pop Ghita and colonel Damaceanu - signed the truce agreement. It contained the following terms: Romania will take part, alongside the Soviet Union, in the liberation of Hungary, Czechoslovakia and Austria[180] with 12 divisions;[181]

---

[175] Lipcsey, Ildikó: The chronicle of a fateful day: Wednesday, August 23, 1944 (Egy sorsforduló nap krónikája. 1944. Augusztus 23, Szerda). World History (Világtörténet), 1985, issue 2. pp. 119-135;
Gosztonyi, Péter: Endkampf an der Donau. Vienna, 1969.

[176] Romanescu, Gheorghe - Longhin, Leonida: Cronica participarii armatei la rasboiul anihitlerist. Bucharest, Editura Militara. 1971.;

[177] Ivor Portes: Operatiunea anonimus. Bucuresti, Humanitas, 1991.

[178] Udrea, Traian: Preliminarile semnarii conventiei de armistitiu intre Romania scu Batiunile Unite, Revista de istorie, Buch., 1987, issue 8, pp. 780-790;
Enescu, Ion: Politica externa a Romaniei in perioada 1944-1947. Bucharest, 1979.

[179] Musat, Mircea - Popisteanu, C. - Constantiniu, Florin - Dobrineascu, V.: Dictatul fascist de la Viena - expresie a politicii de forta repudiata de istorie. In Magazin istoric, 1987, issue 6, pp. 22, 32.

[180] Florescu, Mihai: Cucerirea puterii revolutionar-democratic la 6 Martie 1945 catre masele populare in frunte cu P.C.R. Anale de istorie, 1982, issue 2, pp. 43-56.
According to the author, 540,000 took place in the battles West of Romania;
Ceausescu, Ilie - Constantiniu, Florin - Ionescu, M.E.: Two hundred days sooner. Romania's role in shortening the Second World War (Kétszáz nappal korábban. Románia szerepe a második világháború megrövidítésében). Bucharest, Kriterion Publisher, 1986. A monograph notes 466,357 Romanian soldiers.

Romania will pay reparations to the Soviet Union and, for the duration of the hostilities, will make available roads and all means of transportation and communication for Allied use; and the Second Vienna Resolution is null and void.

The terms of the truce were overseen by the Allied Control Commission (Szövetséges Ellenörzo Bizottság).[182] The truce agreements 19th point stated that: "Romania will receive Transylvania (or most of it)."[183] The accepted view in Hungarian historiography is that Transylvania's final national affiliation remained open because it was expected that Hungary would follow Romania in bailing out of the war. The situation changed for Hungary after Admiral Horthy's unsuccessful attempt to do so on October 15, 1944.

Romania and King Mihai managed to do on August 23, 1944 what Hungary and Regent Horthy failed to do: jump at the last second. This was sufficient to garner Romania a more favorable position in the upcoming peace talks. Contrary to Hungary, it managed to establish a common national unity in Romania that united every citizen, irrespective of party affiliation.

[181] Popisteanu, C.:Cronologie politico-diplomatice romaneasca. 1944-1947. Bucuresti, Ed. Pol. 1976, 73-74.
[182] Stanescu, Flori - Zamfirescu, Dragos: Ocupatie sovietica in Romania. Documente. 1944-1946. Bucharest, Editura Vremea, 1998. pp. 6-9.
[183] August 1944. Documente. Bucharest, vol. II. pp. 699-703.

II. The Communist takeover: 1945-1948

The Sanatescu government

For a short period of time, the military government of the National Democratic Block (Nemzeti Demokratikus Blokk) was able to unite the parties, Army commanders, and the King and his circle. The duration of unity was determined by the fact that the two left-wing and the two historical parties agreed on the following issues: the observance of the armistice conditions; gaining the confidence of the Great Powers; the stabilization of prices; the ending of dictatorship; the removal of Fascist and ultra-right-wing elements; but first of all: the regaining of Northern Transylvania. Prime Minister Sanatescu called on the Hungarian government to surrender Northern Transylvania and on August 30 the Romanian Air Force carried out bombing attacks on several Hungarian towns, such as Nagyvárad, Szászrégen, Kecskemét and Cegléd.

Fundamental differences became apparent when it came to the subject of how deeply to reform the structure of the economy and civil society. Are reforms adequate, or are revolutionary changes necessary? Should there be legal continuity between the old and new Romania? And most important, who will lead the country during the transition? Who will wield power?

For the historic parties, the National Peasant Party (NPP), led by Iuliu Maniu, played a more active role in counterbalancing the left, due to its leading role in the withdrawal. There was reason to believe that a 'Maniu-era' would follow.[184] The party's politicians kept emphasizing that only the NPP could manage the country's historical rebirth due to the country's agricultural character and the Party's wide peasant base. Ion Ratiu, who spent decades in exile, returning home after 1989, also emphasized this point.[185]

The National Liberal Party (NLP) emphasized King Mihai's role in the successful withdrawal that "helped the country out of the quagmire into which it was forced by hypnotic totalitarian revolutionary trends of Europe."[186] By 'totalitarian state', the Liberals meant every kind of class-dictatorship. For them, pluralism and constitutional monarchy embodied law and order, which could not be threatened by "any kind of pseudo-democracy haunted by memories of the Weimar Republic."[187] According to the Grand Old Man of the party, I.C. Bratianu, the model for the country's structure must be western democracy.[188]

The National Democratic Front (Országos Demokrata Arcvonal /NDF/) was formed following a conference with the Romanian Communist Party (RCP) held between October 12-19, 1944. The NDF Council passed an unequivocal resolution stating that the Party would only find acceptable a government whose program rested on the NDF program and incorporated the left, as well. In the end,

---

[184] Dreptate, /D./ 1944, August 27.
[185] Ratiu, Ion: Romania de astazi. Comunism sau independenta? Bucharest, Condor, 1990.
[186] Viitorul, /Viit./ 1944, August 30.
[187] Ibid, 1944, August 31.
[188] Ibid, 1944, September 7.

the NDF considered the compromise that elected Groza as Deputy Prime Minister a success. The illusory nature of the coalition became more and more apparent - conflicts within the government, demonstrations organized in turn by the left, then the right - and assumed serious proportions.

The anti-Hungarian atrocities committed in Northern Transylvania by semi-military, semi-civilian units, the Maniu Guards (named after Maniu), came to light during General Constantin Sanatescu's short-lived second coalition government (November 4 to December 6, 1944). For their activities, the Soviet Union ordered Romania to withdraw civil administration from Northern Transylvania and to cease all activities. It also provided an excuse for the Communist Party to blame the mainstream parties and get rid of its strongest rival, Maniu. The NPP was accused of hindering the fulfillment of the armistice conditions, thereby acting against overall national interests. The main objective of the RCP was 'to denounce and isolate the NPP and, in the long term, destroy it, i.e., to oust it from power'.

The Radescu government

General Radescu, well known for his anti-German feelings, was of the opinion that: land reform is necessary but only after the war; war criminals had to be punished but only after trials (military tribunals were not acknowledged); the regular home forces to increase, primarily to be used against the left-wing - to disarm their 100,000-strong militia.[189] The government, under the pretext of maintaining law and order, took an armed stand against the 'revolutionary demonstrations'. When Gheorghiu-Dej returned from Moscow at the end of January, the Communist Party decided to sideline Maniu and those historical parties, which did not want to collaborate. In his speech delivered on February 3, Gheorghiu-Dej stated, "Maniu is the greatest danger to the country as all the dark reactionary forces band around him."[190] Maniu tried to fend off the attack when he pointed out that *the Left hid its dictatorial plans behind the slogan of democracy.*

The Yalta Agreement handed greater influence for the Soviet Union in Central and Eastern Europe.[191] It was also a trump card in the hands of NDF, that is to say, the RCP, that a Romanian administration could return into Northern Transylvania only if a so-called 'democratic' government, that is a government under Communist influence, came into office.

Groza - on behalf of the Left - called upon the government to resign during the meeting of the Council of Ministers of November 21, 1944. Taking stock of the situation, senior officials of the NPP and the NLP called on Western diplomats and asked for support against the left wing. They were refused on the

---

[189] Radescu, Nicolae: Sowjetische Bajonette. Paris, Comite International Paix et Liberte. pp. 16-27.
[190] Livezeanu, Vasile: Transformarile revolutionare premise ale proclamarii Republicii Populare Romane. In. Studii, 1964, issue 4, p. 863.
[191] Viitorul. 1945, January 17. p. 21.

grounds that, on behalf of the Allied Control Commission, the Soviet Union had full authority in Romania. The ministers of the NDF asked King Mihai, in a letter, to take a stand on the restructuring of the government. Since the King insisted on Maniu and Bratianu, on February 27 - 15 days after Yalta - Soviet Deputy Commissar for Foreign Affairs, A. J. Vishinsky, the chief prosecutor of the Moscow show trials of the '30s, traveled to Bucharest and demanded the reshuffling of the government as proposed by the NDF, claiming that the forces gathered around Radescu endangered and provoked the Soviet Union. The King resisted for some days, but when Soviet tanks surrounded the royal palace, he surrendered.

It was the Radescu-government that issued the *Minority Statute* on February 7, 1945.[192] The Statute declared that every Romanian citizen was equal in the eye of the law; that they enjoyed the same civil and political rights regardless of origin, nationality, mother tongue or denomination. Those courts of justice and county/district courts, as well as village and county administrations, located in an area where at least 30% of the population's mother tongue was not Romanian, were obliged to accept petitions written in the minority language and listen to the parties address the court in their mother tongue. Minorities representing 30% of the population had the right to address official forums in their mother tongue and street signs should be written in the minority languages, too. In these regions, civil servants should be familiar with the local language. In non-Romanian language schools, exams should be held in the language of instruction. The Statute guaranteed the freedom of worship and raised the prospect of punishment of those who violated it. The Statute of 1945 - like the one of May, 1938 - was directed at the outside world since as Vishinsky had already stated: Romanian administration could return to Northern Transylvania only if Romania offered solid proof of solving the minority issue.

Anti-Hungarian Romanian atrocities in Northern Transylvania

The Soviet-Romanian armistice agreement, signed on September 12, 1945 annulled the Second Vienna Resolution and declared that Romania would regain (most of) Transylvania and that Romania would enter the war, with full military force, on the side of the Soviet Union against Fascist Germany. On October 11, when the envoys of Regent Horthy signed the preliminary armistice conditions in Moscow, the Hungarian delegation expressed its hope that a plebiscite would decide the future of Transylvania.

Romania's breakaway opened the road for the Soviet army. Marching along Birlad, Bákó, Roman, Tirgu-Neamt, Focsani, Tecuci, Buzau, Soviet troops reached Bucharest on August 29. The following day, the Romanian high command ordered the 1st and 4th army corps, as part of the armistice agreement, to take part in maneuvers as part of the Second Ukrainian Front. Soviet-Romanian joint operations were launched from Havasalföld (Balkan Wallachia) on

---

[192] Three years of nationality politics in a democratic Romania (A nemzetiségi politika három éve a demokratikus Romániában). Bucharest, 1948.

September 5, towards Southern Transylvania and Szeklerland, the very day when the Hungarian 2nd Army began its push to recapture Southern Transylvania. On September 7, the joint Soviet-Romanian attack, launched from Birlad, spearheaded towards Brasov (300 km. to the West), Sfântu Gheorghe (Sepsiszentgyörgy), Odorheiu Secuiesc (Székelyudvarhely), Reghin (Régen), Aiud (Nagyenyed), Baraolt (Barót), Rupea (Kohalom), the valley of Nirajului (Nyárád), then the region of the rivers Aranyos, Maros, Küküllo and finally Torda, where severe fighting took place. Beginning September 15, the Hungarian forces held their ground for three weeks.

In September of 1944, the Hungarian government ordered the evacuation of Northern Transylvania, while at the same time, the advancing Soviet troops forced out Hungarian administration. Maniu, just like Benes, hoped that - in spite of representing Transylvanian regionalism since 1920 and discussing the possibility of a mutual Hungarian-Romanian breakaway - Hungarian could possibly be deported from Romania and Czechoslovakia.

Politicians spoke openly about the collective guilt of the Germans and the Hungarians leading naturally to its consequence: collective punishment.[193] They advocated deportation to be rid of them.[194] Forcible removal to labor camps also found favor during 1945.[195] The rounding up of a significant portion of the German population by the Russians was matched by the internment of a part the male Hungarian population. From Cluj Napoca alone, 5,000 Hungarian men were rounded up.[196]

At the meeting of the Romanian Council of Ministers on September 27, Maniu proposed the formation of a "government commission" to administer liberated Northern Transylvania. Paramilitary units, the so-called Maniu Guards, approx. 50,000-strong, were formed behind the front in order to maintain law and order, terrorized the Hungarian population of Transylvania during the following month. The Guardsmen killed nearly 100 people, interned several thousand (in total around 40,000). Wherever these 'volunteers of death' appeared in the counties of Háromszék, Csík, Szilágy and Szatmár, book burnings, beatings of Hungarians and looting followed.

The active participants in the anti-Hungarian atrocities – and who should have had a share for the responsibility – were the Maniu Guardsmen, the staffs of the local Romanian administrations (the gendarmerie), the armed local population (driven by personal revenge for petty disputes), after August 23, the Transylvanian battalions mobilized by the Romanian high command and under the command of the regular army, and the raw recruit units, which were ordered to carry out operational tasks, such as garrison duty. These latter were thrown into action against the so-called paratroopers and 'Hungarian partisans'.

---

[193] Dreptate /D./, 1944, September 23.
[194] Ibid, 1944, September 25.
[195] Transylvania (Erdély), 1945, January 29.
[196] Gál, Mária: Death camps in our midst (Haláltáborok itthon). Transylvanian Diary (Erdélyi Napló), 1997, May 20.

However, the Soviet-Romanian armistice did not satisfy Romanian politicians. Urged on by Benes, they wanted Hungarians declared as war criminals, to suffer all the consequences, including resettlement, as happened in Czechoslovakia. Thus, the 'batalioanele fixe,' the voluntars (volunteers in Romanian) become the means of intimidation to force the Hungarians to flee, or to leave voluntarily. The most threatened regions were Háromszék (30,000 people left) and Csík (110,000 fled and only 60,000 remained). Removal of the people started in early September and Romanian administration took charge immediately.

The reign of terror started in Northern Transylvania on September 22, while in Southern Transylvania, it began immediately after August 23, when some 50,000 people were interned.[197] The prime objective was to expel the Hungarians, but among the others were to damage or destroy the Orthodox churches in the Szeklerland, accuse the population of anti-Romanian partisan activity – hence, the label for Aita-seacá (Szárazajta) as a 'partisan village' - and personal revenge.

The leftist Romanian and Hungarian press began to publish the text of the official report compiled on October 14, 1944 by the representatives of the Communist-influenced United Trade Unions. The facts were as follows: Gavril Olteanu, accompanied by 35 volunteers, showed up in Aita-seacá, Háromszék County, on the evening of September 25. They accused the villagers - without ground - of crimes against the Romanian army. One Mrs. Albert Szép had nursed and hid a wounded Romanian officer in the village. However, Olteanu claimed that Mrs. Szép robbed and killed the officer. In retaliation, they took 26 hostages and herded them to the school building, where they were executed the following dawn. Sándor Nagy was led to a stump in the middle of the yard; the axe struck him four times before killing him. András Nagy was luckier; he died on the second stroke. (The ill-famed stump was on display in the yard of the Szekler Museum in Sfântu Gheorghe [Sepsiszentgyörgy] for a long time.) The other victims - their names reported in *Scinteia*, the Romanian Communist Party's daily - Lajos Elekes, Lajos Szabó, Benjámin Szabó, Gyula Német, Izsák Német, József Málnási, Albert Szép, Mrs. Albert Szép, Béla Szép, József D. Nagy, Béla Gecse and László Lázár - were shot. When the wounded Romanian officer's son was informed of the events, he proved that Olteanu's charges were a frame-up.[198]

---

[197] Romania Libera, 1944, November 6.

[198] Lipcsey, Ildikó: The Maniu Guards (A Maniu gárdisták). Critique (Kritika), 1989, issue 10. pp. 24-26;

New Hungarian Central Archives (Új Magyar Központi Levéltár) Budapest, 1964. The situation of the Hungarian minority in Romania. Transylvanian material. The atrocities committed against Hungarians since the 1944, August 23 Romanian military occupation;

Frunza, Victor: Istoria partidului Comunist Roman. Nord, 1984. vol. II. p. 174;

Reuben, L - Markham, H.: Le Roumanie sous le joug soviétique. Paris, Colman-Lévy, 1949;

Frannck, Nicolette: La Roumanie dans l'engrenage. Comment le Royaume est devenu republique populaire. /1944-1947/. Paris, Ed. Révesier Séqueia, 1977.

Besides Aita-seacá, several other villages in Csík, Háromszék and Gyergyó were the scenes of atrocities: the casualties of the massacre at Sindominic (Csíkszentdomokos) on October 8 totaled 11: Sándor Tímár, László Kósa, József Kurkó, Antal Szakács, Imre Szakács, Lajos Zsók, Albert Péter, Lajos Bíró, Ferenc Kedves, Mrs. Sándor Bodó, and the 84-year old Mrs. József György -- many of them relatives of Gyárfás Kurkó, President of the Hungarian People's Alliance (Magyar Népi Szövetség) and of Bishop Aaron Márton. The victims were buried in the Gábor garden.

Leaving Háromszék and Csík counties, the guardsmen, or *voluntars* as they were still called, swept through Cluj (Kolozs) and Szolnok-Doboka counties. In these two counties, Hungarian men were abducted in the greatest numbers. It is widely known that the workers of Aghiresu (Egeres) prevented the Germans from blowing up the power plant supplying Cluj Napoca with electricity. Everyone was shocked, when, on October 22, Sergeant Hartia and his forty-member gang marched 13 people out of Egeres and shot them in the back of their heads, leaving their naked corpses at the edge of the woods. In the days following October 11, 5,000 men were taken away from Cluj Napoca. In mid-October, the majority of men from Floresti (Szászfenes), Gheorghieni (Györgyfalva), Chinteni (Kajántó), Luna de Sus (Magyarlóna) and Rascruci (Válaszút) were taken to an unknown location. At about the same time, men escaped from several villages for fear of being shot.

It needs to be said that in this plight, it was only the Romanian left wing that took action against the Maniu Guardsmen threatening the defenseless Hungarian population. Naturally, in the jockeying for power, the terror reputation of the Guard gave the mainstream parties ammunition, especially against the NPP, whose outstanding political figure was Iulio Maniu.

"Maniu's volunteers are terrorizing the Hungarians in Transylvania," warned Ana Pauker in her address during a ceremony on November 7. Petru Groza's government report, delivered at the meeting of the Council of Ministers on November 13, 1944 admitted that Maniu's guardsmen flooded Northern Transylvania and revenge, blood and death marked their passage. "In the 20th century, it seems as if only Hitler's era existed, innocent Szeklers were beheaded," and the world already knew of the tragic events, which deeply compromised Romania. In reaction, on the following day, November 14, 1944, the Soviet Union, citing the endangerment of the Hungarian population of Transylvania, called upon Romanian authorities to withdraw from Northern Transylvania within 24 hours. Vishinsky justified the decision as follows: as long as the Romanian government is unable to guarantee law and order, democracy and the equal rights of minorities, transitional status would be maintained. Thus, on November 14, Northern Transylvania came under the control of the Soviet military government.

Between January 1945 and April 1946, that is, during the time of the ostensibly democratic Groza government, anti-Hungarian actions continued. By the autumn of 1944, the concentration camps of Feldioara (Földvár), Haghig (Hídvég) and Tirgu-Jiu were filled with Southern Transylvanian Hungarians. Despite the horrible state of affairs - 20 to 25 people a day died of typhoid - the internment of Hungarians and Saxons continued. From Torda-Aranyos county, 1,000 Hungarian men were taken to an unknown location; as late as mid-1945, 43 Hungarian men and women were being held in flimsy huts in Caracal, sick and in rags, without being charged with any crime. In June, several hundred citizens were kept from returning to their homes in Szilágy county. In all, about 50,000 Hungarians were kept in internment and labor camps.[199]

According to the August 2, 1945 issue of *Independent Word* (Szabad Szó) of Tirgu Mures (Marosvásárhely), complaints were arriving from some 60-80 settlements, from every county of Transylvania, almost flooding the offices of the Hungarian People's Alliance. The situation was no better in the towns: Hungarian from Arad were interned, in Cluj Napoca, the 1848 plaque was torn from the wall of the Redout, and Hungarians who gathered to welcome Romanian soldiers returning from the front were battered. Ferenc Nagy and Pál Kovács were killed; Unitarian Bishop Jozan was insulted in the street after the celebration on August 23. The authorities attempted to settle Romanian families into the building of the Teleki Library and the principal of the Hungarian secondary school, Paul Gusztáv, was assaulted in Tirgu Mures.

It was also reported from Cluj Napoca that the paperboys selling the paper *Transylvania* (Erdély) were repeatedly beaten up by Romanians. Hungarians were harassed, especially in the suburbs, on a daily basis. Similar reports arrived from Oradea (Nagyvárad). Between September and December, complaints about the endangerment of Hungarians continued to flood in.[200]

In light of this, the Hungarian People's Alliance, which had already publicized most of the cases, wrote the following letter to Vasile Luca on March 6, 1946: "We have received numerous reports that Hungarians, especially members of our organization, live in such fear as to make it impossible to urge our people to support our democratic government... We ask High Sheriff Pogaceanu (Lord Lieutenant of the county) to take firm steps, because the sad state of the Hungarians are a result of his inaction. With this request, we wish to serve the interest of the democratic government as his weakness drives the masses into the clutches of the reactionary elements. We have in our possession several reports already forwarded to the High Sheriff, but no serious steps have been taken. These outrages must end in the interest of Hungarian-Romanian reconciliation. It is high time that democracy prevail, not only in words but in practice."[201]

A group of Maniu Guardsmen was brought before the military court in Brasov in April 1945. At a time when the Bucharest Tribunal Court passed 28 capital sentences in the case of war criminals, the Court in Brasov delivered the following judgments: Captain Gavril Olteanu was sentenced to life, Stana Traian (he was the one who executed Mrs. Albert Szép) to 3 years. The others merely received a few months of jail.

---

[199] Molnár Gusztáv talks with Méliusz József. „Confess, keep confessing" (Vallani, egyre vallani). Forum. Bucharest, 1983, March. pp. 20-21.
[200] New Hungarian National Archives. sz.n./1964. The situation of the Hungarian .... op.cit.
[201] Illumination (Világosság). 1946, March 7.

The contemporary Romanian Left, members of the Allied Control Commission, the Romanian embassy in Moscow, as well as the senior officials of the British military and diplomatic missions in Bucharest were all of the opinion that the anti-Hungarian terror of the Maniu Guardsmen justified the imposition of Soviet military government in Northern Transylvania, between November 14, 1944 and March 13, 1945. Romanian civil administration was forced to - temporarily - withdraw from the area. Romanian circles in Transylvania whispered that Moscow appointed a governor with the title of 'Governor of Transylvania'.[202]

Even Iuliu Maniu was surprised by this action. In his letter of protest addressed to the Soviet Deputy Commissar for Foreign Affairs, A. J. Vishinsky, he claimed that the action is contrary to the Soviet-Romanian armistice agreement. He justified the Maniu Guardsmen's activities - as recent Romanian historiography still does - that they only punished the Hungarians for the persecution of Romanians after the Second Vienna Resolution.

The government of Northern Transylvania[203]

A provisional coalition government, named Central Advisory Board of Northern Transylvania (CABNT), was established in Kolozsvár on December 1, 1944, in order to fill the void and "to manage public affairs, free of external pressures, relying on itself and resources at hand." The coalition included the representatives of the Democratic Alliance of Romanians in Transylvania (Erdélyi Románok Demokratikus Szövetsége – 12 persons), the Northern Transylvanian Provincial Secretariat of the Romanian Communist Party (Román Kommunista Párt Észak-Erdélyi Tartományi Titkársága), the Social-Democratic Party (Szociáldemokrata Párt), the Hungarian People's Alliance and the Trade Union (Szakszervezet – 6 persons each), the Plough Front (Ekésfront – 4 persons), the Patriotic Alliance, the Jewish Democratic People's Alliance (Zsidó Demokrata Népi Szövetség) and the People's Defense Unit (Népvédelmi Egység – 2 persons each). The Central Advisory Board of Northern Transylvania was empowered to both initiate and execute laws and operated through special commissions of ministerial authority. The two major objectives of the Board were to lay the foundation of self-government in Transylvania and to launch the process of democratization of everyday life. It also assured an orderly day-to-day life, organized production and distribution, took steps to head off conflicts between minorities, ran soup kitchens, dismissed the Gendarmerie and aided people returning from the war and concentration camps. The CABNT was of the opinion that the armistice agreement left the question of the territorial status of

---

[202] Nagy, Zoltán Mihály: Cluj Napoca in the period of Northern Transylvanian Soviet military government. Cluj Napoca's 1000 years (Kolozsvár az észak-erdélyi szovjet katonai közigazgatás idoszakában. Kolozsvár 1000 éve). Cluj Napoca, 2001. p. 314.

[203] Lipcsey, Ildikó: Northern Transylvania under Soviet military government, November 15, 1944 - March 13, 1945 (Észak-Erdély szovjet katonai közigazgatás alatt. 1944, November 15 - 1945, Mácius 13). History (História), 1989, issue 4-5.

Transylvania - at least part of it - open; therefore it condemned those who wished to join Romania.[204]

Due to constant problems, the committees held sessions frequently. The Law Commission devoted a lot of time to framing a view of the future Transylvania. It can not be other than - stated Ágoston Bernád, a leftist intellectual from Cluj Napoca - 1) a self-governed part of the country; 2) the reliance on the proportionality of the nationalities in all walks of life; and 3) the acceptance of Romanian, Hungarian and German as official languages of the state. One of the achievements of the Public Education Commission was the drafting of a new educational law by December 29. It allowed using both Hungarian and Romanian textbooks.[205]

The debate on the standing of Transylvania (ed: whether to be part of Hungary or Romania,) was a regular subject of the CABNT sessions, too. At its meeting on February 7, 1945, the major topic was to forge a position on Northern Transylvania. Teofil Vescan, Romanian university professor of leftist sympathies – along with others - interpreted the Soviet-Romanian armistice agreement as intending to attach Transylvania to Romania, if the country's democratic system ensured full equality for every national minority. The Communist Pál Veress shared the opinion: in 1918-19 the Romanian Social Democrats held the view that they did not wish to be part of the Kingdom of Romania; in 1945, the Hungarians said the same thing but they were ready to collaborate with the Romanian people in a democratic country. Ferenc Bruder, member of the Hungarian Committee of the Social Democratic Party, felt it to be of extraordinary importance to ensure the representation of Hungarians in state and public life in proportion to their numbers.

On February 11, 1945, one thousand representatives of Northern Transylvania's 11 counties – Háromszék, Udvarhely, Csík, Maros-Torda, Beszterce-Naszód, Szolnok-Doboka, Máramaros, Szilágy, Szatmár, Bihar and Kolozs – met in the banquet hall of the Council-house of Cluj Napoca (Kolozsvár). The two major points on the agenda were: a statement regarding the standing of Transylvania and the establishment of the Groza-government. Following the opening words of High Sheriff Pogaceanu, Vescan took the floor. He stated that neither the Hungarian nor the Romanian people attacked the Soviet Union in World War Two, only Hungarian and Romanian Fascists elements. As for the status of Transylvania, he was of the opinion that the Hungarians' hopes were groundless. For the Soviet-Romanian armistice agreement annulled the Second Vienna Resolution, i.e., it did not leave Transylvania's status open to question. He went on to say that point # 17 of the armistice agreement, on the introduction of Romanian administration, did not neglect the subsequent approval of it, as drafted in point # 19. The ultimate solution to Transylvania's nationality question lies in a democratic government taking control of Romania, one that can

[204] Ibid.

[205] MOL, Current Affairs collection. Ministry of External Affairs, Peace Preparatory Section files. XIX-J-1-a 63 box, IV-148 folder, 12/ BE. 1946. Northern Transylvania's political situation at the time of separation.

ensure full equality before the law for every non-Romanian citizen, thereby putting an end to all national discrimination.

The conference concluded with the passing of the program entitled: *Northern Transylvania's Parliament has decided*: 1) the free use of the languages of national minorities, extending the franchise for every citizen over 18, prosecuting war criminals; 2) assuring production and transportation, settling the rate of exchange of the Lei and Pengo (the Romanian and Hungarian currencies of the day); 3) guaranteeing the operation of Hungarian schools and university; 4) settling the status of theater, sports and the press; 5) the expropriation of estates over 50 hectares, the just distribution of lands for the minorities, the repatriation of Hungarian prisoners-of-war and Jewish deportees.

The conference authorized the 15-member Executive Committee – elected as the successor of CABNT – to govern the central administration and coordinate cooperation between the counties. The Commissions resumed their meetings on February 15, 1945, keeping in mind the resolutions of the conference held on February 11-12. The Labor Commission discussed the necessity of public works; the Financial and Economic Commission, of taxation and harmonization of currencies; the Public Administration Commission, the transfer of public servants according to requirements. The major topic of the Law Commission was, obviously, the issue of the executive power of the state. The slogan of the Agricultural Commission was 'Not an inch of land left uncultivated' – including the lands abandoned by German citizens.

József Venczel, statistician and economist, and Julian Chitta submitted a draft agrarian reform to the Commission. Social Democrat István Lakatos took a stand for the renewal of the long lasting traditions of cooperatives in Transylvania. The issue of re-establishing Hungarian higher educational institutions, which were closed between the two World Wars, was raised in the Public Educational Commission. A special commission was established to review the Minority Statute passed in Romania on February 7, 1945. The law permitted the use of a national minority language in judicial matters and public administration where 30 percent of the population was of a national minority. However, regarding the Hungarian university, the commission took the stand that only a Romanian university was needed in Cluj Napoca, with Hungarian departments in the arts and law faculties. (The resolution ignored the fact that the Soviet authorities consented, in September 1944, to the operation of a Hungarian university.)

During the February conference, the CABNT was renamed Northern Transylvanian Central Executive Committee of the NDF whose clear and acknowledged responsibility was laying the groundwork of a regional government.[206] It was another matter that with these steps, the Soviet Union was trying to out-maneuver, to corner, the Radescu government.[207] If Groza is not

[206] Lajos Jordáky's personal conversation with the author.
[207] Illumination (Világosság). 1945, February 18.

named to replace Radescu – warned Vishinsky – Romania will lose not only Northern Transylvania but its independence, as well.[208]

The Groza government: March-December 1945 [209]

The home and foreign press media announced at 7 P.M. on March 6, 1945 that the new government had taken the oath of office.[210] Dr. Petru Groza, already chosen to the post by the communists in the autumn of 1944, headed it. Of the 32 Ministers and Secretaries of State, 17 were nominated from the left-wing NDF (see RCP, Social Democrats, Plough Front, Trade Unions, Alexandru's NPP), two from the Patriots Alliance (Hazafiak Szövetsége), and six from Tatarescu's Liberal Party. It was remarkable how the traditional parties lost ground, since both the Patriots Alliance and Tatarescu's NPP were considered as pro-Communist. They secured the Ministries of Foreign Affairs, Industry, Trade and Finance. There were also six high-ranking Army officers as members of the government. The NPP (National Peasant Party) and NLP (National Liberal Party) announced their opposition in an open letter.[211] However, Groza almost completely neutralized this by his first act as premier when he wired the government of the Soviet Union, asking to re-institute Romanian administration in Northern Transylvania. Stalin's reply was: "The Soviet government has considered the Romanian Prime Minister's request of March 8, on the subject of establishment of Romanian administration in Transylvania. Considering the fact that the new government, which has just taken over the administration of the country, *takes responsibility for Transylvania's law and order and assures the minorities' rights as well as* the orderly operation of all local institutions supplying the needs of the front, the Soviet government has decided to meet the request of the Romanian government, and in accordance with the Armistice Agreement, signed on September 12, 1944, approves the introduction of Romanian administration in Transylvania."[212]

The Council of Ministers held a formal meeting in Cluj Napoca on March 13, 1945 attended by the representatives of the Allied Control Commission (ACC), Soviet Deputy Commissar for Foreign Affairs Vishinsky, King Mihai, Secretary of State Tatarescu, as well as the parties and trade unions. The Executive Commission, as the representative body of the leaders of the city and

---

[208]Nagy: Cluj Napoca … op.cit. p. 319.

[209] Lahav, Yehuda: Soviet policy and the Transylvanian Question (1940-1946). Hebrew University of Jerusalem. The Soviet and East-European Research Centre, research paper no. 27. Jerusalem, July 1, 1977.

[210] Lipcsey, Ildikó: In the spirit of a peaceable future (Egy békésebb jövo jegyében). History (História), 1982, issue 2. pp. 37, 67;
Lipcsey Ildikó: The memory of Petru Groza (Petru Groza emlékezete). Our Life (Életünk). 1985, issue 2. pp. 138-144.

[211] Popisteanu, Cristian: Bucuresti, 6 martie 1945. Orale 19. Magazin istoric, Bucuresti, 1975, 3 nr, pp. 14-15.

[212] Russian-Romanian cease-fire agreement. Telegrams between Peter Groza and Marshall Stalin. Cluj Napoca, 1945. pp. 5-6.

region, welcomed the guests. In his reply, Groza stated that the elimination of discrimination of nationalities and denominations was his personal and his government's most sincere intention – a statement carried the next day in every Hungarian-language paper in Transylvania. However, *Illumination* (Világosság), the daily paper of the Hungarian People's Alliance of Romania, HPAR, (Magyar Népi Szövetség) did not conceal either the general view of the majority of Romanians that: "Democracy will be a reality in Romania, only if all the Hungarians depart for Hungary and all the Jews for Palestine."[213]

A grandiose reception was held at the Town Hall, festooned with Soviet, US, British, Romanian and Hungarian flags and the Royal Guard providing the guard of honor. King Mihai and Petru Groza delivered speeches in the Students' House (Diákház) at noon. It was the first time that the Prime Minister spoke publicly about his idea of a confederation in Central Europe. "The happy time has come when we are again at home in Cluj Napoca" he said. "Two nations live together in Transylvania, two nations that have suffered much, the Romanian and the Hungarian nations. That is why the spirit of reconciliation must also spread towards the Hungarian nation from here, in order to finally meet with all the nations of the Danube Basin, in alliance with our great neighbor, the Soviet Union! ... We are going to work and fight in harmony for the development of the great universal community of mankind in our beloved country, a free Romania."[214]

The Transylvanians warned the government that national equality could not be established without self-government and the proportional representation of the minorities. Vescan submitted the memorandum of the Executive Commission on the subject. It included the following points:

1. Hungarians should be represented in the government in proportion of their numbers;
2. The Northern Transylvanian Executive Commission, with a seat in Cluj Napoca (Kolozsvár), should be appointed to control state and public administration;
3. Village, town and county officials should remain in office;
4. If 50% of the population was Hungarian, the leaders should be Hungarians and in areas of mixed population, the leadership should reflect the population's composition;
5. The proportionality should be strictly adhered to in offices, at the railways and postal service, etc.;
6. The Hungarian language should be acknowledged as an official language;
7. The regulation governing language in public administration should be extended to railways and the postal service, as well;
8. Families made to suffer by the Maniu Guardsmen should receive compensation;

---

[213] Illumination (Világosság). March 14, 1945.
[214] Ibid.

9. Joint Romanian-Hungarian commissions should operate at the borders in order to administer the return of refugees and those who were displaced, e.g.- 60,000 people from Csík;

10. Allow the 200,000 Hungarians who fled from the Antonescu's terror to Hungary (Northern Transylvania), to return to Southern Transylvania;

11. Hungarians who fought in the Red Army should be trained in their mother tongue and get commissioned;

12. Instruction should be assured at every level: a university should be established in Cluj Napoca (Kolozsvár), colleges in Cluj Napoca and Tirgu Mures (Marosvásárhely) and a technical university in Szeklerland;

13. Guarantee the equality of churches;

14. Acknowledge the status of visiting Hungarian guest professors;

15. The Hungarian National Theater should enjoy parity with the Romanian one;

16. Every nation of Transylvania should be free in the use of its national colors;

17. A Hungarian Cultural Council should be established;

18. Jobs should be available without restrictions;

19. Equality should prevail during land distribution;

20. Those Jews, who declare themselves as Hungarian, should be considered as Hungarians; and

21. All persecution of nationalities, denominations or races should be punished.

The intention of the Executive Commission was clear: self-government, introduced on November 14, 1944 to be extended over all of Transylvania. The Groza government made promises to this end. However, the communiqué on the session of the Executive Commission held in early June 1945 was one of the last documents issued by that body. The communiqué contained of four important points: the Ministry of Arts should grant aid to the Conservatory of Music; the Foreign Ministry should take an interest in the Romanians interned to Hungary; the College of Agriculture should be re-established in Kolozsvár; and the composition of the county, district and village NDF Committees should be constituted as: RCP and RSDP (Romanian Social-Democratic Party) 25% each, United Trade Unions (Egyesült Szakszervezetek) 20%, Plough Front, HPAR and Patriot's Alliance, 10% respectively.

In the same month, the Central Advisory Board of Northern Transylvania (Észak-Erdélyi Tanácsadó Testület), then the Executive Commission – having fulfilled its historical missions, i.e., contributed to the observation of armistice terms and guaranteed the normalization of life in the period of transition – were deemed terminated. The dream of autonomy, interpreted in a broader sense, lived on in the National Hungarian Committee of the RSDP (Román Szociáldemokrata Párt) during 1945-1946 and in the Hungarian Autonomous Province in 1952-1968.[215]

Romanian laws came into effect in Northern Transylvania on March 31, 1945 but few people took notice of what Lucretiu Patrascanu, Minister of Justice, announced on the radio. He stated that, henceforth, the basis for the legal situation would be that in effect prior to August 30, 1940 and not that of March 31, 1945. In

---

[215] Ibid.

other words, measures and regulations, such as the ones on the operation of Hungarian schools and institutions, passed in Northern Transylvania earlier, were no longer in force.

The formation of the Groza government on March 6, meant for NPP and NLP that they had lost the battle in the political arena. Therefore, both parties made every effort to preserve their positions in government. They did not conceal their belief that the Groza government did not represent the majority of the Romanian people, and that it did not observe the principles of democracy. In his memorandum, sent to the participants of the Potsdam Conference (July 17 – August 2, 1945), Maniu stressed that the prime condition of a democratic system were free, general elections and the formation of a government that represented all antifascist (by that time considered as the opposition) forces.[216]

Taking the advantage of Truman's radio address, in which he stated that real democracy had to be established in Romania and Italy, King Mihai informed the representatives of ACC on August 21, and Gorza on the 27, that unless they include the leaders of NPP and NLP, as well as the anti-Communist Social Democrats of Titel-Petrescu, in the government, he intends to boycott it. The Western Powers' conception was that - although they did not manage to put the Romanian question on the agenda in London - Maniu should take over the government from Groza. The man who, after the German surrender, questioned the presence of Soviet troops in the country and - not without foundation - accused the government of seeking to create a dictatorship. The USA announced in mid-September that it would not recognize the government of Romania as long as it did not include the country's historical parties to a greater extent.

At the ACC conference, held in Moscow on December 16-26, 1945 Great Britain and the USA made the recognition of Romania dependent on the following terms: incorporation of one representative each of the Liberal and the Peasant parties in the Romanian government and the holding of new elections with the participation of all democratic and anti-fascist parties.

Bowing to international political pressure, Emil Hatieganu of the Peasant Party and Mihai Romniceanu of the Liberal Party were elected to the government. Thus, the attempt of the King and the historical parties to return Maniu and Bratianu to power and to relieve the communist ministers (Ministers Patrascanu of Justice and Georgescu of Internal Affairs) of their office, failed.[217]

In the course of 1945, Groza aided the Communist Party in preparing its position, in preparation for the following year's elections – due to the failure of the Hungarian Communists in the 1945 elections, the elections in Romania were postponed – making use of the so called 'salami tactics', to split the traditional parties and advance their dissidents to power. Through the 1945 agrarian reform,

---

[216] Stan, Apostol: Iuliu Maniu. Nationaliism si democratie. Biografia unui mare roman. Buch., Editura SAECULUM I.O. 1997. pp. 468-472. This subject also arose during the January 1, 1946 conference between the American and British ambassadors, Averell Harriman and Archibald Clark Kerr. Maniu did not believe that the West would abandon Romania to the Soviet Union.
[217] Costantiniu, Florin: Istoria Romaniei. 1945. Romniceanu and Hatieganu members of the government.

Groza intended to diminish the influence of the National Peasant Party among farmers, since it was not inconsequential which party wanted to distribute the land. Groza can also be held responsible for misleading and deceiving the Hungarians in Romania. By meaningless and irresponsible statements and promises, he not only wanted to disarm the Hungarians but also to strengthen his own shaky position.

The Hungarian People's Alliance in Romania (HPAR)[218]

"It has sold Transylvania!" "It has saved Hungarian institutions!" "It was the branch office of the Romanian Communist Party, it was the trail-blazer of Stalinism and it oppressed the Romanian people!" These were just three of the numerous and contradictory opinions and emotions, then as now, about the activities of the Hungarian People's Alliance in Romania /HPAR/ (Romániai Magyar Népi Szövetség) – which considered itself the representative of Hungarian interests in Romania, the umbrella organization above and beyond parties, churches and institutions, as well as the Party organized on a national basis.

Two facts have to be taken into account. One, after World War II, the Soviet military-political presence was a defining factor in the region. First Poland, Bulgaria, then Romania were Sovietized and Communist parties came into power in almost every country of the region. This limited the scope of activity of the Hungarians in Romania *to accept only a left-leaning system, the RCP supported Hungarian People's Alliance.* Two, every effort of Romanian policy was aimed at holding on to the annexed territories. In domestic politics, the social-, economic-, labor- and minority-policies were always subordinated to this. This is one of the main reasons why the country's backwardness became chronic and lasting. In other words, nationalism, as well as the anti-Semitic and anti-Hungarian politics of assimilation became a constant factor in a changing historical situation.

The HPAR enjoyed a distinguished position in the federal and nationality policy of the Romanian Communist Party. There were several well-motivated reasons for this:

1. Before 1944-1945, the RCP was a small party - of 1,000-2,000 members, a number of whom were police informers - most of whom were of one of the national minorities and, therefore, the party was unpopular in the eyes of the majority Romanian people.
2. The country had to be stabilized for the peace talks and to create the illusion that, as a result of forced international policy, this part of Europe would never be a powder-keg again. The West and Hungarians, at home and abroad, had to be persuaded by facts.
3. During its struggle for power against the Liberals, but even more so against the National Peasant Party, the Hungarian People's Alliance was every bit as

---

[218] Lipcsey, Ildikó: The Hungarian People's Alliance on the path to self-destruction, 1944-1953. (A Magyar Népi Szövetség az önfeladás útján. 1944-1953). Bp., Possum Publishing, 1998.

important an ally to the Communists as the smaller Romanian parties – separated from the traditional parties by the use of 'salami tactics'.

4. For the time being, the RCP needed the experts of the traditional parties and national minorities.

The Hungarian People's Alliance was a branch office of the RCP. All this dates back to the Fifth RCP Congress in 1931. A resolution stated that a left wing, that is pro-Communist, party had to be carved out from the Maniu-led Romanian National Peasant Party and the National Hungarian Party. This was how the Petru Groza led Plow Front and the National Alliance of Hungarian Workers (Magyar Dolgozók Országos Szövetsége – hereafter: NAHW) were established in 1934. As an aside, Groza was a lawyer and one of the richest landowners in Romania. NAHW failed to gain popularity because, even though its program included numerous social and nationality demands – for example, instruction in the mother tongue from kindergarten to university and the use of mother tongue in public administration – its declaration that *Romania possessed Transylvania by way of historic right.* In addition, the sectarian leftist attitude of its leaders repelled most Hungarians. The Hungarian People's Alliance, established in October 1944, inherited the leftism of NAHW on the one hand, and the mass support of the National Hungarian Party on the other.

There is also a quite easy to answer to the question, Why HPAR pledged itself, almost without reservation, to the Romanian Communist Party?

1. The Soviet military authorities ordered the plundering Maniu Guards out of Northern Transylvania and Szeklerland at the mediation of the Communist Party, and only the communists condemned the anti-Hungarian atrocities publicly.

2. Liberal and Peasant Party politicians were of the opinion that there was no need to ensure the collective rights of national minorities in the Constitution beyond general human rights; another standpoint was that collective responsibility and resettlement should be extended to the Hungarians in Romania, too. Referring to this statement, the Communists – including László Luka – reasoned that if the Hungarians did not vote for them and the bourgeois Romanian parties came to power, they would all be leaving their motherland with a 40 kg. parcel in their hands.

3. But Prime Minister Petru Groza, the "political chameleon",[219] as well as the Communist Party's leaders promised repeatedly that they would solve the nationality issue and assure full equality of rights. During the election campaign in 1946, promises were made about the autonomy of Szeklerland, even of Transylvania, and the elimination of the border between the two countries, a Romanian-Hungarian customs union and confederation in Central Europe.

---

[219] Gáti, Charles: Hungary in the Shadow of the Kremlin (Magyarország a Kreml árnyékában). Bp., Századvég Publisher, 1990. Peter Gosztonyi's opinion of Petru Groza was identical. Hungary in the Second World War (Magyarország a második világháborúban). Munich, HERP, 1984.

4. And the most promising factor was: the Hungarian People's Alliance, representing the majority of Hungarians, was accepted as an organ which had consultative and veto rights in all issues concerning Hungarians life in Romania. In short, while the Left made promises, the traditional parties only voiced threats and accusations.

The uncertain years of Transylvania: 1944-1945

Due to measures and laws passed in 1943-44, Hungarians in Southern Transylvania lived almost outside the law: the draft meant labor service, the internment camps were full of Hungarians, and the confiscation of radio sets and vehicles became common practice. However, just as in Northern Transylvania, the idea of breaking away from the war kept spreading in the ranks of the Hungarian People's Union (Magyar Népközösség) - the only legitimate Hungarian political organization in Southern Transylvania. As well as the idea of approaching certain Romanian groups to prevent the declaration of Hungarian collective guilt and their resettlement, which began to appear in some Romanian sectors. What made their steps urgent was that, as early as the spring of 1944, the Hungarian leadership of Southern Transylvania became aware of Romanian plans to withdraw from the war.[220]

Two days after Horthy's abortive attempt to break out of the war, on October 16, 1944, the members of the National Alliance of Hungarian Workers /NAHW/ convened a national meeting of leftist Hungarians in Southern Transylvania, in Brassó. In accordance with the ideas outlined by Gyárfás Kurkó, delegates from Southern Transylvania, Bucharest, Háromszék and Udvarhely decided to transform the Alliance into a popular-national organization that rallied every Hungarian irrespective of party affiliation and ideology, except those, naturally, who guilty of Fascist war crimes. It would be temporarily located in Brassó. The session elected the 27 person Provisional Executive Committee and its 5-member leadership. Their prime tasks included preparations for the First Congress of the now established Hungarian People's Alliance in Romania /HPAR/, drafting the organization's by-laws, and organizing the movement. They also enjoyed the support of the Hungarian churches. The successor of the NAHW, the HPAR consistently assumed the mantle of champion of Hungarian national interests.[221]

The repeated NPP attacks against Hungarians in Transylvania in October and November provided a good opportunity for the RCP to play the role of the protector of the Hungarians. NPP and Liberal politicians resented the public actions of NAHW representatives. As an example, Corneliu Coposu, publicist of the National Peasant Party, wrote an article in the October 11 issue of *Dreptate*, making very clear that: "we have no need for cooperation with Hungarian organizations or the Hungarians at all ... As for Hungary's role in the war, it can not be claimed that the government forced the country into the war. The whole

---

[220] Molnár Gusztáv talks with Méliusz József. „Confess, keep confessing" (Vallani, egyre vallani). Forum. Bucharest, 1983, March. pp. 20-21.

[221] A lawyer for the MNSZ, Csákány Béla's personal communication.

nation wanted it. The NAHW should operate there, in Hungary... Let them disappear as quickly as possible, we don't even want to hear their names." Many in the NPP demanded the punishment of 'alleged' war criminals in Northern Transylvania, stating: "there is no place in Transylvania either for bilingual government or Hungarians". Liberals shared these opinions and when they talked about war criminals, they focused almost exclusively on the Hungarians (and Germans), forgetting all others.

Following August 23, 1944, in Northern Transylvania, which belonged to Hungary at that time, Béla Teleki, Imre Mikó, Sándor Vita and Béla Demeter of the Transylvanian Party (Erdélyi Párt), József Venczel of the Hungarian Economic Society in Transylvania /HEST/ (Erdélyi Magyar Gazdasági Egyesület), Lajos Jordáky of the Social Democratic Party (SZDP), Lajos Csögör of the NAHW and Sándor Jakab of the Communist Party (RCP) agreed that Hungary should ask for an armistice immediately. One of the major tasks of the Transylvanian Council (Erdélyi Tanács), established on September 12, was to try to achieve this goal.[222] Their memorandum dated September 9, 1944 and addressed to Regent Horthy, urging a withdrawal from the hostilities at the earliest possible time.[223] In this endeavor, a significant role belongs to the Teleki family, count Geza Teleki (son of count Pal Teleki who, as Prime Minister of Hungary, committed suicide when the Germans forced him to break the Hungarian-Yugoslavian Friendship treaty), and count Bela Teleki, who had a role in the preparation of the first, unofficial, Soviet-Hungarian armistice talks.[224]

Shortly after the fall of Kolozsvár on October 11, 1944 and its occupation by Soviet-Romanian forces, the NAHW held a session in the city. A resolutions was born that as long as the war continued and relations between the two countries and the status of Northern Transylvania was not settled, the NAHW should not join either the Southern Transylvanian HPAR or the NDF. It was also remarked that the Bucharest government's attitude towards Hungarians in Southern Transylvania was anything but friendly. What the majority of the participants did agree on was that every Hungarian movement must, in some way, represent the national interests of the Hungarians, that under no circumstances should the search for a peaceful solution be abandoned, and that no hostile intentions must be exhibited towards the Soviet forces.

1945-46 and the first quarter of 1947 was a period of organization and construction for the HPAR. It was able to carry out its nation preserving and saving activities quite undisturbed. Here also, as in the Romanian Communist Party, the leftist and sectarian elements, which were already thinking in terms of socialist revolution, class warfare, unification of nation and society and

---

[222] Pomogáts Béla talks with Vita Sándor. " The anti-war movement against the fall campaign of 1994 in Transylvania" (Az 1944. oszi erdélyi háború ellenes mozgalomról). Tisza Region (Tiszatáj), 1981, issue 10. pp. 53-56.

[223] Demeter, János: In the Current of our Century (Századunk sodrában). Bucharest, Kriterion Publishing, 1975. pp. 321-323.

[224] Bokor, Péter: Endgame over the Danube. Interview for a movie series (Végjáték a Duna felett. Interjú egy filmsorozathoz). Bp., MTV-Minerva-Kossuth Publishing, 1982. pp. 220-225.

homogenization, were relegated to the background. They observed and directed from behind the scenes. Above all, the philosophy of Gyárfás Kurkó - the purest personality of the Hungarian Left - was able to assert itself, namely that "we have only as many rights as we fight for", equality is a battle. He did not accept that democracy comes first, which automatically brings national equality.

It is regrettable that he trusted in Romanian promises, regrettable that he believed that the HPAR was supreme – they all believed it. HPAR maintained day-by-day relations with the government, the RCP and Romanian authorities. While fully supporting the government, HPAR asked for immediate remedy of the following issues: 1) new minority law; 2) the settlement of the citizenship status of Northern Transylvanians; 3) re-employment of those persons who were dismissed from their jobs under the pretext of failing the language exams or other discriminative measures; 4) the settlement of the pensions of Hungarians; 5) release of political prisoners.

HPAR officials felt that the following guarantees were required to meet the requirement of equal rights of nationalities: 1) the appointment of Hungarian experts and officials in the ministries; 2) the proportionate participation of Hungarians in local organizations and institutions in regions populated by Hungarians; 3) the review of the status of Hungarian public servants in Northern Transylvania; 4) the removal of anti-Hungarian elements; 5) the respect of Hungarian language in offices; 6) the improvement of the Ministry of National Minorities; 7) the extension of the scope of action of the Hungarian People's Alliance in issues concerning minorities.

At the First HPAR Congress, held in May 1945, the following plans were drafted: the establishment of a national independent economic center; the development of production, trade and consumer cooperatives in Hungarian populated regions; the improvement of craftsmen's working conditions and the elimination of injustices in land distribution. As for education, the HPAR asked for extending its authority to make decisions on the number and location of state and church schools; the establishment of four independent Hungarian school boards; the establishment of Hungarian sections in state schools where 20 or more Hungarian students were enrolled; the extension of vocational training (industrial, agricultural, trade, cooperative and apprentice schools) system; the equitable distribution of school buildings; the abolition of teachers' qualification exams (made compulsory for minority teachers by the Liberal-government between the two World Wars) and treating Hungarian teaching staff equally with the Romanian ones. The HPAR's further demands included an independent Hungarian university and a college of drama and music in Cluj Napoca, a technical university in Szeklerland, the maintenance of the Transylvanian Museum Association (Erdélyi Múzeum Egyesület – hereafter TMA), Hungarian medical services in Hungarian inhabited regions and the freedom of worship.[225]

The Romanian left was quite content to allow the HPAR to be the repository of nation saving activities. On the other hand, HPAR manipulated public opinion

---

[225] The Hungarian Peoples Alliance of Romania's (RMNSZ) resolutions. Cluj Napoca, Central Executive Committee, 1945.

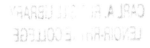

to claim that Hungarian institutions in Romania were established by it. The fact was that a string of institutions (schools, higher educational units, theater and art groups, museums cooperatives, loan-offices, banks and publishers) had a long history, some a century or two.

Due to the circumstances, HPAR was forced to pursue - as the National Hungarian Party did between the two wars - a 'policy of grievances', the daily airing of grievances. The first list of grievances was submitted to the government as early as its First Congress in 1945, and several others on following congresses. The recurring points were the unfairness of land reform, the 50 confiscated buildings of the Kolozsvár University, the complaints of people deprived of their citizenship, the evicted Hungarian schools, the lack of state loans and supply of goods – the 1,200 Hungarian cooperatives were excluded from tax exemption as early as 1945 – failure to observe nationality ratios, that is, the *Romanization* of official and public life (only 2 out of 11 county High Sheriffs in Transylvania were Hungarians, and none of the judges in Kolozsvár).

The end of 1945 also brought the first show trial. Author György Bözödi was arrested on false charges and poet Jeno Kiss for his satirical verses. A military court sentenced László Domokos because he protested the closing of Hungarian schools.[226]

At the peace talks, Romania desperately needed to be able to claim an agreement to the effect that the Hungarians in Romania had accepted the old/new situation. To achieve this, they were ready to make any promise: more universities, independent societal, economic, cultural or academic institutions. Their own armed forces, the use of national symbols – were promises bandied about during 1945.[227] In the first half of 1946, Romanian Hungarians could bask in the glow of several achievements in these areas.[228] At the same time, it suffered several affronts: school closings, exclusion from land redistribution, high taxes, sidelining of Hungarian civil servants and arrests.[229]

HPAR was willing to do them this 'little favor' at the session of the 100-strong Executive Committee held in Tirgu Mures (Marosvásárhely) in November of 1945. The decision made stated that the Transylvanian Hungarians would not contest the decisions of the peace talks.[230] "The Transylvanian question is not a question of borders ... in the future, meaning a Danubian confederation, all borders will cease to exist", they repeated Groza's line. It is for this act that HPAR has been charged - deservedly - with having sold out Transylvania. The memorandum drafted by the senior officials of Hungarian institutions and churches, addressed to the Paris peace conference, more closely expressed the interests and wishes of Hungarians than HPAR. In it, Bishop Áron Márton, along

---

[226] Official Gazette (Hivatalos Közlöny). Bucharest. 1945, May 29, 1.119 edict.

[227] New Hungarian Central Archives n./1964. The situation of the Hungarian minority in Romania.

[228] Ibid; Kelemen, Sándor: The Transylvanian situation (Az erdélyi helyzet). Bp., Hungarian Agrarian Union's publication, 1946. p. 27.

[229] Ibid; Illumination (Világosság). 1946, July 11.

[230] Katona, Szabó István: The Age of Great Hopes (A nagy reménységek kora). Bp., Magveto Publisher, 1990.

with the leaders of the Hungarian denominations and institutions asked the delegates to to listen to their pleas because they do not wish to live under Romanian rule any longer. In deciding the status of Transylvania, their wishes should be consulted.[231]

Following the publication of the Tirgu Mures resolution, the Hungarian opposition also swung into action. Only the National Hungarian Commission of Social Democrats was in the position to voice its opinion - it had its own press – that HPAR was not authorized to speak on behalf of 2 million Hungarians in Romania. It could not voluntarily renounce the right to mark the two countries' boundary in accordance with ethnic principles.

The year of the Romanian elections: 1946

In this period – in 1946, the time of the peace talks and elections – the RCP left no stone unturned to disarm the Hungarians. The Hungarian press was full of Groza's Customs Union, his Central European confederation, nationality politics and the extravagant popularization of his achievements.[232] To forestall placing minority policy under international control and to include various guarantees in the peace treaty, HPAR was commissioned – again as window dressing to the outside, as with the 1938 and 1945 minority statutes - to draft a minority bill, which envisaged establishment of independent national regions at 15% minority presence. László Bányai and László Luka dropped hints that the Szeklerland will be assured of autonomy with Hungarian as the official language, its own gendarmerie and free use of the Hungarian flag and national anthem. All these were meant to show the peace talk delegates that Romania was taking concrete steps to ensure the civil equality of the nationalities. Thus, making unnecessary any action similar to the 1919 agreement which effectively removed the minority question from the country's sphere of influence, i.e., putting it under international supervision.

Naturally, the minority bill was never incorporated into the constitution and never came into force because the communists – with HPAR support – won the elections.[233] As an aside, in September of 1946, Austria was guaranteed protective power status over the 200,000 Austrian living in South Tyrol, now part of Italy.

The reservations of the traditional Romanian parties against Groza proved to be groundless. As Maniu, Tatarescu, the Bratianus, King Mihai, Groza and Patrascanu all shared the same point of view: not an inch of territory to be given up to Hungary as part of frontier readjustment. Groza told the officials of the Hungarian Foreign Ministry that they should stop harping on border readjustment because even a 20-meter change would mean the victory of Hungarian chauvinism, followed by a burst of Romanian chauvinism. Instead, they should

---

[231] Szalay, Jeromos: Martyr bishop's martyred people. Márton Áron (Vértanú püspök vértanú népe. Márton Áron). Detroit, 1958.

[232] What did Groza Péter, Luka László and Kurkó Gyárfás say at the first congress of the RMNSZ. Cluj Napoca, Executive Committee, 1945.

[233] Joó Rudolf talks with Demeter János. Bp., Kossuth Publishing, 1983.

think of the happy, shared future. Before the November elections, Luka skillfully manipulated the Hungarians. If Maniu's group wins, the Hungarians will be expelled. (See the actions of the Maniu Guard from the fall of 1944.) Therefore, the only possible solution for them to remain in their homeland is if they support the Communists, i.e., the Block of Democratic Parties (Demokratikus Pártok Blokkja).

The Block won 347, the traditional parties 36, out of the total 414 seats. Some 9.84% voted for the HPAR, rallying half a million members, and the Alliance secured 29 seats in the Parliament. However, a few remarks need to be made here, indicating just how incomplete the research is on the activity of the HPAR and the era. According to Lajos Takács, one of the leaders of the HPAR, some citizens voted two, three, even 11 times – for the leftists. King Mihai was of the opinion that the election numbers – 347 mandates for the Left and 36 for the Right – were simply inverted by the Communists, therefore the election was invalid and a new one should be held. It is another matter that, on the basis of votes garnered, HPAR was entitled to at least 40 seats.[234]

HPAR did not waste its time during the interval: it established the Petofi Fund, to support and operate schools, cultural institutes and to cover the salaries of teachers – state salaries to teachers was always late – the Hungarian Aid Committee in Romania (Romániai Magyar Segélyezo Bizottság) and became the patron of HEST, EMKE, etc. It organized the review of Hungarian publishers for its congress held in Odorheiu Secuiesc (Székelyudvarhely) in June 1946. It established schools for the Csángós (ed: a Hungarian minority and dialect) of Moldova, secured state subsidies for six Hungarian theaters, and attempted to clarify the status of seven Hungarian higher educational institutes.

1946 marked the summit of national minority policy, and at the same time, the beginning of the decline. After the year's Romanian successes – acceptance of the Romanian arguments at the Peace talks and the election victory of the Communists - HPAR became nonessential. In time, and due to changes in the international situation – the Cold War, one-party system, falling out in the People's Democratic camp, common front against Yugoslavia and acceptance of increased class struggle by the RCP – all contributed to HPAR becoming superfluous.

1946 Paris Peace Talks: The Romanian-Hungarian border question

Hungarian Foreign Minister János Gyöngyösi asked the Great Powers, in a memorandum on January 25, 1946 to hear the Hungarian position on ethnic frontiers. Molotov twice warned Hungarian diplomat Kristóffy in Moscow, in 1940 and 1941, that Hungary could only count on the good will of the Soviet

---

[234] Strategii si politici electorale in alegerile parlamentare din 19 noiembrie 1946. Selectia documentelor, sturdiu introductiv, argument si note de Virgiliu Tarau, Ioan Marius Bucur. Cluj-Napoca, Centrul de Studii Transilvane . Fundatia Culturala Romana, 1998.

Union if it did not enter into war against it.[235] In that case, the Soviet Union would acknowledge the Second Vienna Resolution, i.e., the annexation of Northern Transylvania by Hungary. Moreover, the Soviet Union would support a third resolution, regarding Southern Transylvania, because before October 15, 1944 it was hoped that Hungary would turn against Nazi Germany, thereby significantly shortening the war, reducing casualties and damages. Hungary's declaration of war against the Soviet Union changed this political stance. Molotov no longer sided with the permanent annexation of Northern Transylvania by Hungary.[236]

After the aborted Hungarian breakaway attempt, Hungary's chances diminished. During the Hungarian delegation's visit to Moscow in April 1946, it became clear that Molotov interpreted point # 19 of the Armistice Agreement that Transylvania was promised to Romania. (The Moscow group of the RKP - including Ana Pauker, who, as a close associate within Molotov's circle during the peace talks - played a significant role in transmitting the latest turns of Soviet politics.) The USA also took the position that the 1938 border should be used between the two countries, but left the possibility open of a later adjustment.[237] This, however, was left up to the Soviet Union which, for tactical reasons - the Hungarian Communist party was in favor of border modification, attempting to curry favor with the population - proposed that the two countries settle the issue through negotiations.

Predictably, Romania refused to negotiate. The paramount question for Romania was the Great Powers' reaction to Romania's claim of all Transylvania. The RKP interpreted the resolution of the Council of Foreign Ministers, passed on May 7, 1946, as Groza' success and which proved that his government's minority policy based on the equality of rights was the most crucial issue for his government. Groza took advantage of the fact that the Soviet Union handed Transylvania back to him. In his attempt to strengthen his power, especially against the National Peasant Party, he stressed that only a Leftist majority government could retain Transylvania.

None of the delegates to the meeting of the Council of Foreign Ministers, held between October 11 and November 2, 1945, supported the Hungarians' territorial claim of a maximum of 22,000 km^2 but at the very minimum 5,000 km^2. This in spite of the fact that the US made attempts to renegotiate the terms of the armistice agreement and British Foreign Minister Bevin insisted on a just and equitable border settlement.[238] The majority of Hungarian leading politicians did not believe in the finality of the issue. One after another, the members of Ferenc Nagy's government visited the Western countries and the Soviet Union. They reasoned that the new Hungarian democracy could not assume the responsibility for the crimes of the previous regime. Politicians and writers by the score could be

---

[235] Balogh, Sándor: Foreign policy of the People's Democracy of Hungary, 1945-1947.
From cease-fire to peace treaty (A népi demokratikus Magyarország külpolitikája.
1945-1947. A fegyverszünettol a békeszerzodésig). Bp., Kossuth Publishing, 1982.
[236] Fülöp, Mihály - Sipos, Péter: Hungary's foreign policy in the 20th century
(Magyarország külpolitikája a XX. Században). Bp., Aula Publisher, 1998. p. 306.
[237] Ibid, p. 307.
[238] Ibid, p. 309.

quoted here, all of whom could not imagine the unimaginable - a repetition of the Trianon Treaty.[239]

At the Paris Peace talks, Gyöngyösi submitted, on August 14, a demand for only 5,000 km^2 of Transylvania. As none of the 13 members of the Territorial and Political Committee supported the Hungarian claim, the issue was referred to the representatives of the Hungarian and Romanian governments. On August 31, Pál Auer asked the Romanian party to assent to the annexation of 4,000 km^2 to Hungary, where some 500,000 Hungarians lived, making up 67 % of the population. For the remaining 1,200,00 Hungarians who remained in Romania, it was requested that their right to self-rule be guaranteed.[240] Tatarescu, head of the Romanian delegation, rejected the claim. One of his main reasons was the HPAR's Tirgu Mures resolution of November 19, 1945. He also refused to grant self-government to the Szeklerland. The proposal of the Australian delegate – namely, to provide guarantees against the violation and limitation of minority rights and freedoms in Romania - was also refused. It was not only the middle-class Romanian politicians who rejected the proposals of the Hungarian government - the re-establishment of the borders to their pre-Second Vienna Resolution state was the only issue that united both the Left and the historical parties.[241]

Groza on federation and customs union

A Committee of Peace Pacts and Post-war Arrangements was constituted in 1942 by Soviet People's Commissar Litvinov. Regarding Transylvania, Ernö Neulander, Walter Roman as he was known in the movement, drew up a document in which the possibility of an independent Transylvania was an option – under Soviet supervision and control.[242] In British and American post-war peace plans during the war, Transylvanian autonomy was also a possibility – within the framework of an integrated Central Europe.[243] To further study and explore this idea, institutes were established.[244]

After WW II ended, numerous signs pointed to an intention of reconciliation in Central and Eastern Europe. Without quoting a complete list of names and reasons, leading politicians - Dimitrov, Groza, Károlyi, Kurkó and Tito - all worked, between 1944 and 1948, for a permanent and conclusive compromise, of a federation and customs union. These years can be characterized by: 1945, was

---

[239] Gyarmati, György: To cooperate peacefully for the benefit of the entire Danubian valley. Federal plans post-1945 (Békében együttmuködni az egész Duna-völgye javára. Föderációs tervek 1945 után). Plains (Alföld), 1985, issue 4. pp. 60-61.

[240] Fülöp-Sipos: Hungary's foreign ... op.cit. p. 313.

[241] Lipcsey: The Hungarian People's ... op.cit.

[242] Tofik: Russian foreign policy ... op.cit. pp. 42-48.

[243] Bán, D. András (ed.): Pax Britannica. British Foreign Ministry files regarding post-Second World War East-Central Europe, 1942-42. Bp., 1996.

[244] Romsics, Ignác (ed.): American peace plans for post-war Hungary. Secret documents of the U.S. Secretary of State (Amerikai béketervek a háború utáni Magyarországról. Az Egyesült Államok Külügymisztériumának titkos iratai, 1942-44). Gödöllo Publishing, 1992.

the year of cautious inquiries; 1946, waiting with great hopes; 1947, to September, the sudden stalemate and afterwards, the time of indifference. After the break-up of the international anti-Fascist coalition, the days of the idea of a Hungarian-Romanian - or any other - customs unions were numbered. Independent policy could not be pursued in the buffer zone of colliding international interests and sphere of influence - whether called Central or Eastern Europe. In addition, nationalism again became official state policy in Romania.[245]

Petru Groza was educated in the Calvinist College of Orastie (Szászváros) and the University of Budapest. He highly appreciated Hungarian literature. He voted for the union of Romania and Transylvania at the 1918 session of the Grand National Assembly in Alba Julia (Gyulafehérvár). As a minister in charge of minorities, in 1920 and 1926, Groza incorporated in his program the equality of languages at all school levels. In 1935, the alliance of his party, the Plow Front and the National Alliance of Hungarian Workers (NAHW) gave birth to the People's Front in Romania. During the legionnaires' riot one of his former classmates helped Groza to escape to Hungary. In his talks Bajcsy-Zsilinszky and other Hungarian politicians, the ways and means of the two nations' common future in Northern Transylvania were also discussed. He stated at the founding meeting of the Hungarian People's Alliance in Deva (Déva) in November 1944, that Romania, the motherland of Romanians and Hungarians, would be democratic and free for both nations. (He had good reasons for his cautious wording because the two countries were opposing combatants in war and the idea of Romanian-Hungarian alliance was not quite popular in Romania, at that time.) Groza's pro-Hungarian sympathies qualified him for playing his part: to win over and disarm the Hungarians. Petru Groza's idea was that a customs union would be the culmination of Romanian-Hungarian relations, which would, in turn, result in the creation of other customs unions, culminating in the Central-European Federation.

Groza officially raised this issue for the first time at the HPAR congress in Cluj Napoca and at the meeting of the Transylvanian Museum Association (TMA) in May 1945. His oft-quoted words were: "I have come to solemnly unfold the Transylvanian flag of Romanian-Hungarian co-existence ... We, here in Transylvania, in Cluj Napoca, are making an great experiment. If we can successfully eradicate Fascist hatred among both Romanians and Hungarians, this success will radiate all the way to the Black Sea, to the entire Hungarian nation to the river Lajta. (ed: border river between Austria and Hungary) We know, and we feel, that the closer the two countries come together, the greater the brotherhood of nations living here will be guaranteed".[246]

While there are no Romanian statistics at hand, such as those in Hungary – where, in May 1946, 84% of the interviewees approved of a Hungarian-Romanian customs union[247] - there is no question that, with the exception of a few Romanian senior civil servants, only the leadership of HPAR was in favor of the notion. To

---

[245] Lipcsey: The Hungarian People's ... op.cit.
[246] What did Groza Péter, Luka ..... op.cit.
[247] Gyarmati: To cooperate peacefully ... op.cit.

show the extent to which good intention and tactics were step-brothers in the minds of Romanian politicians, we can quote a remark by Swiss educated Vladescu-Racoasa, who reassured King Mihai when he reluctantly signed another minority demand: "You don't need to worry, Your Majesty, just sign it. Then, we shall see what happens after the peace talks".

The exchange of open letters between Groza and Hungarian author Lajos Zilahy created a sensation in September. It encouraged the supporters of reconciliation and angered the historical parties. "We are grateful to the Hungarian writers and the representatives of Hungary's intellectuals", wrote Groza, "because they believe in our efforts. On the Romanian side, we also believe that we will live to see the day of complete agreement, which will be an example for the other nations of the Danube Basin, creating thereby the family of small nations working together and exchanging their material and intellectual values freely among each others and at the same time building a stronghold of peace and progress in this corner of our continent".[248]

These statements, by and large, contain few facts and mainly serve as proof of Groza's oratorical skill. A similar interview in January 1946, especially its last passage where: "The idea of a customs union has to become part of general awareness on both sides, public opinion has to deal with and ponder on it ... both the Hungarian and the Romanian people have to understand that we are can only progress together, in close economic cooperation. We can not be naive enough to think that we can become hermits behind our borders. Romania expects to meet its industrial demands from Hungary".[249] This quotation may also prove that the Groza government received good press in Hungary. It was at the same time that the Slovak Settlement Office announced that denationalization would affect 580,000 Hungarians (the Hungarian-Czechoslovak treaty on the exchange of population was signed at the end of February); the confiscation of Hungarian properties was announced in May; the Czechoslovak Communist Party (CzCP) criticized the Hungarian Communist Party (HCP); and Benes openly declared that they did not want to see any national minorities [in Czechoslovakia]. The Hungarians, like the Jews, wrote Iván Boldizsár, were outlawed in Czechoslovakia.[250] Hungarian politicians both in Hungary and Romania set Tito's Yugoslavia and Groza' Romania as examples. In contrast to Czechoslovakia where the Benes Decrees placed Hungarians outside the laws, a state of affairs still making itself felt in 2003.

Groza, thus, spoke frequently – both publicly and privately - about reconciliation, compromise and customs unions. However, few people were privileged to hear him speak frankly. Among those were the committee members of the Hungarian Foreign Ministry who visited the Romanian Prime Minister on November 1, 1945 to discuss refugee issues. "Good Hungarian-Romanian relations are of prime importance, but it is not a border issue," stated Groza. "A

---

[248] Freedom (Szabadság). Bp., 1945, Szeptember 4.

[249] Ibid, 1946, January 20.

[250] Boldizsár, Iván: These people have already atoned (Megbunhödte már e nép). Bp., New Hungary (Új Magyarország) Publisher, 1946.

meter or two readjustment of the border is insignificant but a 20-meter rectification means the victory of Hungarian chauvinism," stated Groza in front of the Hungarian ministry officials. He also warned them not to harp on this minor issue, instead they should think of the happy common future. "There is no need for Great Powers' mediation in drawing the Hungarian-Romanian border," he added, "the two nations will decide." (The result of similar bilateral Austrian-Italian talks granted Austria a 'protective' status over the 200,000 Austrians living in South-Tyrol, Italy, on September 5, 1946.)

In contrast, during the months preceding the peace talks, it became clear that Groza was unwilling to enter into talks, which would touch on border readjustments based on ethnic relationships. He also refused bilateral government level talks both on the rectification of frontiers and population exchange. He also rejected the principle of balance, i.e., the same number of Hungarians would remain in Romania as Romanians in Hungary, and also considered it unnecessary that the protection of minority rights were to be internationally guaranteed, as in the minority agreement of 1919. Petru Groza was unwilling to give up any part, or the whole, of Transylvania. There was total agreement on this between him and his political opposition in Romania.

"The conclusion of the Peace Talks in Paris make the customs union timely," stated Groza in an interview given to the periodical *Republic* (Köztársaság) in the summer of 1946. "I have worked out the applicable plans," he added. He envisaged the process as follows:

a) Establish economic and cultural cooperation,
b) Sign agreements of cooperation, and
c) Establish a Customs Union.[251]

The last act of Groza's Customs Union campaign coincided with the Romanian delegation's visit to Budapest in May 1947. After this, or more precisely after Vasile Luca's article on May 22, the word was dropped from the vocabulary of politicians.

The year of change: 1947

In short, the showdown between the RCP and its former coalition partners came to pass – first by depriving them of their economic foundations, then driving them out of political life, followed by the purging of the ranks of its fellow travelers: the HPAR, the Plough Front, and finally, the preparations for establishing a one-party system. The signing of the peace treaty on February 10 also gave impetus to the process of completing the so-called people's democratic revolution. Ten days later, a draft resolution of the RCP congress stated that Romania stood on the threshold of a socialist revolution. It meant the acceleration of nationalization and the unification of the two workers' parties. The resolution also declared that the influence of the Communist Party must be increased in all facets of life, from the agrarian realm to the writers' association to minority organizations.

---

[251] The announcement of the tariff union was blocked by Moscow's objections.

The accord between Tatarescu's Liberals and the RCP – under which the latter permitted a limited private sector while the former did not protest against the state's increasing intrusion into economic life – broke up. Financial reform hit not only the wealthy – 1 new Lei was valued at 20,000 old ones – but the planned economy placed the emphasis on the development of heavy industry.

Tatarescu, who rejected both the financial and industrial reforms, was expelled from the Parliament. His party's 4 Ministers and 2 State Secretaries met the same fate in November; King Mihai was forced to resign on December 30. Even more spectacular was the reckoning with Maniu's National Peasant Party. The senior members of the party, who were about to leave the country, were arrested on June 14; all the MPs were barred from Parliament on July 18. The monster Maniu-trial started at the end of October, ending with severe sentences.[252] Some 20% of NPP members were imprisoned, which translated to about 200,000 people. Thus ended Romania's transitional period.[253]

When HPAR-leader Kurkó worked out the Alliance's economic policy in 1947, he envisaged an economically strong and independent, heterogeneous society. In the interest of industrialization of the Szeklerland, the Alliance supported the Mining Institute of the Szeklerland (Székelyföldi Bányászati Intézet), improvement to handicrafts and lumbering, as well as vocational training, including the establishment of a College in Szeklerland. These issues were regular topics at the sessions of the HPAR economic sections and the Congresses of Cooperatives.[254] The Alliance supported the work of the Kaláka (ed: originally the word meant that family members and friends work together, e.g.- building or harvesting bee), Ant (Hangya) and Alliance (Szövetség) cooperative centers. This was quite necessary precisely because, from the summer of 1946 onward, Romanian cooperatives made every effort to obtain the assets of Hungarian cooperatives. Their political concept was that economic institutions should be *unified*, i.e., the existence of Hungarian institutions should be abolished. A joint stock company, named Horizon (Horizont), was established to actively promote the circulation of capital, the exploration of the natural resources of Szeklerland, as well as industrial and agricultural production and marketing. The Hungarian Economic Council in Romania (Romániai Magyar Gazdasági Tanács) did the same on a theoretical level, i.e., its aim was to direct economic life.[255]

Therefore, following the numerous political failures of the previous year, when in 1947 Kurkó was working out a program for the HPAR, he placed emphasis on economic goals. He argued the importance of the issue by saying, "Our work is a pipedream without an economic basis; any attack against our livelihood is equivalent to an attack against our nation. Neither national equality nor national freedom can exist without economic equality and economic

---

[252] New Life (Új Élet). Nagyvárad, 1947, November 7.
[253] Anelli Ute Gabanyi: Partei und Literatur in Rumaniei seit 1945. München, R. Oldenbourg Verlag, 1975. p. 18.
[254] Illumination (Világosság). 1946, May 6.
[255] National Unity (Népi Egység). 1946, May 11.

freedom."[256] His adherence to the independence of economic units, cooperatives, etc., led to Kurkó's dismissal at the third HPAR Congress, held in Timisoara (Temesvár) in November 1947.

The RCP's resolution, published on July 1, 1947, stated that "any political, cultural or economic rejection, any attempts of separatism against the progressive democracy in Romania would lead to the sapping of our people's strength" was preceded by László Luka's stunning article in *Truth* (Igazság) on 22 May, 1947, which may be considered as the first serious attack against the so-called people's front policy – i.e., uniting the Hungarian intelligentsia, bourgeoisie, wealthy peasantry irrespective of party (ideological) affiliation and non-party (independent) individuals – of the HPAR.

On May 22, 1947, Luka, two weeks after Groza's visit to Budapest – where the customs union was not announced because of Moscow's veto – called the intention of nations in the Danube Basin to unify as dangerous and hostile, seeing in it the revival of King St. Stephen's (ed: the founder of the Hungarian state) concept and anti-Soviet policy. (The same statement will be made later when the Rajk trial is announced in Romania, i.e., Rajk, a leader of the Hungarian Communist Party, in opposition with the four leaders returned from Moscow (Mátyás Rákosi, József Révai, Erno Gero and Zoltán Vas), under the influence of Tito wanted to join the people's democracies in a 'confederation' with the block of Western imperialist countries.)[257] The leaders of the Hungarians in Romania had to pretend to believe in the exaggerated dangers of Hungarian reactionaries. Some of them did so out of conviction, others fearing the loss of power, or hoping that by sacrificing some of their colleagues they could save what was still salvageable.

Attacks by the self-styled democrats against reactionaries, that is the parties representing civil traditions and values, became commonplace. They were followed, for now, by dismissals from the leading posts of Hungarian institutions. Some HPAR officials made statements to the effect that the stress put on *the minority's equality before the law* was due to the machinations of the reactionaries, meant to divert attention from a more important issue: the class struggle. As was made clear by the speech of Alexander Kacsó - who agreed to take over from the dismissed Kurkó - to the HPAR meeting, held on November 10, 1947, that it was the opinion of several members, that in Romania, where the minority issue had already been settled, the HPAR should be disbanded. Kacsó gave as his reason that he would rather accept the - by that time not very prestigious - office of the HPAR presidency rather than have it filled by a person indifferent or hostile to the national interests of the Hungarians.

---

[256] Ibid, 1947, January 10.
[257] Truth (Igazság). 1947, May 22.

The nationalization of Hungarian assets in Romania from 1945[258]

Several points of the Soviet-Romanian armistice agreement, signed in Moscow on September 12, 1944, referred to Transylvania. Paragraph 19 is the best known, stating that "Transylvania, or the major portion of it, will return to Romania". Paragraph 2 prescribed that "the Romanian government and military authorities undertake to disarm and intern German and Hungarian military forces on the territory of Romania, as well as to intern the citizens of said countries having residency permits". In accordance with paragraph 4, "the Romanian government and military authorities commit themselves to cooperate with Soviet G.H.Q. in arresting and bringing war criminals to justice".[259]

Paragraph 8 of the armistice agreement created CASBI. Under the terms of paragraph 8, "the Romanian government undertakes to block the transportation and disposition of any kind of property (including valuables and cash) of Germany or Hungary, or of their citizens, or people that lived on their territories or occupied territories, without the permission of the Allied (Soviet) G.H.Q. The Romanian government and Army G.H.Q. will safeguard these properties in accordance with conditions determined by the Allied (Soviet) G.H.Q."[260]

The February 10, 1945 issue of the Romanian Official Gazette published King Mihai's executive decree No. 91 on the establishment of CASBI, referring to paragraph 8 of the armistice agreement. On its basis, it was decreed the forfeiture of the properties of Hungarian citizens (natural persons) inhabitant in Romania, Hungarian citizens or concerns (legal entities) and the so-called 'presumptive enemies'. In other words, it seemed to refer to the following: 1) Germany, 2) Hungary, 3) German citizens, 4) Hungarian citizens, 5) residents of territories occupied by German forces, and 6) residents of territories occupied by Hungarian forces. According to the royal decree, CASBI was to seize German and Hungarian state properties, as well as the properties of German and Hungarian natural and corporate entities, who were residents in Germany or Hungary and, irrespective of their nationality, the properties of those who departed before or with the retreating enemy. CASBI was to control and supervise the industrial and trade entities in which persons of the above nationalities held 20% ownership.

Presumptive Enemy[261]

In reality, the April 2, 1945 enacting clause No. 3822/45 of the CASBI decree defined the above concept. 'Presumptive enemy' was every person,

---

[258] Lipcsey, Ildikó: CASBI. The nationalization of Hungarian propreties in Romania after 1945 (A CASBI. A magyar vagyonok államosítása Romániában 1945 után). Bp., Possum Publisher, 2001. (CASBI: Rom.: Casa pentru Administrarea i Supraveghere a Bunurilor Inamice; Eng.: Treasury for the Control and Supervision of Enemy Assets; Magy.: Ellenséges Javakat Kezelő és Felügyelő Pénztár).

[259] Ibid, p. 2.

[260] Ibid, p. 3.

[261] Political History Institute archives. /162/pol. 1947. 1. Can be found in the ambassador's report of August 27, 1947.

irrespective of citizenship, living on German or Hungarian territories, or on territories occupied by them, or those Romanian citizens who escaped to Germany or Hungary, or to territories occupied by them before and after September 12, 1944. The concept of 'presumptive enemy' was comprised of two groups:

1. Persons who stayed temporarily for a few days, or were registered residents, in territories occupied by the enemy.

2. Persons fleeing to enemy-occupied territories were those who a) moved to Northern Transylvania after the Second Vienna Decision and were Romanian citizens prior to it; b) those Hungarians who, through mutual exchange of residence, moved to Northern Transylvania after the Second Vienna Decision; c) were under medical treatment or hospitalized in this territory; d) fled to Hungary and latter returned to Northern Transylvania; e) were displaced by German forces; and f) left obeying the evacuation order.

The Romanian side needed the concept of 'presumptive enemy' because the Soviet-Hungarian armistice agreement, signed on January 22, 1945, obligated Hungary to declare war against Germany and to pay compensation to the Soviet Union. With the armistice agreement, Hungary ceased to be an enemy country, and thereby paragraph 8 of the Soviet-Romanian armistice agreement ceased to have effect, although it was explicitly stated by a separate act. It is not unknown in legal practice, especially under circumstances of war. However, lawyers also brought forward another argument. At the time of the signing of the Soviet-Romanian armistice agreement, on September 12, 1944, Northern Transylvania did not belong to Romania, therefore paragraph 8 could not be applied there. Despite it all, the Romanian government continued to treat Hungary as an enemy. The final result was that Hungary paid compensation twice. Firstly, because the process was illegal, and secondly, because – as it was also stated in the HPAR memorandum of May 30, 1945 – the concept of 'presumptive enemy' was unrecognized in international law.[262]

Under the pretext of being a 'presumptive enemy', the houses (and contents), gardens, lands and factories of some 30,000 Hungarians, who fled from the front or were in Hungary on September 12, 1944, were seized in Romania. In addition, the premises and buildings of Hungarian institutions, as well as factories, banks and plants owned by the Hungarian state were also seized. (The same happened in 1919-20 to the buildings of the Hungarian University of Kolozsvár, as well as the collections the Transylvanian Museum Association (Erdélyi Múzeum Egyesület) and the Transylvanian Hungarian Museum (Erdélyi Magyar Múzeum), which were confiscated without compensation by the Romanian state.)

HPAR seemingly bombarded the government and the Romanian Liaison Committee of the Allied Control Commission (SZEB) with its memorandums at the end of 1945. At the end of the year, the Allied Control Commission assented that those Hungarians, who wished to repatriate and obtained the written permit from the Romanian government, could take their movable goods with them. It is no exaggeration to state that the authority of CASBI exerted its control over the

---

[262] Lipcsey: CASBI ... op.cit. p. 10.

properties of average citizens and it was one of the most severe grievances of the Hungarians living in Romania.

Uncertain situation: 1946-47

The apex of seemingly positive Romanian minority policy crested between the 1946 peace talks and the November elections, which were decisive in the political-power struggle. This was the period when HPAR worked out the minority act, which was to acknowledge the Romanian Hungarians as an independent political unit, to assure collective rights and which implicitly included the autonomy of Transylvania. Certain advances were achieved with regard to the activity of CASBI, as a result of the memorandum of HPAR sent to the Romanian government and the Romanian Liaison Committee of the ACC in January, as well as the Hungarian government's letters to the Soviet ambassador in Budapest on May 29, and to the Chairman of the Paris peace talks on September 25.[263] It was reported in early October that the ACC-president in Romania, Colonel-General Susaykov, took steps with the Romanian government in the interest of restitution of Hungarian properties. It is a fact that, in the period of preparation for the peace talks, some CASBI inventoried and seized properties were returned to their owners and some Transylvanians who did not return from Hungary were allowed to reclaim their movable goods. However, the concept of 'presumptive enemy' remained.

The new CASBI regulations, issued in 1947, still contained only partial exemptions. Therefore, on January 7, 1947, the Hungarian government asked for new talks on the subject through its mission in Bucharest. The discussions started in Bucharest on April 27, 1947. As a result, on May 16, 1947 – one week after Groza's 100-member delegation's visit to Budapest – the parties signed an agreement that would have satisfied Hungarian demands. It provided for the Hungarian state the possibility to invest itself with the rights of those who fled to the West; it rendered the sale of agricultural properties of Hungarian citizens easier; and it assured the cultivation of lands in the border zone.[264]

Disregarding all this, Petru Groza called the head of the Hungarian mission in Bucharest to his office on July 5, 1947, and informed him that his government would not ratify the Romanian-Hungarian agreement on the CASBI issue, agreed and signed by the two countries' government commissioners, but will relegate it to Parliament directly to decide. The draft bill, said Petru Groza, would include the following points:
1. It would not set a deadline for settling the enquiries for freeing properties;
2. The Hungarian mission in Bucharest can not present enquiries;
3. Citizens about to resettle to Hungary would be examined by the Romanian authorities and, if deemed to be Romanian citizens, their properties would be confiscated;
4. Properties falling under export prohibition can not be taken in cash;

---

[263] MOL, Presidential Department files. 23/b. 2830/pol/46 33 d.
[264] Lipcsey, Ildikó: CASBI ... op.cit. pp. 45-48.

5. Suspension of lease-contracts would come into effect three months after passage of the law. Compensation cases would be judged in accordance with the Romanian decision;
6. Public servants of Hungarian citizenship would also be obliged to present proof of citizenship;
7. Agricultural properties would have 6 years to be sold;
8. It would free Romanian from any responsibilities regarding restitution.[265]

A vast propaganda campaign preceded the signing of the Hungarian-Romanian Cultural Cooperation agreement at the end of 1947. The Hungarian side deemed that the occasion, prior to the Hungarian government delegation visit to Romania in November 1947, could also be used to clarify the CASBI issue, as well. An expert of the Hungarian Ministry of Justice proposed the following in order to settle the pending issues: it must be achieved everybody should be reinstated in their properties, with the exception of war criminals. The expert reminded of the international practice that foreign citizens' property could be confiscated only after compensation. Groza, however, stated well in advance that Romania could not accept the political or economic responsibility of compensation.[266]

The two countries' top politicians – Prime Minister Lajos Dinnyés, Secretary of State Erik Molnár of Hungary and Prime Minister Petru Groza, Secretary of State Anna Pauker of Romania – signed a protocol in Bucharest on November 5, 1947. It included the following terms: the parties would settle the issue of dual ownerships, the contentious issues between the two countries' national banks, Romania would guarantee the transportation of the movable goods of those who wanted to repatriate to Hungary, bilateral foreign trade debts would be settled, a new trade and postal agreement to be negotiated, and finally to settle the CASBI issue.[267]

Nationalization in Romania: 1948-49

During the nationalization in Hungary in 1948, the majority of Hungarian companies in Romania became Hungarian state property. It covered industrial plants, financial institutes, companies and institutions, as well. Disregarding this fact, in 1948 Romania continued to regard Hungarian state properties as capitalist properties and the laws of Romanian nationalization were extended over them. Hungary then, officially, asked Romania to pay compensation for them. A similar agreement was signed between Czechoslovakia and Bulgaria, under which the latter undertook to make payments over a ten-year period. (The terms of the installments for repayment were set at 10 years.) Romania immediately refused the proposal, stating that it did not intend to pay compensation to anybody. (After nationalization in 1948, 899 natural and legal entities made application for various

---

[265] Political History Institute archives. According to the MNK's Political Department, based on the report of the Bucharesti Mission. 354/pol/1946.
[266] New Hungarian Central Archives, 1737/47.
[267] Rom. Admin. 444415/47 36 d.

companies and shares. At the official 1943 exchange rate, they amounted to 330,268,256.26 Pengo.) The Romanians refused to pay compensation, although paragraph II/2 of the agreement signed by both parties on September 21, 1948, stated: "Romania withdraws any claim for the return of movable goods that have been transported to Hungary". Vasile Luca (László Luka) altered the text to read: "Romania will not withdraw…" Luca's reasoning was that: Hungarian assets in Romania were gained from the exploitation of the Romanian people; therefore, their ownership was the legal right of the Romanian proletariat.[268]

In July 1949, the CASBI county organizations were instructed to close issues of minor importance, if possible. Finance Minister Luca, however, refused to allow the sales of the properties, which was requested by the owners to cover transportation cost from a segregated account opened for this purpose. A Hungarian expert following the situation could only report, at the end of 1949, that the transportation of private movable goods was in progress.

CASBI continued to be a recurring subject of secret talks and exchanges of notes between the two countries. The Hungarian delegation raised the CASBI issue at almost every talk on the two countries' relations. Finally, in 1953, the two countries signed an agreement to terminate any financial claims against each other.[269] Nevertheless, despite it all, complaints kept arriving during the '50s – after 1956! – at the Hungarian Ministry of Foreign Affairs, the Ministry of Finance and the Hungarian embassy in Bucharest from average citizens asking for compensation, exemption or the releasing of the legal impediment on their properties, houses, lands and furniture, and permission to sell them and transferring the value to Hungary.[270]

Hungarian claims against Romania were greater by an order of magnitude than those of Romania against Hungary. The fact that the CASBI issue was raised at the end of the 1990's indicates the insoluble character of the problem. Romania asked to be reinstated in the so-called Gozsdu-estate (several properties) in Budapest for its own use. However, Romania signed away its right with the 1953 agreement. Hungary then stated that it would put the CASBI issue back on the agenda - again.

---

[268] Lipcsey: CASBI … op.cit. p. 74.
[269] Ibid, p. 84.
[270] Ibid, p. 85.

III. The Gheorghiu-Dej era

Effects of the power struggle within the RCP on Hungarians in Romania, 1948-1952.

Hungarians in Romania - having been the allies of left wing parties during the struggle against the historical parties - could not sidestep the fight for political power at the time of coalition any more than during the cleansing within the Communist party. Gheorghiu-Dej was called the Machiavelli of the Balkans. His rise in the RCP was accomplished in three phases. Before 1944, he was imprisoned several times for his leftist ideas and activities. While in prison, he cunningly kept events under control and made clever use of the rivalry of the various factions of the illegal Communist Party; the 'home group' vs. the 'Muscovites', i.e., those who returned from Moscow, having worked for the Comintern during the war. Moreover, both groups were opposed to the party's intellectual wing and its prominent representatives, first of all Stephen Fóris (who, on top of it, was Hungarian) and Lucretiu Patrascanu.[271]

Gheorghiu-Dej, being of a particularly suspicious nature, trusted only those with whom he spent some time in jail. The group of comrades, who later became members of his government and senior communist leaders of the country, was recruited almost entirely of those who served time in the prison of Caransebes (Karánsebes) with him. Among them were: Chivu Stoica, Miron Constantinescu (economic posts), Iosif Chisinevschi (ideology), Teohari Georgescu, Gheorghe Pintilie, Alexandru Draghici, László Ady, Piusz Kovács, Sergei Nicolau, Teodor Rudenko (internal affairs and secret service), Emil Bodnaras (armed forces, KGB), Athanasi Joja (Deputy Prime Minister and Minister of Culture), Alexandru Sencovici (Sándor Szenkovics, Minister of Industry), Mircea Grisan (Minister of Trade), Vasile Vaida (Minister of Agriculture) and Ion Vincze (János Vincze, Minister of Forestry).[272] Thanks to their support, he was able to win Stalin's trust and the leader of the Romanian Communist Party, after it became legal in 1945.

In 1944, he physically removed Stephen Fóris; in 1948-49, he ousted Lucretiu Patrascanu, one of the founders of the Party, the most talented, trained and popular figure of the movement and the Minister of Justice; finally, in 1952, he did away with the members of the 'Moscow wing': Ana Pauker, Vasile Luca and Teohari Georgescu. Patrascanu attended the ceremonial signing of the Romanian-Hungarian Friendship and Mutual Assistance Pact in January 1948, but was not present at the unification session of the SDP (Social Democratic Party) and the RCP and the founding of the Romanian Workers' Party (RWP) in February. In his political address to the unification session, Gheorghiu-Dej stated that the minority policy of the democratic system was built on the principle of complete equality - land distribution, the establishment of the school system, the free use of minority language in public administration and jurisdiction - and that

---

[271] Sfetcu, Paul: 13 ani in anticamera lui Gheorghiu-Dej. Bucuresti, Editura Fundatiei Culturale Romane, 2000. p. 17.

[272] Campeanu, Pavel: Ceausescu, anii numaratorii inverse. Bucuresti, Polirom, 2002. p. 44.

the new constitution should reflect that the democratic state was a state of the workers and intellectuals, of towns and villages.

The General Secretary of the Party warned that – having got rid of the Peasant Party, the Liberal Party and the Social Democrats[273] – a review of the party membership was to follow because former Iron Guardsmen, speculators and dissidents were still hiding in its ranks. After the birth of the RWP from the union of the two left wing parties, there were about the same number of Muscovites and local Communists in the Political Secretariat, on the Central Committee, Communists outnumbered Social Democrats three to one. Party leaders thought the time had come to start intensive Romanization, i.e., to pare down the proportion of minorities; primarily Jews and Hungarians, or more precisely, Hungarian Jews whom the RWP Secretary-General especially disliked. When he realized that the 'Hungarian comrades' working in the state and party apparatus were actually of Jewish origin – 60% at the Central Planning Board, and 12 out of 13 general directors at the Ministry of Health – he felt cheated and felt the need to take revenge.[274]

February 1948 was a turning point in Romania: transition to the Soviet system became inevitable and overt. One character of this change in people's republics - read Soviet satellite states - is the intensification of class struggle according to Stalinist theory and practice; enthusiastically adopted by the Hungarian Left.[275] At the end of July 1948, HPAR resolution #100 of the Executive Committee of Miercuera-Ciuc (Csíkszereda) also accepted the thesis presented at the RWP Plenary Session of June 10-11, 1948 that "The development of the People's Democracy and the transition to the building of Socialism is going on concurrently with an intensifying and shifting class struggle."[276] The HPAR resolution in truth reflected the view of its factional and dogmatic communist members, who gained the upper hand. It was they who praised the Communist Party's forcible nationalization, compulsory food requisitions and minority policy.[277] They were the ones who condemned the [Hungarian] Roman Catholic Church because it protested against nationalization.[278] The resolution signaled the launch of attacks against the Catholic Church because it protested the nationalization of its educational bases, the church schools. In the following school year, one after another, Hungarian high schools were closed under the pretext of nationalization, reorganization and such. Despite all this, the number of minority schools was far greater, enrolment too, than in the Ceausescu-era!

The last, December, congress of HPAR was preceded by the RWP resolution of December 1, which defined for every national minority the concrete tasks for the class struggle. For HPAR, the assigned targets were Hungarian unity, the

---

[273] Gheorghiu-Dej, Gheorghe: Selected articles and speeches (Válogatott cikkek és beszédek). Bucharest, 1951.
[274] Sfetcu: 13 anii... op.cit. pp. 105-107.
[275] Truth (Igazság). 1948, June 28.
[276] Ibid, 1948, June 26.
[277] Balogh, Edgár: Man's Work. Memoirs 1945-1955 (Férfimunka. Emlékirat 1945-1955). Bp., Magveto Publisher, 1986. p. 284.
[278] Illumination (Világosság). 1948, June 22.

isolationism of culture and economy, and to counter the propaganda of the agents of the Vatican.[279] These accusations and concepts constituted a concentrated attack against the Hungarian community and its institutions. 'Hungarian unity' meant – disregarding class struggle aims – the failure to remove from their posts those intellectuals of bourgeois origin, who began to work between the two wars but did not support Communist ideals. 'Isolationism' was the code word for the Hungarian community's desire to preserve its century old institutions. 'Vatican agents' were simply those who opposed to the Party's atheistic ideology, educational policies and principles.

Distrust, in general, grew steadily in Romania against Hungarians and Hungary, the Western neighbor. The Romanian-Hungarian bilateral economic and cultural committees did not hold sessions, foreign trade slowed. The Romanian side did not observe agreements on water management, refused to compensate the owners of assets frozen by CASBI, Hungarian state properties were treated as capitalist properties; private travel was restricted, as well as travel on Hungarian passports. Romania failed to execute the resolutions of the annual sessions of the Joint Water Management Committee, the exchange program of cultural cooperation kept idling and Hungarian-Romanian, as well as Romanian-Hungarian Societies were dissolved; the establishment of the Hungarian consulate in Cluj Napoca was postponed and the circulation of books and newspapers from Hungary were restricted with the argument that they hindered the assimilation of Hungarians in Romania. Mátyás Rákosi made the following acerbic remark in one of his letters to Gheorghiu-Dej: "... today, the Hungarian democracy, building socialism, is immeasurably more isolated from the Romanian democracy, building socialism, than the countries of Horthy and Antonescu ever were... and the longer we Communists are in the saddle, the worse the situation becomes."[280]

The function of HPAR after its last congress, held in Cluj Napoca in December 1948, was limited to relaying to the Hungarians the actual tasks of the class struggle - the battles of coal mining and sowing, the peace priest movement, the struggle against 'wealthy' farmers (kulaks) and the denunciation of institutional Hungarian forces of reactionaryism, nationalism and cosmopolitanism - as determined by the RWP. At the same time, paragraph 24 of the new constitution of the Romanian People's Republic, enacted in 1948, guaranteed free use of the mother tongue and the availability of instruction at every level of education for every national minority in the country. In areas where Romanians lived together with minorities, their languages could be used in both verbal and written communication in public administration and jurisdiction. Public servants should be appointed from their ranks or from different nationalities, who spoke the local minority's language.[281]

---

[279] For lasting peace and for a peoples democracy, 1948, October 16.

[280] Political History Institute archives, 276.f.65/112.

[281] Democratic solution to the nationality question in the People's Republic of Romania (A nemzetiségi kérdés demokratikus megoldása a Román Népköztársaságban). Bucharest, Romanian Institute for Fostering Foreign Relations. 1949.

But in fact, as it was acknowledged during the election campaigns of the same year, the world had split into two: the camp of the people's democratic states and the block of imperialist powers. Although it was the period of unprecedented flourishing of literary societies, public educational organizations and minority cultural life in the writers' association, ever increasing energies were spent every day on detecting an enemy that cunningly infiltrated the party's ranks, exposing the crafty schemes of reactionaries, kulaks and agents of the Vatican.

A peculiar twofold situation developed. On the one hand, the new Romanian constitution decreed the equality of minorities, the free use of minority mother tongues in education and cultural life, but the promised minority law was not passed and Hungarians increasingly suffered from the class struggle. The same can be said about the implementation of the resolution on the revision of Party membership. This is the period when the minorities' situation was also deteriorating due to internal and external political circumstances. The world had split into two, cold war tensions, isolation and the arms race intensified. The socialist countries broke with Yugoslavia and other disparites also surfaced in the people's democratic camp. Changes in the life of minorities served as a sensitive instrument indicating that democracy shifted towards dictatorship in internal policy. Due to their special status, dictatorship afflicted minorities doubly: first as a citizen of the country, second, as a minority.

From 1948 onward, HPAR activity was limited to mobilizing Hungarians for the class struggle and to relaying Party resolutions.[282] The issue of minority equality was officially taken off the agenda. The working class, it was emphasized, should subordinate all problems concerning the minority issue to the main task: the building of socialism. It was admitted that the State machinery had not yet been cleared of the remnants of Romanian chauvinism, and all difficulties were attributed to this.

The RWP fully accepted the Stalinist dogma that the minority issue was one, but not the most important, part of revolutionary transformation. There are certain periods of the revolution when it may be raised to the strategic level but generally it remains a tactical Party issue. The Party resolution of December 1948 included severe criticism of every national minority: the Hungarians for nationalism, the Germans for Fascism, the Serbs for Titoism, the Bulgarians and Ukrainians for being kulaks, the Turks and Greeks for sympathy with western imperialism, and the Jews for Zionism.

Internal enemies, supported by external imperialist circles - emphasized the Party - had been defeated on the political battlefield. Their economic power had been crushed; because of that, they intensified their attacks in the ideological and cultural spheres. "We object to the uncontrolled influx of various press items and books from the People's Republic of Hungary - said Luca at the fourth HPAR Congress in Cluj Napoca in December 1948 - because they are full of references to Western sources and the remnants of bourgeois ideology and culture."[283]

---

[282] Political History Institute archives, 276 f. 60/38.
[283] Scinteia. 1948, December 15.

Although not significantly, the number of Hungarian papers, books and cultural institutions in Romania decreased at that time. In 1947, 17 dailies and 45 periodicals were published in minority languages, including 7 papers and 35 periodicals in Hungarian. But by 1948, this was reduced to 28 items. Only three out of the six Hungarian theaters remained in operation, in Cluj Napoca (Kolozsvár), Oradea (Nagyvárad) and Tirgu Mures (Marosvásárhely) respectively. (There were 25 Hungarian theaters in Transylvania in the time of WW1.) Some 1,500 books were published in minority languages between 1945-48, including 669 in Hungarian - an average of 160 a year.

Between 1949 and 1951, 'kolkhozation' (forced collectivization),[284] compulsory requisition of agricultural products,[285] the development of heavy industry, the repeated sowing and harvesting campaigns and especially collectivization (see: Fight against kulaks in Szeklerland. – in reality, due to natural conditions [this is mountainous country] there were actually no wealthy farmers) seriously afflicted the minorities in Romania: Germans, Serbs and Hungarians. In many cases, a peasant with 9 hectares (22 acres) of land became a kulak. A grand industrialization program was launched in June of 1948 with it, due to a lack of a labor force, internment. In a resolution, which the RWP Central Committee passed on March 3-5, 1949, it declared the necessity of collectivization in order to improve the alliance of the working class and the peasantry and to eliminate the backwardness of agriculture.

The same also applied to the so-called 'verification' – to the discrimination of the minorities. A resolution was passed on June 13, 1949 on the review of Party membership. As a result, some 192,000 people, 20% of the membership, were expelled from the Party before 1951 (In one of his speeches, in the 1970s, Nicolae Ceausescu mentioned about 300,000 people), mainly former Social Democrats, intellectuals and minorities. As a heritage of its illegal past – 90% of the 2,000 party members between the two world wars were of minority origin - there were still too many non-Romanians in the party and the Secretary-General was determined to change this, i.e., to Romanize the party.[286]

When, in the last week of November 1949, the newspapers reported that the Party praised the HPAR for its exemplary enthusiasm in interpreting the speeches of Malenkov and Gheorghiu-Dej and drew the correct conclusions from the Rajk-trial - which was that vigilance could never be alert enough if the extermination of the last remnants of bourgeois nationalism and class enemies was at stake - Gyárfás Kurkó was already in prison, a victim of the first wave of the strike against the 'internal enemy'. Some days later, in the first days of December, Edgár Balogh, Lajos Jordáky, Áron Márton, István Lakatos and József Venczel, and then in 1950, János Demeter came to share Kurkó's fate. The charge was Hungarian

---

[284] Gheorghiu-Dej: Selected articles and speeches (Válogatott cikkek, beszédek). Bp., Szikra Publishing, 1951.

[285] Hunya, Gábor: Romania - an extreme case (Románia - szélsőséges eset). The Hung. Scientific Academy's (MTA) World Economic Research Institute's Scientific Information Service publication. 1987, August. p. 208.

[286] Scinteia. 1949, June 15.

nationalism, separatism, aiding reactionary elements and that the HPAR supported the Rajk-line in Romania. Kurkó was in a difficult situation as he had met with László Rajk several times, and he declined to repudiate a word of his political beliefs, according to which the same rights were due to Hungarians and Romanians (in economy, politics and culture). He was sentenced to life imprisonment.

Almost the entire leadership of the HPAR, clergymen, Social Democrats, writers and members of the former illegal Party, as well as the senior officials of Transylvanian Hungarian Farmers Union (EMGE) and EMKE, were imprisoned on trumped-up charges. There were three concurrent trials in progress against the HPAR leaders, professors of the Bolyai (Kolozsvár) University and clergymen. Some of the charges resulted from the unique situation of the Hungarians. Based on their views on where Transylvania should belong, they were charged with revisionism. Although one of the defendants, Edgár Balogh, supported the notion of joining Transylvania to Romania as early as in 1945, they were also accused of conducting talks with the Left wing (actually Communist) Hungarian Peace Party not about getting out of the war, but about reattaching Northern Transylvania to Hungary. Naturally, among the charges were those included in other show trials - of Slansky, Rajk, Clementis, Kostov - plots against the state and party leaders, espionage, Titoism and Trotskyism etc.[287]

The RWP plenary session on January 23-24, 1950, discussed the elimination of traitors hiding in the ranks of the Party and the necessity of stepping up the class struggle in the transition from Capitalism to Socialism. Secretary-General Gheorghiu-Dej gave a statement on the developments. The process of eliminating the exploiting classes had yet not been completed – he said – not in the people's democratic states advancing toward Socialism. The working class of Romania, in alliance with the working peasantry, completed a transition that changed class relations: strengthened socialist industry and collectivization in agriculture but private farmers and kulaks still held important positions. The capitalists, utilizing their external relations, would like to regain their power, said Gheorghiu-Dej.[288]

Class struggle - continued the Secretary-General - is intensified by the aggressive policy of British-American imperialists in the hope of restoring capitalism in the people's democratic countries. That is why they support Fascist elements here; deploying spies and saboteurs in these countries. The most depraved – the most flattering attribute he used – is the Tito-Rankovic spy organization, which used Fascist-nationalist-chauvinist-kulak elements to carry out provocations in order to achieve their goal. Class struggle in the villages – he continued - consists of preventing the creation of collectives, but the complete victory of socialism will not be achieved without the destruction of private ownership of land and the means of production. Bourgeois nationalism and chauvinism are the major weapons of the 'class enemy' in the matter of ideology and culture. The areas inhabited by different nationalities are especially receptive to these, as well as to cosmopolitanism - the reverse of nationalism. And

---

[287] The trials of 1949-50.
[288] Truth (Igazság). 1950, April 9.

commencing from this, the class struggle affected all facets of life: "in the villages, the kulaks, in the religion, the agents of the Vatican are wreaking havoc", opined the RWP leadership.

In the interest of destroying literary unity, in the spirit of the battle against nationalists, deviants, cosmopolitans, the literature department of the Bolyai University was the first to be put under close scrutiny in 1950.[289] It was not done just in general terms; individuals were named. The Department of History was the next to be scrutinized in June; its professors summoned before a Party panel. The assessment of the activities of the Hungarian higher educational institutions during the spring and summer of 1950 was aimed at removing a large number of Hungarian teachers in order to justify their liquidation and merger with suitable Romanian institutions. Every Hungarian college, the Hungarian State Theater, the Cluj Napoca (Kolozsvár) branch of the writers' association, publishers and literary papers were reviewed during the course of that summer.

At this time, socialist realism was the only accepted form of artistic expression, and it was expected that the subjects of literary works deal with the birthdays of Stalin and Gheorghiu-Dej, for example.[290] Gábor Gaál (He took part in the Hungarian Soviet Republic, led by Béla Kun in 1919, then fled to Romania and founded the leftist periodical Our Age [Korunk]. However, due to his Hungarian origin, he later became dispensable to the Romanian Communist Party) condemned the Literary Almanac (Irodalmi Almanach) that "neither August 23, nor November 7, nor that great holiday of the Party and the people, the Party Secretary-General's birthday, have been the subject of literary works" published in issues 4 and 5 of 1951.[291]

Subsequently, independent Hungarian cultural and art institutes ceased to function independently, absorbed into similar Romanian institutions - operating as their auxiliaries. Among others, the reasons given were nationalism and the influence of bourgeois ideologies, for which reason 'they had to be put under supervision and control.' Moreover, the separate structure of institutions carried the potential of 'national isolationism.' This purge was aimed primarily at scholars of classical studies; the following round eliminated them from commercial sphere, the military and police forces.

By this time, the HPAR sessions did not differ in any way from the Communist Party meetings. Through its media, the HPAR condemned the departments and individual professors of the Bolyai University. They did not spare Hungarian literature in Romania, either. They met expectations, and in this the two rival groups were in agreement, although one of them had, for quite some time, wanted to dissolve the Hungarian People's Alliance of Romania.

The Communist Party passed another resolution on the collective movement in March 1951. The HPAR seminars for farmers discussed not only the ways and means of proper production but also the advantages to be found in the collectives. After the resolution, the organization of collectives picked up momentum in the

---

[289] Our Way (Utunk). 1950, April 13.
[290] As composed by Gáll Erno.
[291] Literary Almanac (Irodalmi Almanach). 1951, issue 4-5. pp. 785-789.

areas inhabited by Hungarians in Transylvania, the Szeklerland and among the Csángó Hungarians in Moldova.

Effects on Romania of developments in the Soviet Union and Hungary after Stalin's death

Gheorghiu-Dej launched the second round of his fight for autocracy in 1952. This was, incidentally, the point at which the development of the other people's democracies and Romania began to diverge. Taking advantage of Stalin's anti-Semitism – this was the time of the trials of Jewish doctors in Moscow – and under the pretext of rightist deviation, Gheorghiu-Dej expelled the leaders of the Muscovite wing of the Party, Secretary of State Ana Pauker, Finance Minister Vasile Luca and Interior Minister Teohari Georgescu. He justified Luca's expulsion by making him responsible for the country's catastrophic economic-financial crisis. The press suddenly began to spell his name as Luka, alluding to his foreign - non-Romanian - origin. Georgescu was charged with hindering trials similar to the Rajk-trial in Hungary to eliminate traitors to the Party. In the same year, Groza was eased out of the post of Prime Minister, to be appointed President of the Grand National Assembly, a ceremonial position of no power.

The expulsion of Luca, Pauker and Georgescu indicated the party leaders' determination to be rid of non-Romanians. Under the guise of anti-Zionism, an anti-Semitic campaign was launched, with the ultimate aim to encourage Jews to emigrate, closely followed by the displacement of 'class enemies', i.e., tens of thousands of Serbs, Germans, Hungarians and even Romanians. The article, "Expose Zionism, the Poisoned Weapon of Imperialism" written by György Kovács, of Hungarian-Jewish origin, is instructive.[292] Gyula Csehi and László Erdélyi were exiled around this time, in spite of the fact that they had served Romanian communists to the utmost. Like others, Erdélyi also condemned László Rajk in his article, "Spies, Imperialists Sentenced."[293] The thread of its logic is illuminating, stating that Rajk and his accomplices "wanted to bind Hungary to Titoist Yugoslav Fascism." Without a doubt, rejection of the "Danube Confederation" plan, supported Groza and the HPAR, was a warning signal.

To get a sketchy picture of the state of the other two main minorities of Romania, the Germans and the Jews, we need only refer to some statistics. In the 1930 census, 745,000 Germans were recorded in Romania; circa 148,000 Germans left during WWII. The 1948 census counted 344,000 Germans; the fate of the difference, i.e., 253,000 people is unknown. (RCP Secretary-General N. Ceausescu admitted in March of 1971 that Germans were displaced from Romania.)

As for the Jews, the national census in 1930 found that 756,930 Romanian citizens professed to be Jewish. Between 1939 and 1955, 146,068 left for Israel. This is the highest number of emigrants from any European country. Detailed figures indicate far more interesting trends: 38,904 people left between 1944-

---

[292] Scinteia. 1949, February 23.
[293] Our Way (Utunk). 1949, October 1.

1948; 17,668 in 1948; 13,595 in 1949; 46,430 in 1950; 40,206 in 1951 and 3,627 in 1952. In 1978, 350,000 Jews lived in Israel who came from Romania; 265,000 of them arrived after 1944. (Today, some 20,000 Jews are registered in community records. The tally does not include those who have converted to Christianity, or atheists.)

After Stalin's death in 1953, there could have been an opportunity to put an end to the exaggerations and distortions of economic and political life, the excesses of the Cultural Revolution and to follow a healthy path of social development. Two aborted attempts for de-Stalinization were made (in 1953 and in 1956-57) in Romania, mostly in literary life and to a lesser degree in political life where, with the exception of a few minor 'plots against the Party' - as they were officially called - little happened. All in all, the thaw of a few months in Romania that followed Stalin's death and the XX. Congress of the Communist Party of the Soviet Union (CPSU) was probably due to uncertainty in the country. After the CPSU's XXII. Congress, the RWP blamed responsibility for the Romanian show trials on Ana Pauker.

Imre Nagy, launching his reform Communist program is July 1953, introduced significant economic and political reforms in Hungary. This was a warning sign for the Romanians, and the resolution of the RWP's Central Committee, passed in August, was designed to address social discontent. The reasons for it were high prices – they increased by 200% between 1947 and 1952, – shortage of commodities, compulsory requisitions of products, low living standards and lack of consumer goods. The resolution[294] envisioned relaxation of the compulsory product gathering, loans for agricultural producers, the production of consumer goods and slowing down the pace of industrialization. One or all of these promises appeared from time to time in Party resolutions of the following years, depending on how the Party leadership gauged society's tolerance.

After Stalin's death, groups of political prisoners were released from prisons and labor camps in the Soviet Union and Hungary. But Gheorghiu-Dej's attitude towards changes and especially towards freeing his political opponents was influenced by fear. This explains why the military court, following a one-week session in mid-April of 1954, more than a year after Stalin's death, closed the Patrascanu-case, which had already been delayed for six years. Patrascanu – who could have been the Romanian Imre Nagy – as the head of the plot, as well as his brother-in-law and several others were sentenced to death on charges of treason, being Gestapo-agents, British-American spies and hindering the withdrawal from the war, and were executed.[295] There were Romanians, Hungarians and Jews both among both the defendants and plaintiffs.[296]

---

[294] Forward (Elore). 1953, August 22.
[295] Serbulescu, Andrei: Monarhia de drept dialectic. A doua versiune a memoriilor lui Belu Silber. Bucuresti, Humanitas, 1991.
[296] Forward (Elore). 1954, April 18.

Regarding responsibility, the entire Romanian Party leadership was involved.[297] It also extended to Nicolae Ceausescu, who ordered the review of the show trials and the rehabilitation of the condemned (except the anti-Hungarian trials) in 1968. At the time of the trial, Ceausescu was Deputy Interior Minister and also in charge of the Securitate. He was appointed Secretary of the Central Committee after the trial, in April of 1954.[298] As for the Soviet Party leaders, a certain degree of reservation could be experienced in their behavior, similar to the Imre Nagy trial. Gheorghiu-Dej would have liked to have Khrushchev's written assent to Patrascanu's execution. Khrushchev refused by saying that it was an internal matter of the Romanian Party.[299] It has since come to light that Gheorghiu-Dej annotated the records of the inquiry and determined the kinds of confessions to be extracted.

Albeit a year earlier, another trial was planned to bring death sentences similar to Patrascanu's, the so-called Oradea-case (Nagyvárad)[300] against Transylvanian Hungarians. In 1955, the former senior officials of the HPAR were released; some were rehabilitated by retrial (Edgár Balogh), while others' terms were cancelled (József Méliusz). But HPAR president Kurkó, Roman Catholic Bishop Áron Márton, university professor József Venczel and István Lakatos, a zealous backer of Transylvanian autonomy, were only released in 1964 under a general amnesty. The fresh currents in literary life were unable to give impetus to changes in the political. However, in response to growing civil disobedience, tens of thousands of political prisoners, laboring on the construction of the Danube Canal, were released.

The Hungarian Autonomous Province (HAP)

At the end of January 1953, Gheorghiu-Dej announced: the minority issue had been solved in Romania. Obviously, after this statement, everything that cast doubt on it was deemed to be nationalism. This spawned the operation of a method reminiscent of the Fanariot era - in the 19th century Romania 'imported' modern institutions from Western Europe – so that the most sensitive,

---

[297] Raduica, Grigore: Crime in lupta pentru putere. 1966-1968: ancheta cazului Patrascanu. Bucuresti, Editura Evenimentul Zilei, 1999.

[298] Nicolae Ceausescu was kept in check for decades by the Soviet Communist Party because his name appeared on the document endorsing the execution of Patrascanu. Related by Crikó Lorincz of Bucharest.

[299] Raduica: Crime...op.cit.

[300] Forward (Elore). 1954, October 10.

objectionable directives, like those concerning minority issues, were disseminated verbally to the people involved. Consequently, since the minority issue 'has been solved', there was no longer a need for the Minority Ministry or the independent minority organizations, including the Hungarian People's Alliance, as well as similar organizations of the German, Jewish, Serbian and Ukrainian minorities. It was justified by stating that they had become the hubs of nationalism and hindered the fraternal rapprochement of Romanians and the other nations; these organizations were eliminated by 'self-dissolution.' It marked the end of the institutional representation of the Hungarian nation. Consequently, the Minority Ministry was also closed.

In his fear that the issue of Transylvania's status would be raised in international organizations, Gheorghiu-Dej established the Hungarian Autonomous Province (HAP) in 1952. Accordingly, the primary consideration before the new territorial-jurisdictional division of the Romanian People's Republic was Section 19, stating that, "the compact Szekler-Hungarian populated area constitutes the Hungarian Autonomous Province. The Hungarian Autonomous Province has its own independent public administrative board, which is elected by the population of the Autonomous Province. HAP extends over the following regions: Csík, Sîngeorgiu de Padure (Erdoszentgyörgy), Gheorgheni (Gyergyószentmiklós), Tirgu Secuiesc (Kézdivásárhely), Toplita (Maroshévíz), Tirgu Mures (Marosvásárhely), Reghin (Régen), Sfântu Gheorghe (Sepsiszentgyörgy) and Odorheiu Secuiesc (Székelyudvarhely). The administrative center of HAP will be Tirgu Mures (Marosvásárhely). Section 20: the laws and statutes of the Romanian People's Republic are in full force in the entire territory of the Hungarian Autonomous Province. And Section 21: the bylaws of the HAP is to be laid down by the Autonomous Province's People's Council to be presented to the RPR's Grand National Assembly for ratification."

The population of the Hungarian Autonomous Province in 1953:[301]

County & center	Hungarian	Total population
County Udvar	123,959	127,330
In Székelyudvarhely (Odorheiu Secuiesc)	9,549	
County Csík	127,481	146,685
In Csíkszereda (Miercuera-Ciuc)	5,280	
County Háromszék	121,491	138,441
In Sepsiszentgyörgy (Sfântu Gheorghe)	12,670	
County Maros	166,738	327,925
In Marosvásárhely (Tirgu Mures)	34,943	
Total	539,669	740,381

---

[301] Romanian Hungarian Voice (Romániai Magyar Szó). 1948, March 18.

Significant Hungarian-inhabited counties according to the administrative division of 1948:

County & center	Hungarian	Total population
County Kolozs	118,823	566,195
In Kolozsvár (Cluj Napoca)	67,977	
County Szilágy,	141,363	372,220
In Zilah (Zalau)	6,566	
County Temes,	108,481	528,662
In Temesvár (Timisoara)	16,139	
County Bihar,	164,896	515,591
In Nagyvárad (Oradea)	52,541	
County Szatmár,	104,419	312,391
In Szatmár (Satu Mare)	30,635	

As can be seen, only about one-third of the Hungarians in Romania lived in the HAP. Section 21 promised a separate law that would have assured self-government, but this never came to pass. The "Socialist Territorial Autonomy" of the 1936 Stalinist Constitution served as the model for the HAP, which provided for greater possibility for the use of the mother tongue. The state's laws and regulations were to have full force; local people's councils, the militia and courts reported to the appropriate central bodies. Local institutions and bodies were in charge of managing local public administration and controlling local political and cultural issues. The situation was promising, unlike the period between the two World Wars, when Transylvania was flooded with Romanian public servants and officials. It was stressed that priority was to be given to local, Szeklerland experts in the selection of staff and senior officials of councils, public administration units and courts, as well as teachers and educators. In the beginning this was so, but over time, Romanians were appointed to important middle and high level posts instead of the local people.

As far as the free use of the mother tongue is concerned, it was declared[302] that Hungarian would be used at the provincial, regional, city and village levels; the state language, i.e., Romanian, would be the means of communication with central state and public administrative bodies. Resolutions passed by the HAP were published both in Hungarian and Romanian. Basically, the HAP differed from any other region of the country only in that a natural condition, i.e., the majority of the population being of Hungarian origin, was enacted into law. However, what was not apparent then that what was considered the natural situation in multi-ethnic regions of Transylvania, the unimpeded use of Romanian, Hungarian and German mother tongues, would soon be limited to the HAP.

The publication of the *Literary Almanac* in Cluj Napoca (Kolozsvár) was banned in June of 1953 — old charges and numerous criticisms against the periodical were rehashed. (Instead, the publication of the monthly *True Word*

---

[302] Constitutional proposal for the Romanian Peoples Republic. Bucharest, for use by agitators, 1952.

[Igaz Szó] was resumed in Tirgu Mures (Marosvásárhely) in July of the same year.) This was followed by the closing of two Hungarian colleges in Cluj Napoca: the College of Agriculture and the Hungarian section at the engineering faculty. At the end of 1953, the State Literary and Art Publishing office was also moved to Tirgu Mures (Marosvásárhely). With the exception of the HAP, bilingual signs were gradually disappearing from Transylvania; barriers rose against the import of Hungarian press items and books - library orders were not met - and the preservation of Hungarian historical monuments faded. Hungarians in Transylvania could feel to an ever-increasing extent - and it was even stated by Romanian government and Party officials between December 1954 and March 1955 - that the Hungarian Autonomous Province was a 'cultural ghetto' for its inhabitants. On top of it, the use of the Hungarian language was gradually diminishing in petitions, official procedures and documents. They failed to maintain and replace the equipment of the Bolyai University; the salary of the teaching staff was lower than that of the Babes University; several Hungarian and Jewish educators were dismissed; the Hungarian material of the University Library became unavailable. It aroused protest when 'Hungarian literature in Romania' was increasingly referred to as 'Romanian literature in Hungarian' and that the schools established in Moldova, in 1947, were closed in order to speed up the Romanization of Csángó Hungarians.

Romanian minority politics in a Hungarian report[303]

Changes that took place in the Soviet Union and Hungary in 1953 made a greater impact on the Hungarian population in Romania, including several Hungarian senior officials of the party, than on the Romanians. They demanded changes in party policy - minority policy was especially and primarily mentioned - and they did it in such a determined way that the Transylvanian leaders of the RWP could not ignore it and entrusted three members of the Party leadership of the Bolyai University to do a survey and compile a report on *Struggle against Bourgeois-Nationalist Influence Spreading among the Hungarian Intelligentsia.* The more than 100-page report was compiled between December 1954 and March 1955, and presented a true picture of what was demanded by the Hungarians and, not insignificantly, it also mentioned that a situation which was normal in Transylvania in 1954-55 - bilingual signs and the use of both languages in public, Party and official life - would be, in say 20 years, be unheard of.

In section one, it was felt offensive that an exaggerated mistrust could be felt from Romanian official bodies towards Hungary, as well as towards those who maintained contact with relatives and friends in Hungary. It was difficult to obtain passports and scholarships, and opportunities to study abroad were limited. However, what was felt to be most alarming was that "it is more and more difficult to get printed matter and literature". They were unavailable in Romania; subscriptions were being cancelled (ed: by the authorities), so that by 1955, the

---

[303] The Hungarian Scientific Academy's manuscript archive. Csehi Sári, Tóth Sándor and Weizman Endre's account.

demands of 80-90% of the subscribers, including university departments, editorial offices and institutions, were not met.

In section two, the authors listed some reservations that the Hungarians had concerning the situation of the Hungarian Autonomous Province: that Hungarians expected the fulfillment of their rights but the opposite happened. The use of language, which was formerly assured in all walks of life and in all of Transylvania, was now limited to one province. The HAP seemed to serve the objective of moving Hungarian educational and cultural institutions from the other major cities of Transylvania and to eliminate the historically developed cultural center of Cluj Napoca (Kolozsvár). Hungarian commercial and store signs were being replaced with Romanians in Cluj Napoca. Hungarian became increasingly neglected in the execution of public affairs; petitions written in Hungarian were refused. The authors summed up that they thought that neglecting the historical monuments of Cluj Napoca was biased, as well as the cadre policy (ed: positions for members of the in-group; political patronage) of appointing Hungarians only to lesser offices.

Section three, titled 'Minority Issue in Scientific and University Life,' gave a summary of the discriminatory handicap of Hungarians. This shed light on the problem that scientific publication in Hungarian was, as yet, unsolved; Hungarian historians, linguists, teachers, geologists and natural scientists demanded semi-annual and annual publications. According to the authors, a far more severe problem was that Hungarian experts were not being employed in scientific institutions; nationalist attitudes were noted in the management of the Kolozsvár University Library, the insufficient supplies reached the Library of the Bolyai University; and a significant part of the Hungarian material of the Library was inaccessible. Comparing the two Universities in Kolozsvár, salaries were significantly higher in the Babes than in the Bolyai.

The authors of the memorandum, all three were leftist scholars, not only proposed that Hungarian historians, natural scientists, physicists and engineers should be allowed to publish their research results in Hungarian publications but also the introduction of compulsory language instruction of Romanian, Hungarian and German in Transylvanian schools; as well, the establishment of a Department of Hungarian Language and Literature at the Bucharest University.

Finally, the authors' proposals included:

1. In areas of mixed population, town and street signs should be in all the minority languages (e.g. Cluj-Kolozsvár, Sibiu-Hermannstadt-Nagyszeben);
2. Compulsory education of the local spoken languages;
3. The establishment of a Hungarian department in Bucharest;
4. For historians, the command of the Hungarian language should be available and compulsory.

They also took a stand in connection with the principle of dual loyalty - after 1968, several representatives of Hungarians in Romania officially repudiated this concept - namely that the culture of the Hungarian minority in Romania had a dual character: part of the culture of the Romanian People's Republic, as well as that of Hungarian culture. On the same basis, they protested against certain Romanian literary circles, which held that "Hungarian literature in Romania must be considered Romanian literature in Hungarian." They also took a firm stand against the Romanization and assimilation of the Csángós in Moldova. They stressed: the language of the Csángós was Hungarian, Csángó folklore was Hungarian folklore, therefore the Romanian state had to provide the opportunity for instruction and culture in the mother tongue, too, as was done with the building of schools in 1947.

The impact of the XX. CPSU Congress and the events of 1956 in Hungary[304]

The internal and external policies of the period between the spring of 1945 and July of 1958 were characterized by uncertainty and the tactics of tightening-loosening. A large Romanian delegation attended the XX. CPSU Congress, held on February 14-125, 1956. They were all filled with foreboding at Khrushchev's account of the Stalinist crimes. Reflecting on their own actions, they did not feel secure; they hoped Khrushchev would fail and everything remains as it was. In his report in March 1956, Gheorghiu-Dej admitted: the personality cult had exerted its influence in Romania, too, but with the expulsion of the Luca-Georgescu-Pauker faction, it was put an end. He declared the thesis, - 'artificially stimulated enhancement of class struggle' - as wrong, but that the above named were responsible. He repeated that certain state security bodies carried out illegal acts but he, personally, had no hand in it. At the same time, the Secretary-General of the RWP denied the criticism expressed by the writer Alexandru Jar at the Party members' meeting of the Writers' Association, stating Party freedom was repeatedly curtailed and that autocracy characterized the activities of national and Party actions, and that writers were exposed to repeated police attention. Jar and his most vociferous supporters were subjected to disciplinary enquiry, were expelled from the Party and banned from publication. Everybody had to take note: the attempt to change Party policy had failed in Romania.

Led by fear, and to disarm the rising discontent of the minorities, stern measures were taken to stamp out every hint of internal Party opposition.[305] However, the Romanian Party leadership could not remain isolated from the changes taking place in the neighboring countries. Hungarian-Romanian bilateral relations improved; writers, journalist and various delegations exchanged visits.[306] It seemed as if Romania would give up its policy of mistrusts towards Hungary, also begin to address fairly the demands of the Hungarian minority for cultural and educational development. Scientific conferences, exchange visits of artists, memorial services for János Hunyadi (ed: 15th century Transylvanian noble, father of Hungarian king Mathias) held in Hungary and Romania, joint commission to locate the tomb of Sándor Petofi (ed: 19th c. Hungarian poet/soldier, fell on a

---

[304] 1956. Explozia. Perceptii romane, iugoslave si sovietice asupra evenimentelor din Polonia si Ungaria. Editie intocmita de Corneliu Mihai Lungu, Mihai Retegan. Postfata de Florin Constantiniu. Bucuresti, Editura Univers Enciclopedic, 1996.

[305] Lipcsey, Ildikó: Hungarian-Romanian contacts, 1956-1957 (Magyar-román kapcsolatok, 1956-1957). Manuscript.

[306] Ibid.

battlefield near Sighisoara [Segesvár]) – the contemporary press published news of this kind almost daily.[307] Museums and libraries were opened, one after the other: in Cristuru-Secuiesc (Székelykeresztúr), Salonta (Nagyszalonta), Sighisoara (Segesvár) and Satu Mare (Szatmár). The reconstruction of the Petofi House in Bucharest went on at an accelerated pace. The Literary Circle (Irodalmi Kör) of Cluj Napoca (Kolozsvár) was revived; Gábor Gaál, former editor-in-chief of *Our Age* (Korunk) who was imprisoned in 1952, was rehabilitated; the visit of writers Gyula Illyés and Áron Tamási [to Romania] in the summer of 1956 was a triumphant procession.[308]

The impact of the events taking place in Hungary in 1956 can be measured on three levels: 1) they created a real catastrophic atmosphere among the Romanian political leaders. Martial law was declared, primarily in the areas of Hungarian and German populations; armed forces were mobilized in these regions and news from and about Hungary was censored and the frontiers were closed;[309] 2) the public showed unparalleled interest in the news – newspaper circulations doubled in Romania; 3) unrest increased not only in the major cities of Transylvania (Tirgu Mures (Marosvásárhely), Cluj Napoca (Kolozsvár) and Timisoara (Temesvár)) but also in almost every larger industrial and university city. Without a doubt, primarily the Hungarians were in a revolutionary mood but certain Romanian circles also expressed their intention to dissociate from the Soviet Union, the elimination of Stalinism and compulsory produce delivery to the state, and even the demand for a multi-party system.[310]

Romanian papers published reports, without commentaries, regarding the events in Hungary in October and November 1956. Initially, they laid blame on the mistakes of the former party leadership, the economic policy, the infringement of democracy and laws and the decrease of living standards. The enemies of the people took advantage of this situation – ran the reports – but "the Hungarian people are making successful attempts to protect the people's power". "White terror rages in Budapest," appeared in the November 4 issue of the *Forward* (Elore), then in a special edition on November 5, it reported on the establishment of the revolutionary worker-peasant government. On this occasion, Groza and Gheorghiu-Dej wished success on behalf of the Romanian government for the Hungarian government, headed by János Kádár.[311] The Romanian party leaders, as well as those of Czechoslovakia and the GDR (German Democratic Republic, East Germany) urged Soviet intervention the last days of October, and they offered actual - military - assistance. After November 4, they demanded strict reprisals.

On November 21, a Romanian Party and government delegation arrived in Hungary. Gheorghiu-Dej seized the opportunity to lecture and correct the

---

[307] Ibid.
[308] Jordáky, Lajos: Diary. Bear Dance, 1992 (Napló. Medvetánc, 1992). Issue 3.
[309] 1956. Explozia… op.cit. pp. 143-145.
[310] Ibid, pp. 186-187, 199.
[311] Forward (Elore). 1956, November 5.

Hungarian Party leadership for allowing the situation to get so far out of hand.[312] In their joint statement, the two Parties condemned the UN Security Council for its intervention into Hungary's internal affairs, and took a stand for the territorial integrity, independence and sovereignty of their countries and non-intervention into internal affairs. It was announced that Romania was to give a loan of 60 million Roubles to Hungary. The visit's secondary aim was to allow Romanian party potentate Walter Roman to try to persuade Imre Nagy, whom he knew from his Comintern days in Moscow, to resign and thus provide legitimacy for the Kádár government.[313] It is true that Romania granted asylum for Imre Nagy and his companions. At the same time, it contributed to their kidnap and arrest before their show trial that ended with their death sentences.[314]

It was not only the Romanian envoy stationed in Budapest, sending slanted reports (he stated, for example, that the revolutionaries intended to recapture the annexed Hungarian territories), but also the Hungarian or Hungarian-speaking officers of the Securitate followed the events on the spot, i.e., in Hungary. It is interesting to note that Securitate agents appeared in Budapest in the summer of 1956, traveling under false Austrian, West German, French and Italian passports, transmitting their reports back to Bucharest. The action was directed by N. Ceaucescu, aided by the NKVD's Romanian advisor.[315]

The frequent visitor to Hungary, Walter Roman – Erno Neulander – was the source of those baseless reports that Imre Nagy, Pál Maléter and János Kádár all raised the prospect of revisions to the terms of the Paris Peace treaty and reclaiming the lands ceded to Romania.[316]

In the course of November and December 1957, workers, teachers, writers and lecturers in the Hungarian Autonomous Province unanimously condemned the Hungarian events at mass meetings, labeling it as counter-revolutionary. However, these statements were manipulated, falsified, signatures counterfeited but the Hungarian intelligentsia failed, even later, to reveal these manipulations.[317]

The party leadership was in virtual panic. Due to the total lack of democracy in public life, the catastrophic economic policy and broken resolutions, they deservedly feared the discontent of the entire population, especially of the minorities for their long record of offending the national minorities. In the HAP, the security service and secret police prepared a roster of 1,000 names, whom they wanted to arrest.

Since the summer, some Party leaders carried out continued talks the representative of the intellectuals, particularly representatives of the Transylvanians and Hungarians. In order to avoid similar unrest as in Hungary,

---

[312] November 22. Gheorghiu-Dej.
[313] Romanian Hungarian Voice (Romániai Magyar Szó). 1993, October 27.
[314] Rainer, M. János: Imre Nagy (Nagy Imre).
[315] Troncota, Cristian: Istoria serviccilor secrete romanesti de la Cuza la Ceausescu. Bucuresti, Editura „Ion Cristoiu" S.A. 1999. p. 448.
[316] Tugoi, Pavel: Istoria si limba in vremea lui Gheorghiu-Dej. Memorile unui fost sef de cabinet de Sectie a C.C. al PCR. Bucuresti, Ed. Ion Cristoiu, 1999. 138 p. Convorbiri neterminate. Corneliu Manescu in dialog cu Lavinia Betea. Bucuresti, Polirom, 2001.
[317] Our Way (Utunk). 1956, November 7and 8.

134

the session of the RWP Central Leadership held on December 27-29, 1957, passed several measures - already promised in 1954-55 - to improve living conditions for the entire population: compulsory agricultural produce delivery was lifted, decentralization was envisioned to replace strict centralization, salaries were raised by an average 15%, the possibility of introduction of a profit-sharing system, the improvement of living standards and the production of consumer goods were promised.[318] These measures had mainly political, not economic, goals, a fact the Hungarian envoy noted in his report.[319]

Romanian policy toward Hungarians became even more duplicitous: on the one hand, every Hungarian was accused of revisionism; on the other, regulations favourable to them were being passed. The Agricultural College was reopened in Cluj Napoca (Kolozsvár) – only to be closed two years later – and several new Hungarian elementary and secondary schools, as well as teachers' training colleges were opened. The House of Hungarian Culture (Magyar Kultúrház) opened in Bucharest. To manage minority educational issues, the Minority General Directorate (Nemzetiségi Foigazgatóság) was established in 1956; it controlled the activities of several newly instituted Hungarian school boards. Hungarian instruction was allowed with a minimum enrolment of 15 pupils in the fifth grade, and with a minimum of 10 pupils in the sixth and seventh grades. A Party resolution made it possible to pass university entrance examinations in Hungarian. More opportunities were created for Hungarian book publishers; the periodical *Our Times* (Korunk) resumed publication, and new periodicals appeared in the stalls: *Culture* (Muvelodés), *Sunshine* (Napsugár), and *Linguistic and Literary Historical Proceedings* (Nyelv és Irodalomtörténeti Közlemények). However, it is also a fact that while these were happening, the closing of Hungarian schools in several regions already started in 1957.

As a note, in 1957, a total of 460 newspapers and periodicals, with a total of 6.5 million copies, were published in Romania. The minorities' share was 55: 41 in Hungarian, 4 in German and 3 in Serbian, for a total of 600,000 copies. (The number of these publications again decreased, so that in 1967 only 25 newspapers and periodicals were published in Hungarian.) Following the higher educational reform of 1957, it was promised that the Bolyai University would be endowed with new buildings and a laboratory. The practice of taking entrance examinations in Hungarian was resumed. Departments of Hungarian, Turkish, Tatar, Czech and Polish language and literature were opened in the Parhon University of Bucharest. German and Serbian departments were established at the College of Timisoara (Temesvár). New courses – Hungarian history, Hungarian folklore, Hungarian language and literature – were offered at the Bolyai University. A new section for training Hungarian choirmasters and music teachers was established at the Institute of Music (Zenemuvészeti Intézet).[320]

A new series started in *Our Way* (Utunk), the literary periodical of Kolozsvár, in 1956. Several, formerly banned, writers regained their former status

---

[318] MOL, Romanian External Affairs Ministry. XIX-J-1-j. 10.007/1957
[319] Ibid, XIX-J-1-j 001162
[320] Lipcsey: Hungarian-Romanian …op.cit.

in literature. It was openly expressed in the series, that the value of a writer is not defined by state prizes or official honors. The debate (series) in *Our Way*, which lasted until August of 1958, assessed all the harmful consequences of the literary policy implemented by Zhdanov.[321]

Post-1956 trials in Romania

The Party and state leaders of the GDR, Czechoslovakia, Romania and, of course, the Soviet Union – Yugoslavia and Poland wavered - urged immediate steps and reprisals against the Hungarian revolution. The populations of these countries expressed varied sympathies, but on the whole, trials – mainly anti-Hungarian – were conducted between 1956 and 1958. A study of court records leads to the conclusion that demonstrations took place in major university cities in Romania – Cluj Napoca (Kolozsvár), Iasi (Jászi), Brasov (Brassó), Timisoara (Temesvár) and Bucharest. More than 80 persons, mainly students and lecturers, were arrested in the latter two, held in detention and brought to court. Apart from one or two, they were all students and professors. The 81 condemned received a total of 301 years and 5 months of jail.[322]

The memorandum of the Timisoara students contained far fewer demands than the Hungarians'; it did not include, for example, a multi-party system or the termination of the Warsaw Treaty. The crime of those convicted in Timisoara mainly consisted of speaking too often, between October 23 and 30, about the events taking place in Hungary. The main culprit, of course, was the Romanian student, Aurel Baghiu, who declared in front of his 2,500 fellow student that, "There is a revolution going on in Hungary, a whole nation's revolution, which has risen against its oppressors". Reprisal was swift. On October 30-31, 2,500 to 3,000 students were arrested in Timisoara and the military tribunal, "under the charges of attempted murder and terrorist acts against the state" sentenced 31 of them.[323]

The first student demonstration expressing solidarity with the Hungarian revolution took place in Cluj Napoca on October 24. It coincided with the general assembly of the students' alliance, where demands were voiced only for university autonomy, greater control over the refectory and that university entrance acceptance be based on knowledge and not social origin. Despite all this, the two student leaders – a Hungarian and a Romania – were arrested the next day, and the police made strenuous efforts to prove that they were in contact with the counter-revolutionaries in Hungary.[324] Here, in Cluj Napoca, between 20 and 30 sentences were handed down.

---

[321] Our Way (Utunk). 1956, October 26.

[322] Pop, Adrian: The student protests of Timisoara and Bucharest (A temesvári és a bukaresti diákok tiltakozása). Our Age (Korunk).1996, issue 10. pp. 48-50.

[323] Sitariu, Mihaela: Rezistenta anticomunista. Timisoara 1956. Bucuresti, Editura Sophia, 1998.

[324] Fodor, Sándor: Diversion in Cluj Napoca (Diverzió Kolozsváron). Transylvanian Hungarians (Erdélyi Magyarság), 1992, issue 12. pp. 13-14.

In the Hungarian Autonomous Province, approximately 2,500 persons were arrested and imprisoned between 1957-1960 on charges of solidarity with the Hungarian revolution and plotting armed revolt against the state. In the Szoboszlay case, out of the 57 accused 10 received the death sentence – and were executed – while the rest received a total of 1,300 years of imprisonment. Actually, it was a real plot against the state, in which Hungarians, Romanians, Slavs and Jews took part. Romanian officers, Hungarian clergymen, students and workers demanded a multi-party system.[325]

When the members of the illegal *Christian Workers' Party* (Keresztény Munkáspárt) – the organization was established in 1950 – were exposed, some 50 were convicted. Two of the 31 condemned in the Valea Iui Mihai (Érmihályfalva) group were executed. Two of the nine imprisoned for the 'UN-memorandum' – a draft plan of an independent Transylvania in the European Union – died in prison. Nine students in Sfântu Gheorghe (Sepsiszentgyörgy) were sentenced; 6 had charges brought against them in the region of the Tirnava Mica (Kisküküllo); and in the Mezoség, students were sentenced strictly because they expressed their sympathy with the Hungarian revolution of 1956. László Salamon of Gheorgheni (Gyergyószentmiklós) was sentenced to 10 years because he took part in the demonstration in Budapest on October 23.[326] In Oradea (Nagyvárad), 500 were arrested, 59 were sentenced. In Cluj Napoca, along the Nyárád River, (Erdovidéken), priest and church leaders were detained.

The trial of the Bolyai University students, the so-called 'Várhegyi-case' (Várhegyi drafted a memorandum on university autonomy), as well as the trials of other university students and lecturers, whose only crime was that they tended the tombs of famous Hungarians in the local cemetery, provided a suitable reason to close down the university, citing that it was a powder keg counter-revolutionaries and revisionists.[327] In Cluj Napoca, an anti-Communist group was arrested; in Reghin (Szászrégen) 24 sentences handed down.

Of the show trials, the 'UN memorandum stands out. It represented all strata of Hungarian society in Romania: the intelligentsia, the churches, the Right, as well as the Left. The participants felt that when the 'Hungarian question' came up in international forums, the topic should not be restricted to the revolution and its bloody aftermath but also a just arrangement of Transylvania's territorial allocation.[328]

The 1956 trials were a taboo subject for a long time in Romania. Consequently, only a portion of them are known, at all. A ban on research in the archives also added to the difficulties. According to our knowledge, about 600

---

[325] Tófalvi, Zoltán: 40 years ago they executed 12 Transylvanians of 1956 (40 éve végeztek ki 12 erdélyi 56-ost). Transylvanian Hungarians (Erdélyi Magyarság), 1998, issue 4. pp. 44-45.
[326] Takács, Ferenc: Belated candle lighting (Kései gyertyagyújtás). Transylvanian Hungarians (Erdélyi Magyarság). 1992, issue 4. pp. 28-30; Finta, Ella: Szilágysomlyó. Transylvanian Hungarians (Erdélyi Magyarság). 1996, issue 4. pp. 28-34.
[327] Dávid, Gyula: 1956 in Transylvania and what followed (1956 Erdélyben és ami utána következett). Our Age (Korunk). 1996, issue 10. pp. 30-41.
[328] Tófalvi, Zoltán: Transylvanian martyrs of 1956 (Erdély 56-os mártirjai). Manuscript.

persons were sentenced for an average of 6 years, imprisonment or forced labor. Dozens of people died of maltreatment during incarceration or fell victims of the death penalties.

In general, the 1956-58 period in Romania, and Transylvania, saw the introduction of extraordinary measures:

➣ police and Securitate (secret service) forces were increased;

➣ ministerial commissioners were assigned to companies where Hungarians worked and the number of informers increased;

➣ historical Hungarian churches, and the Hungarian intelligentsia in general, was put under strict police observation;

➣ many of them were imprisoned or sent to the Romanian Gulag on trumped-up charges;

➣ armed forces were ordered to deploy and act act if a large crowd gathered;[329]

➣ Soviet advisers played a crucial role in working out the new state security plan, which predicted mass arrests.[330]

From the June 1957 RWP Resolution
until the withdrawal of Soviet troops, July 1958

Economic reforms continued in 1957. New, until now unknown phrases, such as "rational economy" and "we need practical experts, not paper experts", became familiar. A new Act, (re)defining the sphere of the local people's councils, was planned in order to increase the responsibility of local administrative bodies. Steps were taken to scale back aggressive centralization.

The CPSU, during its session on June 22 to 29, 1957, censured Malenkov, Molotov and Kaganovich for formenting 'fractional' behaviour. Thus, their plan to remove Khrushchev through a coup was frustrated. Gheorghiu-Dej, too, was waiting for this event. His hopes, also, were not realized.

It was reported at the session of the RWP Central Committee (CC), held on June 28 to July 3, 1957, that the elimination of the compulsory produce delivery elated the people, the friendship between the Romanian people and the minorities living together had strengthened, living standards had improved, as well as both industrial and agricultural production had grown. At the same session, Chisinevski, member of the RWP CC's Political Committee (PC) and secretary of the CC, and Miron Constantinescu, member of the CC's PC, were relieved of their posts because – the statement emphasized – they gave a false account of the work of the party leadership, and earlier had cooperated with the Luca-Pauker faction.[331] Miron Constantinescu – the statement further noted - did not get disillusioned by the events in Hungary and continued to slander the Party. Moreover, he conducted talks with counter-revolutionary forces of Transylvania in the autumn of 1956. The real reason, of course, for their dismissal was that

---

[329] 1956. Explozia... op.cit. p. 149.

[330] The white book of the Securitate (A Szekuritate fehér könyve). Romania Libera, 1994, April.

[331] Forward (Elore). Scinteia: 1957, July 3.

they, the Romanian representatives of the Khrushchev direction, had called upon Gheorghiu-Dej to admit his crimes.[332]

This party resolution provided the basis for expelling all those from their posts who wanted a Khrushchev-like change. As well, to justify the relatively large number of Hungarian writers in Transylvania who were brought up in front of summary courts. In most cases, the charges were treason and nationalism. Writer Alexandru Jar, who in spring 1956, attempted to effect a Stalinist change in literature, was forced to exercise public self-criticism;[333] as was the Transylvanian Lajos Jordáky, one of the members of the reform generation of 1956, who was sentenced in one of the show trials between 1949 and 1956.[334] Gheorghiu-Dej personally informed Ferenc Keleti, the Hungarian ambassador in Bucharest, of the Jordáky case, making special effort to stress how much damage Jordáky's nationalism had caused to the Romanian Communist Party.[335]

At the same time, the party placed great stress on winning over the minorities during the parliamentary elections in February 1957. Thirty-nine Hungarians were elected into the new Parliament, and a series of articles appeared detailing their role and proportion in state administration. At this point, the national minorities had 77 MPs, 10,000 representatives in people's councils and 6,500 people's judges. Several actors of the Tirgu Mures (Marosvásárhely) Szekler Theater, which celebrated the tenth anniversary of its establishment, were conferred with high state honors in the beginning of 1957. Several new Hungarian theaters were established in those years: Hungarian Theater in Satu Mare (Szatmár) in the autumn of 1956, the Hungarian Folk Ensemble, instead of the promised theater, opened its doors in Brasov (Brassó) in June 1957. Hungarian, German and Serbian theaters were established in Timisoara (Temesvár). No less than 8 theater companies were in operation in Cluj Napoca in 1958: separate Romanian and Hungarian theaters, Romanian and Hungarian operas, Romanian and Hungarian puppet theaters, Romanian stage studio and the Hungarian Revue theater.

A Hungarian delegation (János Kádár, Gyula Kállai, Antal Apró, Károly Németh and István Szirmai) paid a visit to Romania from February 20 to 28, 1958. The Hungarians were anxious to settle outstanding and acute issues between the two countries.[336] The wish list contained the following significant items: agreements on civil rights assistance, on health care, on traffic access to the closed border zone. It went on with a need to address the problem of strict Romanian visa requirements, the possible opening of a consulate in either Cluj Napoca or Tirgu Mures, the freedom of movement of travelers, the clarification of the ownership rights of Hungarian citizens residing in Romania, the mutual support of aged parents in the other's country and issues arising out of multi-ethnic marriages.

---

[332] Tóth, Sándor: Report from Transylvania, vol. II (Jelentés Erdélybol. II. köt.). Hungarian Booklets, Paris, 1987. p. 168.
[333] Our Way (Utunk). 1957, August 15.
[334] Ibid, 1957, November 28.
[335] MOL, XIX-J-1-j 004816
[336] Ibid, 001164/6

139

It was a great disappointment that the Romanians primarily stressed the achievements made in the minority issues. The statement made by Kállai and Kádár was another disappointment. The Romanian press ran frequent and lengthy reports on the visit, paying particular attention to the speeches delivered by Gyula Kállai and János Kádár. In his speech delivered in the HAP (MAT) center in Tirgu Mures (Marosvásárhely), Gyula Kállai stated: "We can clearly state that we have no territorial claims. It is a special pleasure for us that... our neighbouring stats ensure all the minorities living within their borders complete equal rights and all the conditions for independent development."[337]

According to press releases, the Hungarian guests were received everywhere amid great fanfare. However, what they did not add, until it leaked out, was that Kádár informed his Romanian comrades that Hungary did not claim an inch of territory and that he was perfectly convinced that minorities enjoyed complete equality of rights. The Hungarians living in Romania interpreted his statements that Hungary had abandoned Transylvania, once and for all. It, however, set the Romanian leaders' minds at ease and they took the next step in minority policy – backwards.

Two days after the death sentence was carried out on Imre Nagy and his companions, the Central Committee of the RWP, at its session on June 19 to 23, 1958, announced further expulsions from the Part. Illegal Party members, Constantin Doncea, Ileana Receanu (nee Ilona Papp) and Iacob Catoveanu were expelled, because they demanded that the RCP Secretary-General should give an account of the mistakes made by the leadership in front of a committee of old party members. According to the official account, cited by the Hungarian ambassador, the steps were necessary because of late 'disgraceful views' were making inroads among the Party members. Also, burgeois activity increased, along with treasonous actions against the Romanian People's Republic by Catholic priests and well-to-do peasants.[338] In December of 1959, fourteen people were sentenced to death on these charges, four of them carried out immediately by the military tribunal.[339]

As Romania proved to be reliable in 1956, Soviet troops were withdrawn from the country on July 25, 1958, a step requested by the Romanians in 1955. Shortly after that request though, they strongly supported the deployment of Russian troops in Hungary. A portion of the representatives of Hungarians living in Romania interpreted this step as meaning that their institutional protection ceased. Indeed, seven lean years followed in the life of the national minorities.

From the withdrawal of Soviet troops to the IX. Party Congress: 1958-1965

An article, entitled "For the ideological clarity of our literary criticism", appeared in issue 21 of *Our Way* (Utunk), on August 14, 1958, less than in a month after the important event [the withdrawal of Soviet troops]. Its effect was

---

[337] Forward (Elore). 1958, February 26.
[338] MOL, XIX-J-1-j 001117
[339] Ibid, 005835

so dismal that almost nothing remarkable can be found in literary activity in the following seven years. The author of the article was László Földes, who was known as an advocate of the democratization of literary life and the re-discovery of national values, but his series of articles was in total contradiction with his former words... and whose articles suitably fit in the anti-revisionist campaign that culminated in summer 1958.

He attacked Áron Tamási and the group of peasant writers as counter-revolutionaries. He called insufferable such phenomena as nihilism or skepticism – citing Zádor Tordai's Madách-study published in *Our Age* (Korunk) as "conveying a false message for contemporary people". According to Földes, József Méliusz was unclear and conciliatory toward bourgeois ideology; Tamás Deák mistook the study of world literature for cosmopolitism; Zsolt Gátfalvi befogged national values and his Hungarianism had no class content, and so on. András Szilágyi added some more remarks: that Jeno Kiss was pessimistic. The poet Miklós Kallós, who lost his standing, passed sentence and declared that "national communism is an imperialist diversion; humane socialism a slogans of the new revisionists". Földes was won over to write his series of articles by showing him the proof sheet of the upcoming issue of the *True Word* (Igaz Szó), running an article attacking him. However, Földes denounciation of the Hungarian writers in Transylvania, from bourgeois writers and poet to those of worker's and peasant's origin, was in vain – having done his allotted task – he was expelled from the running of *Our Way* (Utunk) in September 1958. Shortly afterwards, he was publicly accused in public and expelled from the Party. He was able to return to the literary mainstream only at the end of the 60s, when the publication of *The Week* (A Hét) started.

The merger of the Bolyai and Babes Universities, in 1959, was seen as the first assault against the education of Hungarian intellectuals, accomplished by Central Committee secretary N. Ceausescu. (The document of the merger has never been made public. Some people claim that the reason for it was to render it impossible to refer to existing Hungarian departments and sections that still existed in 1958.) According to the official reason, the existence of the Hungarian university hindered the closer ties of fraternity, and stood for isolationism and nationalism. Following this example and under the pretext of 'unification', schools were relegated to sections of other institutions, and finally, closed down. Under this method, between 1958 and 1968, the number of Hungarian schools was decreased by half; similarly in the cases of theaters, art ensembles and cultural houses. Instruction in the mother tongue for vocational and apprentice training and shriveled to a minimum, with the hiddent intent to restrict the number having an advanced technical training and know-how.

The Romanization of the most important institutions of the administration also started. From that time, neither Hungarians nor Jews were allowed to hold senior posts in the Ministries of Defense, Internal Affairs and Foreign Affairs. Minority managers and technicians of industrial and manufacturing companies were replaced under various reorganization schemes. New measures provided the grounds, in that: 1) the State had the right to restrict the workplace of every individual; 2) through secret decrees, the proportion of minority employees was restricted to 10% – in Transylvania, too – almost certainly shutting certain jobs and careers from them. Another regulation severely restricted – selected – who could, or could not, relocate into towns. The fact that, as a result of the resolutions, the results were serious drops in production did trouble the authors and executors. The most important conditions for moving in Transylvania were Romanian nationality and being a member of the armed forces: army, Securitate or police.[340]

The Secretary-General of the RWP unashamedly announced these measures, in March of 1960 in Cluj Napoca, supporting them with the reasoning that Rákosi and his clique did not fill the leading positions with Hungarians subsequent to 1956. Similar instances occurred in Romania, where leading positions not filled by Romanians but by members of a minority were only handed out to those who exhibited animosity towards the realities of Romanian life and against the Romanian people.[341] Not too long after, in December of 1960, the Hungarian Autonomous Province was reorganized. The proportion of nationalities was as follows in 1956:

	Háromszék, Maros, Csík, Udvarhely	Romania
Hungarian	567,509	1,589,443
German	3,171	382,400
Jewish	2,904	144,198
Romanian	145,718	15,001,190

As the part of the reorganization, the districts of Sarmas (Sármás) and Ludus (Ludas) in Beszterce-Naszód (75% of the population was Romanian) were attached to the HAP, and the regions of Kézdi and Sepsi (80-90% Hungarian) were detached. HAP's name was also changed to Mures-Hungarian Autonomous Province (Maros-Magyar Autonóm Tartomány). Its territory and population:

	Before Dec.1960	After Dec. 1960
Territory	13,500 km^2	12,250 km^2
Hungarian	74.6 %	60 %
Romanian	19.3 %	36.8 %

The pace of industrialization in the Szeklerland was slowed down in order to urge the emigration of Szeklers from areas entirely populated by Hungarians to other regions populated mostly, or entirely, by Romanians. (At its session on February 16, 1968, the Grand National Assembly rescinded the provincial divisions and reinstituted the old county system, thus the HAP ceased to exist.) From then, the Hungarian ambassador was forced to remark in his annual reports that Romanian-Hungarian relations were not without problems but that the Romanian side showed no inclination to remove those impediments.[342] In August of 1961, when a Romanian delegation was in Budapest, the Hungarians raised

---

[340] Ibid, XIX-J-1-j 26570/64
[341] Forward (Elore). 1960, March 17.
[342] MOL, XIX-J-1-j 00294/3/60

objections that only immediate relatives were allowed to travel to Romania. Their reply was that: because most of them were spreading hostile propaganda.

The III. Romanian Workers' Party Congress, held the same year of 1960, and laid out the five-year plan's major targets for the economy, including the improvements to the technical/material foundations of socialism, and the completion of the establishment of socialist production relations. At the COMECON summits in August 1961 and June 1962, the Romanian side refused Khrushchev's proposal for integration stating under it Romania would be paying more for Czechoslovak and GDR goods than world prices.

After returning from the XXII. CPSU congress, the RWP held a session between November 30 and December 5, 1961, and again rejected any changes to the status quo, opting instead to smear all the mistakes of the past on the Luka-Pauker group and the expelled Chisinevski and Constantinescu - condemned as the representatives of personality cult. In 1962, Romania was unwilling to accept the plans of labor division in the COMECON countries, according to which agricultural development and production were to be increased.

In 1964, when the Sino-Soviet conflict broke out, Romania sided with China and protested against its condemnation in international forums. In 1963, the Gorky Institute was closed and the Russian language ceased to be a compulsory school subject. In 1964, Romania revisited the Bessarabian problem, as it would from time to time, depending on which issue was timely on its agenda: anti-Hungarian or anti-Soviet. The RWP CC passed a resolution on April 24, 1964, that stated: "It is every socialist country's sovereign right to determine, choose and adapt the forms and methods of its own socialist structure. No state has the right to present its own interests as general interests..." The resolution requires no further comment. However, it is examine its consequences on the Ceausescu-era: 1) in foreign policy, the anti-Soviet nature of the rapprochement with China, as well as a limited mediator role in international politics (e.g.- its relations with Israel, which seemed not to be incompatible with the semi-official anti-Semitism); 2) in economic policy, extensive industrialization; and what seemingly derives from the previous two 3) in minority policy, the declaration that Romania is a homogeneous state.[343]

Contrary to such statements, the policy of assimilation was stepped up by the Romanian state, removing the majority of not only the upper but middle tier of experts and Party appointees of minority background.[344] Gheorghiu-Dej was always concerned with 'a solution to the Jewish question' in Romania. Beginning in 1959, a wide-rnging propaganda campaign was begun to encourage their emigration.[345] Hence, while Gheorghiu-Dej eliminated the various factions within the Romanian Communist Party and, like Stalin, seized state and Party power, at the same time he progressively distanced himself from the Soviet Union and

---

[343] Ibid, 003407/1/Szt,/1964; Elore (Forward). 1964, April 23 and 26.

[344] Ibid, 006664/64

[345] Marcou, Lilly: Une enfance stalinienne. Paris, Presses Universitaires de France, 1982. pp. 194-195.

defined a unique road to Romanian national Communism – a heritage he left to his successor.

IV. The Ceausescu-era: 1965-1989

Gheorghiu-Dej died on March 19, 1965. The new Secretary-General, Nicolae Ceausescu, addressed the IX. Congress of the Romanian Communist Party, held on July 19 to 24, 1965. (At the time of Gheorghiu-Dej's death, Ceausescu was the secretary of the CC, and in charge of administration and organizational departments, he controlled the Ministries of Defense and Interior. Ceausescu convinced Maurer, Bodnaras and Stoica – who later committed suicide – that it was unnecessary to appoint a successor in Gheorghiu-Dej lifetime. Gheorghiu-Dej's designated successor was Gheorge Apostol, whom Ceausescu later compromised and overthrew.) In the 75-person Central Committee, the opponents of Ceausescu remained in the minority.[346] They debated and accepted the multi-faceted program for the development of socialist Romania. The new Secretary-General announced that henceforth Romania would no longer be called a People's Republic but as the Romanian Socialist Republic.

They confirmed the resolutions of April 1964, strenuously stressing that the RCP pursued a policy of non-intervention. Continuing Gheorghiu-Dej's economic policy, the Party took as its main objective, the continued industrialization. To that end, the amount of investments earmarked for agriculture for the next 5 years were of the same magnitude as of the previous decade.[347] Industrialization actually referred to heavy industry, a veiled code for the real target – the development of military industries. Thanks to these steps and armament imports, Romania became the 5th largest military power in the last years of the Ceausescu-era.

The new Party leadership took initiatives in various directions: it intended to win the Romanian intelligentsia, at home and abroad, as well as the national minorities. The representatives of Stalinism were expelled from the writers' unions, and the works of some previously banned authors were again published. The Nationality Committee (Nemzetiségi Bizottság) working beside the CC, headed by Nicolae Ceausescu, with the cooperation of several senior party officials, and Lajos Takács, András Süto and one German and one Serbian representative, was re-established in 1965. During the constitutional debates of 1965, it was admitted that the proportion of minorities in the country was 9.5% and one-third of the population in Transylvania was Hungarian. It was also stressed that the number of civil servants should reflect this. For example, four of the 18 members of the Cluj Napoca People's Council, and one of the four vice-presidents were Hungarian. The Secretary-General, during his visits to factories promised that the impoverished Transylvanian counties would receive more incentives. The Party's current direction was that equality of the minorities meant equality to work. While providing equal opportunity for economic activities, it carefully avoided mention of equal rights to culture and language.[348]

---

[346] Cimpeanu: Ceausescu ... op. cit. pp. 241-244.
[347] Ceausescu, Nicolae: Romania on the road to achieving socialism. Report, speeches, articles vol. I (Románia a szocializmus építése kiteljesedésének útján. Jelentés, beszédek, cikkek). Bucharest, Politikai Publisher.
[348] Ibid, p. 61.

The Party delegation visiting Budapest on November 4 to 6, 1965, emphasized the indissoluble friendship of the two nations. At the same time, the Romanian Party confirmed its vision on following a separate road from the COMECON, i.e., that every Party had the right to determine its own political line. In every instance, the national ideal and the importance of patriotic education were stressed. Bessarabia and Bukovina were Romanian territories – stressed several historical studies – and Cluj Napoca (Kolozsvár) and Oradea (Nagyvárad) were ancient Romanian cities.

1968 marked an important milestone in the history of Romanian Communism. The plenary session of the RCP Central Committee on April 22-25, 1968, was an outstanding event of political, social and economic renewal. After the session, representatives of the minorities were allowed to speak publicly about their grievances suffered during the period of the personality cult. This process accelerated after the armed forces of five Warsaw Pact countries (Romania did not take part) entered Czechoslovakia in August 1968. Romania, to avoid similar consequences caused by the country's discriminative and assimilative minority policy, was again, as many times in the past, forced by an external event to make promises of future changes. During his visit to the Szeklerland at the end of August, Nicolae Ceausescu promised to put an end to the neglect of the region and to provide greater state subsidies.

Bilingual commercial and street signs appeared once again in Transylvania. New papers were published. A minority book publisher, Kriterion, was established, and the others – Political, Scientific, Eminescu, Albatros, Creanga, Facla, Ceres, Dacia and Medridiane – also published books in Hungarian. Minority secretariats and directorates were established in some ministries, e.g.- the Ministries of Public Education and of the Arts. A work-group was established in the Bucharest-based "Nicolae Iorga" Institute for Historic Sciences to conduct research into the history of national minorities; joint Romanian-Hungarian research into history gained impetus. New museums, literary commemorative houses, public educational institutes, libraries, 500 Hungarian drama groups, 400 choirs, orchestras and dance ensembles were established. Intellectual life teemed in Transylvania. Although there was no independent university established (to replace the old one), but Hungarian schools were opened, one after the other. Instead of the 20-30 books published annually, more than 200 books were published every year in the early 70s. The Hungarian language broadcasts on television and radio were also extended. The most remarkable products of Hungarian poetry, drama, prose, fine arts and scientific achievements were created in Transylvania at the end of the 1960s and early 70s.

Following the October 24-25, 1968, session of the RCP CC, the Councils of Hungarian-Nationality Workers (Magyar Nemzetiségu Dolgozók Tanácsa /MNDT/) and of German-Nationality Workers were founded. Its tasks were – as the published statement ascertains – not merely to involve nationalities in the political-economic activity of the Party and the building of nsocialism, but also to study, and solve, the particular situation and the Hungarian population. The Councils had to contribute to scientific, artistic and literary creativity in the mother tongues of the minorities. Hungarians in Romania believed that the

CHNW would be able to represent its interests, at an institutional level, as the Hungarian People's Alliance of Romania (MNSZ) did in the past.

These positive changes were dogged by negative ones. While the Constitution ensured the legality of the regulations issued by the National Council, later the Secretary-General issued them. In practice, he governed the country by decree. When it came to minority issues, secret and verbal orders were commonplace.[349] The new constitution of 1968 declared Romania a nation state, therefore it made no mention of other nations, nationalities and minorities that were living in the country, besides the Romanians.[350] The constitution of 1948 still contained, omitted now, that every citizen was entitled to use his/her mother tongue "both in private and public life without limitation."[351]

Romania, not having taken part in the invasion of Czechoslovakia in 1968, Secretary-General Ceausescu gained prestige among the Warsaw Pact countries as well as among Romanian and Hungarian intellectuals and the West. At the same time, Romania introduced a new defense policy: priority was placed on protecting the country's territory. The concept of 'people's war' was introduced, that is, the militarization of the society and the Secretary-General became the commander-in-chief. A special elite unit was set up, whose only task was to protect the Secretary-General, his family and inner circle. (It failed to fulfill its task in December 1989).

From 1968 on, Romania took part in the sessions both of the Warsaw Pact Organization and the COMECON[352] but its representatives made it clear that Romania refused the application of the Warsaw Pact to Romania and that it pursued an independent foreign policy. By doing so, Romania and its leader gained even greater adulation West. The essence of the Ceausescu dictatorship – forced labor and forced medical treatment, reminiscent of the darkest Soviet dictatorship – became known to Western politicians only in the 1980s.

In this context, the party leadership deceived the minorities by establishing of the Council of Hungarian and German Nationality Workers. During the Council's session in March 1971, the Party leadership promised that all issues connected with the use of mother tongue, culture, education and economic discrimination would be solved. The party leadership promised, and delivered, everything as the Groza government did in its first three years between 1945-47.[353] Disenchantment and cold reality soon arrived for the Hungarian minority in Romania.

---

[349] Personal communication of Fazekas János and Kányádi Sándor.

[350] Fazekas, János: A Hungarian politician in Romania and his age (Egy romániai magyar politikus és a kor melyben élt). Manuscript. Zrinyi Publisher, 1990.

[351] Tóth, László: An analysis of the Romanian Socialist Republic's national, economic and political system's legal regulatory basis (A Román Szocialista Köztársaság állami, gazdasági és politikai rendszere jogi szabályozásának politológiai szempontú elemzése). Bp., 1980-1981. Doctoral dissertation.

[352] Epoca Nicolae Ceausescu. Cronologie istorica. Buc. Ed. Stiintifica si enciclopedica. 1988.

[353] Forward (Elore). 1971, March 22.

Economic policies at the end of the 1960's

Regarding economic policy, its organization and control, from 1967 the Party leadership announced a greater degree of independence and self-determination: local planning and initiatives were to be allowed to rise to the forefront as opposed to central planning. It was decided that new economic units, cooperative companies, trusts and groups of workshops were to operate under the control of ministries and county Party committees. Some ministries were reorganized; the administrative apparatus was decreased by 39%, affecting 8,500 people. However, the Secretary-General was not satisfied with the results. Ceausescu exhorted the ministries, the local Party organizers to effect more and better agricultural production. He was dissatisfied with the utilization of agricultural employment. He justified it by saying that in 1969, each farming cooperative worker's share was 120-125 work units. Many only fulfilled 2 work units per day. Therefore, it was obvious that they were not utilizing their time effectively. The machinists did not work more than 200 days a year. The Party leadership decided that, to correct these problems, under the county Party organization, county agricultural executives were to oversee local technical supervision. Lacking any market research, industrial and agricultural goods produced were priced well above world prices on the export markets. Obviously, exports were not growing according to plans. To address it, it was decided that a business unit's profits were to be tied to export and internal sales; the cooperative that sold more would pay out more in profit sharing.

In the wake of a resolution of the Council of Ministers, passed in March 1969, Romanian industry was divided into 200 industrial centers between April and December. The Secretary-General was not satisfied with the reorganization. Uncertainty - and chaos - was everywhere, from the running of ministries to the operational rules of the industrial centers. Finally, in 1973, the number of centers was reduced to 64.

The reforms were to have been introduced in the beginning of 1970. In the meantime, several contrary measures were taken. Although the Agricultural Bank was established, it was not followed by the establishment of the Industrial and Trade Bank. The Committee for Material-Technical Supply was set up alongside of the the Central Planning Committee, which was designed to be the supervisory organization over the ministries and the industrial centers. A bonus system was introduced in 1968. Bonuses could amount to 20-25% of workers salaries. Simultaneously, salaries were raised. Theoretically, productivity and the fulfillment of the plan were taken very seriously; managers' salaries could be decreased by as much as 3% if the unit failed to meet the plan.

The complete roll-out of the new economic measures was postponed from 1970 to January 1972. However, from September 1971, the industrial centers had to follow the targets of the central plan. Measures on decentraling investments and foreign trade reform were revoked during the following years. The country had to face up to another problem in the beginning of the 1970s: its foreign debt had almost doubled. In 1966, it was $424M US, which increased to $700M US by 1968. The introduction of Western technology and equipment ended in obvious failure. The level of Romanian products did not meet international standards, had to be sold cheap or were unmarketable. Autocracy continued to live on.

Two views formed in connection with the modification of the economic policy. At the end of 1968, a group represented by Ion Gheorghe Maurer, Maxim Berghianu and Alex Birladeanu held a more realistic concept, favoring moderating plan targets, supply-side development projects and increasing export. The other group, including Nicolae Ceausescu and Manea Manescu among others, wanted to continue the forced development of heavy industry. Aside from its irrationality, it placed an enormous burden on the country. It became clear during the X. Party Congress that the second group's views prevailed.

At the May 1971 session of the RCP CC – two months after the remarkable session of the Councils of Hungarian and German Nationality Workers – plan targets were further increased: industrial growth was targeted for 12-13% and agriculture for 6.3 to 8.3%. All efforts by the opponents of the Ceausescu-group – Berghianu (Head of the Central Planning Board, at the time) and Prime Minister Maurer – failed to convince the public of the dangers of the targets set in the current five-year plan (1971-75), which did not take the country's potentials into account.

The reckless economic venture of the Ceausescu-group reached its summit at the party session in July of 1972. That session constituted a turning point, – of 'historic importance,' as they called it – and not only in economic life. The adjective 'historic' indicated far more: a turning point in Romanian foreign, internal and minority policy. Put more precisely, the overt, unvarnished and ruthless expression of Romanian nationalism: anti-Hungarian, anti-German and anti-Semitic. It sounds eerie, but logical, that who should be blamed for the failures of the oversized economic targets and the consequent deterioration of the economy and living standards? The nationalities were offered as scapegoats! So far, neither events nor critical evaluations, analyses have contradicted this statement.[354]

The Beginning of Disintegration in Minority Policy

In his address to the 1972 July session of the RCP CC, Secretary-General Ceuasescu declared that "Romania is a developing socialist country", which would take the next 15 years to erase the economic differences (he meant the standards of capitalist countries). By 1980, industrial production should increase to 6.7 to 7.5 times the level of 1970 and agricultural production should increase at an annual pace of 23-24%. On average, a 12% annual growth was planned. These targets were raised in every subsequent year. It was also forecast that the country's population would reach about 25 million by 1990, and 9.5 million out of the 11.5 million working population would be employed by industry. Aggressive industrialization, forced centralization, severe ideological and cultural policy, as well as administrative measures, again had a negative effect on minority policy.

---

[354] Tóth, Sándor: Report from Transylvania (Jelentés Erdélybol). Hungarian Booklets, Paris, 1987.

The events of 1948 repeated themselves, when the minorities paid the costs of the hard-line industrialization program.

Another attempt was made to homogenize society (the nation) at the XI. RCP Congress in 1974.[355] A debate was begun in the fall of 1973 openly discussed in Party forums on the issue of the assimilation or, alternatively, emigration of the minorities. Addressing the Congress – held on November 27-28, 1974 – Ceausescu stated that, "Some outside our borders are worried that industrialization will eliminate some defining national characteristics. We are not worried at all."[356]

The Congress resolved to further strengthen the role of the Party in everyday life. The Secretary-General held it unimaginable that the leading and middle strata of societal leaders – actors, journalists, teachers – were not Party members. In November of 1974, Party membership stood at 2,480,000, a half a million more than during the X. Concress in 1969. Party membership reflected the national make-up of the country: 89% Romanian, 8% Hungarian. Here too, as in the case of the councils and representatives, the composition was careful that the ratio should not be out of balance with reality.

At a joint session of the RCP CC and the Romanian Supreme Council for Economic and Social Growth, on July 22, 1975, they approved the five-year plan to cover the years 1976 to 1980 – three years after the 1972 statements of direction and a year after the XI. Congress. The Secretary-General declared the following strict orders and objectives:[357]

1. Industrialization;
2. Increase the stock of raw materials and energy;
3. Effective use of raw and basic materials (i.e., recycling);
4. Effective use of energy and heating fuels (the first step towards rationing);
5. Continuous improvement in the technical and material supplies;
6. More intensive use of agricultural capacity;
7. Improvement in the quality of production and modernization of products;
8. Industrial output to grow by no less than 54% - during the course of the five-year plan – or 9.1% annually (3% higher that originally planned in 1972);
9. Reduction in the cost of production and capital investments, streamlining of the workforce;
10. Growth in the areas of communications and marine transportation;
11. A policy of maximizing invested capital; investments were on the order of 1,000 billion Lei (between 1951 and 1955, the amount was 62 billion Lei);
12. Increase in international cooperation and barter trade.

It is worth to stop here for a second and reflect. Decreed growth in export was targeted at 90% (15% higher than the original target) and imports at 60% (a reduction), to help the balance of payments. The aim was to reduce foreign debts and increase foreign currency holdings. According to Ceausescu, Romania's

---

[355] Scinteia. 1974, November 26.
[356] The resolutions of the XI. Congress of the Romanian Communist Party. Bucharest, Politikai Publisher, 1979.
[357] Forward (Elore). 1974, November 28.

150

situation was perfectly normal from the perspective that – with the exception of several long-term loans – every opportunity was present to reduce the size of the debt. Unfortunately, the Secretary-General's prognosis proved incorrect.

The RCP Central Committee held a working session on October 17, 1975, in the closing months of the current five-year plan. It was obviously the moment of reckoning.[358] Already, the capital was plagued by shortages with bread supply and public food distribution was inadequate, the selection poor. Due to organizational shortcomings, vegetables were not harvested, meat was in short supply and deliveries to markets were continually interrupted. The Secretary-General offered one practical advice after the other: "...each household should erect plastic foil tents to cultivate vegetables ... every household plot should raise at least two pigs!" The Secretary- General and his advisers failed to consider the social consequences of industrialization. Agricultural workers, who formerly cultivated household plots, in short order became unskilled city dwellers and appeared in the markets as consumers and not producers. The county was not prepared for the rapid transformation. The first signs of tension soon appeared. For the time being, the country's Romanian majority was enthralled by being told: the fabulous figures that projected a vision of a multifaceted, developed country; the country's successes in foreign policy; and with the continuous reiteration of Romanian national ideals and nationalism, in fact, their continued stimulation.

In order to build up the Party's leading role, Ceausescu declared that the roles of local Party First-Secretary and county, city and village people's council presidential posts should be amalgamated. It simply meant the fusion of Party and state administrative functions, the strengthening of the role of Party state, which was controlled by a close-knit inner circle, really a family group. Elena Ceausescu, the Secretary-General's wife, became the country's second leader. Everything depended on the Secretary-General, standing at the top of the hierarchy. Instead of a democratic centralism, built from bottom up, the recurring replacement of Party and state leaders became the everyday practice. (The replacement of office holders started as early as after the RCP CC session in February of 1971 and picked up momentum after the CC meeting of April, 1972.) The unity of the Party and the nation, glorious achievements and the perfection of socialist democracy were articulated, but it was all a façade. The reality was a pervasive fear, deteriorating living standards, administrative decrees, the continuous modification of plan targets and the personality cult and its attendant acts: cleansing (Party, jobs), censorship, despotism and the increase of severity in everyday life. The party's influence on cultural life also increased after the session of June of 1972. It is not an overstatement to speak of a kind of regression. Literature's role again became to popularize the achievements of socialism, the glorification of socialism, depicting positive-negative characters and a falsified historical-social atmosphere. The country was again cut off from Western ideas and intellectual trends. Change in the minority policy was just as expected as in the era of the personality cult of Gheorghiu-Dej.

---

[358] Scinteia. 1975, October 18.

The Eastern-type of dictatorship of Ceausescu again imposed a double burden on the national minorities: once as the citizens of the country and second, as member of the Hungarian, Saxon, Jewish, Serbian, Lipovan, Greek, etc. minorities, suffering from overt or covert discriminative measures.

New paths in Minority Policy.
Homogenization and rural redevelopment theories

Ceausescu was always occupied with the idea of making the minorities 'disappear.' Immediately after coming to power, he delivered a speech in Republic (Republicii) Stadium, and he drew a comparison between Hungarians living in Romania and in America. He stated that the latter were Americans of Hungarian-origin, consequently, Hungarians living in Romania were Romanians of Hungarian-origin.[359] Perhaps, it was his intention to mix citizenship and nationality,[360] perhaps not. Nevertheless, it was same thought that provides the basis for the model: everybody should be Romanian or, if not, – as it was discussed in inner Party circles almost a decade later, in 1973-74 – they should leave.

In a speech on Teachers' Day, in June of 1968, Nicolae Ceausescu declared, "When I speak of the Romanian nation, I mean that every inhabitant of the country is part of the Romanian nation – Romanians, Hungarians, Germans, Serbs and other nationalities – who constitute an integral whole and who have to act as part of that whole in making the country prosper."[361] It was the first time that the program of homogenization was openly raised in the Ceausescu-era, but not the first time in the modern history of Romania. First in 1948,[362] then in 1954-55,[363] Gheorghiu-Dej tried to have the concept gain acceptance but resistance was so strong that he was forced to drop the plan. The line of reasoning used by the Secretary-General to arrive from the equality of the Romanian nation and co-existing national minorities to the homogenization of society and the nation, i.e., to the unification of the society, the disappearance of differences between classes and strata, and the conclusion of the differences between the nation and nationalities, is interesting. The disappearance of those differences was at stake and not the enforcement of the principle of equal standing before the law and equal opportunity, which were the characteristics of a nationality: language, culture, historical past and traditions. After June 1972, the Romanian Communist

---

[359] Fazekas: A Hungarian politician ...op.cit.
[360] Ibid.
[361] Related by Demény Lajos, professor, Nicolae Iorga Historical Research Institute, Bucharest.
[362] New Hungarian Central Archives, 0032290/1/65
[363] Ibid.

Party felt secure enough to show its hand and play with open cards; few understood the meaning.

The Hungarian Autonomous Province was dissolved in 1968. During its existence between 1952 and 1968, it did not escape Romanization but its official staff remained Hungarian. Its dissolution provoked resistance. Protests were the strongest in Miercuera-Ciuc (Csíkszereda) and Orodheiu Secuiesc (Székelyudvarhely), the two entirely Hungarian towns of the Szeklerland. Army had to be reinforced in the region. Miercuera-Ciuc (Csíkszereda) was promised to become the county seat, while Orodheiu Secuiesc (Székelyudvarhely) was promised to receive municipal rank and that the Szekler railway would be built. The building of this important infrastructure item has not yet been built.

With the redrawing of the county boundaries, the aim was to establish new counties where Romanians were in the majority (gerrymandering).[364] The establishment of the system of closed cities in Transylvania – which included Cluj Napoca, Oradea, Satu Mare, Sibiu, Brasov, Arad, Timisoara and Tirgu Mures (Kolozsvár, Nagyvárad, Szatmár, Nagyszeben, Brassó, Arad, Temesvár, Marosvásárhely) – was an extention of Gheorghiu-Dej's concept designed to prevent Hungarians from moving to those cities.[365] As an example, 95% of inhabitants in Tirgu Mures (Marosvásárhely) were Hungarians in 1944. In 1968, 20 Romanian villages were amalgamated into the city and the proportion of Hungarians dropped to 55% by 1970, and to 45% by 1990.[366]

It is interesting that in March of 1971, Secretary-General Ceausescu announced at the meeting of Hungarian Nationality Workers that during the 1971-75 five-year plan period "...in order to develop the counties and for the better arrangement of villages and settlements ... we are to begin the construction of new centers, which will grow into significant towns in 15-20 years; we will establish 7-8 centers of this kind in every county – some 250 on the national level – and as a result, the living conditions of the population will radically change in every county. This means that we are about to deliberately establish the preliminary conditions of the foundation of our communist society."[367]

However, the Secretary-General kept repeating the dubious argument that the Party was following the path of Marxist-Leninist nationality policy – which actually did not bode well. At the same time, he did not want to hear about devoting time to the collective rights of national minorities, or the restoration of minority rights that they had previously had, i.e., the practice of self-determination of minorities in Romania in cultural life and public administration. It was clearly worded at the XI. RCP Congress that the country's economic-social character would be radically changed in the interest of a planned redistribution of the labor force on a national level. Nicolae Ceausescu did not equivocate any longer; he declared plainly, "We will start the implementation of plans on rural

---

[364] Fazekas: A Hungarian politician ... op.cit.

[365] Tóth: Report from Transylvania. op.cit.

[366] In 1944-45, the Soviet military authorities ordered a census in Transylvania.

[367] The resolutions of the XI. Congress of the Romanian Communist Party. Bucharest, Politikai Publisher, 1979.

redevelopment and town and village re-arrangement in the next five-year plan period. We have to take measures in order to begin at least 100 village-centers on the road of modernization and transform them into agricultural or agrarian-industrial small towns".[368]

The state of the rural planning project was revealed from time to time by slips in the press, by politicians and the speeches of the Secretary-General. At the working session of the RCP CC held on October 17, 1975, the Secretary-General ordered local Party organizations to post the rural economic-social development plans at every village hall, houses of culture and schools in order to provide an opportunity for the people to discuss them and to decide on what the village would be in 1980, and to determine the intervening tasks. It can be presumed that rural planning was not yet a priority project at the top of the Party, while those at the bottom had no idea how to carry it out.

The new phase of rural planning

The Congress of county, municipal, town and village People's Council, held on February 4, 1976, paid special attention to the implementation of 'the comprehensive planning program of towns and villages.' The program's core aim was 'the rational utilization of land, the amalgamation of agricultural units and the compression of housing developments into compact districts that will blend harmoniously into the unique character of each settlement. Along with housing, care must be given to commercial establishments, technical and community facilities, as well as the necessary network of roads and transportation, along with recreational facilities. Appropriate attention should be paid to environment protection standards." (Remember these words! I.L.)[369] At the time, in 1976, the implementation of the rural planning concept was imagined as follows: the transformation of 3-4 settlements into agrarian-industrial towns in every county – altogether 12 villages in the country – would be started in the 1976-1980 five-year plan period. (300-400 new centers were planned in the long run.) Priority was to be given to the following condition during the transformation process: 1) the most important agricultural, social, cultural, business and health care activities should be concentrated into the centers; 2) folk architectural traditions should be considered beside the requirements of modern construction processes (Remember these words, too! I.L.); 3) the network of roads should be expanded and improved; 4) the final aim of the establishment of new towns was the construction of the multi-faceted, mature socialist society, and – as an important step toward communism – the elimination of differences between town and village. (Drastic methods were used in the course of the implementation of the rural redevelopment project: whole villages, buildings, churches and cemeteries were razed by bulldozers in 1988.)

---

[368] Ceausescu: Romania on the road ... vol. XI. op.cit. p. 61.
[369] Ibid, vol. XII. p. 412.

At the working session of the RCP CC, on December 28, 1976, the Secretary-General expressed his dissatisfaction that the counties had not completed the arrangement of plans for the villages and settlements.

In preparation for the XII. Party Congress on July 22, 1979, the Romanian press published the Guideline-Program for 1981-90 and up to the year of 2000. It regulated the smallest and most remote areas of economic-social-cultural activities (e.g.- geological research, organic micro-chemistry, medical sciences, the development of fish farming, the duties of a diligent Communist citizen, etc.) The Guideline-Program provided details for the necessity of the normalization (standardization?) of towns and villages. Rationality demands, the answer went, the redistribution of the means of production in order 'to provide proportionate sources of materials and energy and labor reserves for the counties,' and 'to assure equal economic-social development for every county, thereby providing an opportunity for each citizen of Romania to equally enjoy the benefits of labor and civilization', stated the Guideline-Program. As an example for unevenness, it was cited that while 200,000 people were living in one county, 800,000 were living in another. This was felt to be irrational. The country's settlement should be standardized; the people homogeneous. The plan was that 140 rural centers would be transformed into agrarian-industrial towns in the first round, and a further 200-300 before 1990.[370]

The Council of Hungarian Nationality Workers, 1974-75

It is an obvious truism that a strong, centralized power does not tolerate any viable political or social organization. Romanian society – which has actually never been a self-governing model – has long acquiesced to this practice. Thus, the meetings of the Council of Hungarian Nationality Workers have also become merely formalized *pro forma* events; fundamental questions could not be tabled. Eight days after Nicolae Ceausescu's election as President, on March 28, 1974, the Councils of Hungarian and German Nationality Workers was convened, on April 5, after a three-year interval.[371] At the joint session, the Secretary-General voiced his appreciation of the contribution of the Hungarian and German nationality workers toward the implementation of the plans. Then, he raised criticism that the majority of speakers did not speak about the great, common task but got lost in the petty troubles of their respective nationalities. Whereas, the Secretary-General pointed out, the solution to those problems lay in the overall development of the means of production. It is easy to recognize the Stalinist dogma in his statement; namely that, nationality issues will automatically be solved in socialism. Regarding the particular educational difficulties, he stated that they were the outcome of the general problems of the Romanian educational system. Everybody can attend the school they want, said Ceausescu, and reproached those who criticized parents for sending their children to Romanian schools. His change of view, and its consequences, and its attendant change in

---

[370] Forward (Elore). 1979, July 22.
[371] Forward (Elore). 1974, April 6.

educational policy can best be illustrated in his statement that "In the future, it will be more important for a Romania - building Communism and Socialism - what is being taught and not the language of the teaching." Those who were stubbornly insist on tuition in the mother language were still "captives of an old mentality, derived from a state of obsolete inequality", stated Ceausescu.[372]

He mentioned, as an example, that the rise in world market prices forced the introduction paper austerity, but he denied that it only affected the minorities. It is true that, in the beginning, Romanian papers and books were also published in limited copies. Later, however, their circulation returned to the original levels, but the publications in nationality languages remained slim and the number of copies of books printed was reduced. At the same session, Ceausescu accepted that an annual meeting of the Congress was necessary, but he rejected the notion on the establishment of new municipal, town and village councils, stating that it was contrary to the constitution of the organization. In conclusion, he emphasized again that the councils of Hungarian and German Nationality Workers should concentrate their efforts on solving the great challenge facing the country. Nicolae Ceausescu's criticisms, if not in its wording but certainly in meaning, corresponded with the criticism aimed at the Hungarian People's Alliance of Romania. The councils of minority workers should pay greater attention to enhancing the political work aimed at the development of socialist consciousness, concluded the Secretary-General with great stress. The atmosphere of the meeting and the peremptory tone of announcing directives damped any enthusiasm of the gathered representatives of the Hungarian and German minorities. A year and a half later, they arrived mentally prepared for the next session of the council.

The joint session of the Councils of Hungarian and German Nationality Workers: December 3, 1975

The meeting of two nationality councils was held in the last month of the current five-year plan period. To the satisfaction of the Romanian Party leadership, it went off smoothly and without a hitch. The participants now thought better than to raise sensitive questions, where before they took considerable risk to do so. Nicolae Ceausescu was pleased to hear that the speeches and comments covered only how the citizenry, disregarding their nationality, could contribute to rapid transformation of society. He repeated the official statement of the XI. Party Congress that, "the minority issue is merely a part of the proletarian revolution and the construction of Socialism and Communism."[373] These words may sound familiar. Ceausescu only slightly altered Yosif Visarionovich Stalin's statement of 1913, published again in 1927, that there are certain phases in the revolutionary process when issues of minor importance, such as the minority question, are raised to the level of strategy. After the victory of the revolution and the seizing of power, these problems are dropped.

---

[372] Ibid.
[373] Ibid, 1975, December 4.

The Secretary-General hinted at the difficulties facing the construction of socialism but emphasized that there was one, and only one, model of socialism, and it could not be implemented according to nations and nationalities. Therefore, he continued somewhat mixing his methaphor, the difficulties could only be overcome in one language, "in the language of unity and labor, in the language of the struggle we are pursuing, under the leadership of the Communist Party, for the implementation of the program worked out by the XI. Congress, which provides the only road to the equality of rights through the development of the means of production. Romanians, Hungarians, Germans and the other minorities have one common task: to fully implement the program of the XI. Congress and support the Party's policy without question."[374]

The nationality councils worked satisfactorily in order to enhance the harmonious cooperation of collective organizations in the Socialist Unity Front, which coordinated their unity, stated unanimously the speakers following the Secretary-General's introductory speech. Reflecting on the cautious remarks on the inadequacy of instruction in a mother tongue, Ceausescu replied that, "When all is said and done, regardeless of what language songs are sung, poems are recited, plays are performed, or in what language works of literature are written, the point is what is said and what is written."[375] It was only one small step away from making the statement that everything can be said in a common language, i.e., in Romanian, and consequently there is no need for the theaters, newspapers and schools, etc. of the national minorities. This step, however, was 'only' taken in December 1984, at the next RCP Congress.

Several regulations, detrimental to the minorities' interests, were passed in the period between 1973 and 1976. Primarily, Educational Act No. 273/1973, which decreed that separate classes for national minorities could be formed in cases of 25 pupils in elementary schools and 36 students in secondary schools. The forming of Romanian classes, however, was independent of the number of students. It meant that a Romanian class had to be provided even for one Romanian student. The law No. 225/1974, on the accommodation of foreign citizens, banned the accommodation of foreign tourists, or foreigners visiting the country for any other reason, in private homes, except direct relatives (children, parents, brothers, sisters and their spouses and children). Its violation was declared a crime and imposed fine of Lei 5-15,000. Acts No. 206 and 207/1974 ordained the state administration of 'art treasures of history and civilization.' In other words, everything became state property - document archives, works of arts in galleries, even birth certificates. According to decrees No. 24 and 25/1976, every citizen was obliged to accept the allotted workplace and post. Decree No. 372/1976 modified decree No. 225/1974 to the extent that the ban did not extend to citizens of Romanian origin.

Equality was, therefore, limited to the equal right to work; economic equality did not exist at all. Transylvania and the Bánát were the most developed industrial regions of Romania. Equalization of differences had already begun under

---

[374] Ibid, 1975, December 3.
[375] Ibid.

Gheorghiu-Dej by cutting back development in these regions. The Szeklerland was left out industrialization before 1965 and the excess labor force was urged to find work in the Regat. A slow tempo of industrialization, as compared to Muntenia and Oltenia, was launched in the mid-1970s, however, labor and living conditions were worse, in fact hardly changed. For example, a Szekler worker's wage was lower, no attention was paid to infrastructure, roads and water supply remained at pre-WW1 level, and food distribution was significantly worse than in other regions of the country. Preposterously, natural gas rich Szeklerland was lacking in gas or other means of heating and not one new hospital was built.

In the second and more intensive period of industrialization, in the Ceausescu era, through more drastic measures than in the Gheorghiu-Dej era, local people were excluded from job opportunities. After the successful Romanization of towns and cities in Transylvania, the aim was to break up the Szeklers still living in one compact block. It did not matter that it was a very expensive undertaking, as huge apartment blocks had be built for the unskilled Romanian working masses moving into the region. It also contributed to a great extent to undermining the Romanian economy.

Pertaining to the state of agriculture in the Szeklerland, although Szekler communal properties – forests and pastures – were nationalized under Gheorghiu-Dej, villagers were allowed to lease them, generally free or for a modest fee. Ceausescu put an end to this. This was how 'the right to work' was interpreted for the Székelys.

Creation of a new, higher phase of socialist society: The 1976-80 Five-year Plan

The accelerated development of industry was the central concern of economic policy. In addition, other targets were also centrally determined, such as a 9% increase in labor productivity, an average of 37% growth in real incomes, a 47% increase in purchasing power and a 50% increase in state subsidies for cultural and welfare activities. The central plan was broken down by counties and its fulfillment was strictly administered. Industry's share of the investments amounted to over 50%; priority was given to chemicals (Elena Ceausescu ran the industry), machine production and energy. In spite of all efforts, energy conservation was imposed in 1979. It goes without saying that plan targets were raised every year.[376] Production was totally centrally controlled and products for internal consumption gradually decreased.

In agriculture, state money went mainly to state owned farms and cooperatives; private producers were forced to sign production and sales contracts

---

[376] Ceausescu: Romania on the road ... vol. XII. op.cit. p. 409.

with the state to receive any subsidy. Although individual, private farmers cultivated a relatively large tract, they suffered from several disadvantages (their pension was one-eight of their colleagues working in the state sector). There was a excess of unskilled workers in agriculture. The number of workers employed in industry increased by 570,000, while 800,000 persons left agriculture during the five-year plan. Slumping living standards, increasing debts, low productivity and poor infrastructure characterized Romania.

Comparative international figures on infrastructure are quite revealing; Romania's ranking among the 26 European countries, excluding the USSR:[377]

	1965	1970	1974	1978
Transportation	25	26	26	26
Communications	25	25	25	25
Housing	26	26	25	25
Health	22	22	22	22
Education, culture	21	22	23	25
Total	25	25	25	25

Romania's level of economic development in comparison with some European countries:[378]

	1960	1970	1980	1983
Romania	100	100	100	100
East Germany	251	279	215	227
Czechoslovakia	248	250	199	187
Hungary	151	164	149	138
Bulgaria	122	129	140	146
Poland	148	150	128	102
Yugoslavia	97	107	103	
Austria	271	321	284	270
Spain	118	171	166	156
Greece	100	129	128	116
Portugal	100	114	92	88
USA	714	714	469	437

While neglecting the real internal situation of the country, Ceausescu played a leading role in a number of international issues, claiming, among other things, that he was the first who suggested a 10% cutback in military spending. He proposed, and not without self-serving reasons, to cancel the COCOM-list; his pro-Arab attitude was guided by the country's reliance on oil; his pro-Israel stand

---

[377] Hunya: Romania - an extreme ... op.cit. p. 15.
[378] Ibid, p. 10.

was inspired by a desire to attract foreign capital. The considerately offered exit-visa for Romanian Jews produced the desired result: the USA granted the most favored nation status to Romania. During this period, 1975 to 1980, the main target of his foreign visits was to secure access to Western technologies, to obtain loans and to declare Romania's independence from the socialist Bloc.[379] One trip around the world, accompanied with immense internal and external propaganda campaigns, followed another. (Romania maintained diplomatic relations with 126 countries and economic contacts with 130 states.)

In the meantime, Ceausescu not only played the role of an apparently independent politician at the meetings of the Warsaw Treaty Organization and COMECON but also condemned 'imperialist aggression' against Third World countries. A series of professions of allegiance in the socialist Bloc, on the one hand, and harping on bilateral problems, primarily between Romania and the Soviet Union, and Romania and Hungary, on the other, characterized Ceausescu's policy. Typical was the visit of a Soviet delegation in November 1976, headed by Brezhnev, who last visited 10 years before. Ceausescu referred to their differences of opinion, while Brezhniev stressed that Romania did not always meet its obligations as an ally.[380] In spite of it all, Brezhnev was honored with the Order of Merit 'Star of the Socialist Republic of Romania', first degree, during his visit to Bucharest. Likewise, Ceausescu was honored with the 'Order of Lenin' when he visited Moscow, although he raised the problem of Romanians in Moldova.

During 1976-77, Ceausescu met with every other Communist Party leader: Erich Honecker of the GDR, Eduard Gierek of Poland, Gustav Husak of Czechoslovakia, Todor Zhivkov of Bulgaria and János Kádár of Hungary. The Kádár-Ceausescu meeting produced a real sensation.[381] The animosity between the party leaders was well known, both in the Warsaw Pact and NATO-countries, as well.

The Kádár-Ceausescu Meeting: 1977

The leaders of the two nations held meetings in two border towns, Orades (Nagyvárad) and Debrecen, on July 15-16, 1977. Ceausescu was on the offensive, Kádár on the defensive, during discussions of thorny problems. Actually, both parties endeavored to preserve the appearance of superficial good relations, to further weaken the unity of the socialist Bloc, a unity demanded by the Soviet Union. Kádár's modest proposals concerning improvement in the situation of Hungarians living in Romania, Ceausescu repeatedly deflected. In order to preserve the semblance of agreement, trite agreements were signed, including a few concessions and more promises made by the Romanian Party. Kádár was of the opinion that their proximity provided a good opportunity to maintain economic cooperation and direct contacts between the two countries' populations. He stressed that both parties were ready to settle issues to be solved in the spirit of

---

[379] Epoca N. Ceausescu. Cronologie... op.cit.
[380] Scinteia. 1976, November 27.
[381] Scinteia. 1976, November 28.

friendship and internationalism. Ceausescu agreed that the meetings of populations and the leaders of the two counties were of particular significance, and did not deny the bridging role of the nationalities, but he definitely underlined that, "the solution of minority issues in the two countries is the task of the respective country's Party and state leaders." (As an aside: at the time, about 2 million Hungarians lived in Romania, and around 25-30,000 Romanians lived in Hungary.)

The joint communiqué, signed by both János Kádár and Nicolae Ceausescu, included the passage, "The solution of the problem of national minorities – citizens of the respective countries – constitutes an internal matter, and falls within the area of responsibility of the respective countries. The parties are of the opinion that the minorities in their countries should be seen as a bridge to promote the bond between the Romanian and Hungarian peoples."

Despite the usual format and binding promises – such as stressing the importance of the relations of the two sides, the significant development of economic relations (they doubled between 1975-80, compared with the figures of the previous five-year plan period), the support of the work economic joint-committees, promises for the improvement of cultural relations – the meeting can not be regarded as a mere formality. As proof, let us cite segments from the joint communiqué signed in Orades (Nagyvárad) on June 14, 1977:

"...during the highest-level meeting, the parties signed agreements on the extension of the barter trade; on postal and telecommunication cooperation; on the modification of the agreement on traffic access in the border zone; on the mutual establishment of consulates; and a protocol on the renewal of the agreement on water-supply management."

..."The parties concluded that the extension and development of cultural relations plays an important role in strengthening the friendship between the Romanian and Hungarian nations, mutual understanding and confidence and in appreciating their ongoing historical traditions."

..."The parties agreed to further extend their cooperation in the fields of ideology, culture, education, science and arts in order to augment Romanian-Hungarian friendship and cooperation. They established the course of the work of joint committees of cultural cooperation and historians in accordance with these principles."

..."The parties noted in agreement that the existence of the Hungarian minority in the Socialist Republic of Romania and that of the Romanian minority in the People's Republic of Hungary has resulted from the centuries-long proximity, and is a significant factor in the development of the two countries' friendship."[382]

In reality, Salonta (Nagyszalonta), Satu Mare (Szatmár), Arad and Oradea (Nagyvárad) were not included in the traffic access to the border zone under the pretext that they were not prepared for mass tourism. It is laso a fact that neither the Houses of Hungarian Culture in Bucharest and Cluj Napoca nor the House of

---

[382] Forward (Elore). 1977, June 18.

161

Romanian Culture in Budapest were opened (though an agreement on the latter was signed as early as in 1947); during their operation, the Romanian Consulate in Debrecen (up to 1985) and the Hungarian Consulate in Cluj Napoca (up to 1988) played an important role in the relations between the two nations and the assistance of the Hungarians living in Romania. (It, unfortunately, included the aid through the distribution of food-parcels.)[383]

The 1977 Census and the Hungarian minority

The ten-year census in Romania took place on January 5, 1977, and it results were published during the Kádár - Ceausescu meeting. (It is a well-known fact, censuses did not provide reliable figures either in Hungary since the Dualism or in Romania after 1920.)

The following table displays the changes of Hungarian population in Transylvania, Romania after 1920:

1910	1,664,000	156,000 lived outside Transylvania
1920	1,326,000	The drop attributed to 197,000 people moving to Hungary
1930	1,554,526	- by mother tongue
	1,425,507	- by nationality
	73,000	- living outside Transylvania
1948	1,499,851	- 125,00 people moved to Hungary after 1944
	17,848	- living outside Transylvania
1956	1,656,700	- by mother tongue
	1,587,675	- by nationality
	appr. 30,000	- living outside Transylvania
1966	1,651,873	- by mother tongue
	1,619,592	- by nationality
1977	1,750,000	- by mother tongue
	1,706,874	- by nationality
	appr. 200,000	- living outside Transylvania

As the census was considered a political and not a statistical act, the figures on Hungarian nationality – as well as the other minorities – are very questionable. For example, the data do not include the group of about 80,000 Roman Catholic Csángós of Moldova. Other sources – such as János Fazekas, former secretary of the RCP CC – estimated the number of Hungarians in Moldova at 200,000. In the course of preparations for the 1976 census, a proposal was laid before the RCP Executive Committee to the effect that those who declare themselves Csángós in

---

[383] Personal communications of Transylvanian Hungarian intellectuals.

Moldova be automatically registered as Romanians. Though Birladeanu, Bodnaras, Maurer and Fazekas protested, the EC did not reject the motion.[384]

Census-takers were ordered that, in cases of mixed marriages, unless the persons concerned protested, the children should be registered as Romanians.[385] The "Csángó" issue was yet finished: local army units were reinforced during the census in Moldova and the theory that the Csángós were, and would remain Romanians, was published in scientific and popular literary works.

After they succeeded in reducing the number of Hungarians living in Romania by registering the Csángó Hungarians as Romanians, they took further advantage of the census opportunity and began to spread again the theory that the Szeklers were not Hungarians, at all therefore they had be ennumerated separately. As a reminder: Nicolae Iorga formed the doctrine of the "Romanian origin of the Szeklers"; he left no stone unturned to prove by 'scientific arguments' that the Szeklers were Hungarianized Romanians. If it had succeeded, it would have significantly reduced the number of Hungarians by deducting the 600,000 Szeklers. They failed to finish the Romanian Hungarian community off as they wished. As it is, the census figures are false, as proved by the following analysis.

It was easier to handle smaller minorities. We must recognize that every minority was treated differently and that the Romanian leadership was motivated by the most contrary facts. Jews were quietly - more noisily in the 80s - hated out of the country. The Germans were up against extremely intricate political components, too. Elements included, among other things, the traditional German-Romanian clash, the remote mother country, especially the existence of the Federal Republic of Germany (FRG), as well as the fact that, due to geographical separation, there were no, there could be no, territorial conflict between the two countries. From the late 1970s on, some 10-13,000 Germans left Romania each year.

The exodus of Hungarians resettling in Hungary began in 1973. The process rapidly gathered speed from 1977 on. It is estimated that the number of people, who due to uncertain ethnic awareness or to take advantage of declaring themselves Hungarians one day and Romanian the next, amounts to 7-800,000. It is quite typical that in mixed marriages, the party belonging to the majority nation absorbs the minority one – it is natural that their children become the members of the majority nation. It happened in Transylvania both 'during the Hungarian era' and 'during the Romanian era'.

The relevant birth rate for Hungarians: statistics registered growth by 87,000 between 1950 and 1956, 31,917 in 1956-60 and 82,216 between 1966 and 1977.

The 86-87,000 increase (5.4%) during 1956-60 and 1966-1977 seems more factual than the 31,917 growth (0.5%), far less than half the births in 1956-60. There are no adequate reasons for this stagnation. The proportion of Hungarian decreased from 9.1% to 8.5% between 1956 and 1966 and further, to 7.9%, by 1977. Károly Király, Romanian party politician of Hungarian origin, statistician

---

[384] Fazekas: A Hungarian politician ... op.cit.
[385] Related by Demény Lajos.

Zoltán Dávid of Hungary, Romanian historian Mihnea Berindei living in Paris, and Sándor Jónás, living abroad, were of the unanimous opinion that, taking an average 1% increase, the Hungarian population in Romania numbered 1,800,000 in 1970, and around 2,000,000 at the time of the 1977 census.[386] The country's population increased by 2.5 million during 11 years, between 1966 and 1977. It represents a total increase of 12.9%, i.e., 1.1% increase annually. Consequently, presuming that the increase in Hungarians' birth rate lagged a little behind the national average, an annual 1% growth, as the above-mentioned persons assumed, is realistic.[387]

Birth-rate statistics

Hungarian country-wide average differences:

Year	Hungarian	Nat'l avg.	Difference
1966	12.8%	14.3%	1.5%
1967	21.2	27.4	6.2
1968	22.9	26.7	3.8
1969	21.4	23.3	1.9
1970	19.8	21.2	1.3
1971	17.9	19.5	1.6
1972	17.4	18.8	1.4
1973	16.6	18.2	1.6
1974	18.2	20.3	2.3
1975	17.3	19.7	2.4
1976	17.1	19.5	2.4

The 'answer' to the Representatives of Hungarians in Romania: 1977

The writer Paul Goma, who was imprisoned after 1956 for expressing his sympathy with the Hungarian revolution, declared his solidarity with the Charter movement of Czechoslovakia in February 1977 and he labeled the countries of the Soviet-block: the states of the truncheon, the muzzle and corruption. (Shortly after, left Romania and immigrated to Paris.) The same year, the year of the workers' strike of the Jiu (Zsil) Valley, when a picture of a unilingual nation was projected in front of the minorities, when one could openly say that minority languages are redundant, when essential issues were raised at national and local Party meetings held in preparation of the national census – that year György Lázár (a fictitious name, hiding the well known Romanian-Hungarian Leftist Sándor

---

[386] Discrepancies exist between Transylvania's official and estimated population data.

[387] Dávid, Zoltán: Census data in the Carpathian Basin (Népszámlálási adatok a Kárpát-medencében).

Tóth, who in 1954-55, with Sári Csehi and Imre Weiszmann, summed up what the Hungarians were wishing in Romania) published a study on minority policy in which he summed up, among other things, that the situation of the minorities had turned for the worse. It was the year when several Hungarian politicians and writers – including Károly Király, Lajos Takáts, János Fazekas, Edgár Balogh and András Süto – sent their petition to Romanian Party and government leaders. In the year of change, in 1968, Károly Király, a Romanian communist politician of working-class descent, was the First Secretary of County Covasna (Kovászna). At the Party plenary session, Király spoke glowingly that all the conditions had been created in Romania for the workers to enjoy the fruits of their labor. He, as a representative of the Hungarian minority, pledged that the Hungarians in Romania would use all their efforts and powers in the construction of socialism.[388] Király's study, "The proportionate industrialization of the country is the firm basis for equality before the law"[389] was published in 1972. In it, he accepted the Party's stand that the equal rights of minorities was the equality of the right to work and of the proportionate economic development of the regions inhabited by the minorities. Király, the successful young party functionary, was expelled from political life in April of 1972. Beside his study, he kept raising his voice for the use of the Hungarian language and the restoration of Hungarian signs. Five years later, he wrote his first letter on the grievances of Hungarians and the other minorities to Ilie Verdet, the leader of the Party CC. The same year, he set pen to paper again, but the addressee was János Vincze. In his letter, Király pointed out that the activity of CHGNW was contrary to the principles that were promised by the Party Secretary-General in March of 1971. He raised his voice against the closing of Hungarian educational institutions of various levels and against the expulsion of Hungarians from offices, senior post and finally from the area of Transylvania. He declared plainly: radical assimilation and the complete lack of tolerance characterized minority policy. He did not hide the responsibility of the personality cult, either. The 'answer' to Király's petitions was a Party disciplinary action and appointment as manager of a factory far out in the countryside.

János Fazekas, over and above preventing the arrest of some 1,000 Transylvanian Hungarians in the autumn of 1956, delivered a speech in County Harghita (Hargita) - before the XI. Party Congress - in which he openly protested against the homogenization plan. He also protested against the fact that troops were deployed in the Hungarian-inhabited areas of Moldova in order to frighten the population during the national census in 1977. He wrote petitions to the Party leadership demanding the reopening of the Bolyai University of Arts and Sciences, training schools for Hungarian kindergarten teachers, teachers' colleges, vocational schools, as well as music, fine and dramatic arts schools, the teaching of minority history, the revision of textbooks, and the erasure of parts inciting national hatred - just to mention a few.

MP Lajos Takáts, former Rector of the Cluj Napoca (Kolozsvár) University, was one of leaders of HPAR before 1952, then member of the CHGNW

---

[388] County Mirror (Megyei Tükör). 1968, October 29.
[389] Ibid, 1969, June 13.

Presidium. In the spring of 1977, at a county Party meeting, he pointed out that Hungarians lived a life full of care and woe in Romania. He repeated this statement in the Party Central Committee, where he was summoned to clarify those cares. To make his enlightening sentences 'credible', Takáts, on his return home, compiled a 27-page statement (consisting of 18 points), which became known as the 'memorandum' among those in the know in Romania. In the memorandum, he clearly stated that there would be no equal rights in Romania as long as the Minorities Act of 1946 was not enacted into law. It would put an end to the situation where the minority issue could be a pawn of politics, but that those who breach the law could be brought to account and punished. He demanded the free circulation of Hungarian language journals, papers and books published in Hungary, Czechoslovakia and Yugoslavia; the expansion of TV and radio broadcasts; the increase of the circulation and quality of scientific and technical publications; the transformation of CHGNW into a group organization, like HPAR was; the establishment of a Minority Commission, to function beside the National Assembly; the transformation of the Minority Secretariats in the Ministries of Education and Arts into bodies vested with executive powers; the unfettered use of mother tongue in official and public life; the use of mother tongue in public administration where 15% of the population belong to a minority; the restoration of bilingualism; the provision of ideological training in the languages of the minorities; the increase of the circulation numbers of papers in accordance with demand; the publication of a high quality scientific periodical; the expansion of publishing activities; the admission of Hungarian experts to libraries and archives possessing Hungarian source materials and bibliographies; the revision of the anti-Hungarian parts of textbooks; an end to the practice of relocating minority intellectuals to remote, Romanian-inhabited regions.

The Takáts Memorandum seemed to achieve certain results. It can be considered a certain retreat that the Education and Training Act of 1978, as well as the Act on Healthcare, dealt with education in the languages of nationalities living together. János Fazekas had great merit in achieving it and, of course, the fact that they still tried to keep up appearances. Beside the oblique statement, i.e. equal conditions should be provided for the sons of minorities in all forms of education, the Act included the following hard facts: instruction in mother language in settlements inhabited by minorities should be assured in faculties, branches or groups in the educational units (schools). In order to obtain a command of the Romanian language, beside Romanian literature and grammar, other subjects should also be taught in Romanian; freedom of choice between Romanian and minority schools. The law enabled that entrance examinations were allowed to be taken in the language they were given; the Ministry was charged with supplying textbooks and appointing teachers in the required numbers; the Hungarian educational network included kindergartens, elementary and secondary schools, colleges, vocational schools and higher educational units in 16 counties and Bucharest.[390] The Act, like many other things, was quietly forgotten.

---

[390] Fazekas: A Hungarian politician ... op.cit.

The CHGNW National Conference: March 14-16, 1978

After the leaders of Hungarians in Romania made their positions felt, and following adequate preparations, the CHGNW was convened in the spring of 1978. The Party wanted to demonstrate two things: one, that equal rights of minorities were in exemplary order in Romania, and two, it would reject most vehemently – calling it even anti-establishment – anything that questioned the first statement. The CHGNW annual plan was published. The plan contained several targets, including the promotion of Party ideological education and the rational deployment of working forces, i.e., the national planning project. The agenda included the state of education in Romania, the "We sing to you, Romania" festival, the activity of theaters and other artistic institutions and the contribution of the Hungarian press, the Hungarian community in general, to the implementation of the Party's economic, social and cultural programs.[391] At the conference, the broaching of certain sensitive questions by the Hungarians was a delicate situation. The debates, however, were not made public. As they did 30 years earlier, the leaders of the Hungarian community once again achieved the impossible. In order to protect and preserve certain past achievements, they continued to consider the Romanian Party leadership as a partner. They thought that the CHGNW was a forum that provided publicity and protection. At the time, the proportion of Hungarians was 3.2% in the Grand National Assembly, 8.1% in the People's Council, 9.44% in municipal councils and 9.48% in town councils. The ratio of Hungarian town aldermen was 27% in County Cluj (Kolozs), 66.67% in County Covasna (Kovászna), 73.16% in County Harghita (Hargita); Hungarian municipal aldermen made up 86.49% in County Harghita (Hargita), 40.68% in County Bihar and 47.08% in County Satu Mare (Szatmár). Three thousand ensembles took part in the "We sing to you, Romania" festival in 1976-77. The six theaters and theater sections and the opera and the puppet company put on 4,200 performances in Hungarian in 1976.[392] The radio aired 2,072 hours in Hungarian (10 years earlier it was 1,500 hours) and 156 hours of TV programs were broadcast in Hungarian (it was 78 hours in the 1960s: a total of 7 hour per day were broadcast in Bucharest, Cluj Napoca (Kolozsvár) and Tirgu Mures (Marosvásárhely) stations, e.g- a 2-2.5 hour program was broadcast in Hungarian on Mondays.) Thirty-two Hungarian papers and periodicals were published; 216 books were published in Hungarian in 1975; 223 in 1976 (including brochures, decrees and propaganda materials) in 2,500,000 copies.

In his address, Nicolae Ceausescu spoke that it was a common effort, including the minorities' that achieved the goals of the five-year plan. He declared that the equal rights of the national minorities could only be assured by the general improvement of the level of civilization of the country, and it could only be achieved through the equalization of economic differences.[393] The Secretary-General admitted to some shortcomings and advised the ministries concerned to

---

[391] Forward (Elore). 1978, March 15.
[392] Ibid.
[393] Ibid.

employ qualified minority teachers and health workers to their native areas. It is worth quoting a portion of the Secretary-General's speech, "Greater attention should be paid to the proper deployment of young people in education and to their placement in counties and settlements where their mother tongues are known. It has to be encouraged, in general, that graduating students – especially teachers, but also those in health care and agriculture – should be sent back to their places of birth, and not to the other end of the county or even the country."[394] This statement raised unfounded hopes that everything would turn to the better if Nicolae Ceausescu promised - in public - the Hungarian intelligentsia of Transylvania would not be banished into other language areas. It was a long held practice that Hungarian doctors found employment in Romanian-inhabited regions and Romanian teachers worked in Szekler counties. All this, of course, continued unaltered after March 1978; despite the Secretary-General's promise, nothing changed. Ceausescu also spoke about the 'severe abuses' committed after the war against citizens of German origin. However, he fiercely refuted that anybody encouraged them to leave their native villages. "The place of our country's citizens is nowhere else but here where they were born, where their parents and ancestors lived," orated the Secretary-General in an exalted voice. He declared that Romania wanted to solve the problems in a humanitarian way. As regards marriages and family unification, he stated that "foreign reactionary circles, the press and radio stations" and "foreign temptations" were luring people to leave the country (he did not argue, as he did in 1971, that families were free to be united in Romania).[395] We don't know whether anybody posed the question to the Secretary-General during the session of the Council of Hungarian Nationality Workers on March 14, 1978: "What is his opinion on Romania issuing exit visas for 5,000-10,000 German Marks for members of the German minority and for $10,0000 US for Jews?" Citizens who have lived generations, centuries in the country; in other words, "What does he think about the fact that Romania, which is said to be building Socialism, sells (markets) its citizens speaking different languages, from different origins or of other faiths?"

There is another phenomenon worth noting: the relation between the minority issue and international affairs. On this topic, Nicolae Ceausescu said the following: "We do not allow anybody to interfere in our internal affairs. Listening to some 'men without character' and 'morally corrupt elements,' certain foreign circles slander our county and encourage our citizens to leave the county by exaggerating the problems and misinterpreting the facts." His expressions that 'one or two golden thalers, a bowl of lentils' or 'a plate of goulash' is the payment of the traitors suggested who those foreign circles might be. Leaving no doubt, a mere year after the meeting of the two Secretary-Generals of the Hungarian and Romanian Parties, Hungary was the 'tempter' and the Romanian Hungarians were the 'morally bankrupt deserters.' In addition, the writer Paul Goma also caused

---

[394] Ceausescu: Romania on the road ... vol. XV. op.cit. p. 556.
[395] Ibid.

great mischief as he was among the first, on escaping the country, to denounce the Ceausescu-regime.[396]

The minority councils also got what they deserved: they were ordered to play a more active role in the work of the Party and state bodies, and they should not become the places of isolation. The Hungarian People's Association of Romania was charged with isolationism first in 1947, then in 1953, and now the same charge was raised against the sham-organization of the Hungarians, the Council of Minority Workers. This charge was confirmed at its next session, a year later, when the Secretary-General was conspicuous with his absence and the agenda included merely the great cultural festivals.

The XIIth RCP Congress: November 19-23, 1979

If we take a look at the most important events of the year, the propaganda was similar both in content and atmosphere to the ones preceding previous Party congresses. Exceptional similarity can be traced in at least three aspects: the meeting of consumer demands in the weeks preceding the Party congress; some gestures towards the national minorities; and a shift in emphasis on results instead of the merciless scourge of the shortcomings and mistakes. Slogans were also in abundance: "The five-year plan has to be completed before schedule," "We have to take advantage of the mobilizing force of labor competitions," and "We need reduced energy consumption."

The Romanian Communist Party had 2,842,064 members on December 31, 1978. Membership increased by 142,000 in a relatively short time (the 59,000 Party organizations counted 2,700,000 members in 1957; 51% were workers, 19% peasant and 22% intellectuals). The CC session in March of 1979 inaugurated a new election system in order to more adequately represent the county Party organizations in the national leadership. As a result, unprecedented in the international Communist movement, the number of Central Committee members was increased to 450 and that of Party Committee to 45.[397]

The most important foreign political events of the year of the XII. Party Congress were the visits to Bucharest by Valery Giscard d'Estaing, Konstantin

---

[396] Ibid, p. 573.
[397] 1 member delegated to the CC after 12,000 party members, 1 alternate member delegated to the CC after 18.000 party members and the county PC representatives number 71, the capital 151.

Karamalis, Antonio Ramalho Eanes, Josif Broz Tito, Meir Vilner and the Japanese Crown Prince and Ceausescu's visits to Bulgaria, Libya, Gabon, Angola, Zambia, Mozambique, Sudan, Egypt, Syria and Spain. Included in almost all the joint statements issued were words to the effect that efforts should be increased complying with the Helsinki Accord (to end the nuclear arms race) in the interest of European and world peace, signifying Ceausescu's dedication to universal peace. At a UN conference in Manila on May 7, Ceausescu presented a 10-point plan on international relations based on equality. During his August 1 visit to the Crimean Peninsula, Leonid Brezhniev honored Ceausescu with the Lenin Order of Merit. On these visits, his uneducated wife, Elena Ceausescu, who first became a scholar and then a politician, accompanied Ceausescu. On her birthday, she was honored with the Star Order of Merit of the Socialist Republic of Romania, First Class. In its letter of praise, the Political Executive Committee of the RCP CC thanked her not only for her 40 years of revolutionary work "for the victory of the social and national ideals of the Romanian people" but also her achievements in chemistry. On July 24, in Bucharest, Comrade Dr. Elena Ceausescu, engineer and academician, accepted the Award of the Institute of Rome for her contribution to the technical and scientific development of Romania and the world.

Only one year remained in the five-year plan period. Nevertheless, the Party congress and the CC sessions were unplanned moments of reckoning. The following indices were published, covering a long period, 1950-1975, and the next five-year plan, 1981-1985: (billions of Lei)

	1950	1965	1977	1978	Planned increase in 1981-85
Industrial production	27.5	178.4	109.1	317.1	9-10%
Agricultural production	32.4	62.5	102.4	127.7	4.5-5%
Foreign trade	27.0	13.1	110.1	76.8	8.5-9.5%
Consumer goods & services			106.8		
National income (GDP)	35	146	107.6	35.3	6.7-7.4%
Social & cultural spending			106.9	46.4	
Economic investments	6.3	47.0	116.2	196.8	5.4-6.2%
Real wages					3-3.4%

Marked changes took place between 1977 and 1978: industrial production increased by seven times and investments also grew vigorously. While national income increased by four times, foreign trade and social-cultural expenses dropped back almost to half and consumer goods and services to one-third. In the meantime, a total of 166,000 apartments – or 20,000 per month – were delivered in 1978.

All reports on the Congress used the phrase that 'the participants debated' this or that issue, although it is difficult to state that it was a debate. It is more accurate to say that they "accepted the Guideline plan" for the socio-economic development of Romania for 1981-1985 and, indeed, up to 1999. They "approved the Guideline program" on technical development and energy exploration With the exception of the aged Constantin Pirvulescu – one of the last Communist veterans in Romania, who became the member of the CC in 1928 – no one dared to raise criticism for his practice of shifting the efforts and mistakes of economic policy entirely upon the population. When Pirvulescu expressed harsh and unexpected criticism, he was interrupted and led out of the Congress hall. His contemporary, Leonte Rautu (Roitman), the former head of the Romanian section of the Moscow Radio, who loyally served every directive since 1944, took a stand in the name of the illegal (pre-1944) Party members on the side Ceausescu's policies.(Rautu was only expelled later when his relatives applied for exit visas to Israel.)

The Congress did not say anything new. Expressions such as "the expansion of our own raw material and energy bases," "far reaching agrarian reform," "the utilization of the achievements of the technical-scientific revolution," "the further development of the well being of the entire nation," "Romania's active and effective participation in the international division of labor," "the continued improvement of socialist democracy," "the strengthening of the leading role of the Party," "a demographic policy that provides firm basis for the labor force" (by 1985, the country' population should reach 23.4-23.7 million and an average life-span of 71), "the increase of expenses allocated for education" and "the continued educational training" - it concerned 2 million people annually – all echoed phrases from the previous speeches of the Secretary-General.

On March 29, 1978, at the national conference of Presidents of People's Councils, Ceausescu repeated that little progress has taken place in the county planning program. "You must understand that there will be no progress in living and working conditions until the program completed," said Ceausescu. It was his answer to those who opposed his grandiose ideals (meaning that there were opponents to the program in the country) and urged the improvement of the water supply, sewage system and electricity network, as well as the construction of streets, roads and highways. Ceausescu, however, considered these issues as incidental functions of the county planning program, and would be solved by the reduction of built-up areas and the construction of multi-stored buildings. Therefore, "before 1980, we have make the final decision about the model of the 300-350 settlements we are going to transform into agrarian-industrial towns by 1990," stated the Secretary-General, adding that they actually must deal with the problems of other settlement, as well. Naturally, special attention was paid to the county planning program at the Congress, too. It seemed that the program had made no progress and failed to reach the level the Secretary-General expected.[398]

The intensifying crisis, the 7th Five-year Plan

During the elections on March 8, 1980, out of the 15,631,351 eligible voters, 15,398,443 (98.52%) voted for the slate of the Front of Socialist Democracy and Unity (Szocialista Demokrácia és Egység Frontja) and 230,011 (1.48%) voted against.

---

[398] Scinteia. 1979, November 28.

The Grand National Assembly reconfirmed Ceausescu, on March 28, 1980, in his post as the President of the Republic. At the same time, József Kovács and Ferdinánd Nagy were elected into the State Council; János Fazekas and Lajos Fazekas became members of the government, the latter as the President of the People's Council Committee.

One of the outstanding events of the year was the celebration of 'the 2050th anniversary of the establishment of the first centralized and independent Dacian state' in the Republicii (Republic) Stadium in Bucharest on July 5. Almost all of Bucharest's population participated in the event. Looking down from a bird's eye view, the participants formed spectacular pictures. In the center, of course, was the portrait of Nicolae Ceausescu. The other important event was a scientific session, entitled 'Romania's contribution to the development of universal culture and civilization' on August 7-8. The 15th International Historian Congress, with 2,000 participants from 50 countries, which was also dedicated to the 2050th anniversary of the establishment of the Dacian state, was held in Bucharest on August 10-17. The differences of opinion of the Hungarian and Romanian historian ended up in an open debate, a continuation of the dispute between Gyula Illyés and Gheorghiu Mihnea of 1978.

The five-year plan period beginning in 1981 was the main topic of the RCP CC plenary session, and the conference of the Grand National Assembly in December, as well as at the meeting of the Council of Hungarian Nationality Workers on December 26, 1980.

Three important items were on the agenda of the plenary session of the Grand National Assembly, both in December 1980 and January 1981. The first was the new economic mechanism and the body passed several resolutions: a) the extension of workers' self-government; b) the introduction of independent asset, money and hard currency management, in order to expand foreign trade and international economic cooperation; c) the utilization of county and local sources of meat, vegetable and fruit supply of the population, and the organization of its distribution. The second main point was concerned about international issues. More precisely, about praising the international politics of Nicolae Ceausescu and Romania, striving for the decrease of the nuclear arms race and freezing the UN's military budget. Huge peace demonstrations were organized all over the country in 1981. Schools, factories and workers were mobilized to present the appearance that the entire country was at a fever pitch, the fever of peace. The slogans included not only variations on the theme of 'We want a world free of weapons' but also 'Ceausescu-Peace,' designed to suggest that the party leader was a believer of peaceful solutions. Moreover, that he, and only he, could preserve peace.

The 20th Year of the Ceausescu-era

Parliamentary elections were held on March 17, 1985. The list of registered voters included 15,733,060 people, and 99.99% cast a ballot. Of those, 15,375,522 (97.73%) voted for the Front of Socialist Democracy and Unity and 356,576 voted against. The latter stated their opposition to the Ceausescu regime. A total of 369 representatives were elected: 91.4% were Romanian, 7.3% Hungarian and 1.3% German. This proportion reflected the official census figures, although, in reality, the proportion of minorities was much higher. Many declared themselves Romanian - some changed their names - in order to gain a better life and carreer.

One Hungarian, Lajos Fazekas, was elected to the Political Executive Committee of the CC, and two, Mihály Gere and József Szász, were elected as alternate members. None of the nine members of the CC Secretariat wwere Hungarian. For the first time, during the 1985 elections, several Hungarian candidates were nominated not in Transylvania but in exclusively Romanian-inhabited areas. The CC plenary session on March 26-27 re-elected Nicolae Ceausescu as President of the Republic, who accepted the insignia of office, the mace, and title of Conductor (Leader in Romanian, Führer in German).[399] The new government of Romania was formed at the March session of the Grand National Assembly; Árpád Páll represented Hungarians as one of the five vice-presidents of the State Council, which did not have a Hungarian member. Constantin Dascalescu continued to head the government and one of his ten deputies was Lajos Fazekas. Ferdinánd Nagy was the State Secretary, with ministerial rank, of the Ministry of Agriculture and Food Industry. A scientific session and cultural-artistic festivals were held on July 17-18 to celebrate the 20th anniversary of the election of Ceausescu as Secretary-General of the RCP. The festive event, entitled 'The Ceausescu-age,' was held on Republic Square, and the festivities were closed by the march of 150,000 people in folk costumes.

But Romania refused to sign the resolution of the Budapest Cultural Forum in October 1985, where, for the first time, an open and heated debate ensued concerning Romania's minority policy. For the first time, Romania's leaders were called to account on democracy and the observance of human rights. Romania, of course, called all this an intrusion into its internal affairs.[400] While the official 'representatives' of the Hungarians in Romania, who, according to the Party's invariable claims that they were represented in accordance with their numbers in Parliament and the People's Councils, the statements made at the XIII. Congress that there were no nationalities in Romania only Romanians who spoke Hungarian, German or Serbian etc., were preceded and followed by deeds, i.e., the closing down of Hungarian institutions.

When identity cards were replaced in the Szekler county of Covasna (Kovászna) in 1982, the practice of name analysis was resumed; names that were easily translatable into Romanian were arbitrarily changed. The entire editorial staff of *The Week* (A Hét) was fired. The cause: the periodical raised peripheral (Hungarian) issues and did not properly reflect the Romanian reality. In 1983, the celebration of the centenary of Transylvanian Hungarian polyhistor Károly Kós' birth was banned and the Romanians launched vicious attacks against him.[401]

Beginning with the XIII. Party Congress – which the publication of *The History of Transylvania* (Erdély története, Akadémia Publishing Office, Budapest)

---

[399] Scinteia. 1985, March 25.
[400] Budapest, 1985, October 15.
[401] The date in question is July, 1987.

only sharpened – vague hints changed to open innuendoes, accusations and slander, including such provocation as the alleged blowing-up of a Romanian statue in Sfântu Gheorghe (Sepsiszentgyörgy). Anti-Hungarian measures followed one after the other ceaselessly in 1984-85. At the order of the Ministry of Education, contracts were signed with the Hungarian freshmen of higher educational institutions, which ensured their employment outside of Transylvania after they received their diploma. On the other hand, Romanian students were attracted with various incentives to Transylvanian universities; mixed marriages were officially encouraged – and financially subsidized.[402]

Actor Árpád Visky, of the Hungarian Theater of Sfântu Gheorghe (Sepsiszentgyörgy), who was imprisoned for agitation, was released in September of 1984. However, Visky was banned from returning to acting; he was employed as an unskilled wlaborer and died soon thereafter under mysterious circumstances. (He was found hung ... was he hanged?) Ethnographer József Gazda of Cluj Napoca (Kolozsvár), who was one of the victims of the 1956-trials in Transylvania, was expelled from Moldova, where he was doing research work among the Csángó Hungarians.[403] In September of 1984, the entire graduating class of the Tirgu Mures (Marosvásárhely) Medical University were assigned to jobs in the Regat.

The re-arrangement of the collections of Transylvanian museums started in the autumn of 1984. All materials relating to minorities were removed. The aim was to arrange the materials exhibited in the museums of Miercuera-Ciuc (Csíkszereda), Orodheiu Secuiesc (Székelyudvarhely), Sfântu Gheorghe (Sepsiszentgyörgy) and in the Transylvanian Museum of Cluj Napoca (Kolozsvár) so that 30% should be of pre-10th century origin to prove the notion of Romanian continuity. For example, the entire collection of the Szekler Museum of Sfântu Gheorghe (Sepsiszentgyörgy), including the paintings of Miklós Barabás, a noted 19th century painter, was transported to Bucharest. The same with the artefacts of the Tirgu Secuiesc (Kézdivásárhely) museum. In its place, a permanent exhibit, entitled 'The Ceausescu-era' was opened. At the end of the same year, in the month of the Congress and under the pretexts that they did represent bourgeois tastes or that they were fakes, Hungarian local historical collections, folklore houses and museums were closed. The dismissal and retirement of Hungarians also started the same year. The Hungarian History and Philosophy sections of the Babes-Bolyai University were closed down and Hungarian lecturers of retirement age were discharged.[404]

Ödön Bitay, head of the Hungarian section of the Political Publishing Office, was fired because he refused to publish a monograph, edited by Mihai Fatu, containing a reies of obvious falsehoods concerning the atrocities of the Horthy-regime. Next, the Kriterion Publishing House and its manager, Géza Domokos, became the target of attacks. The last straw for the authorities was when Domokos

---

[402] Related by of Demény Lajos.

[403] It was at this time that identity documents were confiscated from the Moldavian Hungarians.

[404] Related by of Ara Kovács Attila.

protested in a letter, addressed to the Writers' Association, against the extremely anti-Semitic tone of Corneliu Vadim Tudor's book, *Saturnele*.[405] Incidentally, the anti-Semitic and anti-Hungarian Elena Ceausescu was in charge of personnel (cadre) policy in Romania.

The Minority Directorate at the Ministry of Culture was also closed. The State Secretariat of Minorities of the Ministry of Public Education shared a similar fate. The practice also changed where the Propaganda Secretary was a Hungarian in Hungarian-inhabited regions. The number of Defense and Interior Ministry employees increased ten-fold in areas inhabited by Hungarians and Szeklers, as compared with other regions of the country. In 1985, in the 20th year of the Ceausescu-era, the Hungarian language broadcast of the Tirgu Mures (Marosvásárhely) and Cluj Napoca (Kolozsvár) radios were halted, under the pretext of necessary economization, the time of the Hungarian broadcast of the central Bucharest radio was cut back to half an hour and TV broadcast was terminated. About 600 employees were dismissed, the radio tapes and archives were destroyed.

It is worth noting how Hungarian language broadcast time rose and fell:

	Radio	Television
1975	5.25 hrs.	2.42 hrs.
1981	6.54	2.69
1985	0.5	0

György Beke, the only representative of Hungarian sociography in Transylvania, was dismissed from *The Week* (A Hét). The Hungarian classic historical drama "Bánk bán" by József Katona and Ferenc Erkel's historical opera, 'Hunyadi László' were banned from Hungarian stage in Romania. From that time on, permission had to be obtained from Bucharest for every theater production. The collection of the Cluj Napoca Lapidary (Kolozsvár Lapidárium) was transported to Bucharest. Folkdance-houses, the hubs of Hungarian nationalism in the eyes of the authorities, were closed one after the other. Identity cards were taken away in several Csángó villages in order to hinder people changing residence (ed: to stop them from moving elsewhere). [The Csángós of Moldova are one of the branches of Hungarians. They speak the most archaic dialect of Hungarian. The only group that has been living in the same place for 700 years, surrounded by Romanians and, as a result, many have become Romanianized. Their religion is Roman Catholic. The Csángós have been asking the Pope to send Hungarian Roman Catholic priests for years to spread the faith in Hungarian. The Vatican keeps sending Romanian priests.]

The Hungarian population of the Zona Calatei (Kalotaszeg) and Rimetea (Torockó) regions, famous for their wealth of folk art, were sternly warned not to visit Hungary. At the same time, family members were prohibited from traveling abroad together. In spite of it, 7-8,000 Romanian citizens left Romania via Vienna

---

[405] At this time and for the first time, Chief Rabbi Moses Rosen publicly exposed the situation of the Jews. He condemned Romanian antisemitism in a similar vein at a January 1994 press conference in reference to the news that several towns want to erect statues and name streets after Antonescu. Evenimentul Zilei, 1994, January 28.

between June of 1985 and October of 1986. Also unprecedented as an act, several well-known Hungarian writers were refused visas for private or official tours abroad.

The closing down of Hungarian schools was going on at top speed all over the country. Twenty students graduated at the Hungarian Faculty of the Babes-Bolyai University of Cluj Napoca (Kolozsvár) in 1985. Although there were 29 posts vacant in Transylvania, none of them got a job in the region. Pairing a foreign language with Hungarian literature and grammar ceased in the 1984-5 academic year. In the same year, the exclusively Hungarian language schools were shut down in Cluj Napoca (Kolozsvár). Students were taught in Hungarian special classes in schools. *Numerus clausus* (restricted admission), applied in education before, was replaced with *numerus nullus*. From Oradea (Nagyvárad) to Orodheiu Secuiesc (Székelyudvarhely), senior educational directors of Hungarian origin were replaced one after the other with Romanians.

Open conflict between Hungary and Romania

Addressing the Political Executive Committee's session on January 30, 1987, Ceausescu voiced his concern and displeasure at the slow implementation of the plans: in mining, in oil (where the bulk of investments were made) and energy, where two to three times the financial and material resources had been expended than was necessary. Heavy industry, which was to manufacture machinery for the chemical industry, metallurgy and energy sectors, also fell behind plan. The Secretary-General deemed it a serious problem that exports decreased 11% in 1986 as compared to the year earlier. The main reason, he pointed out, was the substantial increase in internal consumption. If only 50% of internally consumed goods were exported, there would be no decline. The logical consequences were that rations were to be reduced even further. And so it happened. In many areas of Transylvania, people did not get even the ration-card portions of butter, egg or meat.

Austerity and continuous challenges for the surpassing of the Plan characterized 1987, the second year of the Five-year Plan period. Severe austerity was a requirement and a duty, and it was taken for granted that the severity was to be further raised. The new austerity measure was published in *Forward* (Elore) on February 8, 1987.[406] Excess energy consumption was taken very seriously (constant control was continually threatened), 1 Lei was due for every kilowatt-hour in the case of 1-5% over consumption, 2 Leis in the case of 5-10% over consumption and the consumer was given a stern warning. For natural gas use, over consumption of 1-5% brought a fine of 1,500 Lei per 1,000 m^3, and 3,000 Lei for 5-10% over consumption. The gas was disconnected if over consumption exceeded 10%.

What emerged at the Political Executive Committee of the RCP CC on July 3, 1987, was that despite all strict measures there were severe problems in agriculture. Accordingly, the country failed to meet export projections. Wheat and

---

[406] Forward (Elore). 1987, February 8.

176

barley were unharvested in several regions of the country, and all summer and fall tasks were behind schedule. Phantom enterprises, with phantom results, characterized the age. Ceausescu often visited various parts of the country, and it often transpired that a phantom plant - with machines, equipment, workers and high production figures - was built. After the Secretary-General's visit, the scenery was taken down.

In addition to increasing austerity measures, the slow implementation of large investments characterized 1987. This included the construction of the nuclear plant of Cernavoda (the Canadian contractors were not satisfied with the safety equipment, among other things), as well as the broad avenues and the Palace of the Republic (Köztársasági Palota) of Bucharest, which was designed to showcase the Ceausescu-era. However, several charming old districts, streets, monuments and churches of Bucharest were destroyed, falling victim to its construction. Workers went on strike in Brasov (Brassó) on November 15, 1987. Poor supplies, unemployment and the unscrupulous graft of the local authorities were behind the spontaneous protest. Immense forces were mobilized to suppress the strike.

Publication of *The History of Transylvania* and Reaction in Romania The Session of CHGNW: February, 1987

After several Romanian authors, such as Stefan Pascu and Ilie Ceausescu, had written historical works published in various languages, the Hungarian Academy Publishing House (Akadémia Kiadó) published a 2,000-page, three-volume historical work: *The History of Transylvania* (Erdély története), in November of 1986. That day represents a clear change of direction in relations between the two countries. The study's tone is extraordinarily moderate but it could not ignore the most blatant falsifications of history, refute them and prove the opposite by scientific methods and documents. In line with the RCP CC's resolution, passed in January, that Hungarians in Romania should also take a stand against the Hungarian historiography, a session of the Council of Hungarian Nationality Workers was convened on February 26-27, 1987. It was part of the almost year-long national campaign that followed the publication of *The History of Transylvania*. At a meetings organized for teachers, research scientists, journalists and clergymen (e.g.- the teachers of the Cluj Napoca Calvinist Theology College) the organizers and speakers of the conference unanimously described the monograph, edited by Hungarian Minister of Culture, Béla Köpeczi, as a Fascist, revisionist, revengeful and Horthy-ite work, derogatory to the Romanian people and their history. The fact that the book was banned in Romania did not trouble the authorities, and if it was found during house searches, possession was equal to capital treason. Therefore, there were only a few dozens people who were able to obtain the book legally. The atmosphere of the CHGNW meeting was as gloomy as that on December 26, 1984. Emil Bobu, Lajos Fazekas and József Szász attended the meeting, which was addressed by Mihály Gere. Many people contributed to the debate, well-known and less known ones (even a few whose identity could not be established later): editors-in-chief Gyozo Rácz of

Our Age (Korunk) and Gyozo Hajdú of the *True Word* (Igaz Szó), county Party Secretary István Rab and the President of the farming co-operative Sándor Czégé.

According to the script, every single representative of the Hungarian minority taking part in the February session took the opportunity to express "their firm conviction" that only the Romanian Communist Party could ensure total equality of rights, especially through "the implementation of those visionary programs which were determined by Nicolae Ceausescu in the five-year plan, disregarding the differences in nationalities and through the continuous increases in material and intellectual wealth." Ceausescu personally appeared at the session and called *The History of Transylvania* a "Horthyist, fascist, chauvinist, revenge-seeking compilation."[407]

Gyozo Hajdú, as was his habit, outdid the prescribed text and overacted his part. His speech was full of expressions describing his admiration and veneration of the Secretary-General. In his speech, Ceausescu was "the genius leader of the Party and the State," "the builder of modern Romania," "a valiant and heroic man," "the champion of freedom and national independence," "the hero of peace," "the symbol of present and future Romania, of equal rights and fraternity," "the legendary warrior," "our great leader," "the symbol of our unity," "the hero of world peace," "the wise leader" and "the far-sighted revolutionary" whose every idea he accepted, even that there was a common language beside (rather, above) the mother tongue, - the Romanian language - the language of that nation which established a strong state in the Carpathian basin 1,000 years before the settlement of the Hungarians.[408]

Hungarians in Romania found themselves in a difficult situation. Refusing to take part in the debate might mean that the person would lose his job, but what was a greater loss, and his privileges. Some people – well-known Hungarian scholars and intellectuals Lajos Demény and András Dancsuy, as well as worker Ferenc Bálint of Szászrégen – had the courage to remain silent. Bálint, under suspicious circumstance, fell from the window of his hotel room, shortly after the meeting.

The RCP party conference, held in December of 1987, passed a resolution, which declared: "Romania is a nation-state ... where, over the centuries, citizens of various nationalities have settled alongside the Romanian people."[409] The resolution rejected any attempt of Hungary to intervene in Romania's internal policy, under any pretext or issue, especially minority issues. Hungarian publications on dealing with Transylvania were again criticized and condemned. The party resolution of December, 1984, was confirmed, stating there was to be no more mention of minorities in Romania, only of Romanian citizens speaking Hungarian, German, etc. The 'results' of minority policy soon became apparent

---

[407] Ibid, 1987, February 28.
[408] The Week (A Hét). 1987, April 23.
[409] Forward (Elore). 1987, December,

and in a spectacular way: what remained of Hungarian institutions were eradicated.[410]

As a result of population (Romanian) resettlement into Transylvania, unemployment increased further (the number was estimated at 300-400,000, affecting mainly the young and the minorities). By way of its Army exercises in April of 1987, Romania concentrated its military demonstrations on its Western border. Through statutory procedures in July, the Hungarian, German or Serbian languages could no longer be used. The retirings and dismissal of Hungarians continued. The staff of the Teleki Library (Teleki Téka) was decreased by 17, and that of the University of Medical Sciences by 82, both in Tirgu Mures (Marosvásárhely); only one secretary of Hungarian origin was left in office at the party committee in County Harghita (Hargita); the last high school (lyceum) was closed down in Cluj Napoca (Kolozsvár), instruction in Hungarian was ended in Bucharest. If one is at all permitted to speculate on the gravity of these effects, the closing of schools threatened the very existence of Hungarians in Romania.

Before WWI, there were 25 buildings suitable for theatrical performances in Transylvania. Between the two wars, there was only one theater-company to holding performances in the small and large settlements of Transylvania. There were 6 independent Hungarian theater companies in 1947, then four. The situation improved in the years of 1956 to 1958; there were four companies – a drama, a puppet, an opera and a chamber theater – just in Cluj Napoca (Kolozsvár). There were numerous Hungarian theatrical companies in operation in 1978. During the CHGNW session in February, pointing to a Romanian section established in Sfântu Gheorghe (Sepsiszentgyörgy), the Hungarian company was terminated, and only two independent Hungarian theaters remained in operation in Cluj Napocs (Kolozsvár) and Timisoara (Temesvár) respectively. The mass exodus of Hungarian intellectuals in the following years worsened the situation. The number of actors in Cluj Napoca (Kolozsvár) dropped from 55 to 18 (a total of 100 Hungarian actors left Romania). Twelve actors played the roles of the play *Stonehearted Man's Sons* (Koszívu ember fiai, originally a novel with a great number of characters by Mór Jókai on the 1848-9 Hungarian revolution and War of Independence) in Satu Mare (Szatmár) in 1989.

Draft labor service from the Hungarian-inhabited settlements of Transylvania also began that year. From Sfântu Gheorghe (Sepsiszentgyörgy) 228 persons, from Miercuera-Ciuc (Csíkszereda) 558 and from Cluj Napoca (Kolozsvár) 1,000 – altogether 3,000 people from Transylvania – were drafted for work at the nuclear power plant at Cernavoda, for an average of 6 months. They wore uniforms, had their hair cut, lived in barracks on the construction site and daily shifts exceeded 8 hours. Hungarians accounted for 85% of the labor force at the site and convicted common criminals the remainder. In turn, Hungarian families were encouraged to resettle in Cernavoda by promises of favorable salaries and living conditions.

---

[410] In 1978, including technical publications, 26-28 were published in the Hungarian language, 9 theatres mounted Hungarian language productions, 6 of which functioned as subsidiaries.

As between the two wars, Hungarians then living in Romania believed that the nationality's very existence depended on instruction in the mother tongue; its elimination would necessarily lead to the liquidation of the nationality itself. If the learning and teaching of the mother tongue were terminated, soon there would be no need for books, magazines and theaters where the language can be used. The mother tongue of the minority would retreat to the family – and in mixed marriages it would be driven from there, also – and the deterioration of the language would became unavoidable, its oblivion inescapable. The minority would thereby lose its means to maintain a link with its history, literature, cultural memories - its past and future.

On the one hand, they were deprived of their most primary *human right*, the use of mother tongue, on the other, lacking the means (language) they could not develop self-recognition. Therefore, the destruction of its national and ethnic existence was inevitable and final. The administrative staff of Hungarian schools were reduced by 48% in February of 1987; only two of the graduating class of the Babes-Bolyai University in Cluj Napoca (Kolozsvár) secured jobs in Transylvania, but in Romanian villages. This was due to an order issued that year that no Hungarian graduating students, from secondary schools and universities, were allowed to work in Transylvania. Compiling confidential personnel reports was resumed at educational institutes in July of 1987, and it covered topics such as ethnic origin, ideology and relatives abroad. In Szeklerland, Hungarian-language classes in elementary and secondary schools were closed overnight through administrative measures. Ten years earlier, the ratio of Hungarian-Romanian schools was 3:1, the situation was reversed by the 1988-89 school year.

Territorial (county) Development and Homogenization.
The Refugee-situation

By 1988, Romania had: 1) paid off its foreign debts at the cost of immense efforts, but the promised improvement in consumer goods, etc. failed to materialize; 2) became an anachronistic phenomenon in the eyes of the world because of the trappings of the personality cult, which vied with Eastern despotism; 3) due of its refusal of reforms, had isolated itself from the developed Western countries, as well as within the Warsaw Pact; 4) the globetrotting journeys were cancelled as politicians in several Western countries felt embarrassed to admit they were taken in by the Romanian myth of independence and openness; 5) international pressure increased because of the changes in the historical-cultural-ethnic traditions of villages and towns, the ruining of the country and the elimination of the minorities; and 6) by the end of the 80's, faint signs appeared indicating that some opposition movement was germinating within the Party and the intelligentsia.

The dismissal of leaders came into fashion at the CC sessions, the moods of which were not only gloomy but frightening. The more figures were declared as confidential, the thinner the yearly statistical reports became. Figures published in Party publications were unconfirmable and, moreover, false but even there the drop in foreign trade was detectable. Other data on incomes, budget expenditures and the around-100% figures of production seem to be very 'rounded-up' - in light of knowledge of the disastrous state of the Romanian economy, even for those who were not economists.

The Fourth National Conference of the Presidents of People's Councils started on March 3, 1988 in Bucharest. Nicolae Ceausescu announced that the territorial-administrative reorganization of the country had reached its crucial phase. "In order to accomplish the harmonious socio-economic territorial and organization programs of all the counties and settlements, we have to take emphatic measures to effect county planning and organization, to execute programs confining built-up areas, modernizing our country's townships and villages. Considering that we have 900 settlements of less than 3,000 inhabitants and 290 of those have less than 2,000 inhabitants, we have to realize the establishment of bigger settlements of at least 3,000 inhabitants. The re-organization program should envision a total of 2,000 settlemets. At the same time, we have to radically decrease the present number of villages from 13,000 to, at most, 5,000-6,000.

From 1987, Romanians who settled in Transylvania received 15-30,000 Lei in aid and were actually being recruited. Sfântu Gheorghe (Sepsiszentgyörgy) was a small town of 22,000 inhabitants in 1968, and grew to 81,000 by 1981, of which 51% was Romanian. In two other Szekler towns, Orodheiu Secuiesc (Székelyudvarhely) and Tirgu Secuiesc (Kézdivásárhely), the ratio of Romanians was 20%. The construction of blocks of apartments started in the county with the largest Hungarian population, Covasna (Kovászna). It meant the destruction of 28 villages. New Romanian dwellers were moved into Tirgu Mures (Marosvásárhely) under army protection. In Cluj Napoca (Kolozsvár), the old Hungarian civil servants' district in Hoof (Pata) Street and in its vicinity was demolished. Construction went on at a great pace, and even the destruction of the St. Peter Roman Catholic Church was also considered.

Approximate figures show that 4 million Romanian were resettled in Transylvania: mainly untrained, first generation (off the land, ed.), workers. Despite the intensive construction, the Romanian infrastructure could not budge from its dismal place. (It was in last place, 25th, in Europe.) Moreover, due to the development of technology and increase in consumption - with the exception of Poland, and at the end of the 1980's, the Soviet Union - the situation grew even worse as a result of the restrictions introduced since the early 1980s. This included transport, decreased train service, restrictions on automobile use and, after catastrophic reduction of mass transit, telecommunications, education and culture. Health services stagnated and the state of housing was extremely inconsistent. Although conveniences of city flats, compared with old village houses, improved, the flat could be heated only to 12-14° Celsius and lightbulbs were limited to 25W output. Power outages were frequent at hospitals and public institutions toward the end of the decade. Although there was a program for machine production, it did not include household appliances. Citizens were unable to buy color TV sets, videos and household appliances in Romania.

Starting after the April 29, 1988 meeting of the RCP CC Political Executive Committee, Hungarian place-names again disappeared from the magazines and publications: Nagyvárad was replaced by Oradea, Nagybánya by Baia Mare, Csíkszereda by Miercuera-Ciuc, and names that could not be translated into Romanian were prohibited. The world had already been shocked by many of the events that took place in Romania, but no one expected the flood of refugees. What the assimilation policies of the liberal governments between the two world wars failed to achieve, and later that of the extreme right, and the left wing under Gheorghiu-Dej, Ceausescu managed successfully. The smaller minorities were vanishing, at least in statistics. Some 20,000 Jews remained in the country out of the 350,000-strong Jewish community in 1945. The average decrease amounted to 1,000 annually. The same has happened to the German minority. The regime's anti-minority laws affected every minority. The attacks were, however, primarily aimed at the Hungarian minority living in contiguous territories: Zona Calatei (Kalotaszeg), the Szeklerland and the Hungarians of Moldova.

The resettlements from Romania, started in the early 70's, accelerated between 1984 and 1988. 1988 and 1989 marked the years of mass exodus. According to official figures, 26,132 persons moved from Romania to Hungary between January 1, 1988 and September 30, 1989. They arrived by land or on water, however they could. The nationality distribution of the refugees was as follows: 16,805 Hungarian, 3,097 Romanian and 1,144 German. Only few Romanian citizens staying in Hungary returned, or were sent back by Hungarian authorities, to Romania. According to the report of the Office for Refugees, a further 3,000 persons arrived between September and December of that year.

During the session of the National Council of the Front for Socialist Democracy and Unity and the Grand National Assembly, more than 100,000 people held a silent demonstration on the streets of Budapest, on June 27, 1988, against the destruction of villages and the infringement of human rights. The next day, the RCP CC was convened and Nicolae Ceausescu reported that the RCP Central Committee sent a letter to the Hungarian Socialist Workers' Party (HSWP – Magyar Szocialista Munkáspárt) Central Committee in which it stated that the Hungarian press and the unforgivable statements of some Hungarian officials were responsible for the deterioration of bilateral relations. Romania considered it an intrusion into its internal affairs, which was in contradiction with the Friendship Treaty between the two countries and severely effects the two nations' relations. The demonstration provided a long awaited pretext to close the Hungarian consulate in Cluj Napoca (Kolozsvár). (The Romanian consulate in Debrecen was closed in 1985.)[411]

Following an unprecedented swift exchange of notes, General Secretaries Károly Grósz of the HSWP and Nicolae Ceausescu of RCP met in Arad on Sunday, August 28, 1988. The communiqué issued after the meeting reconfirmed that both parties expressed their wish to explore ways of strengthening friendship between the two nations and to solve emerging problems. They also emphasized that strengthening fraternity and developing bilateral relations are in the interest of the two nations, Socialism and universal peace.

---

[411] Scinteia. 1988, June 28.

The negotiations, which were urged by the Romanian Party – due, in all probability, to the ever-increasing international pressure – lasted eight hours. The Romanian Party's major wish was to have the Hungarian mass media cease its criticism of Romania and Romanian internal policy. At the same time, the Hungarians had a series of concrete requests: 1) increased economic cooperation; 2) the resumption of the work of cultural joint committees; 3) the resolution of the refugee situation; 4) the re-organization of the joint committee of historians; 5) the opening of the consulates; 6) the joint promotion of current historic traditions; 7) lifting resolutions that hindered tourism; 8) permission for a delegation of Hungarian journalist to visit Romania to study the situation first-hand; 9) the review and termination of the settlement reorganization programs in Romania; 10) high-level joint declaration on minorities.

The Romanian side agreed to the following:
1. the joint declaration on minorities would be made in a year;
2. a parliamentary and journalist delegation would be allowed to study the settlement reorganization plan first-hand;
3. the work of cultural and historian joint committees would be resumed;
4. steps would be taken for the expansion of economic relations;
5. family unification will be enabled and roadblocks removed from the path of emigration;
6. tourism will be unimpeded. Of all the promises made by the Romanian side, effectively none were kept. It was not accidental that many people had reservations about the basis of the meeting.[412]

The last days of the "Golden Era"
The XIVth RCP Congress, November 20-24, 1989 and its aftermath

The agenda of the RCP CC session of April 9, 1989 included several important topics. One, a proposal to hold the XIV. RCP Congress in the second half of November. Two, the organizational, ideological, political activity and the core policy of Party organizations were examined and evaluated. It was stressed that priority must be given to Party programs that lead to a comprehensively developed Socialist society and further progress toward Communism. Three, a review of the territorial and settlement reorganization and modernization. It was stated that these measures represented "the comprehensive and revolutionary program which was initiated by comrade Ceausescu and worked out with his definitive contribution after the RCP IX. Congress..."[413] The Political Executive Committee made a proposal to implement the necessary modifications to the territorial-administrative reorganization plan passed in March of 1988, and to work out the socio-economic development program for every village, city and county for the 5-year plan period of 1991-1995. Fourth, the PEC consented to

---

[412] The members of the Hungarian delegation did the same.
[413] Forward (Elore). 1989, April 10.

183

cancel, or to reschedule, certain debts of farming cooperatives in order to assure a better food supply for the population. Fifth, they listened to a report concerning the sanctions raised against individuals with assets derived from illegal sources

The RCP CC held a plenary session on April 12-14, 1989. The body heard reports on the results of the national economy, the state of employee bonuses, the changes in costs and prices. They proposed to cancel or reschedule some agricultural debts, examined the current state of county planning (village destructions, e.g.- the Szekler inhabited Bözödújfalu which was simply flooded. Today, only the church spire can be seen. The inhabitants were carted away). A report on the Party's activities was approved; preparations for the XIV. Congress were launched. Nicolae Ceausescu opened the plenary session with the following announcement, " ... I would like to inform the plenary session that Romania has discharged its external debts as of the end of March." According to the Secretary-General's report, Romania repaid a total of $21 billion US in debts and interests between 1975 and 1989. As a result, Romania's economy and political activity became unfettered! During its session of April 17-18, the Grand National Assembly issued a statement to the effect that Nicolae Ceausescu was to be personally credited for the repayment of debts. In addition, an act was passed to ban Romania from taking out foreign loans in the future.[414]

One of the important events of the year was the meeting of the Czechoslovak and Romanian leaders in Prague in May where the parties could take an opportunity to coordinate their stand on the latest developments in Poland and Hungary. After the CC session held at the end of June, which passed a resolution on the re-election of Nicolae Ceausescu, the General Secretary took every opportunity to express his concern that certain socialist countries had chosen the mixed economy path. He warned that it would lead to no good because it raised the threat of the return of capitalism. While the Brezhniev-doctrine, which introduced greater Soviet control both in the internal and external workings of the socialist Bloc countries, was no longer in force in the Soviet Union, it made its appearance in Romania. Ceausescu tried to convince the Warsaw Pact allies to prevent – by armed intervention, if necessary – the Solidarity Union from coming to power in Poland.

Romania's official representatives continued to represent their country as the model of peace, disarmament and independence; a society on the path to Communism. Only a very small group of Romanian intellectuals ignored the expected threat of reprisals and expressed the opinion – attempting to clean the stain cast on the nation's and their reputation – that the Romanian people want no part of the 'golden-era' and did not want to live in the country of 'famine, freezing and fear' (in Romanian: *foame, friga, frica*) any longer. The Romanian opposition had begun to toy with the idea to launch a signature-collection campaign opposing the re-election of Ceausescu and to hold a plebiscite instead. [Mrs.] Doina Cornea (her daughter was a leading figure of the Romanian émigrés, providing her with a certain amount of international protection), at the top of the opposition list, wrote several open letters to Nicolae Ceausescu. She made him personally responsible

---

[414] Ibid, 1989, April 15.

184

for the country's abysmal situation and asked for the re-establishment of the normal operation of the economy and the society, as well as stopping political persecution.

She also protested – along with author Aurel Dragos Munteanu – against the destruction of villages, i.e., 'land use rationalization.' Several people, including Communist writer Dan Desliu, blamed Ceausescu for destroying the historical past and monuments of the Romanian people. In his letter of March 10, 1989, he wrote, among other things "...every crime is committed in the name of the people: all the offenses against the laws, the Constitution, the privacy of the mail and the non-observance of international agreements."[415] Ana Bandiana, Mircea Dinescu and Geo Bogza were among the few who salvaged the reputation of Romanian writers and intellectuals, those who kept quiet or served the regime. The public, naturally, knew little about these protests. Samizdat (underground) publishing was almost unknown. Society was controlled through electronic listening and eavesdropping devices. Opposition behavior, especially in its open forms, was a infrequent occurrence in Romania. Even Mircea Dinescu admitted it in December of 1989, "Intellectuals, the writers and journalists, are today the greatest anti-Communists. But they are the same ones who yesterday led the campaign idolizing Ceausescu."[416]

Opposition inside the Party also made its voice heard from time to time: Gheorghe Apostol, János Fazekas and Alexandru Birladeanu made the first attempt in 1983, then in January of 1989, the petition signed by Apostol, Birladeanu, Silviu Bucan, Corneliu Manescu, Constantin Privulescu and Grigore Raceanu became known as the "Letter of the Six."[417] In it, the former senior officials of the RCP called upon Ceausescu to change his policy before it was too late. They blamed him for not respecting the Helsinki Accord and the country's Constitution, for ruining the peasants' lives, forcing workers to work overtime, persecuting intellectuals, violating the privacy of the mails and human rights. Also, that the planned economy was bankrupt, the country was drifting further from Europe, foreign companies were closing their Romanian branches, the nation was starving and frightened and that he had driven the minorities out of the country.[418] The Secretary-General foamed at the mouth and raved. He called the signers of the letter Soviet, US and Hungarian agents, but gave not the faintest sign of listening to the counsel and warning of 'the old comrades.'

The Congress of the Romanian Communist Party began in an atmosphere of total dissatisfaction on November 20, a Monday. With the exception of remote China and Cuba, the country had lost all its nearby supporters: Erich Honecker of the GDR and, to his great sorrow, Milos Jakes of Czechoslovakia just a few days before. All this did not deter Nicolae Ceausescu in the least and he made no

---

[415] Became widely known after the 1989 regime change.

[416] For a long time, Ana Blandiana was under a government gag order, Doina Cornea was continually harassed by the Secret Police and Mircea Dinescu was freed by Domokos Géza and his circle.

[417] Corneliu Manescu in dialog cu Lavinia Betea. „Convorbiri neterminate". Bucuresti, POLIROM, 2001. pp. 343-345.

[418] The authors were kept under house arrest by the Secret Police.

changes to the agenda of the Congress. The country's borders were closed on Saturday, November 18, and the security forces ringing the capital were reinforced. The opening ceremony was held in the Great Hall of the Palace of the Republic with 115 guests from 82 countries and 3,308 Romanian party delegates in attendance. Hungary did not send any official representatives,[419] however, General Secretary Roland Antoniewicz of the János Kádár Society greeted the Congress in a telegram and he attributed the deterioration of bilateral relations to the Hungarian 'counter-revolution' (in 1989!). It was also notable that neither the Austrian, Italian nor the Finnish Communist Parties were represented. No sooner had the Secretary-General started his speech – which lasted five and a half hours and was interrupted by thunderous ovation 115 times – a chant built in the hall: "Ceausescu will be re-elected by the XIV. Congress!"

Chapter three of the 'Report' summarized the history of the Romanian nation, starting with the establishment of the first Thracian-Dacian state 2060 years previously. He mentioned the Hungarians indirectly by referring to the wandering tribes who settled down in the land of the Romanians and "adopted the culture and way of life of the native population."[420] The Secretary-General repeatedly mentioned, anonymously, foreigners whose crime was spiriting out of the country assets worth several hundred billions of dollars between the two wars – the backwardness of Romania at the time was attributable to this – and they continued their destructive activity until the RCP IX. Congress. One of the historical achievements of that Party Congress was "to put an end to concepts and solutions alien to Socialism, and copying and kowtowing to everything foreign...", i.e., Hungarian, Jewish and Soviet.

The unified National Plan assured socio-economic development, stated the Secretary-General, adding that the per hectare grain harvest placed the country as best in the world. Official reports stated that 60 million tons of grain was harvested, but after December it became known that in fact it was only 16 million tons. Ceausescu also stated that private consumption increased, but in fact, it decreased. Law and order was strictly enforced in Romania and law was applied in all its rigors against those who "intrigue against the Socialist achievements of the Romanian people and put obstacles in the way of Romania advancing toward Socialism." It was an open threat to Party opposition, but it was also plain to that segment of the Romanian intelligentsia who accepted literary censorship, muzzling and even prison, and yet openly confronted the dictatorial power of the Ceausescu-clan.

The Secretary-General, as well as the other speakers, catalogued the "outstanding achievements of the golden-era" for hours during this Congress. But let's read how emigrant playwright Eugène Ionesco saw this period. "Poverty has been a common experience since the beginning of the 80's, and it became institutionalized. Basic commodities such as meat, sugar, oil, bread, flour, etc. are available, if at all, only for ration coupons. Even a plain potato is sold by the

[419] Tokés, László: The Siege of Timisoara, 1989 (Temesvár ostroma. 1989). Bp., HUNGAMER Ltd., 1990.   p. 264.
[420] Scinteia. 1989, November 22.

186

piece. Baby formula, if available, can only be obtained by prescription in drug stores. Everyday life is a nightmare not only because the endless queues, but also because of the frequent lapses in gas and electricity service, the poor condition of mass transportation, the draconian cutbacks in central heating in winter, the deteriorating housing, the lack of medical services and the shameful condition of intellectual (mental) hygiene. In these circumstances, it is not surprising that – according to official figures – the average lifespan is decreasing in Romania, despite the 'barbarian' birth control policy." What Ionesco described was everyday reality for the population of Romania. The only exception was the new class, the beneficiaries of the dictatorship and their representatives, whose repeated thunderous applause made this very lengthy Congress even longer.

Nicolae Ceausescu was re-elected Secretary-General on the Friday session of the Congress. One of the three children of the Ceausescu-couple, Nicu Ceausescu, who was also elected into the Central Committee, took the floor as the delegate of County Szeben and said "It is my exalted moral responsibility to express the will of Szeben County's Communists and workers to reelect comrade Nicolae Ceausescu, the glorious hero of the Nation, the determined revolutionary and ardent patriot, to the highest rank of Secretary-General of the RCP. Also, all our respects are due to comrade Elena Ceausescu for her work in making Romanian education, culture and science prosper." The Party had 3,831,000 members at the time of the XIV. Congress. No Hungarian was elected as a member of the RCP CC Political Executive Committee, and only two of the 26 alternate members were Hungarian.

In November of 1989, Ceausescu missed the last opportunity to peacefully retire from the political stage, to enjoy his remaining the years, and yield his office to a young Party leader who might espouse the ideals of reform Communism. He was obsessed with power and clung to the titles of Secretary-General, Head of State, Commander-in-Chief and Leader (*Conducator*). Moreover, those surrounding him made him believe – it was not difficult – that the bond between the Secretary-General and the Party, and the Secretary-General and the people was unfaltering and staunch. Ceausescu heard what he wanted to hear at Party congresses and CC sessions; he read in the papers what he wanted to read, i.e., that Comrade Ceausescu enjoys the deep and full trust of the entire nation, that the report of Congress - supremely important, a brilliant scientific analysis of the state of development of Romanian society, and the brave and far-reaching picture of the splendid future of the nation...

One who missed the last opportunity to save his and his family's life.

The End of the Ceausescu-era

The RCP CC Political Executive Committee held a session on December 1, Friday. Naturally, the participants took the opportunity to express their 'warm appreciation' to Ceausescu for working out the socialist development program of the country. In his directives, Ceausescu distributed the tasks for the implementation of the 1990-plan. Finally, the members of the PEC Standing Office were elected: Nicolae Ceausescu, Elena Ceausescu, Constantin Dascalescu,

Manea Manescu, Gheorghe Radulescu, Emil Bobu, Gheorghe Oprea and Ion Dincu.

By December 4, Ceausescu was in Moscow at the Warsaw Pact leaders' meeting. In a joint statement, the leaders of Bulgaria, the German Democratic Republic, Hungary, Poland and the Soviet Union admitted, that the entry of their troops into Czechoslovakia on August 21, 1968, was an intervention into the internal affairs of that country, an affront to that country's sovereignty and, therefore, a reprehensible act. This not only constituted an apology to Czechoslovakia but also provided the opportunity for Romania, rather Ceausescu himself, to deliver a speech in the defense of the Romanian model of Socialism.

Calvinist pastor László Tokés had been a thorn in the authorities' flesh for a long time and – unfortunately – the senior clergy who ardently served the government, particularly Bishop Dr. László Papp. It was Tokés who protested against not only the diminishing scope of activity of the minority churches, i.e., the Catholic, Calvinist, Lutheran and Unitarian churches, which were treated as stepchildren. He raised his voice not only for his own flock but also for the reinstitution of the rights of Hungarians and every other minority living in Romania and exposed the true nature of the Ceausescu dictatorship. And he did this not in secret but openly – writing a letter to the Romanian leaders and to well-known personalities of international politics.

In his letter of December 8, 1989, addressed to Jimmy Carter, Tokés asked the US President "to use his faith, power and political influence" in the observance of human rights - in the spirit of Helsinki - for himself, his flock and the 2 million Hungarians living in Romania.[421] In another letter written the same day to Chief Rabbi Tamás Raj of Budapest, Calvinist pastor László Tokés stated nothing less - he who has been expelled by the authorities from Timisoara (Temesvár) and whose congregation had to enter the church in a gauntlet of policemen - than "the Hungarians have become the Jews of Romania".[422] The government wanted to retaliate immediately, but the supporters of Tokés launched a sit-down strike, on December 15, Friday, to keep authorities from arresting their pastor.

And a miracle happened. The multi-cultural population of Timisoara (Temesvár) - Romanian, Hungarian, Serb, German, Jewish, Polish and Bulgarian - understood: there was far more at stake than refusing the order of a Bishop and they stood guard, arm-in-arm, around the vicarage. In the early morning hours, at 2 a.m. on December 17, a group of about 20 Securitate officers deported László Tokés and his family to the village of Menyo in County Szilágy. The sympathy demonstration of 10,000 people for Tokés suddenly changed into a protest against Ceausescu. The militia and even the army opened fire at the unarmed demonstrators. There was, of course, constant direct contact between Timisoara (Temesvár) and Bucharest. The arrogance of the government was typical.They thought that the punishment - liquidation - of the leaders, as well as the intimidation of the masses with gunfire, would solve the problem.

---

[421] Tokés: The Siege of ... op.cit. p. 264.
[422] Ibid, p. 265.

Although Ceausescu, morbidly suspicious, distrustful and loathing crowds, who made his most trusted supporters, the special units of Securitate, practice the operation of 'the last hour,' did not find the current situation dangerous and did not alter his schedule, which was made public during his visit to Moscow on December 4. President Ceausescu of Romania arrived on a so-called 'official, friendly visit' to Tehran on December 18, Monday. At the dinner given in his honor, Ceausescu tried to convince his host that Romania's economic and financial status was stable, and, as was his habit, he tried to dazzle the Iranian leaders with figures (such as a 10-fold increase in industrial production and 40-fold increase in gross domestic product) in order to provide grounds for continued, mutually beneficial, cooperation in the future. Grasping the situation, Ceausescu preached that the developed capitalist countries continued to exploit the less developed countries, like Iran and Romania.

But events at home took a tragic turn that day. Casualties in Timisoara (Temesvár) numbered over 100. Armored units surrounded Timisoara (Temesvár) and Arad. The army took control of the airport in Bucharest, and only those who held diplomatic passports were allowed to enter Romania. The country's borders essentially sealed and next day emergency measures were introduced. Despite news blackout, the world soon learned that martial law was introduced in Timisoara (Temesvár) on December 19, that soldiers who refused to obey orders to shoot were themselves shot, many people - even children - were arrested, tortured and killed. (Since then, the photos of the victims have been seen around the world.) Despite the severe reprisals, unrest spread to several other cities in Transylvania. The people of Bucharest, however, remained silent. Reinforced patrols were in the streets; public buildings and factories were ringed by armed guards.[423]

Returning home from Iran, Ceausescu alerted all available military units (army, police and the Patriotic Guard /Hazafias Gárda/) on December 20, Wednesday. In his radio speech aired that evening, he described the events in Timisoara (Temesvár) (the army sided with the demonstrators that day) as a disturbance of foreign terrorist, Fascist and hooligan elements who were encouraged by foreign spy networks. He named Budapest as the instigator and claimed that the breaking up of the territorial integrity of the Country was the ultimate aim of the plot. The same day, on December 20, the temporary Hungarian Chargé d'affaires was called into the Foreign Ministry (State Department) and was personally informed of the same. In Timisoara (Temesvár), the militia volley after volley into the demonstrating crowds. News agencies reported disturbances in Arad, Cluj Napoca (Kolozsvár), Oradea (Nagyvárad), Constanza and Buzau.

Thursday morning, December 21, people in factories and offices were ordered to march, as usual, in front of the party headquarters – the former royalpalace - in Bucharest to hold a so-called sympathy demonstration for of the Secretary-General. Everything started off as planned. The crowd had been shivering in the cold for hours, the applause prompters and slogan shouters were

---

[423] Christmas Revolution. Report on Romania (Karácsonyi forradalom. Riportkönyv Romániáról). Népszabadság Villám Books, 1989.

ready when Ceausescu finally appeared on the balcony. But he scarcely began to speak, when the crowd, instead of chanting the usual cheers and slogans, suddenly interrupted the Secretary-General with yells abusing the regime and Ceausescu himself. The television, which broadcast the event live, stopped its transmission and played music for several minutes. Many people, so many people, had waited for this moment for so long! In the meantime, Ceausescu, having composed himself inside where his security detail pulled him, returned to the balcony to continue his speech. To calm the crowd, he promised an increase in salaries and pensions and asked everybody stand on guard for socialism. Hs speech was far shorter than he originally planned. He hurled serious charges at László Tokés, "inciting revolt in Timisoara (Temesvár) and being in the service of Hungarian irredentists and imperialists."[424] His words missed their mark. On the contrary!

Finally, Bucharest stirred! People went into the streets, chanting: "Timisoara (Temesvár)!" " Freedom!" "Down with Ceausescu! Down with dictatorship!" The state emblem was ripped out of the center of flags, Ceausescu's pictures were torn apart. According to eyewitnesses, tanks appeared in the streets in late afternoon and the militia deployed armored vehicles and water cannons to disperse the crowd and "they shot at anything that moved." As in Transylvania, they did not allow the bodies to be taken away in Bucharest. The Securitate planted explosives at several points in the city. News arrived from an ever-increasing number of places that the Army had changed sides. In the early hours of December 22, an immense crowd gathered in the streets of Bucharest and started off toward Republic Square, to force Ceausescu to resign. Here and there, security forces fired into the crowd, but the Army and the militia joined the demonstrators and finally some officers of the Securitate, the circle around its future General Director, Virgil Magureanu, also. In the short time left for Ceausescu, he informed the country on the radio that "the traitorous" Minister of National Security, Vasile Milea, committed suicide. But, as it came to light later, the Securitate killed Milea. The crowd occupied the headquarters of the radio and television and for days formed a human chain around them to prevent the Securitate from re-occupying the buildings. The crowd attacked and occupied the Palace of the Republic (the former royal palace), also. The Presidential couple and their closest retinue were forced to escape by helicopter.

A few minutes before noon, local time, the two most slandered members of opposition beside László Tokés, Doina Cornea and the poet Mircea Dinescu – the latter was liberated from prison by Géza Domokos – announced that the Ceausescu-regime had been overthrown and the National Front for Salvation (Nemzeti Megmentés Frontja) had assumed power. Revolution was victorious in Romania! The Ceausescu couple was not brought to trial, rather a military Summary Court-martial sentenced them to death and executed them. The most plausible reason was to prevent them from implicating many collaborators who, as 'reform communists', took a role in political power in the following years.

---

[424] Bodor, Pál: The necessity of a state of hysteria. An unpleasant handbook on Romania (A hisztéria szükségállapota. Kellemetlen kézikönyv Romániáról). Bp., Szabad Tér Publisher, 1990. p. 286.

V. Transition Attempts

Concerning the events of 1989, which swept away the Ceausescu-clan, some speak of a popular uprising while others consider it as the first real revolution. The extremist papers *Romania Mare* and *Vatra,* however, insist that "hooligans and Hungary's agents paved the way for" the events in Timisoara (Temesvár). (This red herring phraseology recurs throughout the regime's visible deterioration.) The statement of Silviu Brucan, one of the ideologists of the Communist Party since 1945 and an opponent of Ceausescu, can be considered a dependable assessment. According to him, it was a plot of a small circle of generals and Reform Communists – in Romania 35% of the population was a Party member, while in the other 'socialist countries' it was only 15-20% – which brought about the popular revolution. The 'revolution' had 1,104 victims. It is characteristic of the state of inner turmoil that 942 persons died after December 22, 1989.

Some experts are of the opinion that the three Muscovites - Ion Iliescu, Petre Roman and Virgil Magureanu (captain of the Securitate in 1972 and later a Colonel – born Imre Asztalos) – who were not content with the Romanian version of Glasnost and Perestroika, or the lack of it, made preparations for the change in government during their regular meetings. According to recent Romanian articles, Gorbachev himself encouraged them and the KGB experts supplied them with advice. Consequently, no real change of regime took place in Romania in December of 1989 - not in the classical sense - in spite of the fact that Iliescu and his supporters were forced to accept the idea of a multi-party system on December 31. We can speak of a coalition only during the first two weeks of the operation of the Provisional Committee of the National Front for Salvation (NFS). After that, several representatives of the opposition quit and, due to a sudden halt in the implementation of the revolution's program – the establishment of a constitutional state, democratization, economic reforms, market economy and real multi-party system – street demonstrations again became a frequent occurence.

It is an important momentum that even Romanian intellectuals acknowledged, "László Tökés was, and remains, the symbol of the spark of the revolution."[425] Almost all sources agree that according to the takeover script, several attempts were made in 1988 and 1989 to remove the Ceausescu-clan from power. The second last attempt was the XIV. Party Congress.

The proclamation of the National Front for Salvation, issued on December 21, 1989, included a promise of complete equality before the law for the national minorities.[426] One of the prominent representative of the Party leadership, Károly Király, in the opposition in the 70's, was elected Deputy President of the Provisional Council. László Tökés and Géza Domokos were elected into the 145-strong Council. All anti-nationality and anti-minority laws passed in the Ceausescu-era – including the Acts on abortion, accommodation, territorial development and the system of restricted access towns – were abolished on December 28. A National Committee for Minorities was established within the

---

[425] L. Florian's article appeared in the April 14, 1990 issue of Timisoara.
[426] Romanian Hungarian Word (Romániai Magyar Szó /RMSZ/). 1989, December 24.

National Front for Salvation. The NFS communiqué of January 5, 1990, on the rights of minorities in Romania, also gave grounds for hope. They considered it necessary that: 1) the new constitution of the country should acknowledge and guarantee the individual and collective rights of national minorities; 2) an act on national minorities has to be worked out, and this act should be passed by Parliament in six months time after the enactment of the new constitution; 3) the institutional framework necessary for the enforcement of basic minority rights should be established, in line with the legal measures for the free use of the mother tongue, to support nationality culture and to protect nationality identity. For this purpose, a Ministry of Minorities also to be established.[427]

Many are of the opinion – wrongly – that the anti-Hungarian activities were begun after the speech French President Mitterand on the unfairness of the Trianon Treaty, made in Budapest on January 19, 1990. It is, however, true that after the speech, slogans like "Down with the Hungarians!" and "We won't yield Transylvania!" were chanted at mass demonstrations in Romania. Vatra, which had become an extreme nationalistic Romanian organization, and which the government tacitly acknowledged, incited the hysterical hatred of Hungarians. But this is just part of it. The Mitterand speech was merely a pretext. The chronology of the events in Romania indicates different conclusions.

In the first days of January 1990, the leaders of the Hungarian community in Romania focused their efforts to regain their schools, as soon as possible. The state of instruction in the Hungarian language was catastrophic when compared to the situation in the end of the 1940's. The following table is clear proof:[428]

	1948/49 school year	1989/90 school year
Hungarian kindergarten	447	92
Elementary, grades 1-4	1064	408
Elementary, grades 5-8	459	700
Secondary	68	None, only sections in Romanian schools
Higher education	7	

The National Minority Department of the Ministry of Public Education summed up the Hungarian and German demands for independent instruction in their mother languages, in a statement of January 10, 1990.[429] Immediately after its issuance, the Ministry's Hungarian State Secretaries took steps to fulfill these demands. Some schools were regained in Counties Harghita (Hargita) and Covasna (Kovászna) and Oradea (Nagyvárad), Satu Mare (Szatmárnémeti) and Timisoara (Temesvár). Hungarian attempts met vehement Romanian resistance in Cluj Napoca (Kolozsvár), Arad and Tirgu Mures (Marosvásárhely), even in the case of parochial schools.

The open campaign of the re-established opposition parties was motivated by anti-communism against the National Front for Salvation and by nationalism against the Hungarian community. The overt operation was complemented by the

[427] Ibid, 1990, January 5.
[428] The Week (A Hét). 1990, March 1.
[429] Romanian Hungarian Word (Romániai Magyar Szó /RMSZ/). 1990, January 14.

'whispering propaganda' of the Securitate, the officially dissolved political police. "The Hungarians want Transylvania" or "Hungarian agents are operating in the country" were recurring elements. In its statement sent to MTI (Hungarian News Agency) on January 8, 1990, the Hungarian Foreign Ministry, in the name of the Hungarian government, rejected the Romanian charge that the Hungarian government or its citizens were interfering with local affairs in Romania in an attempt to regain schools.[430] This statement preceded the Mitterand speech by 11 days. On January 25, Romanians attacked the local headquarters of the Democratic Alliance of Hungarians in Romania (DAHR) in Szászrégen, and Romanian public servants protested against the use of the Hungarian language in Marosvásárhely.[431]

VATRA – Romanians' self-defense organization in Transylvania – a Neo-fascist Movement[430]

According to some sources, Vatra Romaneasca (Romanian hearth, motherland, home, land) was formed in December of 1989,[432] but officially two months later, on January 19, 1990, in Tirgu Mures (Marosvásárhely). This organization has been organizing every important action against the non-Romanian citizens of Romania. According to Vatra, the sole masters of Romania are Romanians. By wakening a strong sense of nationalism, it wishes to protect the Romanian national character. It protects the historical rights of the Romanian nation in Transylvania. Its ultimate aim is to establish a Romanian state where no alien elements are tolerated – it was the Iron Guard's slogan between 1936 and 1946, "We want a Romania without Hungarians and Jews." The time has come, said the ideologists of Vatra, to take possession of a Transylvania where there is no longer room for Gypsies and Bozgors (a derogatory nickname for Hungarians).

Vatra considers it important that its headquarters be located in Tirgu Mures (Marosvásárhely) - to restrain Hungarian demands - as the city's vicinity to the Szeklerland makes it a critical focal point of Transylvanian Romanians. Resettlements have put an end to the 90% Hungarian majority the city used to have. Romanians think that if they rule Tirgu Mures (Marosvásárhely), they will be a step closer to controlling the Szeklerland where one-third of the Hungarian population of Romania lives in one compact block and in the majority. Vatra calls itself a cultural organization for two reasons. One, it allows it to operate in workplaces, e.g.- the armed forces, which is forbidden for political parties; two, in order to embrace the entire Romanian population. Its ranks include the representatives of the former communist regime, the Securitate, as well as judges, university professors and teachers. Like other Romanian nationalist movements

---

[430] People/Freedom (Népszabadság). 1990, January 8.
[431] Takács, Ferenc László: Romania's government politics re Hungarians, 1989, Dec. 22 – 1996, Sept. 17 (A román kormányzat magyarság politikája. 1989. December 22 - 1996. Szeptember 17). Bp., Office of Dispersed Hungarians. Manuscript. p. 6.
[432] Kincses, Elod: Black March in Tirgu Mures (Marosvásárhely fekete márciusa). Bp., Püski Publisher, 1990. pp. 18, 21.

from the 18th century onward, Vatra was also born in Transylvania and blankets the country. In short analysis, it professes the right wing ideals of the period between the two wars and rests on the existing infrastructure and mass support base of the left.

According to Octavian Ghibu, one of the leaders of Vatra, "Hungary's long developed diversionary action plan endangers the safety of the Romanian State." The Hungarians enjoyed a privileged position for a thousand years and then oppressed Romanians in the Communist era. Now their main thrust is separatism. By separatism, they mean three things: their schools; their political parties and institutions established on a nationality basis to differentiate themselves from Romanians; and ultimately to separate Transylvania from Romania. All this is typical of the Romanian mentality. In its program, the Romanian Cultural League demanded the same things at the end of the 19th century – independent schools, associations and institutions – for Romanians living in the Austro-Hungarian Monarchy. The notion that the Romanian-cultural nation is one and indissoluble, despite boundaries, was just a preparation for the ultimate goal: to unite Romanians in one country.

The expression 'separatism' and the anti-Hungarian charges connected with it first appeared in 1947, on the eve of the one-party system, when the Romanian Left began to eliminate the Hungarian institutions and infrastructure organizations, including the Hungarian People's Alliance. It was raised for the second time in 1958, after the revolution in Hungary, when, quoting Lenin, the Hungarians were charged with nursing the ideals of nationalism in their schools. Lenin was of the opinion that following the victory of the socialist revolution both society and nation would merge. Consequently, the main charge in the anti-Hungarian trials in Romania following the 1956 Revolution was Hungarian nationalism. Using separatism as the pretext, in 1958 Secreatary-General Gheorghiu-Dej worked out a 10-year plan for the elimination of the network of Hungarian schools. Actually, Nicolae Ceausescu's only contribution was to require every citizen of Romania, disregarding nationality, to speak the same language, the language of socialism.

Unbridled anti-Hungarian hatred was also behind the bloody events in Tirgu Mures (Marosvásárhely).

Part of the election campaign: Tirgu Mures, March 19, 1990

The events are well known.[433] In the run-up to the elections, a meeting between Hungarian and Romanian intellectuals, designed to promote reconciliation, was held in Budapest on March 19 (Vatra called the Romanian participants traitors). On the same day, Romanian-Hungarian clashes in Tirgu Mures (Marosvásárhely) resulted in several deaths and injuries. In order to prevent the Senatorial nomination of Elod Kincses and Smaranda Enache, several hundred armed Romanians, incited by Vatra, arrived in the city from nearby villages,

---

[433] Ibid.

which were solid bases of the extreme right-wing Iron Guard, which accepted Hitler's ideas, i.e., a Fascist organization, between the two wars.

They broke shop windows and committed other acts of vandalism while marching in the streets of the city to the radio station and the Hungarian theater. The assault on the DAHR headquarters, with some 75 people inside, began at 4 PM. The attacks were repulsed until 9 PM when the militia arrived to rescue them. But police did not provide protection for the Hungarians leaving the building and the Romanian mob kicked them and beat them with chains. Several Hungarians had to be taken to hospital. Writer András Süto suffered the most serious injuries. Discounting eyewitness testimony and film footage, the Romanian government to this day holds the Hungarians responsible. The (Lutheran) Gypsies who rushed to the aid of the Hungarians were immediately convicted. It is a pity, that the Romanian government and Vatra repeated that, "the Romanians in Tirgu Mures (Marosvásárhely) were enraged by the 10,000 nationalist provocateurs from Hungary, disguised as tourists, who arrived to celebrate March 15."

Although the aggrieved minorities – Hungarians, Jews and Gypsies – should have turned to the international courts and charged Vatra with incitement of, and instigation to, violent acts, Hungarians both at home and abroad were guilty and responsible. At least, that is the conclusion of an investigation submitted by a Reserve Major General to the Public Attorney's Office on June 15, 1990 – published by Cuvintul Liber (Szabad Szó) on November 1, 1990 – which raised the following charges against András Süto: 1) denunciation to the police; 2) inciting the public; 3) disgracing a monument; 4) criminal offence against a representative of authority; 5) incitement to commit mass murder; 6) damage of public property; 7) misuse of authority; 8) divisive acts; 9) sabotage; 10) theft of weapons and ammunition; 11) undermining state power; 12) unlawful detainment [deprivation of freedom]; and 13) unsanctioned organization of a mass meeting. Editor-in-Chief Corneliu Vadim Tudor of the *Romania Mare*, infamous for his anti-Semitic poems, proposed at a mass meeting in Tirgu Mures (Marosvásárhely) that the DAHR should be banned as a Fascist organization. (Some government party officials proposed on December 5, 1990 the arrest of Calvinist Bishop László Tokés on charges of anti-state and anti-national activities.)

The ongoing electoral rivalry the between populist parties, i.e., the opposition and the governing post-Communists of the NFS, provided the undercurrents to the events. The opposition held massive anti-government demonstrations on January 12 and February 18, 1990.[434] The government immediately adopted the opposition's extreme nationalist slogans, made concessions to their demands and forgot its former promises regarding the collective rights of minorities and the Act on Minorities. This constituted a significant step towards rapprochement between the government and the opposition. It also emboldened Vatra to take more serious steps against the Hungarians than mere demonstrations and threats. As Cluj Napoca (Kolozsvár) had already become Romanianized, Tirgu Mures (Marosvásárhely) became the main target of the Romanian attacks. Both Vatra and the local representatives of

---

[434] Adevarul. 1997, February 4.

the government openly broadcast that, "Hungary has a three-tiered plan for the detachment of Transylvania."[435]

Naturally, this slander had little to do with facts, yet the Hungarians were exposed daily to various atrocities such as break-ins to the Protestant vicarage and threats by high-ranking officers that the Army will take care of "irredentist, revisionist Horthy-ites."[436] By mid-March the molestation of Hungarians became commonplace – Calvinist parish was burgled; high-ranking Romanian officers threatened the Hungarians with having the Romanian army to wind up "irredentist, revisionist and Horthyist" Hungarians in Romania.[434] After the tragic events which left 6 dead, 3 Hungarian and 3 Romanians - as well as 180 Romanian and 88 Hungarian injured - came the Romanian allegation that the provocation of 10,000 Hungarian agents under the pretext of celebrating March 15 caused the bloody eruption.[437] Hungarian Secretary of State Gyula Horn was labeled as an 'aggressor' in the Romanian media. The events have not yet been officially investigated. Of those arrested, only 14 Hungarians and Gypsies were sentenced. The events gave an impetus to a new wave of Hungarian emigrations.[438] Some circles considered László Tokés as responsible for the events.[439] This was the starting point for the attacks against Tokés to this day.

The first election after the changeover and the DAHR

In the first half of 1990, Romania was also making preparations for the first free elections following the Communist dictatorship. Two phenomena are worth noting: one, DAHR became a potential rival of the Romanian parties; and two, unlike the period between the two wars, when the parties considered it important to win the support of the minorities, the nearly 100 parties entering the election race – apart from a few exceptions – vied with each other in anti-minority views.

It was no accident that those insignificant parties and splinter groups, most of which disappeared after the election, introduced far more radical minority policies than those parties which had broader based support. For example, the interview with Gh. Popileanu, President of the Christian Republican Party – "10 minorities: signs in 10 languages!" – sounds almost ridiculous now, but it represented exactly the attitude that the Hungarian minority expected from the majority nation. Popileanu declared that, "the minorities' place and role in society is exactly the same as the Romanians... Minorities had the right to use their own language in education, regardless of where they lived. These rights had to be guaranteed, even if there were only five children living in a given community... There is need for instruction in the mother tongue at every level of education, including universities... Then he added: I know that they wish settlement names to be written in both in Romanian and Hungarian in Transylvania. My proposal is

---

[435] Kincses: Black March ... op.cit. p. 47.
[436] Ibid, p. 59.
[437] Reporter. 1990. March, 29.
[438] Takács: Romania's government ... op.cit. p. 12.
[439] Scandal. 1990, issue 4.

that if, let's say, ten minorities are living in a settlement, then the place-name should include inscriptions in all the ten languages... Minorities – in one way or another – should have representation in the parliament, too."

The Romanian Europe Party, another small party, declared that it supported "the right of autonomy of every (social, political, ethnic, ideological, religious, etc.) minority." Radu Campeanu of the Liberal Party, as well as Adrian Motiu of the National Peasant Party called the right to cultural autonomy desirable. Radu Dimitriu of the Social Democratic Party went the farthest because he supported the reopening of the Bolyai University, as well as Hungarian art and agricultural colleges, and the establishment of a Ministry of Minorities and the enactment of the Act on minorities.

But, an election campaign with its non-committal promises is different from reality. Romanian reality and everyday life was characterized by unbridled emotions.

The Democratic Alliance of Hungarians in Romania (DAHR), established in December of 1989, representing Hungarian interests in Romania, can be considered the successor of the National Hungarian Party (1922-1938) between the wars and of the Hungarian People's Alliance (1944-1953). It encompassed the newly formed Independent Hungarian Party, the Hungarian Smallholders' Party and the Hungarian Christian Democratic Party in order to form a strong Hungarian faction in Parliament. In the course preparing for elections, it became clear that DAHR had the most comprehensive platform of all the parties in Romania, including the reform of property rights, economic decentralization, attracting foreign capital, new land law, environmental protection, infrastructure development, introduction of unemployment benefits, a tax law, the restoration of the properties of the churches, health and educational institutions, freedom of scientific research, the free establishment of companies, societies and alliances of everyday life, the general introduction of self-government. All these based on the historical examples that Hungarian society, as well as the Hungarian community in Transylvania, was poised to benefit more from the secular transition than the Romanian.

In its election program, the DAHR national presidium defined two important areas of activity. First, the establishment of a parliamentary constitutional state and civil society. A prerequisite to these is the creation of political, economic and cultural autonomy of citizens and the establishment of local self-government. Second, representing the interests of Hungarians living in Romania. DAHR stressed that the Hungarian community constitutes a part of the Romanian state but, from a historical and ethnic point of view, it is part of the Hungarian nation. It does not consider collective rights for freedom as a gift but as something that derives from universal human rights and the part of the fabric of a nation. The Romanian state has to guarantee them in its constitution, based on the UN Charter, the Universal Declaration of Human Rights, the Helsinki Accord, the Vienna post-conference, and the Alba Iulia (Gyulafehérvár) Resolutions of 1918. In part, this formed the basis for the DAHR draft act on national minorities and autonomy concept, published in November 1993.

In 1990, DAHR nominated 147 Parliamentary and 34 Senatorial candidates in 37 counties. It won 41 seats in the elections on May 20, 1990, and became the second largest party in Parliament, and the largest opposition party, yet 20% of Hungarians did not vote and another 20% cast their ballots for the National Front for Salvation. Naturally, Vatra announced immediately that it did not recognize the national scoped and organized DAHR. It was among the first to deny that a minority could establish its own party, thereby launching a series of media attacks in which several contributors exposed their ignorance by stating that political parties, organized on nationality or minority bases, do not exist anywhere in Western Europe.

DAHR's stand – already counting 700,000 members, almost half of the Romanian-Hungarian population – was to take the following actions: co-ordinate its policy with the other minority parties; refuse to enter into a government coalition; not form a coalition with the other (Romanian) opposition parties; rather, pursue a policy of 'constructive opposition.'[440]

The Petre Roman government: the anti-Hungarian attitude continues

The new government, headed by Petre Roman, was established in mid-June of 1990, Ion Iliescu remained as President. The national minorities raised severe objections against the President's speech as he failed to touch upon either culture, or the churches or the national minorities. The Democratic Forum of Germans in Romania was of the opinion that the government of the National Front for Salvation has abandoned the promises it made in December of 1989. It pointed out, as an example, the rejection of the notion that the representation of national minorities in local organizations should be proportional. In addition, the government decided that prefects (county chief administrators) and mayors would be government appointed until the local elections, much the same as the Liberal governments did between the two wars and during the Communist-era.

Since 1990 to this day, Hungarian parliamentary representatives have been expressing their opinions concerning various questions under less than satisfactory conditions. According to Romanian logic – as already expressed in Parliament in 1990 – their coherent and organized manner must be a result of treason; their institutions more than likely based on a secret, underground organization. These opinions repeatedly yield undeniable evidence of suspicion and ignorance, because since the 13th century, political life of Transylvania has been characterized by the existence of local governments, social, economic and cultural institutions and not by a strong central power. And those institutions they complained about, complain about today, irrespective of party affiliations, Hungarians in Transylvania established one, two or more centuries ago. The National Unity Party of Romanians in Transylvania (NUPRT) protested against the establishment of minority schools, claiming that their existence encourages revisionism and separatism.

---

[440] The decision of the Romanian Hungarian Democratic Alliance /RMDSZ/ at their 1990, May 29-30 session.

MPs Zsolt Szilágyi and László Zsigmond were physically assaulted in the Romanian Parliament because they demanded bilingual, Hungarian and Romanian, signs in Szeklerland. NUPRT submitted a proposal that the state should not subsidize schools for national minorities, at most only classes, and that entrance examinations to higher educational institutions should not allowed to be taken in minority languages. This last one, according to a decree passed in 1978, was possible in the Ceausescu-era. It became an endless refrain that "the Hungarians, whom the hospitable and noble Romanian people received into their homes, provided them with everything and protected them, now demand – in the name of democracy - institutions not existing anywhere in the world." Horror stories were invented to fan the flames of anti-Hungarian emotions. Some politicians and journalists recounted tales claiming that Hungarians were cutting off Romanian peasants' heads with sickles in Counties Harghita (Hargita) and Covasna (Kovászna).

Gigantic preparations were launched in August of 1990 for the celebration of the 50th anniversary of the Second Vienna Award. Many Romanians wanted to change the anniversary into the day of reckoning and revenge, claiming that the lives of Romanians in Transylvania were in danger and demanded punitive actions. According to the absurd statements published in *Romania Mare* (Greater Romania), Hungarian agents have organized and trained military units among the Hungarians in Romania in order to break away. Supposedly, half a million Hungarians were organized into 42 divisions who were prepared to carry out Budapest's order to conquer Transylvania. Although, in response to the protest that DAHR addressed to the President, in his television speech on September 14, Iliescu called upon the Romanian extremist elements for moderation but failed to firmly and explicitly condemn their anti-Hungarian attitude.

A fire broke out in a machine-tool factory in Oradea (Nagyvárad) in the dawn hours of September 3, 1990, at 5.45 a.m. During the night of September 6 to 7, an explosion shook the chemical plant of Fogaras. ROMPRESS news agency published the following statement: "in mid-August of this year, Mr. Corneliu Vadim Tudor, editor-in-chief of the publication *Romania Mare*, came into possession of a Xerox copy of information on diversion and sabotage planned by reactionary Hungarian forces in Transylvania." It is not difficult to recognize the connection between the deteriorating political and economic situation, the opinion of the West that Romania was halfway to Europe (ed: and the Third World) and increasingly anti-Hungarian feelings.

It was under these circumstances that a society of reserve officers, headed by Avram Iancu, was established in Tirgu Mures (Marosvásárhely) in October of 1990, to protect the country's borders against the Hungarians. Not coincidentally, the writer Mircea Dinescu said that "people's minds had further deformed since the change in government in December of 1989"; that this was the "great drama of Romania". Dinescu was one of the few Romanians who expected and demanded his fellow citizen to think according to European standards, and rejected the forcible assimilation, the discrimination or persecution of minorities. Both Dinescu's warning and László Tokés' open letter – "to the Romanian opposition in support of national reconciliation" – of September were in vain: as in the

Ceausescu-era, Hungarian street-signs were replaced in the towns of Transylvania and Hungarian statues were defaced. DAHR's warning was also neglected – even the government newspaper *Azi* (Today), which launched a full-out attack against Hungarian programs on radio and TV[441] – that the continued emigration of minorities, the Securitate and political police infiltrating the parties and the dictatorial trappings would cast out Romania from Europe.[442]

Romania's New Constitution

The new parliament was elected for limited term not to exceed 18 months. Its primary task was to work out the new election law and the new constitution to replace the previous one modified by Ceausescu. The draft text of the new Constitution, the so-called "Theses", prepared for the debate stated that, "Romania is a sovereign, united and indivisible nation-state," reiterating the fundamental idea of the 1923 Constitution. The "Theses" declared unconstitutional political parties and organizations formed on ethnic foundations and stated explicitly, that the language of education should be Romanian at every level. The "Theses" banned walkouts, rather strikes, for political reasons as well as minority separatism. (The Peasant Party's draft included the concession to permit instruction in the mother tongue in private and parochial schools.) At the other extreme, Vatra founder Radu Ceontea said the following in Parliament, "according to this, any MP's can express any opinion about the Constitution. For example, a Senator could request that the country be renamed the United States of Romania - and that its capital should be Budapest. National minorities should be called nations, and they could be lead by a Monarch, a Governor or a Gypsy chief. There should be many official languages so that people can only communicate with hand gestures and through mime."[443]

The acrimonious debates of Romanian and Hungarian MP's over the new draft Constitution in the spring of 1991 – according to Radu Ceonteau, every Hungarian carries a piece of rope in his pocket to hang at least one Romanian with it[444] – fortuitously radicalized the DAHR, which publicized, through its parliamentary faction, the tenets the Hungarians could not give up: Collective rights guaranteed by the new constitution; free use of the mother tongue in public administration and before the law; the restoration of teaching in the mother tongue from kindergarten to university; the proportional participation of national minorities in legislation, executive authority, the judiciary, as well as economic and social institutions; the formation and operation of minority cultural, artistic and scientific institutions; the new constitution should recognize the national minorities' languages as official languages in areas where the minorities' proportion was 20%; establish the Ministry of National Minority Affairs; pass the National Minorities Act; restore the system of schools and continued education

---

[441] Romanian Hungarian Word (Romániai Magyar Szó /RMSZ/). 1990, November 3-4.
[442] Ibid, 1990, October 15.
[443] Ibid, 1991, February 27.
[444] Cites from the paper Baricada: RMSZ, January 3, 1991.

opportunities to be guaranteed in the mother-country; regular TV and radio programming in minority languages should be aired daily.

Not coincidentally, in May – concurrent with the parliamentary debate on the constitution – Romanian television broadcast several times a film shot at a conference held in Eger, Hungary, on April 13-14, 1991, entitled "Transylvania's Past and Future." For his participation at and contribution to the conference, not only the Romanians but Transylvanian liberal (cosmopolitan) circles also criticized László Tokés. This in spite of the fact that Tokés voiced his opposition to redrawing the map of Europe. Instead, he saw the solution of the minority issue in the democratization of public life and the extension of collective rights. It was a widely held opinion that all the 60 persons who attended the conference from Romania should be expelled from the country.

Press reactions, TV commentaries and the negative statement of Parliament were all designed to establish a 'suitable atmosphere'[445] for the Constitutional Assembly. Case in point. On May 7, the topic under discussion was section 2, paragraph 4, point 6, dealing with the use of languages. Károly Király, Vice-President of the Senate, proposed the 20% minority population as the threshold for the compulsory use of the mother tongue, written as well as spoken, in public and official life, in a given area.[446] In reply, a comment was made that, "the European Parliament should understand that this is the Parliament of Romania, and we make the decisions here ... and if the Hungarians withdraw [from the plenary session], let them leave and keep going until they are on the other side of the border."[447]

Despite all the criticism, the Council of Europe extended the status of 'special observer status' to Romania in its session of January 28 to February 1, 1991. During the summer of 1991, international opinion of Romania again turned unfavorable, mainly due to the flare-up of anti-Semitism on the pages of *Romania Mare*. Yielding to external, mainly American, pressure, the government banned its publication between August 15 and September 15. In May, the paper printed an article calling for the establishment of "National Guard units for the protection of the motherland against internal enemies." These National Guards were designed to play the same role as the Iron Guard commandos of the 1930s, and Maniu's similarly called National Guards in 1944-47. At the same time, members of Right-wing political circles voiced ever more frequently the re-introduction of 'numerus clausus' policies, claiming that 60% of the State's institutions were headed by Jews, and that the press, theaters and even the government were controlled by Jews. (They were actually hinting at Petre Roman, Silviu Brucan, Adrian Severin, Dijmarescu, Teodorescu and Plesu.)[448]

Anti-Semitism reached its peak during the visit by Elie Wiesel, winner of the Nobel Prize for Literature born in Sighetu-Marmatiei (Máramarossziget), during which nationwide commemorations were held in memory of the Jewish victims in Romania. The Right was reluctant to acknowledge that 400,000 Romanian Jews

---

[445] Azi, 1991, April 19 & 22.
[446] Romanian Hungarian Word (Romániai Magyar Szó /RMSZ/). 1991, April 20.
[447] Ibid, 1991, May 7.
[448] Ibid, 1991, June 24.

were killed during the deportations. On the contrary, they spoke about a Romanian Holocaust in which outstanding personages of Romanian culture fell. The country is in danger, they emphasized, because what Chisinevski, Pauker, Rautu, Brucan and Sándor Jakab started was now continued by Teodorescu, Sora and Plesu. Their voice reached America, always sensitive to the Jewish issue, and Congress passed a resolution denouncing anti-Semitism and provocation against the national minorities in Romania. Some one hundred Romanian intellectuals joined the condemnation. However, after September 15, *Romania Mare* continued to agitate with renewed efforts. The refrain remained the same. Namely, that the Romanian people were ruled by those who accounted for 0.001% of the population, and thus the Romanians, through the actions of the Hungarians and Jews, have become a minority in their own country.

However, as Romania was in dire need of American capital, in the form of trade agreements and such, it was forced to make concessions in order to improve its image. One of these was President Iliescu's well-publicized visit to the Holocaust Museum in America in the spring of 1993. Officially, at the government level, they reject Chief Rabbi Moses Rosen's appeal for a condemnation of anti-Semitism. However, the $130 million aid received after the President's visit to America was greatly welcomed by Romanian official circles.

The draft constitution passed on November 21, 1991 was sanctioned by a plebiscite on December 8; 20.4% of the citizens voted against it. Although the constitution accepted the international agreements signed by Romania, it was never adhered to. On the other hand, all proposals curtailing the rights of minorities were enacted and scrupulously observed.

New Bill on Education

The conference in Eger presented a good excuse to backtrack on the education of national minorities. The government decree, 521/1991 V. 21, provided that the language of instruction was to be Romanian. Romanian-language classes were mandatory where minorities lived, even if the number of pupils enrolled was under ten. Hungarian could only be used as an 'auxiliary,' or 'explanatory,' language. Organizing kindergarten groups and classes in elementary and secondary schools for minorities was allowed. However, instruction in lyceums and vocational training was not included in the draft bill. It meant that 18 Hungarian lyceums in Romania found themselves outside the law. The Educational Superintendant of County Cluj (Kolozs) passed a decision in September that Romanian classes had to be offered in three Hungarian parochial schools in Cluj Napocs (Kolozsvár) in the 1991/92 school year. In protest, the pupils, teachers and parents formed a human chain around the schools. One argument they employed was the fact that Russian and Romanian schools were separated in Bessarabia.

The use of mother tongue has always been a very sensitive issue among Hungarians – the state-creating nation of the past, now in the minority in Romania – always proclaiming: *a nation lives in its language!* If it is deprived of its language, its national existence will become endangered. The need for instruction in the mother tongue and – although covertly – for cultural autonomy (TV and radio broadcast, book publishing, press, theaters, museums and cultural societies, etc.) were already defined in the years of dictatorship, and – although greatly limited – were guaranteed until the beginning of the 1980s.

To reiterate, there were 3,000 educational entities in operation in Transylvania in 1918, at the time of the handover, which fell to under 1,000 between the two world wars. Except for seminaries, teachers' colleges and art schools, all Hungarian higher educational institutions were taken away. Until 1958, the number of Hungarian elementary, secondary and vocational and higher educational schools numbered around 2,000. For example, there were 7 universities and colleges in operation in 1947. The cutbacks in education was begun in 1958, under the pretext of unification. In the early 70s, several new Hungarian educational facilities were opened, but at the end of the decade another wave of reductions came. Only one or two Hungarian classes were left in operation in formerly independent Hungarian schools, and statistically they were registered as independent units.

From 1989 on, Hungarians are free to openly demand the restoration of their schools, including parochial schools, and the reopening of autonomous Hungarian universities, primarily the Bolyai University of Cluj Napoca (Kolozsvár). Bolyai, as the successor of the first Hungarian university in Transylvania, established by István Báthory, Prince of Transylvania and King of Poland, in the 16th century, has a very long and rich heritage. In its present form, it was opened in 1872, in some 50 buildings. The Romanian State confiscated it without compensation in 1919. After the Second Vienna Award, the Hungarian university was able to move back from Szeged to Cluj Napoca (Kolozsvár). King Mihai guaranteed, by decree in 1945, the operation of the facility – jam-packed into a couple of buildings. Nicolae Ceausescu finally closed down the Hungarian university in 1959, by unifying it with the Babes University in the days of Gheorghiu-Dej. Today, neither the Romanian intelligentsia nor the Romanian opposition support the Hungarian demand for an exclusively Hungarian-language university.

A national strike was called in protest against the new Act on Education on July 11, 1992, because the law would ban the establishment of a Hungarian private university in Cluj Napoca (Kolozsvár), and because the Mayor did not want to acknowledge that Hungarian churches owned the Báthory, Apáczai and Brassay Lyceums. The DAHR program struggled for instruction in the mother language as a means of protection of national identity. Protests were held in Cluj Napoca (Kolozsvár), Deva (Déva), Hunedoara (Vajdahunyad), Satu Mare (Szatmárnémeti), Sfântu Gheorhe (Sepsiszentgyörgy), Gheorgheni (Gyergyószentmiklós) and Tirgu Mures (Marosvásárhely).

In the 1991-92 school year, 62,616 pupils were entered in grades 1 through 4 in 80 sections of 326 schools, or 5.2% of the total number of pupils in Romania. The 4.8% Hungarian pupils registered in the 1st grade indicates a decreasing tendency. It was estimated that 23,000 Hungarian pupils attended Romanian schools. Compared to the previous year, the number of Hungarian schools increased by 43; those of grades 5 through 8 decreased by 10. There were 217 schools, 483 sections and 3,367 Hungarian grade 5-8 classes in the country. This represents 5.8% of the total grade 5-8 classrooms and represents an increase of 294 classes. The registered pupils - 71,870 children – make up 5.1% of the total 5-8 graders; 27,000 Hungarian grade 5-8 pupils were being educated in Romanian schools. The Hungarians officially make up 7% of the population (estimates run at 10-11%). Therefore, the proportion of Hungarian students educated in Hungarian vs. Romanian schools stood at 72.4% vs. 27%. As for secondary schools: Hungarian was the language of instruction in 26 Hungarian secondary schools and 110 sections. The national proportion of students taught in Hungarian increased from 4.2 to 4.6 %.

Draft on local administration and the autonomy of Szeklerland
The Stolojan government

It was the previous Roman-government that passed the State Security Act. Separatism, the most frequent charge against Hungarians, was deemed to be a seditious act. Preparations for municipal elections took to the forefront of Romania's internal politics from September 1991 on. A stalemate developed since neither the Right nor the Government's reform-communist opposition was able to attract enough support to take power. The government tried to escape the internal political crisis by sacrificing Prime Minister Petre Roman. Electrifying the situation, a trainload of striking miners from the Jiu (Zsil) Valley arrived in Bucharest in the last week of the month to protest against the deterioration of their living conditions. Concurrently with the miners' strike, Romanian televison gave wide coverage on September 23 that an emigrant Transylvanian government was formed in Budapest. That the event was a pure fabrication, there can be no doubt. Nor, that the so-called Transylvanian Emigrant Government was the brainchild of the Romanian secret service. Just as a reminder, we are in the period immediately after the anti-Gorbachov coup in Moscow at the end of August of 1991.

Simultaneously, DAHR sends greetings to the recently seceded and newly independent Moldova Republic.[449] In Parliament, they introduce a study done by the Polish Foreign Ministry, which examined the possibility of an independent Transylvania.[450] Romanian radio and television broadcast, with ample anti-Hungarian commentaries, the September 29 celebratory Mass from Alba Iulia (Gyulafehérvár) in honor of its elevation from a bishopric to an archbishopric. According to Romanian nationalists, the future directions for the secession of Transylvania from Romania will come from here.[451]

A financial expert, Theodor Stolojan, took over the office of Prime Minister on October 1. The idea of DAHR participation in the government was raised, and they would have been willing to accept ministerial and State Secretarial posts if

---

[449] Ibid, 1991, August 28.
[450] Ibid, 1991, September 10.
[451] Ibid, 1991, October 5.

democratic local self-governments and a rule of law were established. The other bombshell exploded, figuratively speaking, when the so-called Szeklerland political group of DAHR, headed by Ádám Katona, announced that it would declare the autonomy of the Szeklerland on October 19. The Romanian response was swift. On October 11-12, demands for the introduction of emergency measures in Szeklerland were demanded in Parliament; Hungarian MP's were accused of spying on October 15. A few days later, in a special session, MPs heard a 6-hour account, compiled from a 4,000-page report from a committee investigating the complaints of Romanians in Counties Harghita (Hargita) and Covasna (Kovászna), who were settled there in the Ceausescu-era and who left after December 22, 1989. This was broadcast live on TV.[452] Their voluntary leaving – their workplaces closed and jobs disappeared – was represented as the result of Hungarian persecution.

Anti-Hungarian lynch hysteria swept the country. László Tokés summed up the situation most accurately: " a scripted, vast anti-Hungarian plot is in progress." Whereas, the Hungarian community of Romania is the only nationality (see the Irish, Basques, Albanians), which still lives in minority and has never resorted to force when demanding its rights.

It was the Stolojan-government that submitted the Act on Local Administration for debate in Parliament. The Prefects would have the power to suspend decisions made by the local Councils, the Mayors, as well as county offices. (The Prefects would continue to be appointed by the government.) MP's voted by roll call on the Constitution during the last week of November. Naturally, the NFS members voted unanimously for it, and DAHR members against it. However, the fact that several Romanian MP's also voted against the Constitution and proposed the drafting of a new Constitution indicated that a new, albeit, small political group exists, following European standards.

Preparations started in November-December of 1991 for the national census on January 7, 1992, local elections, the drafting of the Hungarian-Romanian Bilateral Agreement and, in the far distance, the Parliamentary elections. According to published figures, the birth rate was declining: 4.1 per 1,000 in 1990 and 1.5 per 1,000 in 1991. One reason was the large-scale official and unofficial (illegal) emigration. During 1990, 22,000 Romanian citizens received exit visas. While 132,000 applications were submitted during that year, 141,500 applications were received during the first five months of 1991. According to preliminary estimates, Romania's population decreased by 440,000, however, official reports do not reflect this. It came as a shock that the number of Hungarians in Romania declined by 93,738, whereas in all official circles they estimate between 2 and 2.5 million Hungarians. This provides all the more justification that DAHR, the churches or other organization should conduct its own census.

The census handbook included four categories for identifying Hungarians: Hungarian, Ungur, Szekler and Csángó. DAHR recommended that everyone should 'Hungarian' in both columns under the headings of 'Nationality' and 'Mother tongue.' At the same time, the handbook for the census-takers suggested

---

[452] Ibid, 1991, October 17.

that the questionnaires do not have to be filled in right on the spot and that pencils could be used – providing a great opportunity for fraud! Worries about cheating and manipulation proved to be well founded. A great number of shady practices were found and reported by the local press. Although DAHR announced that it would take a census with the assistance of the Churches, it has not been held yet. (Another census took place in 2002. By that time – within 10 years – Romania's total population decreased by one million, and the number of Hungarians declined by almost 200,000.)

The year of elections: 1992

The publication of the Harghita-Covasna (Hargita-Kovászna) report, which examined the complaints of 5,000 Romanians who were "bodily threatened and expelled from Szeklerland" began the coordinated slander campaign launched against László Tökés. The memorandum of the Romanian Foreign Ministry of February 23, criticizing (Hungarian Minister of Defense) Lajos Für's speech, delivered in Miskolc on the 14th, and the interview with Géza Entz, published in Magyar Hírlap on the 19th of the same month, was aimed at turning public opinion against Hungarians in Romania. Romanian society was also reminded, on the eve of the elections, not to forget point number 8 of the so-called Timisoara Manifesto (Temesvár Kiáltvány), which excluded the members of the old administration and the Securitate from public life. After these events, i.e., the forging ahead of the extremism on one hand and reminders of the rule of law, on the other, came the municipal elections that were meant to establish a new social and administrative structure in Romania. In the first round of elections, 21% of 16,404,149 citizens exercised their right to vote. Of the 40,178 aldermanic positions, 38,946 were filled. This yielded the following party distribution:

National Front for Salvation (NFS)	40.24%
Democratic Convention (DC)	20.77%
Agrarian Party	11.64%
Democratic Alliance of Hungarians in Romania (DAHR)	6.96%
Independents	6.23%
Romanians' National Unity Party (RNUP)	3.87%
Romania Mare	0.42%

1,340 of the 2,951 mayoral positions were filled.

NFS	57.01%
Independents	14.25%
DAHR	8.73%
DC	7.46%
Agrarian Party	5.22%
RNUP	2.34%

The incumbents garnered the majority of votes in Moldova and Muntenia (Havasalfold), as well as in Medias (Medgyes), Rupea (Kohalom), Oradea (Nagyvárad), Hétfalu and Hunedoara (Vajdahunyad), which elected government-party mayors.. The mayors of Brasov (Brassó), Fogaras, Sibiu (Nagyszeben), Deva (Déva), Arad and Sighetu-Marmatiei (Máramarossziget) were members of the DC (Democratic Convention, a coalition of 14 parties). Many were of the opinion that DC was the model of a possible government coalition of the future. DAHR elected 117 mayors.

The RNUP posted a strong showing in Transylvania, electing mayors in Cluj Napoca (Kolozsvár), Torda, Satu Mare (Szatmárnémeti), Blaj (Balázsfalva), Sighisoara (Segesvár), Reghin (Szászrégen) and Zalau (Zilah). The President of the DAHR called the elections fair in general, but pointed out some deficiencies in the Elections Act. For example, it was possible to order military personnel to other posts, as it happened in Cluj Napoca (Kolozsvár) and Oradea (Nagyvárad). This influenced voters, and changed the voter demographics. Mures (Maros) County, Tirgu Mures (Marosvásárhely) occupies a particularly significant position in Romanian politics. Official organizations refused the nominations of several Hungarian mayoral candidates. The stand of DAHR in the case of László Pokorny, one of the mayoral candidates in Tirgu Mures (Marosvásárhely), was that it was "personal carelessness but not deliberate violation of laws" - and counseled restraint.

In the second round, the NFS won 617 mayoral mandates with 38%, and the DC won 151 posts with 29.6%.

The County Council was elected in Cluj Napoca (Kolozsvár), the capital of Transylvania, in early April. The party distribution of the 45 council posts was as follows: Romanians' National Unity Party 14 seats, National Front for Salvation 10 seats, DAHR 9, DC 6, the National Liberal Party, the Republican Party and the Romanian National Agrarian Party 3 seats each. The main objective of the Romanian parties, especially the right-wing ones, were Cluj Napoca (Kolozsvár), the center of Hungarian scientific and cultural life, and Tirgu Mures (Marosvásárhely), the center of the Szeklerland.

The national presidium of DAHR stated on February 17 that, despite the show of strength extremist parties spouting nationalistic and demagogic slogans, DAHR and DC both achieved satisfactory results in the elections. DAHR contributed to the DC's success with half a million votes. However, the presidium was too optimistic in evaluating the situation. To wit, it was obvious that (1) the NFS achieved a significant, but not overwhelming victory in the election of aldermen and mayors, (2) the Romanian right wing wanted to, and did, achieve success mainly in Northern Transylvania, and (3) the DC and DAHR were not able to counterbalance these two forces.[453]

After the municipal elections, it became clear that local autonomy was not guaranteed, and the operation of self-governments was hindered by the lack of its tradition in Romanian society, the continued survival of centralization, including

---

[453] Ibid, 1992, February 17.

the unequal distribution of funding. Personal contacts continued to take an important role in this (ed: it helped to know the right people).

In September 1992, came the Parliamentary and Presidential elections. Of the 180 parties and political organizations, 82 fielded candidates, among them 19 from minority groups. Some of the parties did not agree on holding both the parliamentary and presidential elections concurrently. However, political analysts figured that both wings of the Front were in favor of early elections as this would improve Iliescu's chances. The election campaign started on July 24. The Romanian opposition voiced its concern that equality was not observed in the election campaign. Since the press, the radio and television were controlled by the NFS, it had an advantage over the opposition.

In the course of the elections, certain Romanian peculiarities became evident in their actuality.

1) Iliescu and his party, the Democratic National Salvation Front (FDSN in Romanian) were elected to victory by the rural population. According to the 1990 statistical yearbook, the country's population exceeded 23 million and 11 million of them lived in the countryside. It has to be said here that the Democratic Agrarian Party, a collection of the representatives of the former agricultural party-officials, unexpectedly won more than 3% of the seats. The fact that the media, especially television, was controlled by his party - the best means to reach the countryside - contributed to Iliescu's victory.

2) The victory basically meant the success of the economic anti-reformers. Iliescu cunningly manipulated the widely known fact that the reformers' aim was personal wealth creation. The masses of peasants who lost their lands during the Communist dictatorship did not support this. Iliescu and his party were still able to make people believe that they could stop inflation, unemployment and the economic crisis and the rise in prices.

3) A Romanian peculiarity is that the Left and the Right are almost identical. The Left often professes rightist aims, means and ideology, while the Right is quite ready to appear in the guise of the Left. The common ground for both was their hatred of foreigners.

4) Many were surprised by the noticeable inertia and absence of the youth vote. As well, the fact that the industrial workers – a decisive majority of the RCP was made up of them and of the state mandated unions – did not ally themselves with any Party, but spread their votes around.

Many could not understand why the Democratic Convention lost the elections. Although its popular leader, Emil Constantinescu, contrary to the hopes of the DAHR, only made superficial promises instead for the solution of the minority issue, won a majority of votes in Transylvania while Iliescu did the same in the Regát. The reason for this was simple: Romanian nationalism won. The Romanian's National Unity Party, which was exclusively established for hindering, avoiding and eliminating the 'Hungarian subversion,' garnered votes from the DC in Transylvania.

To sum up, the winners of the election in September of 1992 were the former party faithful, the formerly outlawed Communists reestablished under the name of Socialist Labor Party, extremist forces in Transylvania and right wing nationalists.

At the same time, Reform Communists, technocrats and pro-westerners, lead by Petre Roman, showed significant strength. (Beginning with the second quarter of 1993, there began a well orchestrated, documented campaign against them - ostensibly against corruption - which received widespread media coverage.) The winning Party initially formed a minority coalition government with the support of the Romanian National Unity Party, the Greater Romania Party and the Socialist Labor Party. The RNUP officially joined the government in March of 1994, and the four parties formed an official coalition in January of 1995.

The DAHR received about 150,000 fewer votes than in the previous election. Due to the split of the NFS and RNUP, the Hungarian party dropped to fifth place in Parliament with 27 MPs and 13 Senators.

DAHR as "Umbrella over the Hungarian community", platforms and parties From internal self-determination to autonomy: 1989 - 1992

In its statement, the DAHR Provisional Executive Committee, issued on December 16, 1989, declared that it interpreted self-determination as the basis of the operation of secular society (e.g.- institutions, hospitals, universities, towns and regional self-governments) and of national equality. The document was signed by Géza Domokos, who - partly due to bad memories and partly to his habitual loyalty - always looked to the Romanian party to ascertain its mood, trying to augur what they might think. Surprised and frightened by Romanian nationalism that erupted, volcano-like, Domokos accepted that any attempt at autonomy was contrary to Romanian interests and became one of the most resolute opponents of autonomy.

That DAHR was not a unified organization became evident at its First Congress in April of 1990[454] and at its Second Congress in May of 1991.[455] Hungarian intellectuals in Romania held Géza Szocs to be too pro-Western and liberal, while Géza Domokos was considered a reform-Communist. The general opinion was that DAHR was dominated by former, now reform, Communists. One faction only demanded cultural autonomy for the Hungarians and another added administrative autonomy to their demands, while a third group – its numbers unclear – wanted to establish an independent Szekler Party. (Writer, poet Géza Szocs was an opponent of the Ceausescu regime. He and others - including Bishop László Tokés – prepared the first Transylvanian samizdat *Counterpoints* /Ellenpontok/. Géza Domokos studied in the Soviet Union, as did Iliescu, and was a Communist Party official and in the management of Kriterion publishing.)

The DAHR National Presidium and the National Council of Delegates held a joint session in Oradea (Nagyvárad) on March 28-29, 1992.[456] The political body decided to modify the statutes and to launch preparations for the Congress. They stated that the Hungarians and the Csángós had lived in the area for more than a thousand years and consider themselves Romanian citizens, but as a community,

---

[454] RMDSZ I. Congress: 1990, April 20-21.
[455] RMDSZ II. Congress: 1991, May 24-26.
[456] RMDSZ Delegates National Council /KOT/: 1992, March 28-29.

they consider themselves a state-creating constituent who should be due the same rights as the majority nation. Inherently, they consider themselves a part of the Hungarian nation and, on this basis, they wish full freedom for maintaining relations with the mother country, Hungary.

The DAHR National Presidium held its next session in Cluj Napoca (Kolozsvár) on April 9-10, 1992. It heard the report of the Platform Committee, stated that the registered goals tally with those of DAHR and that the activity of the various workshops added to the success of the Alliance's overall activity. According to MP Imre Borbély, there are basically directions in DAHR, (1) those that focused the national issue down to the free development of the individual, and (2) those wishing to guarantee collective rights. In addition – not to be mistaken for party platforms – leftist, liberal (cosmopolitan), and some moderate and radical shift could be experienced within DAHR. Going on, Imre Borbély thought that the Hungarians in Romania were in a similar situation as the Hungarians during the Reformation, i.e., the banning of the Hungarian language in public administration, suppression of national culture, assimilation or emigration of the intelligentsia and tremendous economic backwardness. The way out could be provided by national liberalism based on Christianity, i.e., Western Christianity, the fostering of national consciousness, the ideal of liberty and liberal values, and the union of political course assembled by DAHR.[457]

Two events caused a great stir in mid-summer of 1992. 1) On July 7, sentences were announced in the trial of the persons arrested in the wake of the events, which took place in Tirgu Mures (Marosvásárhely) in March of 1990. DAHR was of the opinion that the sentence of Pál Cseresznyés and his companions – exclusively Gypsies and Hungarians – unjustly received 10 year sentences and a fine of nearly one million Lei in the 'self-defensive struggle of the Hungarian population,' under paragraph 20, section (1); paragraph 174, sections (1) and (2); paragraph 176, section (1) point (a) and section (2); paragraph 21; paragraph 74, section (1), point (a); and paragraph 78 of the Mures (Maros) County Penal Code.[458]

2) Considereded as the continuation of the report of the complaints of Romanians in Szekler counties of Har-Kov(Hargita and Kovászna), Imre Pataki, Prefect of County Harghita on December 22, 1989 - where 85 % of the population are Hungarians - was relieved of his post on July 21 by Prime Ministerial Decree 389. The event was described as a provocation of the government and was followed by a mass demonstration in Miercuera-Ciuc (Csíkszereda). A proposal was put forward that, if the government neglected the wishes of the Hungarians, i.e., to have a Hungarian Prefect in the counties of Harghita and Covasna, the Hungarians should wear yellow stars from August 1st onward, as they felt themselves as disenfranchised as the Jews did during their persecution.

László Tokés, Honorary President of the Hungarian Democratic Alliance of Háromszék and Csík, put it bluntly: Ceausescu at least kept up appearances but Iliescu, aware of his power, provoked Hungarians with demagogery and cynicism,

---

[457] RMDSZ National Presidium. Cluj Napoca, 1922, April 9-10.

[458] Regarding the matter of Cseresnyés Pál, they rendered a decision on July 7, 1992.

relieving the prefects from their post. The event was also an attack on Romanian democracy. Prime Minister Stolojan upheld the decision and temporarily solved the problem by appointing two prefects, one Romanian and one Hungarian. It must be taken into consideration that prefects have a great deal of power, they have the right to review and override decisions made by aldermen and mayors.

Around this time, the Hungarian community was satisfied with the apparent changes within their ranks, the crystallization of opinions and the forces gathering around certain groups. Its members agreed in one thing: the Hungarian nation, as a community, represented an entity, that is, the union of traditions, culture, national consciousness, language and history. This entity was represented in political and other spheres by DAHR, or should be represented by DAHR in the future, as only this activity would justify its existence. It must avoid exercising dictatorial rule on Hungarians and tolerate internal opposition. Essentially, it must act like an umbrella for the Hungarians living in Romania, embracing and protecting them, moving together with them where and when necessary, while tolerating different opinions.

This was the reason that DAHR was the last one to work out a draft proposal on the self-determination of Romanian-Hungarians, even though the Hungarian, Szekler and Saxon communities in Transylvania had had social autonomy and self-government going back to the 13th century, and this would have been the most natural act. This was preceded by the Democratic Community of Hungarians in Voivodina (DCHV – Vajdasági Magyarok Demokratikus Közössége) issuing a draft on triple autonomy in April of 1992. The Hungarians in Slovakia were also quicker in announcing their program of 'self-determination for the nation and self-government for the minorities,' not to mention the demand of the Hungarians living in the Sub-Carpathian region [now part of the Ukraine] for the Special Zone of Sub-Carpathia and the autonomy of Beregovo (Beregszász). (At the commemorative ceremonies at Agyagfalva in October of 1991, in the midst of heavy police presence, Ádám Katona was successfully condemned, with Romanian help, because he dared to speak about Szekler government - and his local Hungarian compatriots disassociated themselves from him.)

The III. World Congress of Hungarians was in progress in Budapest on August 19-21, 1992, when the extremist paper *Romania Mare* published the DAHR's draft proposal for autonomy, in Romanian, on August 21.[459] Following the regular National Council of Delegates session held in Cluj Napoca (Kolozsvár), the DAHR published its Declaration on the minority issue on October 25, 1992. The participants of the session expressed their conviction that it is necessary to end the damaging practice of self-sacrifice, the subordination of nationality interests to the process of Romanian democratization. These bore no fruit so far, we may add, since the obstacles were not, are not, these but the lack of historical traditions and experience. They stated that the defining of 'new priorities' in DAHR policy was a life and death issue for the existence and future of the Hungarian community. Setting self-government as a goal on the basis of the

---

[459] Romania Mare. 1992, August 21.

right of self-determination and – later on – working out the Act on national minorities and the autonomy concept is essential.

The NCD session ended with a solemn oath-taking ceremony in St. Michael Church of Cluj Napoca, where the leaders of the DAHR and the Hungarian community took a vow that, "as a faithful Hungarian, I shall serve my people, which trusted and authorized me to represent its interests, to fight for its full equality of rights, the rights of its communities, liberty, and for its survival, the sole solid guarantee of which is internal self-determination."[460]

The Declaration of principle - the contents of which were defined by Imre Borbély as meaning that self-determination is a right to manage one's own affairs, the first step of which is cultural autonomy, then a Hungarian Council and a national (individual) census and, finally, the establishment of regional self-government - created a great stir. President Iliescu claimed that Romania was a nation-state, but that Romania pursued the most democratic minority policy. Both the Senate and the House of Representatives elected to put it on their agenda: the condemnation of the DAHR declaration.

Romanian media and Parliamentary bulletins all spoke of a agitation directed from Budapest, treason by DAHR and irredentism. Cimpeanu, the leader of the failed Liberals, said that he foresaw the treason of the Hungarians; Petre Roman spoke about a coup d'etat against the unified Romanian state. RNUP leader Ioan Govra was of the opinion that it was always the Hungarians who started the hostilities; moreover, this was a case of nothing less than Hungarian terror in Romania. A columnist of *Tineretul Liber* claimed nothing less than that Hungary was looking for support for its revisionist claims in Russia – as in the Ukraine earlier – and, as a prelude, was demanding autonomy for the Hungarians living in the neighboring countries.

Many, on both the Romanian and Hungarian sides, were convinced that Reformed Bishop László Tokés was responsible for DAHR's radicalization and that a breakup of the leadership of the Alliance would become inevitable. It was unfortunate that in November, a Cluj Napoca (Kolozsvár) daily, *Freedom* (Szabadság), published a series of articles about Hungarian politicians and public personalities, criticizing László Tokés. They reproached him for, among other things – like former MP Péter Eckstein (nee Kovács) did – that he should not have provoked the Romanians with the question of internal autonomy but instead should have submitted a compendium of the most urgent problems to President Iliescu.[461] In his open letter of mid-January, 1993, László Tokés explained that a series of actions were begun against him and some DAHR leaders, starting in November of 1992, to which the Cluj Napoca (Kolozsvár) newspaper *Freedom* (Szabadság) gave prominent place, to which the Romanian Radio Free Europe and some propaganda materials disguised as private letters joined. Éva Cs. Gyímesi held László Tokés, Géza Szocs and Imre Borbély responsible for the lack of

---

[460] Freedom (Szabadság). 1992, October 25.

[461] The attack against Tokés László began here, in the same month, in the Cluj Napoca paper Freedom (Szabadság).

internal democracy, and thus joined the Romanian opposition, which considered the three to be Hungarian secret agents.

Third DAHR Congress, Brasov (Brassó), January 15-17, 1993 [462]

Romania's greatest problem in the first half of 1993 was to improve its image, by any means, in order to win membership in the European Council; DAHR had to solve its internal problems in order to preserve its, and consequently, the Hungarian's unity, and to work out the autonomy concept. László Tokés, who declined the presidential nomination, forwarded a 6-point proposal which was unanimously accepted. The proposal included, among other things: DAHR committed itself to the 1989 revolution and the change of regime; it took point 8 of the Timisoara Manifesto (Temesvár Kiáltvány) as a guideline. The Honorary President suggested the creation of an economic council. In accordance with the last proposals, DAHR turned to the US Congress and requested the granting of the 'Most Favored Nation' status for Romania, even though it did not meet the necessary requirements.

In his speech, László Tokés stressed[463] that Romania merely paid lip service to democratization, privatization; constitutional rights and freedom of the press remained idle words. The re-arrangement and preservation of power and the survival of the old structures could be seen everywhere. The new regime made no effort to find the murderers of the victims of the 1989 revolution; the previous anti-Semitism was replaced by anti-Hungarianism. In addition, said Tokés in his speech delivered on January 15, "The vice-laden regime of pseudo-democratic, post-Communist government hallmarked with the name of Iliescu has failed to deliver revolutionary-socio-political justice. And yet, without it, there can be no talk of a real change of regime, a revolutionary renaissance and democratic development begun on new foundations. Without justice and moral rebirth, the regime remains unchanged and inward looking; a society ruined by dictatorship continues to struggle in the chains of the regime. To state the situation simply, all the miseries of our country's present transition can be directly traced back to this socio-political state. We can not hope to overcome the economic crisis as long as the supporters of the old regime - preserving the old structures, privileges and power - cling tenaciously to their positions; as long as privatization, market economy and economic prosperity are idle words and demagogery in their mouths. We can not speak of a constitutional state and democracy as long as the old representatives of Communist - those deprivers of rights - are still swagger in Parliament, are present in the government, have a grip on key jobs in the judicial branch and are even sabotaging the few democratic laws, and the Constitution itself, which the 1989 changes finally compelled."

"There will be neither pluralism, nor social reconciliation, nor stability, nor a balanced civil society as long as distrust and intimidation, caused by the secret

---

[462] RMDSZ III. congress. Brasov, 1993, January 15-17.

[463] The speech by Tokés László was given at the same place on the 15th. Romanian Hungarian Word, January 19, 1993.

police and the Communist-type of misleading mass manipulation continue to keep the nation ignorant and divided. This includes the nationwide intolerance, xenophobia, anti-minority and anti-Hungarian sentiments and awakening anti-Semitism, the scale of which is bordering on Fascism itself. By actively inciting it, or by tacit support, the present regime makes political capital for itself and distracts attention from society's real problems, trying to find support from nationalists on both extreme Right and Left. Extreme Romanian nationalism is fundamentally anti-Romanian, as it damages Romania's international image."

With regards to autonomy, the following text was included in the draft resolution: taking historical and geographical peculiarities into consideration, local and regional self-administration and individual cultural autonomy are the desirable directions and targets for the members of the Hungarian nation minority living in Romania. Personal autonomy extends to all spheres of culture, the use of the mother tongue, religion, education, social organizations and the free flow of information. The III. DAHR Congress elected Béla Markó as President and László Tokés as Honorary President. The national leadership was taken from the members of the National Council of Representatives.

On the one hand, the statement by Tokés that "a sort of ethnic cleansing was under way in Romania," and in light of the alleged Kohl-Gorbachev pact of 1990, which divided the region to new spheres of influence, on the other, and that the Hungarians of Romania were suffering repeated provocations, historical circumstances seemed to favor the representatives of self-sacrifice, the so-called "moderates", at the DAHR III. Congress in January of 1993. This reversed in the second half of the 1990's and the radicals – in Hungarian historical parlance, the rebellious 'Kuruc' – gained ascendancy.[464]

The DAHR draft bill on minorities

The DAHR Federal Representatives' Council approved and forwarded the "Draft Bill on National Minorities and Autonomous Communities" in Tirgu Mures (Marosvásárhely) on November 14, 1993. The draft consists of three sections, of 63 paragraphs.[465]

The twelve paragraphs of Chapter I, the general chapter, included the following: A definition of the concept of autonomous community, i.e., one established by a minority by its own will and on the principle of internal self-determination. This autonomy expresses itself in various forms in which a minority enforces its rights. It is the inalienable right of every national minority to define itself as an autonomous community and thereby, as a state-creating factor, personal autonomy as well as local and regional administrative autonomy on the basis of individual minority rights are the rights of an autonomous community.

Paragraph 5 states: A community which has personal autonomy has the right to self-government - including decision making and executive rights - in education, culture, public life, social activities and information.

---

[464] Borbély, Zsolt Attila: Transylvanian Hungarians (Erdélyi Magyarság). 2002, issue 50.
[465] The RMDSZ put forward their minority law proposal on November 13, 1993.

Paragraph 6 stresses: In public administrative units, where individuals of a minority or autonomous community are in the majority, they can exercise local administrative autonomy as well as regional autonomy, operating on territorial principles, in their associated units, and the minority's language can be used as the official language.

Paragraph 7 guarantees that the geographic distribution of minorities and autonomous communities must be taken into consideration in drawing the borders of administrative units and electoral districts. (The draft minority bill of the Hungarian People's Alliance, worked out in 1946, proposed that the union of territories having a 65% minority population be respected.)

Paragraph 8 says that in administrative units where a national minority and an autonomous community are in the minority, they have limited veto rights in issues concerning their identity.

The section also deals with the freedom of conducting relations with countries with which there are ethnic, religious, language and cultural ties. Also, the banning of discrimination, [forced] assimilation, changing of traditional ethnic structures of historically developed regions, deportations, the destruction of historical and cultural monuments. It also emphasizes that although the institutions of minorities enjoy state subsidies, other sources of funds – foundations, donations, etc. – are available.

Section II, paragraphs 13 to 59, deals with the general rights of national minorities and autonomous communities.

Point A. Individual minority rights include: the right to national identity, dual or multiple national ties, banning [discrimination based on] name analysis; the free use of the mother tongue in private and public life, public administration, before the law, as well as in minority associations, organizations, political parties and the educational system; fostering the mother tongue and history, exercising religion, participation in the work of non-governmental international organizations, the protection of personal data, the free choice of family and first names, the use of the mother tongue on signs, inscriptions, information sheets, religious and civil ceremonies and family holidays.

Point B. Collective rights of national minorities and autonomous communities are set out as follows: the right of preserving traditions and the choice of identity; the right of being an independent and political entity, internal self-determination, the free enforcement of one's collective identity through the various autonomies, for unimpeded contact with foreigners, having influence over public radio and television programming, being able to apply for legal remedy to state bodies or international forums if collective rights are violated, the free use of the mother tongue in place-names, institutions and street signs, etc, in regions where their population amounts to 20%.

Paragraphs 24 and 25 deal with state budget allotments, and with national and religious holidays and the use of national insignia.

Point C sums up the wishes concerning the use of the mother tongue. It includes the right of instruction / training in the mother tongue at every level of state institutions, the right of natural entities, churches, etc. to establish educational institutions; state guarantees for instruction in the mother tongue in kindergartens, elementary and secondary schools, colleges and universities, vocational schools and postgraduate institutions, the right of obtaining scientific titles / designations in the mother tongue. Where there is not the required number of students to form a class, it should be formed with only 4 students in primary and secondary schools and 7 students in institutions of higher education. The state and local public administration are to be in charge of operating state and parochial educational units, and they should contribute to the expenses of private educational institutions, also. The national minorities have the right to know the history of their mother nations, to operate their own school boards; the State must acknowledge foreign diplomas, and the majority nation has to get acquainted with the culture and history of the minority.

National minorities and autonomous communities must be treated equally in public education, scientific life and book publishing; those public administrative areas, where their proportion reaches 10%, should be declared as bi- or multi-lingual. Here, they should be able to use their mother tongue, both in speech and writing. Public institutions and street signs should be identified in two or more languages. Notices and decrees should be published in the languages of the national minorities and autonomous communities, official reports can be written in their languages and public servants of the same mother tongue or having command of their languages should be employed. (This was assured by every Romanian Constitution passed since 1948.)

Significantly, the draft bill extends the use of the mother tongue, both in speech and writing, not only in the law, judicial processes and economic life but also in health services and the armed forces, although in the latter only in private conversations and personal correspondence. (Many objected that the authors of the draft bill did not demand that minority soldiers should be trained in the region where they lived.)

Point D sums up the criteria of individual / personal autonomy. It stated that those national minorities, which determine themselves to be autonomous communities should have the right to personal autonomy. Within this scope, self-government and executive rights are due to the community in the fields of education, culture, and social and welfare activities; the autonomous community has the right to elect its own officials and to work out the statutes of its self-government.

Points E and F deal with the local self-governments of special status and regional autonomy.

Point E: Local self-governments of special status.

Paragraph 54: in those public administrative areas, where national minorities and autonomous communities are in majority, they can, on the basis of local self-government autonomy, obtain special status and the mother tongue of the given national minority and autonomous community can also be used as the official language.

216

Paragraph 55: in the self-governments of special status, the participation of persons of Romanian nationality or of other minorities should be assured.

Paragraph 56: the provisions of the European Charter on local governments are germane to the authority of self-governments of special status.

Point F: Regional Autonomy

Paragraph 57: the union of self-governments of special status is assured on the basis of local self-administrative autonomy.

Paragraph 58: in the union of self-governments, established on the basis of regional autonomy, the language of an autonomous community can be the official language.

Paragraph 59: the autonomous communities exercising regional autonomy are free to determine its own organizational and operational rules and regulations.

The most important part of Section III, entitled Closing Regulations, is concerned with the return of properties, libraries and archives expropriated from national minorities after 1945.

The defining activity of DAHR, up to 1996, was the intent to publish its proposals for the legal basis for right to autonomy of the Hungarians in Romania. The proposal to introduce the draft bill in Parliament for discussion was voted down. In February of 1993, the government established the National Minority Council, which dealt exclusively with the division of monies handed out to minority institutions and the organization of procedural conferences. In response, DAHR withdrew from the National Minority Council.[466]

Council of Europe report on Romania

The so-called "Koenig-report" was tabled in Strasbourg in mid-May, 1993. In his report on Romania's membership in the Council of Europe (CE), Friedrich König underlined that Romania should provide guarantees to the passing of the Minorities Act assuring education in the mother tongue, including the Bolyai University. Visiting the country, Max van de Stoel, former Dutch diplomat and Commissioner of the European Conference on Security and Cooperation (ECSC) in charge of minority issues, could see that political trials were in progress targeting Hungarians and Gypsies, they were constrained in the use of their mother languages and were excluded from certain jobs – like posts in the Ministries of Defense, Foreign Affairs and the Interior – since they were considered unreliable. The Commissioner also stated that police forces were significantly increased in the Szeklerland and their unlawful acts were not punished; the people were correct to speak of police terror in the region. Despite all this and in spite of the fact that Romania promised even less than Slovakia did in connection with minority and human rights, following the acceptance of the Czech Republic and Slovakia, Romania also received a green light to membership in the Council of Europe. Following a short debate, the plenary session passed a

---

[466] Takács: Romania's government ... op.cit. p. 15.

217

resolution recommending the admission of Romania to full membership of the CE. The Romanian delegation was pleased to interpret this as confirmation that Romania's foreign supporters felt that it had solved the minority issue according to European standards.

The two CE representatives, Friedrich Koenig and Gunnar Jansson - whose task it was to review twice a year to see if Romania met the CE membership requirements it undertook in October of 1993 when it became an CE member - visited Romania between March 27 and 30, 1994. In their report, they were pleased to find that Parliament ratified the European Convention on Human Rights. However, they made further proposals.[467] Romania should ratify the CE agreements on privileges and immunity, the European Charter on Self-Government, and the European Charter on Regional and Minority Languages. Furthermore, the situation in Romanian prisons was condemned and it was also urged that Romania should sign the agreements on torture, punishment and cruel and inhumane treatment.

The CE representatives also found an unsatisfactory situation in connection with an independent judiciary and a constitutional state, e.g.- the police were still organized according to a military model. They also criticized the practice of wiretapping and that the Romanian Intelligence Service (SRI – the internal intelligence) was still controlled by a parliamentary special commission and not by a politically responsible ministry. They also objected to the fact that no advancement had been achieved in the restitution of nationalized properties and that those, who were drafted into military service in foreign armies during WW II, were excluded from the War Veterans Act, which provided a number of advantages.

A long chapter of the CE representatives' report dealt with the situation of the minorities. The situation of the Hungarians had not improved, - it reads - the Prefect of Cluj Napoca (Kolozsvár) has introduced further discriminatory measures; Parliament rejected the Minority Act; the Education Act was not in accordance with Recommendation No. 1201, the addendum Protocol on Minority Rights to the Convention on Human Rights (history and geography are not taught in the languages of the minorities). The removal of signs in two and three languages is also contrary to the recommendation. Koenig and Jansson also noted the fact that vocational and medical training in the mother tongue was reduced, and that only Hungarians were still in prison in connection with the events that took place in Tirgu Mures (Marosvásárhely) in 1989 and 1990. To remedy of this observation, President Iliescu signed the clemency plea of 24 victims, including former members of the RCP PEC and a few Hungarians sentenced in the cases of 1989-90. (Pál Cseresnyés was an exception, he was freed only in 2002.)[468] Only the Orthodox Church's properties were returned and the others, including the Hungarian churches, were not. (In responding to these complaints, Secretary of State Melescanu promised the opening of the Hungarian Consulate in Cluj Napoca (Kolozsvár) and of further border-crossing points and elimination of border fees.)

---

[467] Adevarul. 1994, May 19.
[468] Romanian Hungarian Word (Romániai Magyar Szó /RMSZ/). 1994, March 25.

The report was tabled, discussed and accepted in the Political Committee of the Council of Europe's Parliamentary Representatives meeting at the end of May.[469]

Apart from expressions of good intentions, not much happened at the European Conference on Stability in Paris on May 26 and 27. The so-called Balladur-plan – which was a step backward to the Carrington-plan – caused disappointment not only to the Hungarian Foreign Minister but also in Romania, and in a broader sense, among the Hungarians living beyond the frontiers, because:

1) They were not regarded as negotiating partners, therefore their presence was deemed unnecessary;
2) The conference failed to work out a binding minority code;
3) For Hungary, it would be the same as losing the war for the third time, i.e., it would be equivalent to a forced peace treaty after a defeat.

In August of the same year, DAHR President Béla Markó informed ECSC Commissioner Max Van der Stoel that in Cluj Napoca (Kolozsvár), with a population of Hungarians over 20%, the 119-member county council had not one Hungarian member, and moreover, there were no Hungarian factory presidents and engineering directors.

Situation report from Transylvania: summer of 1994

The CE report publicized that since the European Conference on Stability, i.e., the last week of May, the news from various Transylvanian cities, like Oradea (Nagyvárad), Cluj Napoca (Kolozsvár), Tirgu Mures (Marosvásárhely) and Miercuera-Ciuc (Csíkszereda) of anti-Hungarian measures or actions proving that they were coordinated – planned – series of events, or more precisely: provocations. It cannot be considered anything but provocations when (1) the paper *Tinerama*[470] was the first to question the promotion of Tokés to the Bishopric. Then the same paper accused Bishop László Tokés of being an agent of the Hungarian Secret Service, the KGB, the CIA and the Securitate, as well, (2) the municipal authorities of Cluj Napoca (Kolozsvár) decided to begin excavations around St. Michael Church, (3) plans for raising a statue of Ion Antonescu in Marosvásárhely, and (4) for establishing an Orthodox Episcopal residence in Miercuera-Ciuc (Csíkszereda) were published. Raising Antonescu's statue was considered a provocation because his name was connected with the Romanian Holocaust affecting 400,000 Jews. It was to this that Chief Rabbi Moses Rosen referred to in his lecture given to the Jewish World Conference in the beginning of February 1994.[471]

The objectives of these provocations – and it was plainly stated – were not other than to increase tension between the ethnic groups living in Transylvania into conflicts at various points of the region, and to create a civil war atmosphere

---

[469] Ibid, 1994, June 11.
[470] Tinerama, 1994, Mai 14; Azi, 1990, Decembrie 15; Phoenix, 1991, May 21.
[471] Romanian Hungarian Word (Romániai Magyar Szó /RMSZ/). 1994, February 8.

similar to that in rump Yugoslavia. Similar to that situation, it would allow for the forcible expulsion of Hungarians – the last minority of any significant number and a state-creating element, too.[472]

Moderate Hungarian circles in Romania agreed that Tokés was right in his reasoning. He reasoned that the current situation is not related to regular four-yearly election cycle of officers within the Reformed Church. Rather, we are talking about a much more serious phenomenon. The fact that the accusations and slander are part of the continuous and ever widening propaganda campaign launched by those in power – Communist or Nationalist, as they made up almost half the Romanian legislature - with the assistance of the reorganized and reactivated Romanian Secret Service, active at home and abroad. Their targets are the representatives of democratic (Romanian) and minority parties and organizations, and their prominent representatives. (It is presumably correct that the main direction of secret service activity was Hungary.)

According to the *Romanian True Word* (Romániai Igaz Szó), the danger of renewed political and ethnic diversion was threatening Tirgu Mures (Marosvásárhely).[473] It was also generally agreed that those who had prepared the events of 'Black March of 1990' were the same who urged the erection of the Antonescu statue.

The Mures (Maros) County group of War Veterans' Alliance, named after Ion Antonescu, submitted a request to erect a 1.2-meter bronze bust – on a 1.9-meter pedestal - of the wartime Marshal along the former Gábor Bethlen Promenade (now renamed Antonescu Promenade). Marshal Antonescu, who took part in the occupation of Budapest in 1919, had no connection with the city at all. Although no official permission was granted, and in spite of protest in the city, county councils and the DAHR, they made preparation for the statue.

Mayor Gheorghe Funar of Cluj Napoca (Kolozsvár) seems full of ideas. This time, the object of his attack was the statue grouping of King Matthias. Funar's plan was to move the statue from the historical center of the city under the pretext of Roman-era excavations and exhibition. This was severely criticized throughout Transylvania. On behalf of the Association of Inter-Ethnic Dialogue, Dr. Octavian Buracu called his action such a 'provocation' that it 'endangered peace' in Transylvania and the stability of the entire country.[474] The following consequences can be drawn from Funar's newest idea:

1) It is well known that archeological excavations to date have proved that, between the Roman and the Hungarian settlement period in Romania, no evidence has been unearthed to support the theory of Dacian-Romanian continuity, i.e., that the present Romanian nation is a direct descendant of the Romans and Dacians. Therefore, it is quite obvious that the excavations were not another attempt to prove that the Romanian people have been living in Transylvania for 2,000 years as the aboriginal inhabitants and, therefore, Romania has a historical right to Transylvania. On this basis, all successor nations on the territory of the Roman

---

[472] Romania Libera. 1994, July 8.
[473] Romanian Hungarian Word (Romániai Magyar Szó /RMSZ/). 1994, June 21.
[474] Ibid, 1994, June 22.

Empire, from Great Britain to North Africa and from Spain, through Hungary, to the Lower Danube could be considered descendants of Rome.

2) The excavations of the Central Square, which would take place around the Roman Catholic Church, would accidentally endanger the building itself, damaging its foundation and structure.

3) These efforts – proving the Roman continuity and destroying the Hungarian historical character of the of the city center – would serve the covert aim, which has been mentioned before and which was not news to Hungarians or reasonable Romanians, to provoke anti-Hungarian and/or Hungarian-Romanian conflict. Analyzing the events from any point of view arrives at the same conclusion.

Concerning the attempted attack on the King Mathias statue, the DAHR Federal Coordinating Council published the following statement on June 18, 1994: "Cluj Napoca (Kolozsvár) has become the battlefield between the extremist, xenophobic forces attempting to erase our national identity and those of ethnic tolerance in the spirit of European democracy. The nationalistic policies practiced by the Mayor, which do not shrink from cultural barbarism, from sowing dissension among ethnic groups or repeated violations of law, have prepared another attack against the Mathias Rex sculptures and against the main square of Cluj Napoca (Kolozsvár), renowned throughout Europe for its aesthetic and architectural values. Based on scientifically unproven suppositions, he [mayor Funar] has ordered the digging-up of the Main Square of our treasured city and under this cover of manipulative politics is endangering one of our national treasures, the statue by János Fadrusz, one of Europe's five most famous equestrian statues. The excavation plans are not based on scientific reasons but on the location of the statue. The center of the ancient Roman settlement is not located under the statue. The planned excavations are designed to provide further pretexts for changing the characteristic features of the city and for the removal of the Matthias-statue."[475] Emil Constantinescu protested against Funar's idea - the excavations in Cluj Napoca (Kolozsvár) - in the name of the Democratic Convention.[476]

The events unequivocally prove that Romania had again gained an advantageous position (over Hungary) with its membership in the Council of Europe (CE). Many regretted that (1) the EU placed confidence in Romania before it met requirements, (2) the representative of the Hungarian government did not veto it, and (3) not only did national minorities find themselves at a disadvantage but the CE also lost in stature and started down a road to become another irrelevant organization. On the other hand, Romania (1) seems to care ever less for appearances, (2) discriminates even more against national minorities, and (3) at state and government, indeed every official, level tacitly support extremist forces which provoke clashes between ethnic groups.

---

[475] Ibid, 1994, June 18.
[476] Ibid, 1994, July 15.

The Hungarian-Romanian Treaty

As in 1945-46, when Romanian Communists, Social Democrats, Peasant Party members and Liberals, irrespective of political affiliation, were of the unanimous opinion that not one square meter of land, not a single village, should be handed over to Hungary. Now, there was again unity among liberal government parties, Romania Mare or Peasant Party politicians, that the victory of the Hungarian Socialist Party brought a government into power in Hungary that would be ready to sign the Hungarian-Romanian Basic Treaty. "Romania Is Saved!" "Romania Can Breathe Freely Again!" – wrote the *Romania Libera* and *Evenimentul Zilei*.

There was no unanimity regarding the issues about unalterable borders and minorities. Knowing the Romanian policy pursued over the past 75 years, it is easy to guess what the interest of the Romanian side was. Naturally, it was not the settlement of the minority issue, by - for example – enacting a minority/nationality bill, but rather the clause covering unalterable borders. Quite typical of Romanian politics, – hinting that Romania has or may have territorial claims against her neighbors - at the press conference of the President's spokesman on June 3, 1994, the following was said: although the Molotov-Ribbentrop pact and the peace treaties following WW II deprived Romania of significant territories, in order to prove its peaceful intentions, it was willing to accept the current situation even though it is unfavorable to itself.

Some of the public statements reflected the worries of Hungarians: that the same situation could develop after the signing of the Basic Treaty as happened in 1958 when Soviet troops were withdrawn from Romania. The presence of Soviet troops exerted a restraint on the chauvinist Romanian minority policy. Only afterwards was the independent Hungarian Bolyai University closed down and instruction in Hungarian was cut back, - Gheorghiu-Dej gave ten years for winding up the Hungarian schools - Hungarian and German signs disappeared; Hungarian (and Jewish) officials were dismissed from the Ministries of Defense, Interior and Foreign Affairs. The system of sequestered towns was introduced and the national ratio of minority employees in certain work categories was fixed at 10%.

We must remember that Romania observed almost none of the international or bilateral treaties signed in the 19th and 20th centuries. Since 1947, the Romanians have failed to observe any agreement with Hungary on culture, water management or trade. This was the subject of the dispute between Rákosi and Gheorghiu-Dej, as well as Kádár and Ceausescu. It was particularly apparent in the case of a so-called Basic Treaty which:

1) was a political act aimed at demonstrating a new type of relation between two countries;
2) contains no guarantees for its observation;
3) since it was signed by two nations, a third country or an organization can not oblige any of the parties to observe it; and

4) even though it contained clauses for appealing to the World Court at the Hague, the UN or any other organization in case of violations, this would only entail endless, unresolved and futile legal disputes.

If Hungary signed the Treaty in order to (1) attest that it considered the borders permanent (ethnic principles were not taken into consideration when they were first drawn in 1920 or 1946), and/or (2) help Hungarians living beyond its borders, it would fail to accomplish its objective because there are elements which are certain to question its sincerity and would give a green light to anti-minority policies. So, it would gain nothing. The Hungarian-Ukrainian Treaty provided a good example for this, as the Ukrainian government had not the slightest intention of observing its minority clause. (3) Indeed, Hungarians living beyond the borders would feel that the mother country has abandoned them and this might result in ill-considered actions. (This was particularly true for the Szeklers, who still had memories of autonomy, while Szeklerland is dotted with arsenals - possessed by the army and Vatra.) That the two parties intended to sign the Treaty without consulting the 3.5 million Hungarians living beyond the borders, was not a rare opinion. 4) The Romanian attitude concerning national concept and national policy is quite simple and clear: A true patriot is one who would declare and fight for the unification of all territories where Romanians lived, disregarding whether the territory was ever under Romanian rule or if there was ever a Romanian state there - as in Bessarabia in the 18th century - or not, as in Transylvania, where Romania can be mentioned as a state only since 1918. Anyone who does not accept this is not a patriot but a traitor.

This concept is applied to others, as well. Romanians think that the true Hungarian is a revisionist, (they consider every Hungarian, along with the new Hungarian government, a born nationalists) and demands the return of Transylvania. The opposite (perhaps) never enters their mind. Consequently, every Hungarian statement, which appears contrary to this preconception, i.e., that Hungary accepts the current borders and does not intend, either by peaceful or other means, to claim the return of the Hungarian-populated regions or any part of them in Upper Northern Hungary, Southern Counties, Sub-Carpathia and Transylvania, is unbelievable to Romanians.

The Hungarian side wished to prove through the Treaty that the limitation of minority rights destabilizes the entire region. On the other hand, the Romanian side contends that it granted every right and it is the 'revisionist' Budapest that is the destabilizing factor.[477] The Hungarian side wished – in return for giving up border revision and encapsulating it into the Treaty – to include international documents signed after 1989 into the Treaty. As a reminder, the 1201/1993 proposal of the CE Parliamentary General Assembly, which Romania agreed to observe as part of the admission to the Council of Europe, embraced the following: 1) it is prohibited to change the demographic composition of an area inhabited by a national minority to the detriment of the given minority; 2) it is the right of every national minority to establish its own organizations and political parties; 3) where a minority lives in significant numbers, its mother tongue can be

---

[477] Takács: Romania's government ...op.cit. p. 17.

used in public administration and judiciary; and 4) according to Paragraph II., where minorities are in the majority, they have the right to establish their own autonomous public administrative organizations or special status can be granted to them.

It rapidly became apparent through the course of the 1995 talks that Romania would not accept Proposal 1201 – Emil Constantinescu even made a statement to that effect[478] – even if it was not made compulsory or that it should be in harmony with the internal legal framework of the state. Finally, after Hungarian and international pressure, it was included into the appendix to the Treaty. The Romanian public considered it a concession made to Hungarian revisionism.[479] After prolonged debate and compromise, Prime Ministers Gyula Horn of Hungary and Nicolae Vacaroiu of Romania signed the Romanian-Hungarian Treaty – in the presence of Romanian President Iliescu – on September 16, 1995, in Timisoara (Temesvár).[480]

---

[478] Romania Libera. 1995, March 20.
[479] Adevarul. 1995, September 16.
[480] Hungarian News Journal (Magyar Hírlap). 1995, September 17.

VI. The Realities of Romanian Internal Politics

Overview of the general political situation (Summer of 1996).

Despite all efforts, Romania's reputation abroad was appalling. *Le Monde* ran several articles concerning the ghastly situation. In each instance, it concluded that Bucharest was the city of filth and grime, where stray dogs and rats wandered in the streets. Tuberculosis, the disease of the poor, had returned, the mortality rate was high (23.9 per thousand) and life expectancy low (66 years for men). Ion Diaconescu, president of the Christian Democratic Peasant Party stated that the neo-Communist leadership allied itself with corruption.[481] The 'Taracila-list', compiled by the Romanian Ministry of Interior and named after the Minister, was published in July. It listed more than 300 crimes, each of which cost the state 50 million Lei (2.5 million Forint). However, the charges either did even reach the courts or the courts cleared the accused of the charges in return for suitable bribes.

The *Evenimentul Zilei* supplemented the Taracila-report with concrete information. Between 1990 and 1994, two billion dollars disappeared from the country. No one checked the expenditures of the annual budget plans between 1989 and 1992. According to data published by the Audit Office, 86% of joint ventures were in violation of the applicable laws. Moreover, the majority of privatizations, controlled by the National Privatization Agency were illegal, e.g.- assets were significantly undervalued (by 300 %), mortgage payments were interest-free, title to buildings and land were transferred to foreign [business] partners free of charge. Tax fraud, illegal accounting and the disappearance of relevant documents were commonplace.

Official, ministerial reports of the first half of the year did not paint the situation in bright colors, either. The trade balance in June of 1996, compiled by the Minister of Trade, showed a deficit of $353.4 million US. It was due partly to the cost of crude oil imports, worth $151.1 million US, and partly to the decline of exports. Although total imports in the first four months decreased, that of some products – primarily energy demand and basic materials - increased. In early June, a committee representing the Ministries of Trade, Industry, Agriculture, Food and Finance met to analyze the situation.

The national budget was passed only at the end of April; consequently, export financing was late. Financial guarantees for exports were also insufficient. To control the situation, government and ministerial level restrictions were introduced on the import of duty free products. The Romanian customs system was tightened up, with special attention paid to determining which products would cause difficulties to domestic manufacturers if imported in large quantities.

The three large Romanian banks, which conducted significant volumes in hard currencies – Bancorex, the Commercial Bank and the Romanian Development Bank – announced that the Lei / US$ exchange rate would cross the 3,000 'psychological threshold' at the end of June. The director of one of the banks told the press that the presence of the representatives of the International

---

[481] Romania Libera. 1993, September 10.

Monetary Fund was responsible for the official exchange rate surpassing 3,000 Lei per US$, because the IMF disapproved of Bucharest freezing the official exchange rate, causing a significant gap between the exchange rates used by official and private agencies' rates. In February, the IMF prevented Romania from obtaining a $70 million US loan package, due to irregular activities on the interbank market. The World Bank issued an ultimatum to Bucharest: if it did not increase energy prices before June 20, the World Bank would cease to finance Romania.

Under the Vacaroiu government, energy prices were 12-fold, the price of methane gas was 17-fold and that of thermal energy 21-fold higher than in 1992, while minimum wages increased only 8-fold in the four years. Projections showed that close to half a million Romanian were to lose their jobs before the end of the year.[482] According to official sources, the active labor force numbered 11,235,000 persons. During the municipal elections, the rate of unemployment dropped to 7.7%, or 862,736 persons. Among the states in transition in Europe, only the Czech Republic was better off than Romania; unemployment was higher than 11% in Bulgaria and Hungary, it reached 13% in Slovakia and surpassed 15% in Poland. These figures had not changed in the past four years. Premier Vacaroiu promised one million new jobs, but managed to create only 150,000 in five months. Some half a million did lose their jobs in the second half of the year.

What will happen to the 500,000 dismissed workers? Where will unemployment benefits be found? These questions remained unanswered, for the time being. According to 1995 statistics, the most people worked in industry, with the construction industry being second, but it employed 4.5 times fewer people than industry. It offered mainly seasonal employment, same as agriculture, which ranked third. The number of employees grew slightly in education, financial institution and public administration, but that meant a growth in the bureaucracy. Transport and health services were on the decline. The condition of the latter was rather worrisome, especially when shortages were noticeable in the supply of basic medicines.

Therefore, it was no accident that people hit the streets. Organized by the National Trade Union Block, more that 3,000 people protested in Bucharest at the end of June against the bankruptcy of the government's economic policy. The participants protested that the Vacaroiu-government and the current political-caste supported corruption, unfair competition and underground (illegal) labor.

Romanian foreign policy

Romania became a full member of the Central-European Initiative effective on June 1, 1996. On this occasion Foreign Minister Melescanu said that as his country was situated in Central Europe, Romania wanted to be a bridge, linking the Black Sea regions, the Caucasus and the East (the CIS). Following this, the joint session of the two houses of Parliament passed a resolution to forward an

---

[482] Very critical articles appeared in the Adevarul containing crucial facts.

appeal to the 16 NATO countries, asking them to support Romania's admission to full membership.[483]

New trends emerged in Romania's foreign policies. Great importance was placed on good Romanian-German relations, partly for foreign policy reasons – support in joining the North Atlantic Treaty Organization – and partly for economic reasons. Iliescu's visit to Germany, repeatedly delayed by the Germans, took place at the end of June. Iliescu himself said that the host country was "Romania's most important partner" and "the number one economic power in Europe".

German President Roman Herzog assured Iliescu that the Germans considered Romania as a part of Europe. During his talks with Herzog, Iliescu emphasized again that Hungary and Romania should gain EU admission together; discrimination would lead to conflict. Several cooperative agreements were signed, including economic cooperation, investments, defense and transportation. It was felt to be important to take united action on organized crime, especially since there were an increasing number of Romanian criminal gangs in Germany.

The Romanian President met several representatives of Romanians living in Germany, who asked him to return their expropriated properties. (As a reminder, the German-Romanian Treaty assures a protector status for Germany, i.e., the right to intervene in Romanian policy as it affects the German minority.) According to the report of the Romanian Development Agency published at the end of May, Germany was leading in foreign investments $170 million, followed by South Korea with $159.1 million, Italy with $148.1 million, the USA with $144.4 million, France with $132.9 million and the Holland with $132.3 million. Foreign investments totaled $1.101 billion US in 1995, less than the sum invested in Hungary and Poland.

President Iliescu grabbed every opportunity to warn of the consequences of making a distinction between the Eastern- and the Central-European states regarding their integration efforts. He did this at the Salzburg summit on Eastern Europe, too. Another recurring theme of his speeches, both abroad and at home, was that Hungary demanded the respecting of minority rights while it failed to achieve any progress in that field. Minorities were not represented in the Parliament in Budapest and minorities were not educated in their mother languages. The latter was not true, as instruction in the mother tongue is available from kindergarten to university level. Iliescu's third recurring topic was that the Hungarians, after gaining autonomy, would try to secede from Romania.

Congressman Tom Lantos (California), who demanded the opening of the Bolyai University in 1991 while in Cluj Napoca (Kolozsvár), kept his promise to Iliescu and supported the granting of Most Favored Nation status to Romania. But László Hámos (president, Hungarian Human Rights Federation, New York), during his Congressional hearing, stated that Iliescu did not fulfill the obligations he undertook when signing either the ECSC Copenhagen Agreement, or the Paris CHarter, or the European Council's convention on Human and Minority Rights, or

---

[483] It was at this time that an article was printed in Le Monde, exposing conditions unimaginable elsewhere in Europe.

Recommendation 1201, or their most important concept: enacting a bill on minorities, establishing a minority ministry, assuring mother tongue instruction at all levels of education, and returning the properties of minorities, the Churches and individuals.

In Washington, Foreign Minister Melescanu argued that Romania's defense doctrine was based on the principle of NATO membership. In mid-July, after Melescanu's visit, Romanian diplomacy and politics were successful: the US House of Representatives granted Most Favored Nation status to Romania, permanently, overwhelmingly voting 333 for and 87 against. Congress deemed that significant economic reforms had been carried out in Romania, including price liberalization, privatization and the canceling of subsidies. At the same time, Romania was called upon to continue reforms and to settle the contentious issues with its neighbors, the Ukraine and Hungary. Contrary to official US opinion, former Ambassador David Funderburk to Romania – and a significant number of economic and political experts – had doubts about Romania. He was of the opinion that Romania was the only Eastern-European country that had failed to elect a democratic government, to distance itself from its Communist past. He added that there were severe human rights problems, phones were tapped illegally and properties expropriated during the years of Communist power had not been returned.

The act contained an important condition in that the Most Favored Nation status was granted to Romania and not to a Party or the President, i.e., it could not be used in the election campaign. As Romania ignored this clause, several US representatives, Christopher Smith and Frah Wolt, sent a letter to President Clinton proposing the withdrawal of the MFN status. Shortly after was born the American plan to enlarge NATO with Poland, the Czech Republic and Hungary.

Defense Minister Georghe Tinca was among the first who raised the alarm. He was worried because Romania did not gain admission to NATO. In his opinion, there were three factors of uncertainty for Romania: the delicate situation in the East (see the situation in Russia and the Ukraine), anti-Romanian feelings and Hungarian irredentism. The pro-Hungarian lobby in Budapest represented a constant threat. Only afterwards did he mention other dangers, such as extremism, organized crime, drug trafficing and terrorism.

Tinca emphasized that even if Romania did not gain admission to NATO, it would still continue a consistent pro-Western orientation. His statement - among others - also proved that pro-Russian policy has receded in Romania, together with the view that Romania always belonged in the Russian / Soviet sphere of interest, and would so in the future. On reporting the state of the Romanian army in 1995, Tinca stated that they intended to improve Russian-Romanian military relations in order to prove that Romania's integration into NATO would not be directed against Russia. These two contrary statements clearly exhibit the duplicitous nature of Romanian foreign policy.

Not everybody shared the Romanian Defense Minister's opinion. Certain anti-NATO voices were also heard. According to Dumitru Tinu, one of the pillars of the Romanian Communist Party, Budapest was making secret preparations for war. "We have no right to pretend that we don't recognize the severity of the situation and to lessen its importance. With or without NATO, the protection of the united nation is above any economic solutions." Tinu lectured Melescanu, saying that he should concern himself with the improvement of the country's defensees and not with admission into NATO.

Melescanu, on the other hand, stressed during the conference of Romanian diplomatic missions on July 30-31, that the prime target of Romanian diplomacy should be to achieve success in NATO integration during the coming months. This was the reason for the purge – 'refreshing' the corps – launched in August and September in the entire Foreign Service. Melescanu considered it a success that Premier Alain Juppé received him after the conference in Paris and assured Romania of his support.

Municipal Elections (first round: June 6, 1996; second round: June 16)

Surveying the political map of Central and Eastern-Europe in 1996 gives evidence of the advance of Right, Center-Right and Conservative parties: in Estonia, Lithuania, the Czech Republic, Slovenia, Croatia and lately in Romania. In the first opportunity since 1989, there was a possibility for a change of regime in Romania; after the failure of the post-Communist coalition with the extreme Left and Right, a coalition of the Christian Democratic Center-Right and the Social Democrats could secure victory.

In Romania, municipal elections are considered a dress rehearsal for the parliamentary and presidential elections of November 3. More than 60% of the population voted for the opposition, which thus received 1 million more votes than the ruling parties. The opposition came to the conclusion that a good opposition coalition and cooperation would be able to overcome the post-Communist government.

The election procedure, in which citizens choose from various party candidate lists for aldermen and mayors, is a good indication of the people's opinion about the regime. A large percentage of voters, 50%, did not cast a ballot. Experience indicates that the majority of the candidates included on the county lists were unknown, not only in the smaller settlements but also in the cities and county seats. Nationally, of the 17,737,425 eligible voters, 10,016,932 exercised their franchise in the county alderman's lists. On the basis of these results, Constantinescu, leading politician of the Democratic Convention (DC), declared that the opposition won the elections.

The order of parties, with the exception of the independents, did not change after the second round:

Democratic Convention (DC)	1,667,177	19.53%
Romanian Party of Socialist Democracy (RPSD)	1,390,180	16.28%
Social Democratic Union (SDU)	962,474	11.27%
Democratic Alliance of Hungarian Romanians (DAHR)	602,474	7.06%
Romanian National Unity Party (RNUP)	464,471	5.40%
Socialist Labor Party (SLP)	439,648	5.15%
Greater Romania Party (GRP)	344,042	4.03%
Independents	303,459	3.55%
RDAP	273,252	3.20%
PSZP	270,209	3.16%

Party ranking of the 2,742 mayoral results were as follows:

RPSD	26.4%	868 mayors
Democratic Convention (DC)	20.6%	320 mayors
Social Democratic Union (SDU)	16.1%	447 mayors
PSZP + LP'93	8.3%	
Socialist Labor Party (SLP)	7.3%	
RNUP	6.5%	
DAHR	6.5%	139 mayors
RDAP	4.9%	
Great Romania Party (GRP)	3.3%	

DC won mainly in the big cities and county seats. In Bucharest, union leader Victor Ciorbea defeated Ilie Nastase, world famous tennis player, who entered the elections as a candidate on Iliescu's party list.

As for the party results, RCDP again enrolled the farmers behind itself, thanks to the fact that one of its first and most important decisions in 1990 was the liquidation of agricultural cooperatives and state – collective – farms, and land distribution. However, the loss of prestige was obvious. What also was not very helpful forcing almost every civil servant and business leader into the RCDP in 1996, just as they used to in the one party state.

The urgent socio-economic measures of the "neo-nationalist-communist" Vacaroiu-government are dismissed as mere 'smoke and mirrors.' The reality is that the large state industries (subsidized in order to win the election) are on the verge of bankruptcy, as are the banks; agriculture is also subsidized out of taxes. The coalition government was unable to re-organize industry; price increases swept through the economy like a chain-reaction; the number of people living under the poverty level increased; fuel prices went up, and the value of the Lei declined. On the other hand, corruption at the state level blossoms; speculation and smuggling are carried on openly.

The performance of the Democratic Convention is significant but internal conflicts, first of all the rivalry of the successors of the two historical parties - the National Peasant Party and the National Liberal Party - could lead to the disintegration of the DC, predicted some political observers.

The showing of the Socialist Labor Party, led by Ilie Verdet - one-time Prime Minister of the Ceausescu-era - is not surprising. The simple answers can be found in the deterioration of social circumstances and certain nostalgia for the past regime.

The gains of the Social Democratic Union can be credited primarily to Petre Roman, President of the Democratic Party. However the good combination of personalities (economists, etc.), as well as Roman's international reputation, his realistic program built on traditional social democratic values and a plan with socio-economic reforms, also contributed to his success.

Funar's RNUP should still be considered a regional Transylvanian party; the Greater Romania Party is the extremist party of the Transcarpathian territory, despite the fact that it received a few more votes in Transylvania than in 1992. DHAR polled 784,375 votes in 1992, and 602,561 in June of 1996, a decline of 181,814. Loss of confidence was most noticeable in Cluj Napoca (Kolozsvár) where an estimated 15-20,000 Hungarians simply did not vote. The reason for the substantial abstaining was that the DAHR did not enter its own Hungarian candidate and asked Kolozsvár's 20% Hungarian population to vote for the DC candidate. They actually strengthened Funar's position, all the more so as some of the Romanians voted for Funar because the DAHR supported the DC candidate!

The DAHR after the elections

The federal representatives had ample material to evaluate as a result of the municipal elections. For a time, the DAHR was wondering about the reasons for the vanishing confidence (which Markó previously denied), indicated by the fact that, in proportion, fewer Hungarians than Romanians voted in Cluj Napoca (Kolozsvár). DAHR mayoral candidates in Miercuera-Ciuc (Csíkszereda) and Tirgu Secuiesc (Kézdivásárhely) received but a small proportion of the votes; Hungarian candidates were defeated by independents in 14 settlements of Harghita County; five Hungarian mayors were elected in Szatmár County, but they all ran under the colors of Romanian parties. The fundamental question concerning the role of the DAHR was raised: Was it a political party or an organization representing the opposition?

Other Hungarian parties (e.g.- the Romanian Christian Democratic Party) and organizations expressed heavy criticism against DAHR for the development of a elite-group spirit, as well as the inadequacy and corruptness of MPs.

The following also didn't help the DAHR's cause: 1) the conflict between Markó and Tokés; 2) that they were afraid to bring Géza Szocs to account for his financial dealings – who was called 'Transylvania's Berlusconi' by the Romanian press; 3) that it nominated a presidential candidate; and 4) that this candidate was none other than György Frunda, who was held to be too close to the Romanians, i.e., having served Romanian interests.

György Frunda, who was conducting talks with Romanian government members without the knowledge of the DAHR, was nominated for the candidacy with 72 votes for, 12 against and 8 abstentions. Frunda expressed his hopes that he would receive more votes – by picking up votes from the other minorities and some from Romanians – than the total number of Hungarian in Romania. He intended that, in the second round, his votes go to the democratic Romanian candidate who made the minority issue a part of his platform. Frunda and his liberal and cosmopolitan (similar to Alliance of Free Democrats in Hungary) circle (Péter Buchwald, László Fey and others) held it a virtue that Frunda's program was not limited to minority problems but offered a national alternative. Its explicit target was to win Romanian voters. (Just a reminder that, in Cluj Napoca (Kolozsvár), voters cast their ballots for Funar rather than the Romanian candidates of DAHR.)

We must cite the opinion of Ádám Katona, leader of Transylvanian Hungarian Initiatives in Orodheiu Secuiesc (Székelyudvarhely), about Frunda. In an earlier article, he wrote that the DAHR must purge not only those MPs who once belonged to the former Party apparatus and nomenclature but also of those who, in their personal and family connections, were distant from the Hungarian nation.

On July 20, the Romanian government party published a document addressed to the DAHR. It posed a series of questions – expecting answers. Does DAHR accept, without reservation, the Romanian constitution? Will it give up boycotting the commissioners in Counties Harghita and Covasna? Will it clarify its relationship with the Hungarian government, as its representatives are regular participants of the sessions of "the inner DAHR parliament"? Does György Frunda wish to become the President of Romania or only of Szeklerland, whose autonomy has been proclaimed at a Hungarian diaspora meeting in Debrecen?[484]

All in all, the nomination of György Frunda for the presidency evoked displeasure for all segments of society Romanian as well as Romanian-Hungarian.

Presidential election

On November 3, 17,253,093 voters went to 15,117 polling stations in 42 precincts. They were voting for the candidates of 44 parties, five coalitions and more than 10 national minority organizations. The Romanian Democratic Convention won 53 out of the 143 seats in the Senate, and 122 out of 253 mandates in the House of Representatives.

The following parties gained mandates on the list of the Democratic Convention:

That outstanding elder of the Christian Democratic National Peasant Party and one-time secretary to Iuliu Maniu, Corneliu Coposu launched the Democratic Convention and served as its first president. He passed this post on Constantinescu in 1992. DC's economic policy reflected its right-of-center and Christian Democrat character, as it included:
- liberal reforms,
- privatization,
- change of economic structure,
- closing down large companies operating at a deficit,

---

[484] Azi, Romania Libera. 1996, July 21.

232

- tax reduction,
- cheap credit,
- support of economic ventures, and
- social welfare security.

It is evident that the government program did not include any thoughts on minority policy.

But the DC was not a party, but a loose alliance of parties and movements, creating a constitutional absurdity that it was not a party that won the elections but an eclectic alliance of parties. The Christian Democratic National Peasant Party (CDNPP), which brought the DC into being, was the most important among them both in numbers and stature. The CDNPP held itself the successor of the one-time Peasant Party, which united with the Christian Democratic Party. Transylvanian-born Corneliu Coposu, once a close colleague of Iuliu Maniu, and spent more than a decade and a half in Romanian prisons, was one of the influential leaders of the CDNPP. The party accepted the nation-state doctrine; it was ready to support the minorities' ambitions for instruction in the mother tongue (cultural autonomy) but it rejected territorial autonomy. It considered state decentralization as the means of solving the minority issue.

Ion Diaconescu, Coposu's close colleague and prison mate, was the president of the party in 1996. Right after the elections, it was certain that the CDNPP had the best chance to nominate the new Romanian prime minister. On November 19, it was announced that the 42-year-old mayor of Bucharest, Transylvanian-born Victor Ciorbea, a graduate of the law school of Cluj Napoca (Kolozsvár) and belonged to the close circle of Coposu, would be the prime minister. His appointment would take place after Constantinescu took the Presidential oath, which was planned to take place prior to the series of commemorations of the Alba Julia (Gyulafehérvár) National Assembly of December 1, 1918. (That was day the union of Transylvania and Romania was declared by the Transylvanian Romanians at Alba Julia (Gyulafehérvár), before the start of the peace talks.)

The facts that the National Peasant Party reorganized itself by 1996, on the one hand, and that the numerous small liberal parties united, indicated that they were striving after a certain legal continuity. The DC rallied the following member parties: the National Liberal Party (16 Senators, 25 MPs), leader: Mircea Ionescu Quintus, vice president: businessman Viorel Catarama; the National Liberal Party-Democratic Convention, (5, 5), president: lawyer Nicolae Cerveni; the Social Democratic Union (23, 53), lead by Petre Roman and recently admitted to the Socialist International. I was constituted of two parts, the numerically lesser SDP but with great social democratic traditions and the Democratic Party encompassing those who left Iliescu's party.

The new President's scope of political activity

Emil Constantinescu won hands down. Thanks to the Transylvanian voters, the official tally gave following results: Emil Constantinescu: 7,057,905 votes or 54.41% vs. Ion Iliescu: 5,914,579 votes or 45.59%

233

It must be told that Ion Iliescu fell into hysterical rage and demanded to be elected Romania's Prime Minister, otherwise DAHR would carve out Transylvania, landowners would return and take their lands back (in 1992, he swayed the peasants and the so-called 'peasant barons' with the same arguments) and, finally, that the King would return.

The DAHR 'delivered' about 800,000 votes for Constantinescu. It is worth mentioning, for example, that 201,577 voters out of the total of 220,976 in County Harghita (86% Hungarian population) voted for Constantinescu. As in 1992, Constantinescu received most of the votes from the well educated, the workers and voters under 35. It was also unambiguous that he received votes from the Szekler counties in Transylvania, the Partium – Szatmár, Máramaros and Beszterce-Naszód – and from counties Galati, Prahova and Konstanca (Constanta) counties in the Transcarpathian territories and from Bucharest.

Speculation spread about the distribution of portfolios that the CDNPP, in addition to the prime ministerial post, were expected to hold the Interior, Agriculture, Telecommunications, Local Administration and the government's Secretary General. The Social Democratic Union was tipped to be given Foreign Affairs, Defense, Transportation, Environment and Welfare posts.

Although Iliescu lost, if there were to be no change in the state apparatus – which was full with members of the former Party and the Securitate – Constantinescu, who stressed that he would not launch a cleansing, and Ciorbea would find themselves in a difficult situation. It was also not to their advantage that Constantinescu came from Bessarabia and Ciorbea (Csorba in Hungarian?) was of Transylvanian-Romanian origin. Historical experiences indicate – see the short life of the government of the Transylvanian National Peasant Party between the two world wars – that the Romanians of the Regat do not tolerate for long the rule of their Romanian brothers arriving from the region beyond the Carpathians.

The DC maintained its stand for closer ties with the West. Experts pointed out that it would carry the disadvantage of the intensive involvement of the International Monetary Fund, which would result in the closing down of the mammoth companies operating at a loss; that would mean the dismissal of 5 million people whom agriculture would be unable to absorb. Forecasters warned that it could easily cause the fall of the government and the resulting early elections could see the return of the post-Communists.

Constantinescu's statement that Romania wished to act as a mediator between the Balkans and Central-Europe and he wished to strengthen relations first of all with the Czech Republic, Hungary, Poland and Croatia, indicated the revival of the Peasant Party's, more precisely, Maniu's cooperation plan, who tried to counterbalance strengthening German and Soviet influence through an alliance of the above mentioned countries. In 1996, Constantinescu wished to maintain his country's independence from Russian influence.

The president's scope of activity was defined not only by economic problems. On the one hand, Constantinescu had to take into consideration that three political groups determined internal politics in Romania: the National Peasant Party, the Liberal Party and the Romanian Party of Socialist Democracy, i.e., the post-Communists, the strongest party that time. On the other hand, the latter completely dominated the life of the state and the economy. It was the reason for Constantinescu making overtures toward the army in the final days of the election campaign and for appointing former trade union leader Ciorbea as Prime Minister. That is, he tried to counterbalance the unchanged Communist-era structures with the power of the trade union movement.

The DAHR as government-maker

Although, the President of the Democratic Coalition and would-be president of Romania stated that they did not make any kind of secret agreement with the DAHR but according to confidential sources a pact of that kind existed indeed (although it would mean very little as Romania did not observed a single international agreement) about giving three ministerial and several State Secretary posts to the DAHR.

The possible inclusion of the DAHR in the government created quite a stir. The two leading government papers, *Dimineata* (Morning) and *Vocea Romaniei*, led in the agitation of the population. According to *Dimineata,* Hungarian extremists, like László Tokés, Béla Markó and István Csurka wanted not only to recapture Transylvania but also to influence the entire fabric of Romanian political life. *Voceae Romaniei* printed articles stating that the DAHR changed schools into "anti-Romanian powder kegs" and established local armed cells, in actuality "terrorist groups". Vatra Romanesca called upon Constantinescu and Roman in an open letter to distance themselves from the absurd demands of the DAHR. They made references to the DAHR's autonomy-concept. However, the DAHR, in the interest of gaining governmental influence, seemed agreeable to giving up this concept.

News leaking out from confidential sources on November 20, seemed to suggest that the offer for three ministerial posts diminished to one but, on the other hand, the DAHR would receive 10-12 posts of Prefect and Vice-prefect instead. One thing for certain, it became evident the day after the election that the DAHR overestimated its own importance by hoping that it would be the tail that wagged the dog, that it would decided whether the government and Romania took a turn to right-of-center or left. With the signing of the alliance between Roman and Constantinescu, although not really sympathetic to each other, and with their two political groups winning the majority of votes, they actually did not have a pressing need to include the DAHR into the government coalition. Despite it all, Béla Markó kept stressing that the DAHR held the balance and that the Romanian government had an undeniable need for the support of the DAHR. Essentially, Markó spoke the truth. The West kept insisting that Romania's membership in NATO depended on whether or not DHAR was included in the government.

According to official records, 1.6 million Hungarian live in Romania, and about 1.2 million of them had the right to vote. Of that number, 836,790 Hungarians excercised their vote on November 3. Outside the Hungarian populated areas, the DAHR received votes in Vasliu, the oil-fields of Prahova, Braila and Constanta (1,000-1,000 each), and 300-300 votes in Suceava and Giurgiu respectively.

The Hungarian Free Democratic Party reveived 14,000 votes, accounting for 0.01% in the House of Representatives and 0.12% in the Senate. Imre Borbély reveived 2,000 votes in County Harghita, and 2,152 people voted for the Forum of Szekler Youth (Székely Ifjak Fóruma).

Election results of the Democratic Alliance of Hungarians in Romania (November 3, 1996): [485]

-- DAHR presidential candidate: György Frunda   6.02 %
-- DAHR in the Senate   6.81 %
-- DAHR in the House of Representatives   6.64 %

While DAHR had 27 MPs and 12 Senators in the Romanian Parliament in 1992, their number now decreased to 25 and 11 in 1996. National minorities represented in Parliament:

-- Federation of Romanian Jewish Communities
-- Turkish Democratic Alliance
-- 'Bratstvo' Community of Bulgarians in Romania
-- Romanian Greek Alliance
-- 'Dom Polski' Alliance of Poles in Romania
-- Democratic Alliance of Slovaks and Czechs in Romania
-- Italian Community in Romania
-- Turkish-Muslim Tatar Democratic Alliance of Romania
-- Roma Party
-- Cultural Alliance of Albanians in Romania
-- Democratic Alliance of Serbs and Croats
-- Alliance of Armenians in Romania
-- Alliance of Ukrainians in Romania
-- Democratic Alliance of Germans in Romania
-- Community of Lipovans in Romania
-- DAHR.

---

[485] Romanian Hungarian Word (Romániai Magyar Szó /RMSZ/). 1996, November 5, 6.

VII. On the waiting list: 1997

The European Council stated the conditions of admission for the Central and East-European countries at its session held in Copenhagen in June 1993. They are the following:
?? democratic system of administration, rule of law, respect for human rights;
?? protection of minorities;
?? orderly relations with neighbors - a political condition;
?? a working market economy – an economic condition;
?? the ability to meet, as a member, the portion of (financial, defense, etc.) obligations.

According to the official report forwarded to Romania in the first half of the year, the country could only partially meet these requirements, and therefore was put on the waiting-list, for the time being. The detailed reasoning went as follows: Although democratic institutions have been established in the country but they have to be consolidated. A great number of defects were found in observance of basic rights. Greater efforts must be made to strengthen the legal system and to overcome corruption. Complaints were raised against the activities of the police and secret services. The situation of the Hungarians in the country has improved; the same can not be said of the Roma (Gypsies). There is no coordination between economic strategy and legislation. Land ownership rights are not guaranteed. The entire industry is in crisis; agriculture needs to be modernized. The financial sector needs to be restructured, and the European legal system should be adopted. Further efforts are to be made in the development of telecommunications and customs/excise. Problems have been found in Social Security and the creation of new jobs. The entire energy sector has to be re-structured; the same goes for public administration. The model of regional development should be worked out.

In short, present day Romania is still unfit for integrating into the Euro-Atlantic structure. Consequently, it was relegated among the seven of the ten candidate countries that constituted the *waiting-list*. Part of the complaints result from the fact that the process of switching from a one party system and decentralizing central power are proceeding too slowly, similar to Serbia, Slovakia, Belarus and other Soviet successor states.

The party elite, dressed in national colors and chanting nationalist slogans, remained in place until November 1996. As a result of the elections in November, while their ranks were thinned in the political, economic and social life, as well as in legislation, they continued to hold their posts in executive power in public administration and public institutions – mainly in the countryside – with only minor changes.

The anti-corruption campaign is merely one evidence of the failure. Valerian Stan, head of the government supervisory office, compiled a report on illegal assignment and acquisition of flats (apartments) and lands. According to it, during the past seven years 6,000 persons acquired 11,000 hectares of land in illegal ways, mainly through the abuse of authority. The list included Secretaries of State, high ranking Ministry officials, and three politicians of the Democratic Party:

Petre Roman, President of the Senate, and two ministers, Adrian Severin and Traian Basescu. Typically, instead of calling the people concerned to account, Valerian Stan was dismissed from his post.

In early October, the President announced that additional law enforcement organizations would be formed, such as the national agency to collect and analyze information on money-laundering, the anti-corruption council and a national council to study corruption. Corrupt practices in three areas were so rife that they endangered the country's safety: the navy, fertilizer production and the oil industry.

While the Western-European, and especially US, experts demand evidence of the rule of law, associated with properly operating institutions, as well as a market economy from Romania, they are not aware of the peculiarities of the Romanian development model. The leading strata here are alien from Western-European liberalism (both in the political and economic sense), up to the 1950s 78-80% of the population worked in agriculture, and 30% of working-age people are still commuting back and forth from their jobs. Due to the shutting down of factories and the new land law, the number of workers in agriculture is still growing. With the exception of mining, the establishment of the manufacturing industry followed the Soviet model of forced industrialization in the 1950s (during the cold war). Finally, Romanian society knew nothing, to this day, of autonomous social organization. For the present, economic restructuring is still incomplete but not because of a lack of capital. Expertise - owners and entrepreneurs - who are able to work with the accumulated capital, is missing. There is a shortage in the skilled trades, especially trained professionals and skilled workers, the Hungarians, Germans and Jews of the recent past, those who could produce and manufacture marketable goods.

The conditions for the influx of foreign capital have also been established only recently. Now, it is guaranteed that profit generated by production can be taken out of the country, as well as assuring the right for acquiring the property on which the foreign owner's bank, factory, plant, etc., is operating. As far as the concept of marketable products, we are not talking about Western markets, because most products, with some exceptions like furniture, are not marketable even in the former COMECON countries. Concerning productivity, Professor Ion Aluas phrased it the following way: "Here, five people accomplish a task that is done by one person in the USA, and five people share that one's wage."

The Ciorbea-government's economic reforms

The government announced its new economic policy in February 1997, demanded by the West and the IMF. It was followed by deregulation of prices, a rise in energy prices and termination of exchange rate controls on the Lei. The second phase, somewhat longer, was the establishment of the necessary legislative background for economic transition, lasting the first half of the year. This led to the third and more drastic step, the closing down of the 17 companies running at a deficit. In the government's decree No. 9 of August 7, it announced its intention to accelerate the reform process and the closing of 14 state operated companies and 3 oil refineries, because they were 'producing' an annual loss of US$37 million. (The annual output of Romanian oil refineries amounted to 20 million tons, while only 11 million tons were consumed. The refineries were working at 50% effectiveness.) The closing of the 17 industrial units affected 30,000 people. The list of companies scheduled to be closed included another 200 names, which put a further budgetary loss of half a billion dollars. Further costs added to the pressure; for example, these companies, factories did not pay for electricity and water consumption. Even if they managed to produce some profit, it did not cover their expenses. One these plants was the Small Boiler Factory of Cluj Napoca (Kolozsvár) (one of the plants built in Transylvania in the Ceausescu-era, which could be conveniently converted to armament production) employing 1,200 people.

Total assets of the 17 plants	Lei 264 billion
Their total output	Lei 133 billion
Their total deficit	Lei 270 billion (US$37 million)
Their total debt	Lei 1 trillion

Budgetary income decreased in the first half of the year, because companies failed to pay their debts to the state and social insurance funds. The number of deficit producing companies and banks requiring state subsidies increased.

Budget deficit	Lei 2.3 trillion
State income	Lei 13.98 trillion
Profit	Lei 3.74 trillion

Under the agreement signed with the IMF, the country's annual budget deficit could not surpass 4.5% of GDP. (The deficit amounted to 5.7% of GDP in 1996.) This resulted in a reduction of the budgetary plan and some restructuring. (According to projections, the budget deficit had to stay below 3% in 1998.)

Changes in budget items:

Defense	Lei 5.478 trillion instead of 6.2 trillion
Agriculture	Lei 3.7 trillion instead of 4.1
Industry	Lei 2.616 trillion instead of 2.894
Scientific R&D	Lei 804 billion instead of 859
Education	Lei 25.3 trillion instead of 24.6
Health	Lei 7.6 trillion instead of 7.0

On September 4, the government decreed that state monopolies had to be privatized within three months. The deadline for the transformation of the 14 monopolies owned by local municipalities was May 16, 1998. The government decree empowered the Office of Mineral Resources to grant mining concessions to foreigners for 20 years and to close down the most unprofitable mines. This resulted in a loss of 200,000 jobs in the mining sector. IMF delegate for Romania,

Paul Thomsen, expressed his satisfaction with the drastic governmental measures, and held out the prospect of a payment of US$86 million, the second part of the total US$430 million loan granted in April. After another on site inspection in October, the IMF approved the payment of the third part of the loan. The Romanian government submitted 15 sectoral reforms to the conference of the G-24, involving the IMF, the World Bank, the EBRD, the EIB, the EU and the developed countries, held in Brussels in November, in order to be granted a US$1.3 billion loan. (Romania had received a credit of US$1.5 billion up to that time.)[486]

Romania's foreign debts grew drastically. In August of 1997, it was US$7.7 billion, an increase of US$45 million in a month. Bucharest's major creditors – holding US$3.2 billion – were foreign private banks. In first place was Great Britain (30%), followed by Japan, Germany and France.

Workers and miners responded more radically to losing their jobs and livelihood than they did in Hungary, for example. Roads were blocked by trucks in Ploiesti and Brasov (Brassó), the workers of the aircraft factory in Craiova blocked the main road with an airplane. Protesters and police clashed in several cities. Doubling of prices and inflation, which rose to 177.4% in June and lessened to 159.8% in July, also contributed to the worsening situation. Dismissed employees and workers received compensation pay. The amount depended on length of service: 3, 6 or 10-month's salary. This was not enough to start any kind of business; the governments aim, to return people from industry to farming. While it would have been best to wait until after the passing of the land reform law, in September the Parliament was still debating whether to limit land acquisition to a maximum of 50 or 17 hectares. Consequently, many people spent their severance in short order, increasing the number of the have-nots and the masses without any prospects.

Social tension and anti-government feelings increased even further. Romania, like the other ex-Soviet satellite states, became the country of the poor and the rich, more so than at any time in history. Multimillionaires Ion Ratiu, Viorel Catarama, Ion Tiriac, Ioan Bacali, Cristian Burci and Virgil Magureanu, belong to the country's political and economic elite, and media owners. In addition to all this, Magureanu, the former head of the secret service, attempted to gain control over armaments production as well. It came as no surprise when opinion polls reported that 20.4% of the population wished to emigrate.

The State Property Fund reported that 2,710 companies, worth Lei 10.015 billion, were planned to be privatized during 1997. In the financial sector, only the Romanian Development Bank and one other, were designated for privatization. Bankruptcy proceedings were begun against 40 commercial companies, while the privatization of 800 companies, worth Lei 600 billion and employing 100,000 people, was completed. Although only half of the planned privatizations were completed during the year, it represented a 45% increase over the previous year.

---

[486] The statistics appeared in Weekly World Economy /HVG/, a Budapest weekly specializing in economic matters.

240

There was a debate as to who is entitled to the proceeds from privatization. Thus far, 60% of the proceeds went to the privatized company and 40% to the state property agency. According to the new budget bill, 70% would go to the budget, 15% to the property agency and 15% to a non-budgetary, independent state development fund.

The post-communist opposition and the right wing took advantage of the country's disastrous economic state, which stirred up public tension. It was heard more frequently heard that "in the past the Russians dictated in Romania, now it is the Americans," "Romania is governed by the IMF," and "the government's policy leads the county to ruin." Naturally, DAHR is also mentioned as responsible for the situation, or, for example, "Romania is ruled by a Jewish-Hungarian government."[487]

The new Land Act was a modification of the Act 18/1991. Every Romanian citizen, living in any corner of the world, could reclaim his land before February 2, 1998. (This deadline was postponed by 60 days.) The act aimed at restoring property rights. The onus was on Romanian citizenship, possession of which, or reapplying for it were the prime conditions of reinstating former owners in their possessions. (Applications had to be handed in at the mayor's office in whose jurisdiction the reclaimed land was located.)

The following elements of the Land Act modification contained items in the public interest:

Arable land could be reclaimable
    1)   up to 50 hectares, by a private person;
    2)   by churches:
           up to 200 hectares per archbishopric,
           up to 100 hectares per bishopric,
           up to 50 hectares per deanery,
           up to 50 hectares per cloister and order
           up to 10 hectares per parish.
Forested land could be reclaimable
    1)   up to 30 hectares, by a private person;
    2)   up to 30 hectares by churches;
    3)   up to 30 hectares by educational institutes;
    4)   up to the maximum verified by property right by villages, towns, etc.;
    5)   up to the maximum verified by documents by common proprietors.

Extremist Romanian parties, individuals and the media, not without some ulterior motives, drew the conclusion that 'lands would be returned to the nobility in Transylvania.'

---

[487] The Romania Mare, an extreme and incitful weekly, devoted several columns to the question.

Differences between public opinion and opinion poll results

   Polls conducted between August 16-24, 1997 showed a picture contrary with the opposition's opinion, i.e., a 'social time-bomb' is ticking in the country, and the picture indicated by social unrest and strikes. A good number exist who count on the fall of the government , in spite of the apparent resolution of internal differences (Democratic Party vs. Peasant Party, and DAHR vs. Peasant Party). They were of the opinion that the change of ministers was not a solution but mere fire-fighting. However, the opinion poll indicated that confidence grew in the government.

Question regarding the standard of living:
- live in slightly worse circumstances	33%
- the same circumstances	38%
- in very bad circumstances	15%

On class and incomes:
- belonging to the upper class	1%
- middle-class	46%
- lower class	53%

About rapid wealth accumulation:
- did not happen honestly	82%
- it was honest	4%
- don't know	14%

The most important issues for the people:
- increase in living standards	34%
- stop inflation	19%
- decrease of unemployment	17%
- restoration of agriculture	10%
- NATO- and EU-integration	2%

On the consequences of the Madrid resolution that Romanian will not join the NATO in the first round:
- no consequence at all	35%
- drop in foreign capital inflow	11%
- Romania will be isolated	10%
- increase of Russian influence	7%
- economic stagnation	6%
- more money will be spent on defense	3%
- instability in the region	3%

List Parties' popularity:
- Democratic Convention	45%
- Social Democratic Union	9%
- DAHR	6%
- RPSD	14%
- GRP	8%
- Alliance for Romania	7%
- RNEP	3%

If an election were to be held, who would you vote for:

- Constantinescu	56%
- Iliescu	16%
- Corneliu Vadim Tudor	10%
- Petre Roman	9%
- Gheorghe Funar	2%
- György Frunda	2%

A survey made by the National Statistical Committee showed certain differences to the results of the above opinion poll. The survey states pithily: Romanians live similar lives to the people of poor African countries. In August, gross monthly income was Lei 871,591 and net income was Lei 650,641, or slightly more than US$100 (HUF 3 worth Lei 100). Families consume the entire sum due to repeated increases in consumer prices, transportation and travel costs. Consequently, the Committee members are not at all optimistic about the limit of the population's tolerance.

Naturally, in the course of the reform process, the situation further worsens. The majority of the population share this opinion, except the narrow layer represented in the opinion poll. No matter whether present day Romania returns to its own model – an agricultural country with developing industry – or starts off on the road of transition, according to Western, or more precisely, Central-European model, it can be considered an unstable country, and in the long term, instability will be a decisive factor.

The Ciorbea-government's foreign policy
Question of NATO and EU membership

After 1945, with the exception of some attempts to break free – Gheorghiu-Dej's steps towards China, Ceausescu's attempts at Chinese, Arab and Western orientation, and Melescanu's maneuverings between the West and Russia while maintaining a certain duality after 1989 – it was an accepted fact that, due to its geographic-strategic situation, Romania belonged in the Soviet, then Russian, sphere of interest. After the elections in November of 1996, which was seen as Romania has returned to its former self after 50 years (the process was sealed with the restoration of King Mihail's citizenship – he was stripped of it by a decree of the Groza-government on May 22, 1948 – and his returning home in December of 1997), it was expected that Romania would return to its traditional foreign policy which was unambiguously Western- and specifically French-oriented.

Thus, it was surprising when President Emil Constantinescu's first foreign visit on January 13, 1997 – equally unexpected as his foreign minister's – was paid not to Paris or Strasbourg, but to Poland. In a press release issued after his talks with President Kwasniewski, the Romanian president could look back with satisfaction that Poland supported Romania's participation in the Central-European Free Trade Agreement and Romania could look on CEFTA-membership as and important step on the road to EU membership.

However, Constantinescu's visit to Poland had another, no less important, target, which can be interpreted as the creation of a new Bucharest-Kiev-Warsaw axis based on the traditional, historically developed and more or less functional relations in the region. Foreign Minister Adrian Severin announced in Strasbourg on January 29, 1997 that Romania, Ukraine and Poland wished to create a trilateral cooperative alliance. Its enlargement, he emphasized, would not be fortuitous as it would make it ineffective. For Hungary, the creation of the Bucharest-Kiev-Warsaw axis created a distinct possibility that she would be isolated from the Ukraine and Poland.

Polish-Romanian relations contained no elements that posed a problem. The same was not true with the Ukraine. The signing of the Romanian-Ukrainian Treaty, similar to the treaty with Russia, was delayed for a long time by the question of debatable territorial claims. According to Romanian opinion, the Herta Region, the Isle of Snakes (Kígyók szigete), Northern Bukovina and Southern Bessarabia never belonged to the Ukraine. However, what Romania mostly wanted to achieve through the Treaty was a condemnation of the Molotov-Ribbentrop Pact, which resulted in these regions being assigned to the Soviet Union.

Some politicians and public figures openly stated that Romania has territorial claims against the Ukraine. The humor of the situation was that even they realized that regarding the Moldavian, and the regions along and beyond the Dniester River, i.e., the Romanian-Russian debatable areas, Romania could only count on the Ukraine. Therefore, Romania was forced to soften its stance on what was drafted into the Ukrainian-Romanian Treaty.

Regarding Hungary in Romanian foreign policy, a new concept was already heard earlier, 'strategic partnership.' Severin put it very clearly in Strasbourg when he said: "Romania intended to form a strategic partnership with Hungary." This aim was served by establishing joint committees, as well as new agreements on economic relations, frontier traffic and military cooperation. Romania's motives for determining a new 'direction' could be appreciated.

It is quite probable that, as a result of assessing the possible negative impact of the step on the regional political situation, on power relations and on stability, and in the wake of probable significant international 'pressure' behind the scenes, Romanian diplomacy might modify its stand. It is not impossible that Romania would implement its plans in more realistic steps, for example, in the forms of a Romanian-Ukrainian-Polish-Hungarian or Romanian-Moldavian-Ukrainian Treaties. Thus far, the latter can be considered as achieved.

We must mention another circumstance, seemingly not connected with the Romania issues, at least not directly, that Turkey also increased it international efforts and made gestures of rapprochement toward the Islamic countries, which contained an explicit "message" for the NATO partners. After receiving 'no' from NATO, Romanian-Turkish relations became closer, indicated by the signing of a Turkish-Romanian-Bulgarian anti-corruption agreement. (As an aside, Romania willingly signs bi- or trilateral agreements with its Eastern, Southern and Northern neighbors.) Beyond its natural interest in the Black Sea region, the Turkish support of Romania's efforts joining the NATO can also be taken as Ankara's rebuff to its Western allies. As a reminder, Turkish stance about Romania's joining – for the known reasons – was, so far, generally negative.

Dorian Dorin, secretary of the Parliamentary Foreign Affairs Committee, as well as President of the Jewish People Community in Romania (Romániai Zsidó Népközösség), stated that the Israeli lobby also offered its support in achieving Romanian foreign affairs objectives. Romanian-Israeli relations generally were on the rise. It seemed that Israel was most anxious to contribute the development of the Romanian army, especially to the modernization of the air force. The Israeli firm, Rafael, made an offer to sell its new, and top secret, tactical missile, the Python 4. Talks progressed during the year about the purchase of 120 MIG-21.

During his visit to Romania at the end of February and in early March of 1997, King Mihail took an oath that, as an ex-monarch in kinship with other European dynasties, he would make every effort and use all his connections to promote the realization of Romania's integration endeavors. It is interesting to note that the question of the 'resurrection' of dynasties and the restoration of monarchies was often raised in the Balkans – rump Yugoslavia, Bulgaria and Albania. President Emil Constantinescu is a open, ardent royalist. For the sake of interest, it must be noted that in December of 1997, Corneliu Vadim Tudor stated that he was ready to stand, with gun in hand, barring the way for a monarchy in his country.

The new Romanian government was full of hope that the return of the Royal family would encourage Romanians in exile to return or, at least, to increase their extremely modest investments in order to support Bucharest.

Similar to other countries on the waiting-list, there were significant political forces opposed to NATO membership. Their counter-arguments included, on the one hand, that the costs of membership – calculated at US$250-300 – would constitute a significant financial burden for the economy and a budget that was otherwise facing severe problems. On the other hand, joining the NATO would mean that Romania must give up 'ancient ancestral' territories now part of surrounding countries.

Waiting for the invitation

Despite massive Western-European and Hungarian support for Romania's NATO membership, the US 'No' was the decisive factor. Of course, the official explanation made no mention of the fact that Romania never kept a single international agreement and failed to remain faithful to any of its allies. In spite of the fact that NATO Secretary-General Javier Solana made encouraging noises in Bucharest on October 13, that "Romania will be invited in 1999" – the year of US presidential elections – Romania gambled everything in its foreign policy on one card. It meant a dual task for the country, that is, it had to continue relations with all its old partners on the one hand, and on the other, while looking for new partners it had to continue to strengthen regional systems.

In this spirit, November of 1997 saw extraordinary diplomatic activity. Prime Minister Ciorbea represented Romania at the Balkan states' summit on Crete on November 3. The main topic was the establishment of a zone of cooperation in the Balkans. On his visit to New Delhi on November 17, the Romanian president emphasized that the region, and especially India, played an important role in Romania's foreign political strategy. For the host, Romania would constitute a bridge toward Eastern-Europe. Later in the month, in Bucharest, President Constantinescu expressed his thanks to Turkish President Suleiman Demirel for Turkey's "exceptional strong support" of Romania in its efforts for joining NATO. The parties signed agreements on customs cooperation, on improving trade volumes, and on establishing cultural centers in Constanta and Istanbul. During his visit, Demirel officially opened Demirbank, a branch office of one the biggest Turkish private banks. (Up to now, Eximbank played key role in financing investments.)

The presidents of Romania, the Ukraine and Moldova met in Izmail, on July 3, 1997, to sign an agreement on regional cooperation. On November 24, Bucharest hosted the Polish and Ukrainian presidents. Primarily, the parties discussed the practical tasks of Euro-regional cooperation in the so called upper-Prut River region, joint actions against organized crime, the development of small- and medium-sized companies, the development of transport between the Baltic and Black Seas, the importance of the Warsaw-Lvov-Bucharest route and the modernization of the railroad between the harbors of Gdansk and Constanta. It was voiced that the three countries, forming a block of 120 million inhabitants, would represent a potentially solid economic factor in Europe. President Kuchma of the Ukraine emphasized that the parties would really become the guardians of security as NATO members. The Romanian president naturally stressed his country's role in contributing to regional stability by the Romanian-Moldavian-Ukrainian, the Romanian-Polish-Ukrainian, the Romanian-Bulgarian-Turkish and finally the Romanian-Hungarian-Austrian cooperation agreements.

Russia is notably missing from these cooperation pacts. It indicates that Romania was not unintentionally buttressing itself. The ongoing debate over the Romanian-Russian Treaty is proof positive of the not exactly unclouded bilateral relations. Russia is still unwilling to condemn the Molotov-Ribbentrop Pact, but it also demands compensation from Romania for the losses it suffered in WWI; Romania continues to demand the return of the royal treasury, sent to Russia for safekeeping in the same period, assessed at US$40 billion. The Russian answer is always the same: the treasure was somehow lost during the Bolshevik revolution.

Hungarian-Romanian relations and the issue of consulates[488]

Life came to almost a standstill for the two weeks before Christmas of 1996, as the President decreed a general pause in work. That is why the press only commented on January 7, 1997, on Adrian Severin's statements made during his visit to Budapest on December 27. The Romanian Foreign Minister promised the re-institution of the Bolyai University, the restoration of bilingual signs, the modification of the Education Act, the opening of consulates and the indemnification or restoration of nationalized church and community properties.

---

[488] Lipcsey, Ildikó: Addenda to the history of Hungarian-Romanian contacts, 1945-1955 (Adalékok a magyar-román külkapcsolatok történetéhez 1945-1955). External Affairs, 1999. pp. 3-4, 228-238.

Evenimentul Zilei published interviews with two prominent personalities – Radu Tudor, with close ties to SRI, and one-time Securitate general, Ioan Serbanoiu. The latter was in command of the group of 30 intelligence officers, which kept the Hungarian consulate in Cluj Napoca (Kolozsvár) under observation, and compiled a more than 100-page report for Ceausescu. Publishing opinions based on the 'statements' in the report, the paper stated no less than "the Cluj Napoca consulate was closed because Hungarian diplomats pursued intelligence gathering activities and illegal currency smuggling". Consequently, if the consulate were to be reopened, Hungary "would again have spies, protected by diplomatic immunity, in Transylvania."[489]

On the basis of these statements, Funar's party, several representatives of the former government party, including Iliescu and Melescanu among others, the Avram Iancu Society representing army officers and the Vatra Romaneasca protested against the consulate. They reasoned their objections that the re-opening of the consulates was rendered absolutely unnecessary by canceling the obligatory visa, that this action "would disturb the Romanians' tranquillity and the good Romanian-Hungarian relations in Transylvania," that it would re-establish "the nest of spies," as well as it would indicate the weakness of the government by making unnecessary concession, etc.

The coalition of parties (the so called "historical" ones, i.e., the Liberals, the Peasant Party and Social Democrats) in the Ciorbea-government held these worries as gross exaggerations. Moreover, many of them held that the re-opened consulates harkened back to the classical economic, cultural and private transactions, and can be considered as one of the important signs – not without foundation – of calming the formerly tense, almost cold war like, atmosphere between the two countries and promoting relations and rapprochement of the two nations.

The Hungarian Consulate-general in Cluj Napoca (Kolozsvár), closed at the end of June 1988, was finally opened on July 23, 1997. It has since had to suffer the attacks of extremist Romanian politicians, primarily mayor Gheorghe Funar's. Important events took place in the summer and autumn of that year. Joint Hungarian-Romanian chambers of commerce were formed, a joint military unit was organized, and a certain success was achieved in cooperation of criminal investigations. During the visit of Hungarian Foreign Minister, László Kovács, to Bucharest on October 8-9 – making preparations for the Hungarian Prime Minister's visit – the parties spoke of 'an avalanche of negotiations;' the establishment of an inter-governmental joint committee, comprising nine technical commissions, was also held.

Giving pride of place given to Hungarian 'relations' was not, and could not, be overshadowed by the fact that Romanian foreign policy launched an extended 'offensive' in all of the previously mentioned directions. In addition, to prove its commitment to the process of integration, we can assume that the motive of the gambit was that Romania – taking advantage of the general instability in the region, and the internal and external political weakness of the governments of the

---

[489] Evenimentul Zilei. 1957, January 6, 7.

other countries, moreover, it would not be surprising if it was inspired by significant external support – wants to play a leading role in the Balkan region.

Hungarian-Romanian economic relations

Experts reported dynamic growth in economic relations. Increase in bilateral trade was already considerable in 1995, Hungarian exports grew by 81%, amounting to US$357 million, and imports by 12%, – amounting to US$130 million. In 1996, exports dropped to 59% while import increased by 13 percent. That year the bilateral trade balance amounted to US$277.6 million, with a Hungarian surplus of US$131.1 million. Many politicians – on both sides of the government – looked on the improvement of the foreign trade balance, and especially the Hungarian investments in Romania, as a political achievement. MOL (Hungarian Oil and Gas Industries) is buying Transylvania – wrote *Redesteptarea*, the newspaper of Iosif Constantin Dragan who lived as an émigré for his ultra-right views (referring to the fact that MOL invested US$80 million in Romania.) "Hungarian investments in Romania infringe on the Constitution and endanger the country's independence." "Hungarian capital governs County Cluj (Kolozs)." This statement was based on the 313 Romanian-Hungarian joint ventures operating (total capitalization of US$2.1 million), although by number and capital they were ranked second behind Romanian-German joint ventures (total capitalization of US$5 million).

The exaggeration is evident if we, for example, examine the October status report on foreign investments. Hungary's share of the total US$34 billion foreign investment was US$41 million. The Szeklerland was considered as a particularly sensitive region. It is worth mentioning that foreigners invested US$28.9 million in County Harghita – US$4.45 million, or 15.4%, of it was Hungarian. It is a fact that 356 out of 616 joint ventures were Romanian-Hungarian ones.[490] According to Romanian sources, 1600 joint ventures exist in the country and Hungary ranks ninth among Romania's foreign partners.[491]

Signing the document in Bucharest on April 12, and becoming a partner to the Central European Free Trade Agreement (CEFTA), was also expected to further promote Hungarian-Romanian bilateral trade. CEFTA-membership brings significant reduction in tariffs. In particular, duties on 80% of industrial and two-third of agricultural products were reduced to zero, or almost. Both sides expected annual volume to grow to US$1 billion in two years. Romania currently ranked second, after Russia, in Hungary's foreign trade with the former socialist countries. The problem of the accumulated Romanian debt, worth 115 million in convertible Ruble, was resolved in the first half of 1996. Since the CEFTA-document was signed, Hungarian exports to Romania increased by 31% and imports by 110%. In trade volume, Romania was 15th among Hungary's partners, and Hungary was 20th among Romania's. Following the Budapest Bank and MOL (US$80 million), Dunapack intended to invest US$20 million in Romania. The

---

[490] MTI news data bank.
[491] Azi. 1995, October 3.

bulk of investors consisted of mainly small-sized companies. Today, some 2,010 Hungarian-owned companies operate in Romania. The main tasks of the chambers of commerce in Budapest and Bucharest is to further improve relations and assist in job creation in both countries.[492]

Foreign investments, in the amount of US$3.4 billion, were invested in Romania between March 1990 and September 1997. The amount invested by country was as follows:

The Netherlands	US$294.6 million
USA	US$254.5 million
Germany	US$250.1million, an increase of 38 fold
South Korea	US$235 million
France	US$ 227.1 million
Italy	US$199.7 million
Great Britain	US$139.3 million
Turkey	US$124.3 million
Austria	US$99.3 million
Luxembourg	US$94.8 million

The number of corporate investors:	46,685
The number of private investors:	55,694
Italian	5,913
German	5,756
Turkish	4,702

Assessing the 1997 balance, the new Foreign Minister, Andrei Plesu, did not seem dissatisfied. A total of US$3.5 billion was invested in Romania, with Hungary's share about US$38 million, ranking Hungary the 11th among foreign investors in 1997. The proportion of invested Hungarian capital was 1.11% and accounted for 3.2% of the total foreign capital invested in the country.[493]

The regional breakdown of Hungarian capital invested in Romania was as follows:

Bucharest	38.9%
County Covasna (Kovászna)	17.75%
County Harghita (Hargita)	13.26%
County Bihar	8.9%
County Arad	7.8%

All these, once again, refute Romanian concerns.

---

[492] MTI news data bank.
[493] Ibid.

Hungarians in Romania

As mentioned earlier, Foreign Minister Adrian Severin made several promises on his visit to Budapest on December 27, 1996. Government decree no. 22 of May 29, 1997 declared that in settlements where any minority made up 20%, its language could be used in public administration, on signs, etc. This affected 1,200 settlements in Romania: 1,071 Hungarian, 36 German, 57 Ukrainian, 15 Russian, 8 Turkish, 26 Slovakian, 7 Serb-Croatian, 6 Polish, 3 Tatar and 112 Roma (Gypsy) ones. (The National Peasant Party wanted to raise the 20% to 50%.) as a consequence, bilingual signs appeared in some settlements, and the so-called 'sign-war' took off, primarily in the Counties of Bihar, Cluj (Kolozs) and Maros, where the Hungarian place-names were referred to in Romanian circles as Medieval or from the Habsburg- and Horthy-eras.

EC suggestions also included the lifting of educational restrictions, too. It meant to cover instruction in the mother tongue from elementary to university level, the teaching of the history of the minorities, ensuring the instruction of history and geography in the mother tongue, the recognition of parochial schools and the instruction of professional skills in the mother tongue in vocational schools. Widespread protest was launched against the introduction of the decree. The Hungarians collected a petition of 500,000 signatures, demanding the re-instatement of the independent Hungarian university, the Bolyai, in Cluj Napoca.[494]

Both the Romanian government and the President took an ambivalent stand regarding the Bolyai University. By the beginning of the academic year, even the so-called two-staged solution fell into oblivion, i.e., a Hungarian department would first be formed in Cluj Napoca (Kolozsvár) university, followed by the independent Hungarian university sometime later. However, more Hungarian students were accepted. (As an example, 30 Hungarians were allowed into the law faculty from the 1997-98 year.) Instead of a university, 3-year college courses were begun in Sfântu Gheorghe (Sepsiszentgyörgy) and Gheorgheni (Gyergyószentmiklós), but the language of instruction was Romanian. The stand of the governing Romanian political circle on the existence and place of the Hungarian university was conflicting. More precisely: sometimes they took a stand for it, and then against it; and this included both the President and the Premier of Romania.

Church and community properties were not restored, either. As a gesture, the Hebrew Church was re-instated in five of its properties. Then, promises were made that the other minorities would receive a total of 18 properties; that the Hungarians will get the Petofi House in Bucharest, the Transylvanian Museum of Timisoara (Temesvár), the Unitarian Pension Building in Cluj Napoca (Kolozsvár), the Batthyaneum in Alba Iulia (Gyulafehérvár) and the Catholic and Protestant bishop's palaces in Oradea (Nagyvárad). Up to December 31, 1997, none were handed back.[495]

---

[494] Freedom /Cluj Napoca/ (Szabadság /Kolozsvár/). 1997, October 27.
[495] Freedom (Szabadság). 1994, April 9, 10.

The Permanent Conference of the Elders of Hungarian Christian Churches in Romania issued a Memorandum in Cluj Napoca (Kolozsvár) on June 25, 1997. It pointed out that the draft amendment to the 84/1995 Education Act was in contradiction on several points with European Council regulations. The EC rules specifically directed Romania, point by point, to re-instate the dissolved or restricted minority and parochial schools to their full rights, to re-establish the independent status of church education, state subsidies for them, the restoration or compensate for the properties confiscated in 1948 and the re-opening of the Bolyai University, closed in 1959.

The Consulate-general in Cluj Napoca (Kolozsvár), closed down by Ceausescu in June of 1988, was opened on a temporary site on July 23. In the intervening time, the mayor has sent numerous letters to the leaders of the country asking for the closing of the institution and expelling Consul-General Károly Bitay.

Various forms of Anti-Hungarian attitudes

The dailies *Adevarul* and *Evenimentul Zilei* fairly lashed the government for its "short-sightedness" in meeting the demands of the DAHR. Nastase's opinion was that ever since the DAHR got into power, it was blackmailing the government and forced it to issue 120 decrees, all the while circumventing Parliament. Former Foreign Minister Melescanu, who broke with Iliescu and defined himself and his party, the Alliance for Romania Party, as centrist and social democratic, stated that "Transylvania will be Magyarized," if Hungarian signs were allowed to appear, he admitted, mostly in the Counties of Maros, Kolozs and Szatmár, outside the Szeklerland. The explicit target of the Melescanu-led Alliance for Romania Party, which preceded the DAHR on voter popularity lists, was to supersede the DAHR from and take its place in the government. Many politicians crossed the floor lately, the party had 14 MPs and 2 Senators in Parliament.

Interior Minister Dejeu paid a two-day rapid visit to Transylvania in early August to gauge tension between the ethnic groups. Dejeu called it alarming that Romanians living in the Szeklerland might lose their national identity because of imposed, forced Magyarization. His visit to Cluj Napoca (Kolozsvár) caused the removal of the Hungarian flag from the building of the Hungarian Consulate-General and a rise in the anti-Hungarian sentiments. The local arm of the Romanian National Unity Party issued a statement encouraging a settling of accounts with the 'terror organization, DAHR, and its leaders,' which were 'setting up semi-military units and making preparations to settle scores with the police and the secret service.' As a side note, fly-bills with the same content, i.e., encouraging a showdown with the Hungarians, were often handed out in Cluj Napoca (Kolozsvár) in earlier days, too.

After the visit of the Interior Minister, Mayor Gheorghe Funar wrote the Prime Minister a letter, urging him to convene the country's defense council and declare martial law in Transylvania. He claimed that the SRI had ample information about the anti-Romanian activity of the 'Budapest-directed' DAHR. Funar referred to the alleged SRI-report, which was published in series in

National, and which claimed that the Romanian secret service possessed reliable information items about the espionage of Hungarians in Romania. The report claimed that by getting into power, DAHR would get access to state secrets and would disclose them. Niculescu Antal, who worked at the General Secretariat of the government, was mentioned by name, and would be 'smuggling state secrets out on CDs."

After all that, it is not surprising that the three extremist politicians, Funar, Vadim Tudor and Adrian Paunescu celebrated together, on September 12, the 125th anniversary of the death of Avram Iancu in Cluj Napoca (Kolozsvár).[496] The mob gathered and shouted anti-government and anti-Hungarian slogans: "Transylvania was sold to the Hungarians," "Thieves, murderers!" and "Out of the country!" At the end of November, Iliescu's party launched the so called "Transylvania maneuver" and called on all political forces to fight against "the autonomist and separatist intentions encouraged by the new power". A newer report saw the light of that that asserted that Romanians were being Magyarized in the Szeklerland and denying their basic human rights. Some are of interest to be noted.

The Permanent Delegation of the County Covasna (Kovászna) Council sent a letter to the President, the Prime Minister and the Chairmen of the two Houses of Parliament on November 6, 1997. It became evident from the letter that 23.4% of the county's population were Romanians, but the commanders of the armed forces, including the SRI (secret service) local office, were all Romanians, 15 out of 30 heads of state institutions were Romanians, 20 out of 25 local judges were Romanians, and 34.6% of the 32 commercial companies were Romanians, too. As for the number of Romanians, it did not decreased but increased from 23.4% to 25%. In 58 out of the 128 settlements of the county, the language of instruction was Romanian and in 96 settlements, in Hungarian and Romanian.

Prefect Zoltán József Dézsi of County Harghita published his thorough and detailed study both in the Hungarian and Romanian media. Taking the results of the 1992 census the population of the county as a base, the populace was:

348,335		increase over 1997
Hungarian	292,104 = 84.71%	17,517 = 79.53%
Romanian	48,948 = 14.05%	4,154 = 18.86%
Other	4,283 = 1.24%	354 = 1.61%

The number of senior officials: 237, Hungarian: 147, or 62%, Romanian 90, or 38%. The number of education institutions: 618, Hungarian: 519, or 83.98%, Romanian 52, or 8.41%, mixed 47, or 7.61%.

Taking all these facts into account, the Prefect did not uphold the accusations that the persecution of the Romanians was based on facts.

Hungarian-Romanian moderates and radicals in politics [497]

[496] Romania Mare. 1997, September 3.

[497] Szentimrei, Krisztina: „Left" and „Right" in Transylvanian Hungarian politics („Bal" és „Jobb" az erdélyi magyar politikában). Transylvanian Hungarians (Erdélyi Magyarság), 1998, issue 34, pp. 7-13.

It is widely known that after the 1996 elections, when civic powers (ed: democratic) won over the reform and post Communists, President Constantinescu received assurances from the West regarding NATO membership. The West's stipulation: take DHAR into the government. From that moment, the hidden, latent animosity became open and sharp within DHAR, a situation that was brought forwards into the 21st century.

The moderates were the Neptunians, so named after a vacation village on the Romanian seashore where some DHAR politicians, without consulting the DAHR leadership, carried on negotiations during Iliescu's term. They held talks with the government's representatives at the initiative of foreigners, more specifically the Freemason influenced international organization, Project Ethnographic Research (PER). According to other sources, the differences between the 'collaborators' and the radicals became explosive after the unconditional joining of the government ranks in 1994. The radicals clustered around Bishop Tokés. The backers of establishing a national self-government on the basis of the right for self-determination did not form a homogeneous group. It was comprised of various groupings, like the Transylvanian-Hungarian Initiative, the Fidesz-like platform of the Reform Grouping (Reformtömörülés), the Szeklerland Grouping of Transylvanian Civil Society.

By name, the latter's founders were Károly Király, Ádám Katona, Imre Krizbai, Elod Kincses, Géza Borsos, Pál Vilmos Sántha, István Csutak, Miklós Patrubány, Árpád Gazda, József Gazda, József Csapó, whose autonomy draft Funar tore apart publicly, and Imre Borbély and lastly, the bishops and priests of the Hungarian churches. They openly accept confrontation: with Presidential candidate György Frunda, with Minister of Minorities György Tokay, with DAHR Chairman Béla Markó, with DAHR executive chairman Csaba Takács, with Senator Attila Verestóy, with State Secretary László Borbély and the entire leadership of the DAHR. It must be noted that these DHAR leaders were not persons 'cast aside' during the years of the Communist dictatorship. In fact, they made careers in the Party. Both sides were convinced that the differences of opinion sprung from the different directions they must take to define the future of Hungarians in Transylvania.

At the session of the Council of Federal Representatives (CFR – Szövetségi Küldöttek Tanácsa) held in Cluj Napoca (Kolozsvár) on July 12-13, 1997, a mini parliament of Romanian-Hungarians, the radicals conveyed the hypocritical objections widely held by Romanians. In response, László Tokés proposed the recall of Frunda and Tokay, among others, because:

?? the DAHR joined the government without negotiating, i.e., they made no conditions that Hungarian demands to be met,

?? getting into power was the only priority, as during the election campaign they made offers to Iliescu's party that, in exchange for delivering the votes, DAHR would be the tie-breaking minority group,

?? its results were only symbolic,

?? they ignored the program passed by the congress, more precisely, they gave up the demands for autonomy and the independent Hungarian university,

?? they did no work on the preparation of an internal census,

?? they did not consult with the DAHR leadership regarding the distribution of posts, and

?? they supported improving friendship between Budapest and Bucharest, only if the ambitions of the Hungarians in Transylvania were not the subject of any bargain.

Subsequently, the radical representatives proposed another CFR meeting before the coming Congress, to discuss the final versions of the draft statutes on individual autonomy and Szeklerland's autonomy. József Csapó, who drafted the two statutes, was of the opinion that it was incomprehensible that the DAHR be a part of the governing process when it obviously could not govern itself. The DAHR, with its two Ministers and eight State Secretaries – the posts of another State Secretary and of two Ministerial General Directors were appointed recently – was implementing a government program in which no efforts for autonomy was present, even on the level of a declaration.

"Unity remains – as do the debates." On balance, that was the outcome of the Fifth DAHR Congress, held in Tirgu Mures (Marosvásárhely) on October 3-4, 1997. Despite heated debates, the DAHR did not split in two, and it did not give up its government positions, either. Tokés' proposal to authorize Frunda, delegated to the Council of Europe, to ask again for the institutional review of Romania, provoked debate. They called upon Minister Tokay, why, as Minister of Minorities, he had no detailed program regarding the minority question. The Alliance President was pressed as to why he did not compile a list of successes and failures. In his reply, Markó mentioned among the results the new Land Act which provided an opportunity for reclaiming communal properties and lands, the agreement signed with Hungary regarding the reciprocal recognition of diplomats, and the ratification of the Charter on Local Autonomies.

The Congress gave its consent in principle to make negotiations between the Romanian majority and the Hungarian minority a permanent process. They supported the transformation of the István Sulyok College of Oradea (Nagyvárad) into an independent Hungarian university. Regarding instruction in the mother tongue, the Congress passed a decision urging the establishment of a state-subsidized, Hungarian university with its seat in Cluj Napoca (Kolozsvár). (Thereby, they left the opportunity for laying the foundations of either establishing a new university or separating the Babes-Bolyai university.)

The Congress accepted the action program presented by the moderates. Its message to the Romanians was that the DAHR intended not to act as limited-interest body representing the Hungarians but a responsible political factor which would contribute to Romania's efforts for joining Europe and the implementation of reforms. It was a victory for the moderates – the proportion being about 83/17 between moderates and radicals – that the drafts on complete autonomy were temporarily shelved.

Several influential leader of the Hungarians in Romania were convinced that the failure in delivering the government's promises on the one hand, and the postponement of Romania's NATO membership on the other, would radicalize the Hungarian community. For fear that Europe was going to be permanently divided into two, the question of territorial revision in connection with Transylvania and the Partium, and/or the independence of Transylvania, would be raised sooner or later.

Two facts indicated the crisis within DAHR. First, the gap between the Bucharest-based leadership and local authorities had increased. Second, the Alliance seemed to have to leaders: President Béla Markó and Honorary President László Tokés. Tokés proposed Tokay's dismissal and the preparations for another round of Hungarian-Hungarian (i.e., mother country and Hungarians beyond the borders) summit at the next CFR meeting in December. The closing weeks of the year forced some people to reflect on the achievements. The failures of the debates during the autumn Parliamentary session and the DAHR's retreating tactics gave ample reasons to do so.

DAHR's entire program - self-government, autonomy and internal representative reform / turnover – faces a government and its program, one it swore to uphold, where it can not fulfill its fundamental goal. Not only program initiating activities but situational analysis and determining strategy and tactics were neglected. Because DAHR gave up its interest-representation duty in order to become part of the government, it misled the West into believing that all was well in minority politics in Romania. The question, consequently, whether it should remain in the government, was a permanent agenda topic.

Ongoing government crisis: 1998

Romanian nationalism exists on several levels: Pruteanu's onslaughts were accepted, but Funar's ultra-nationalism made even his party pause to think. His expulsion resulted in the split of the Romanian National Unity Party, but the moderates, the Valeriu Tabarac-led wing, did not yet gain complete victory. (In the events, not only Funar's extreme behavior, but also personal and inter-group clashes played a part.) Their statement of November 5 characterized the political environment of the Funar-group: "Where Funar is, we are also there. Traitors can choose between prison, noose and bullet." The two groups held concurrent sessions in Bucharest and Cluj Napoca (Kolozsvár) on the last Saturday of November. The Cluj Napoca meeting was initiated by the party's County Cluj arm, where Funar's expulsion was not accepted.

Romanian internal political crisis arose on two levels during 1998:
1. Society's confidence in the government was shaken. According to the results of an opinion poll taken in early November, 50.6% of the population would dismiss Prime Minister Ciorbea. (The fact that the miners' severance pay was spent played an important role.) Those polled blamed Ciorbea for the increased prices, unemployment, governing through decrees instead of applying constitutional ways, "rolling over" for the IMF, placing the coalition's interests before the nation's interests and for including the DAHR into the government.
2. The clashes between the Christian Democratic National Peasant Party and the Democratic Party in the government coalition risked the operability of the government.

Figures indicate the changes in the popularity of parties and the sudden advance of the nationalist to 39%:

Romanian Party of Socialist Democracy	25 %
Great Romania Party	9
Romanian National Unity Party	5
Total	39 %

Their opposition, the historical parties and their allies:

Democratic Convention	35 %
CDNPP	6
National Liberal Party	1
Social Democratic Union	2
Total	44 %

It was, therefore, not surprising that President Constantinescu resorted to the well proved anti-Hungarian method on December 1, 1997, the 79th anniversary of the Alba Iulia (Gyulafehérvár) National Assembly (where Transylvania's joining to Romania was declared in 1918 - before the Peace Treaty decisions), when he:

?? precluded any assurance of collective rights, although it was totally contradictory to European norms;

?? called "territorial autonomy on an ethnic basis" unacceptable; and

?? when the Army held the first public display of power after the Ceausescu-era, stated that "the Romanian Army carries out its duties, as it has always done".

Ciorbea sought to escape from the crisis by appointing 9 new Ministers. The target of reshuffling in the government – as Ciorbea put it – was to implement global reforms, to accelerate the establishment of stability, restructuring and the creation of a market economy, to complete the agricultural and the public administration reforms. All these precisely corresponded with the objections raised by the Democratic Party. Petre Roman actually kept the government in check by threatening that his party would leave the government coalition if it did not continue to complete the reforms. The Democratic Party's influence was clearly indicated in the structure of the new government, too. Adrian Severin's (Democratic Party) successor in the post of Foreign Minister, Andrei Plesu, and the appointment of Victor Babiuc to the post of State Minister was also to curry favor with the Democratic Party.

On the year-end balance of Ciorbea-government, having gambled everything on NATO membership and the influx of foreign capital, none of them came to fruition. Nevertheless, it was held on a government level that 1997 was the year of repudiation (see the deconstruction of inefficient infrastructures) and 1998 would be the year of construction. To achieve this target – while the opposition was preparing for the advanced elections – and to cross the opposition's scheme, the Democratic Party did not leave the government coalition – the government planned to introduce the following changes:

?? to support small ventures, and those who re-invest profits and those who invest, through a new tax system;

?? to create new jobs;

?? to introduce direct credit;

?? to start to modernize the infrastructure (see the Budapest-Bucharest-Constanta highway);

?? to replace outdated mining equipment;

?? to start environment protection works;

and it counted on an increase in purchasing power.

In a country suffering from an economy agonizing over directions, a confused society, where the implementation of reforms were hindered by old structures left in place, where the managers of bankrupt companies were still living in luxury while 5.5 million pensioners and more than 1 million unemployed were living below the poverty line, where inflation was planned to reach 40%, yet the salaries of civil servants were to be 'adjusted' by 60%, it was strongly questionable that the government experts - or expert's government - would be able to lead Romania out of the crisis.

Romanian governments, irrespective of their political character, are finding it more and more difficult, year after year, to wrestle with the economic problems and the social unrest that follows, culminating in civil disobedience and strikes. It is not surprising that the Director of the Romanian Intelligence Service, Costin Georgescu, stated in his 1998-99 annual report that the greatest threat factors facing Romanian national security are economic collapse and social unrest.

The year 1998 was a black one for Romanian economy. The annual GDP was 338.67 billion Lei, which was a 7.3% decrease when compared to 1997. Foreign investments dropped by 18.6%, unemployment hovered between 9% and 9.4% (in January of 1999, it rose to 11%) and the Lei was devalued by 36%. Industrial output dropped by 17.3%, agriculture by 7.6% and the value of services by 20% as compared to 1997. The per capita GDP was US$3,692 vs. US$3,976 in the previous year.

The Business Central Europe data sheds the following light on Romanian economic life (there are some differences with the above mentioned figures which came from Romanian sources):

	1996	1997	1998
Per capita GDP	$4,560	$4,356	$4,990
Change in GDP	3.9%	-6.6%	-7.3%
Industrial output	9.9%	-5.9%	-17.3%
Unemployment	6.6%	8.8%	10.3%
Average monthly wage	$138	$121.80	$153
Foreign investments	$263 M	$1,224 M	$884 M
Foreign currency reserves	$600 M	$2,500 M	$1,600 M
Foreign debt	$8,300 M	$8,200 M	$9,200 M

The country started 1999 with a long list of problems: privatization came to a halt, inflation and unemployment grew while production enthusiasm waned, large factories employing thousands were closing – mainly in heavy industry and consumer goods – even in industrially advanced Transylvania which accounted for 20% of the country's industrial output and 50% of the heavy industrial output.

Last, but not least, the legal framework was still not in place that would lure foreign investors.

VIII. On the threshold of new elections: 1999

Economic Situation

The annual budget bill was passed on February 16, 1999. It envisaged that last year's 4% deficit would be decreased to 2% of the GDP. Inflation was planned at a monthly 3%, annualized at 25%. (However, by the end of the year, it stood at 50%, far higher than the planned rate.) The budget planned on a revenue of Lei 3,500 billion from privatization, while canceling subsidies granted to foreign investments – who were, in any case, kept away unfathomable regulations and the delays in the meeting of promises – and export incentives. According to the budget, the country would be able to make its 1999 payment on its foreign debts, amounting to US$3 billion. Concurrently with passing the budget bill – the opposition parties abstained from the vote – Parliament increase electric energy prices by 23%, heating by 40% and natural gas by 20%. A further 15% increase in food prices was planned to be introduced in early March, testing the purchasing power of the population. The opposition held it alarming that the deficit of the balance of payments increased by US$765 million in one year. Exports amounted to US$7 billion, while the balance of payments deficit increased to US$3 billion. The fact that businesses failed to take advantage of export opportunities, e.g.- duty concessions granted to Romanian products going to the European Union, also contributed to the situation. As exports dropped by 1.6% in 1998, as compared to 1997, the government passed a packet of export incentives in March.

The delegation of the International Monetary Fund, during its talks conducted in Bucharest at the end of February 1999, did not exclude the possibility of freeing the US$430 million loan frozen in 1998, but only if Romania met certain requirements, among others:

?? draft a detailed plan on restructuring (e.g.- the reform of the banking sector, closing of mines);

?? accelerate privatization, modify the act on privatization;

?? rescue the Foreign Trade Bank and the Bancorex.

Finance Minister Decebal Traian Remes stated that Romania would be able to repay its US$937 million debt in the first half of the year without taking out foreign loans (annual debt to be repaid in 1999 amounted to US$3 billion). However, Remes also pointed out that they would try to reschedule debts due in the second half of the year. According to the ministry's promise made earlier in the year, it contributed to the reorganization of the Bancorex by providing Lei 4,200 billion, because the country's financial system would collapse if it failed to do so.

It was not accidental either that the Finance Minister announced in March the unification of the income tax system. Progressive tax rates were to be introduced and, although incomes under a given level would be tax-free, deposit interest would be taxed. The tax system consisted of five rates: 18% up to Lei 11 million income per year, then 23%, 28%, 34% rates, and 40% tax over an annual income of Lei 60 million. Taxpayers were allowed to reduce their taxes with Lei 800,000 for charitable donations.

A week after the visit by the IMF delegation, in order to stop the rapid devaluation of Romanian currency – it lost 17% of its value within two months, since the beginning of 1999 – the National Bank of Romania raised interest rates, so daily and weekly money-market interest rates earned 200-300%. The fact that it lost 5.8% of its value in one day, indicated the devaluation of the Lei. At the beginning of the year one dollar bought Lei 11,000, while its exchange rate was 15,000 by March. (Consequently, HUF 1 was worth Lei 63.) On March 18 – within one day – the dollar's exchange rate jumped to Lei 22,000. It decreased slightly, to 18,000 Lei, by the end of the year. However, some financial experts thought that the real dollar to Lei exchange rate should be 1:30,000-40,000.

Central reserves amounted to US$2.8 billion, but it would all be used up to cover external debt due to be repaid that year. US$1 billion was due to be paid back in the first month of the year, and further US$1.5 billion during May-June. Romania's gold reserves were 101 tons at the end of June. According to some, by selling the gold reserves of the National Bank worth US$927 million, the country would be able to solve its financial problems. The Bank's management, however, insisted on preserving the country's currency reserves.

In early June, the Governor of the National Bank stated that the country expected US$5 billion foreign financial support during that year, including US$900 million from the IMF, the World Bank and the European Union; US$1.4 billion from privatization and foreign investments; US$900 million from former credit agreements; and a loan worth Lei 1.1 billion from the private sector. The Ministry of Finance planned to issue bonds worth US$300 million, and the central bank expected to receive US$600 million as short-term loan. The International Monetary Fund was ready to open the long-awaited US$300 million loan only if Bancorex, which covered one-fourth of the total banking and 70% of foreign trade transactions, would be saved from bankruptcy by state assistance. In 1998, the state subsidized the bank with Lei 4,180 billion to save personal deposits worth Lei 5,523 billion. In 1999, a further Lei 2,500 billion were lent to save Bancorex in the first round. The bank's crisis stems from the practice pursued between 1992 and 1996, when it granted loans to unprofitable companies – and the new government also followed this practice – even if the company was unable to cover its payroll. On the other hand, the bank was keen to fill loan applications from the political elite. In addition to all this, Bancorex gave credit to individuals working in the armed forces, staff members of the Ministries of Foreign and Internal Affairs and senior officials of intelligence services – and the list of their names was published by the press.

Bank scandals became commonplace in Romania. Some US$2 billion was spent from the budget to keep the banks alive for the time being. Dacia Felix Bank, which was established to buy out land in Transylvania, created a US$160 million loss when its managers made various transactions through Swiss financial institutions. Legal proceedings were commenced against the managers of Dacia Felix Bank in the course of the anti-corruption campaign.

The Director of the National Bank of Romania stated that half of the active debts of Romanian banks, Lei 30,000 billion, were irrecoverable due to corruption and loans granted under political pressure. The hard currency reserves of the

National Bank decreased from US$1.02 billion to US$813.2 million within a month, by the end of June, because it was used to cover the current installment of debt repayment. Experts gave numerous reasons why the expected capital did not materialize in the country:

?? the postponement of promised reforms,
?? the reorganization of the economy did not take place,
?? the financial crisis in Asia and Russia.

A further round of talks started between the representatives of international money-market and Romania in early June, because Romania repaid only US$2 billion of its debts in 1999. The agenda still consisted of the restructuring of the banking system and the postponement of privatization. Urged by international financial organizations, Romania received loans worth total US$120 million from private banks, while the IMF held out the prospect of granting a US$485 million stand-by loan. However, the IMF subjected it to the condition of Romania taking further loans of US$350 million for amortization.

Bucharest hoped that this transaction would help it in gaining the stand-by loan for one and half a years. But the country's population had to suffer further price increases. Fuel, telephone and meat prices went up by 20% on average. They were followed by the increase of beverages and tobacco. It was not accidental, either, that the repayment of debt was followed by the issuance of bonds, that is, the government borrowed from the population to cover the repayment of debt. Gross domestic product decreased further, especially in the energy sector and public services.

In early August, the IMF Board of Directors passed a decision allowing Romania to receive part of the loan of US$547 million and US$73 million of it was transferred immediately. The IMF emphasized again its expectations: the government, asking for credit, should account of its private capital to a greater extent in order to provide an opportunity for the debtor country to use IMF-loan primarily to repay its debts. In this concrete case, the IMF expected Romania to take a US$350 million loan from commercial creditors on the international money-market before October 15. The following reservations were made: inflation should not be higher than 40%, the budget deficit should not surpass 3.7% of the GDP and – as on a number of occasions – the transformation and stabilization of Bancorex.

In early August, it became apparent that attempts to save Bancorex would end in failure. It was followed by the cancellation of its license, which was the prime condition of IMF granting credit, then by the merger of Bancorex and the state-owned Romanian Trade Bank. The State Property Fund redirected personal bank accounts to the Trade Bank. Now, 62% of Bancorex was held by the State Property Fund, 28% by investment funds and 10% by small investors and private companies. Bancorex' desperate debts included loans worth Lei 13 billion, loaned to several hundred companies, and it was planned to be recovered through legal proceedings. Bancorex possessed fixed assets of US$220 million, and their liquidation was quite probable.

The IMF Board of Directors consented to grant a US$547 million stand-by loan to Romania in August. US$73 million out of it was immediately made available, the rest to be in three installments if Romania succeed in obtaining a US$470 million loan on the international money market. As Romania failed to meet the IMF conditions – the latter one as well, among others – it was only promised in December 1999 to get access to the US$200 million already granted. If IMF declined to transfer the credit, Romania would lose the chance the obtain other credits as well.

The fact that the second part of US$200 million of the IMF stand-by loan was not transferred in 1999 played a partial but important – indirect and direct – role in the development of the government crisis in December.

The new government, led by Mugur Isarescu, who had been the President of the National Bank of Romania for ten years, thought the issuance of its economic program for 2000 was its most important task, first of all to win the confidence and the credit of the West.

His program included:

?? a 3% budget deficit;
?? 25-35% inflation;
?? 1.5% economic growth;
?? 25% currency devaluation;
?? privatization to be completed (mammoth companies would be liquidated one by one, big and medium-sized companies would be privatized (bought out) by investment banks);
?? banks to be reorganized and privatized;
?? priority to be given to regional development programs;
?? service sphere to be reorganized and privatized;
?? farmers to be subsidized;
?? 6% of the GDP to be spent on reorganizing banks;
?? priority to be given to the fight against economic crimes and corruption.

This economic strategy, however, seemed absolutely unaccomplishable, when inflation, as compared with the previous year's 40%, increased by 50% between January and November 1999, and it stood at 53.7% in December; food prices increased by a further 3.4%, services by 2.5% and consumer goods by 5.3%. The slightest improvement in the economic situation is not exclusively a matter of a government program; social willingness to implement it was still missing in Romania.

As to privatization in Romania, the State Property Agency (FPS) wanted to complete the privatization of the companies under its control before the end of 2000. According to schedules, 1,800 production concerns were privatized in the first half of 1999, and a further 1,500 small- and medium-sized companies were planned to be privatized before the end of that year. FPS Chairman Radu Sirbu reported that 80% of Romanian companies were still in state hands. (As a reminder: there were 2,000 state-owned companies 10 years ago in Hungary, nowadays there are some 250-300.)

Privatization was closely connected with attracting foreign capital into the country. But the undeveloped state of the Romanian economy kept foreign capital at a distance. For example, the agricultural budget in Romania, which is twice the size of Hungary – the level of mechanization and developed technology – was half of that of Hungary. The Romanian constitution did not guaranteed the ownership of private property. In addition, sales tax constituted the most important tax category in developed countries, but in Romania – which had an underdeveloped industry and a moribund agriculture – individual income tax, profit tax and customs duties were the most important income sources.

In order to achieve certain improvements, in May 1999 the Romanian government passed a decree on granting significant allowances, including:

?? exemptions from corporate taxes,

?? exemptions from customs duties,

?? exemptions from value-added taxes on imported equipment and raw materials,

?? exemptions for those who invest at least US$50 million.

Due to certain international pressure, privatization gathered speed at the end of 1999. The Romanian State Property Fund was able to close the year with success, by completing the privatization of 1,705 state-owned companies, 500 more than in the previous year. However, the number of privatization processes executed with foreign capital dropped. Investors showed interest mainly in banks and food industrial companies. A further 2,570 state companies were planned to be privatized in 2000, and another 330 to be reorganized – stated Chairman Radu Sirbu in the first days of 2000.

Reprivatization (ed: the return of nationalized or seized assets) had also been on the agenda of Parliament for years. Certain goals were reached in 1991 and 1997 on this issue. First of all, the center-right government that seized power in the 1996 elections, wanted to achieve a permanent decision. A draft bill, worked out by the legal commission of the Houses of Parliament in September 1999, provided a chance for restoring the real estate seized in 1945 to their original owners in the near future. In the past, Romanian citizenship was made one of the conditions, and if the property was tenanted, the owner had to provide adequate replacement property instead. In addition to natural persons, legal entities and parties, which were banned in the Communist-era, were also able to reclaim their properties. The draft bill, however, still did not refer to either those who were compensated in the 1970s, or the communal properties of the national minorities, which were fundamental for the re-institution of their institutes. Merely promises were made that a separate act would deal with them.

However, the Romanian reprivatization bill, which was signed by the President on January 10, 2000, decreed that one-time owners, or their agents, could reclaim 50 hectares of arable land and 10 hectares of woods. In the case of common properties – the communal property of peasants – it did not determine the upper limit of reclaimable land or woods, and it was a significant improvement. (Lands held in common in County Csík and the Szeklerland total 64,000 hectares, and the owners want to get it back, if necessary, with international assistance.)

Those Transylvanian Hungarians who left the country but retained their Romanian citizenship, or are able to prove that they have been stripped of their citizenship, could reclaim and be reinstituted in their properties. According to preliminary surveys, land compensation affected several hundred thousand Hungarians who once lived in Romania. Application had to be forwarded to Romanian authorities before March 13, more precisely: to the mayor's office in whose jurisdiction the property lay.

Bilateral trade volume between Romania and Hungary[498] increased three and a half times between 1991 and 1998. In 1998, among Hungary's foreign trade partners, Romania was number 10 in imports, 24th in exports, standing 25th on the overall trade volume list. Of the trade within the CEFTA countries, Romania accounted for 28% of the exports and 11% of the imports.

In February 1999, 2,789 joint-venture companies, with Hungarian capital, were registered in Romania, with the Hungarian investments amounting to US$83.7 million. Hungary thus ranked 11th among investing countries. The list of big investors included MOL Rt. (operating 20 gas stations), Budapest Bank, and Zala Ceramics Ltd. (Zalakerámia Rt.). Romanian Petrom established a branch in Szeged, and began construction of a gasoline service station by investing US$4 million. At the same time, Romania was ready to export 100 megawatts of electricity to Hungary.

Hungarian-Romanian external trade volume amounted to US$766.1 million in 1999, a 50% growth over the previous year. However, this increase was unfavorable for the Romanian side, as its foreign trade deficit, vis-à-vis Hungary, grew to US$327 million. Romanian exports to Hungary amounted to US$49.6 million but imports from Hungary totaled US$81.2 million.

Hungarian-Romanian foreign trade data, January-March 1999:

	Exports		Imports		Balance	
	1999 US$M	99/98 %	1999 US$M	99/98 %	1999 US$M	99/98 %
Food, beverages, tobacco	25.5	74.6	3.9	42.2	21.5	-3.3
Raw materials	1.3	21.3	9.2	188.5	-7.9	-9.0
Energy	3.1	55.6	0.7	353.2	2.5	-3.0
Processed goods	54.3	105.1	27.7	111.4	26.6	-0.2
Machinery, machine parts	10.5	61.3	3.5	101.8	7.0	-6.7
Romanian total	94.7	82.7	45.0	105.4	49.7	-22.2
Hungarian total	5,714.5	108.4	6,348.4	109.4	-633.9	-98.9
Country ranking	11	10	23	25		

Thanks to Romania's CEFTA-membership and customs concessions, bilateral trade increased by 20-30% every month. The Hungarian side expected that disputed matters – duty levied on Hungarian wheat and flour and the issue of Romanian steel deliveries – would be settled within CEFTA. During bilateral talks held in May, the issue of duties levied on Hungarian grains was taken off the agenda, but it became clear that it was Bucharest's firm intention to introduce protectionist measures against pork and poultry, which was strange as poultry

---

[498] Economic indicators differ from those of Romanian sources.

production dropped drastically in Romania. The 1996 output of 139,000 tons decreased to 78,000 tons in 1997, forcing poultry imports of US$108.9 million that year. The amount of poultry imports increased every year afterwards.

In June of 1999, Romania suspended the preferential CEFTA export-duties on Hungarian pork and poultry for a year: instead of the 25%, a duty of 45% was levied. It must be noted that Romania increased export-duties only against Hungary among all the CEFTA-countries. Romania unilaterally suspended the CEFTA-agreed tariff on Hungarian flour in 1998. (Slovakia did the same when it levied higher duties on Hungarian wine.) In addition, the Romanians declared that Hungary was attempting to settle its agricultural problems through Romanian exports and that the entire Free Trade Agreement, i.e., the system of CEFTA, should be revised and discussed. The introduction of Romanian protective tariffs resulted in a 33.5% drop in Hungarian agricultural exports, i.e., by US$26.4 million.

In 1996, Brussels extended the PHARE-CBC subsidies – available to countries bordering on the EU – to the Hungarian-Romanian border region and it provided the foundations for the cooperation of neighboring counties in the two countries. Between 1996 and 1998, this region received 14 million Euro in PHARE subsidies. The next installment of 23 million Euro subsidy was designed to complete the second phase of the establishment of the Central-Eastern-European business information center, to promote economic development in the Bihor (Bihar) region, including its infrastructure, to construct the road connecting border villages Kiszombor-Cenad (Nagycsanád), to rebuild the road leading to the border crossing of Battonya, to modernize the border crossing at Csengersima-Petea, to develop environmental protection in the Crisul Negru and Repede (Fekete- and Sebes-Körös) rivers and to establish a flood-warning system along the Tisza, Crasna (Kraszna) and Turul (Túr) rivers.

It needs to be noted that these institutional contacts constituted only potential possibilities for the development of relations. Their effectiveness was doubtful in the past, as it is today. Consequently, as with many other inter-governmental committees, organizations and institutions, they are 'smoke and mirror' organizations in the two countries' mutual relationship and both parties are quite aware that they are operating them to meet certain foreign expectations.

Changes in Internal Politics
A recurring phenomenon: the miners' strikes in the Jiu (Zsil) valley

The Jiu (Zsil) valley miner's strikes are a traditional event in Romania:
1. In the first event, in 1929, the Liberal Party of the Regat provoked them into a strike in order to overthrow the National Peasant Party government formed mostly by Transylvanian Romanians;
2. It the 1970s, in the Ceausescu-era, the miners' demonstrations can be equally considered as wage fights and anti-regime protests;
3. On January 28, 1990, just before the first elections after the change in regime, Ion Iliescu and Petre Roman, the two prominent figures of the National Salvation Front, used the miners in their struggle against the historical parties,

the Liberals and the National Peasant Party. The miners did their job by demolishing the two headquarters. The reason for the action was that the Peasant Party and the Liberals demanded that the National Salvation Front, as a reform-communist organization, should not organize itself into a party and should not enter the elections;

4. On June 13-15, 1990, the miners were pressed into action on University Square, Bucharest, against students protesting for 50 days against the revival of Communism;

5. On September 24-27, 1991, Iliescu used the miners to overthrow Petre Roman, by now his political enemy. The reason was that the government refused to conduct negotiations with workers on strike in one of the mines of the Jiu Valley.

6. On January 18-22, 1999, in protest against the closing down of mines, 10,000 miners, led by Miron Cozma, started off for Bucharest on buses. Breaking through the police barriers at the entrance of the Jiu Valley, they reached within 150 kms. of Bucharest. The extreme right-wing Great Romania Party, which stood at 20% according to certain opinion polls, its Chairman Corneliu Vadim Tudor and Vice-Chairman Miron Cozma orchestrated the miners' march on the capital. Premier Radu Vasile was forced to open negotiations with the strike committee, led by Cozma, in the monastery of Cozia. Vasile had to promise that he would review the closing of the mines and that dismissed miners would receive significant compensation.

7. On February 16, 1999, some 3-4,000 miners left Petrosani (Petrozsény) for Bucharest to overthrow the government because it failed to keep its promises made in Cozia and because their leader, Miron Cozma, was sentenced to 18 years imprisonment for the role he played in the miners' march to Bucharest in September 1991. The following dawn, militia and police forces dispersed the march.

It can be said that the miners of the Jiu Valley were always used as a tool of the political-power struggle, once by Iliescu's post-Communist party, then by the Romanian opposition (in September 1991, when Corneliu Coposu and Doina Cornea expect the miners to overthrow Iliescu), and lately by another extremist party, the Great Romania Party, to overthrow the current coalition government.

Several trade unions called for a general strike on April 26, 1999. Their demands included both economic and political ones: the dismissal of the management of the National Asset Foundation (Állami Vagyonalap), making public the composition of the managements of property administrative bodies and boards of directors, the modification of tax and customs policies, wage adjustment tied to inflation, the modification of the Election Act and the Constitution, a reduction of electricity and fuel prices or their subsidy, rescheduling the debts of indebted companies, doubling of wages, and the establishment of courts of labor. All this, when the government's financial burdens were extremely heavy. As proof of the unions' strength, on several occasions they prevented the government from privatizing big state industrial concerns or forced the cancellation of privatization contracts. Analyzers of the situation in Romania pointed out that the strikers, by preventing the closing of money-losing mines, companies and plants, did not contribute to stop the swift deterioration of the economic situation but, on the contrary, they postponed the ultimate solution.

There was no big city in Romania where people did not go on strike before November. That month 8,000 student demanded the doubling of scholarship and better provisions in hostels in Bucharest. At the same time the workers of the lorry factory in Brassó went of strike, for neglecting the collective agreement. All this was topped by the railway men's strike in Bucharest. No doubt the railway workers' strike had the greatest result: the replacement of the Vasile-government. However, the slender welfare allowances achieved could not be considered a "result" that could significantly change the life of railway workers or employees of any other branches.

By organizing an internal coup within the Christian Democratic National Peasant Party, Radu Vasile played a key role in overthrowing the previous Prime Minister, Victor Ciorbea. His dismissal, in turn, took place at a very unfortunate moment when, following the EU-summit held in Helsinki on December 9-10, the European Union invited Romanian to take part in the membership talks. According to an official report, Günther Verheugen, EU commissioner in charge of expansion, informed the Romanian government about the Union's reservations:

?? there was no operating market economy;
?? the macro-economy was unstable;
?? State companies were running at a loss;
?? the economic and financial laws were lacking or contradictory.

All these provided sufficient basis for the dismissal of the Prime Minister. As always, there was no shortage of promises. During the inauguration of the Isarescu-government, the new Prime Minister made a promise that US$5 billion would enter the country if his reform package was implemented. The reality is that Romania, on the threshold of the 21st century, is as inconsistent and unstable a society and economy as it was 10, 50 or 100 years ago.

New Transylvanian policy

Sabin Gherman, journalist of the Cluj Napoca (Kolozsvár) television, published his declaration in September of 1998, entitled "*I am fed up with Romania, I want Transylvania*" (Appendix B). He demanded the revival of the regional Romanian policy pursued in Transylvania between the two World Wars. He reasoned his demand stating that the annual budget of Bucharest – symbolically the capital of the Regat – was higher than that of Transylvania, i.e., the capital received more than a whole region of the country, and it administered Transylvania as a colony for 80 years. This is what the majority of Romanians born in Transylvania would like to end. They see only one possible alternative, which aligns with Western-European norms, as well: the granting of economic and administrative autonomy to Transylvania and the Banate.[499] The fall of Foreign Minister Adrian Severin of the Democratic Party was caused by an article

---

[499] Gherman, Sabin: M-am săturat de Romania! (Elegem van Romániából!), *Monitorul de Cluj*, September 16, 1998.

similar in tone to Gherman's, *"Transylvania – the Romanian Padania?"* (Appendix C).

In December, 1998 the Great Romania Party, and its leader C. V. Tudor, claimed the Gherman received US$30,000 from Budapest for his subversive activity. The Romanian National Unity Party and Iliescu's Romanian Party of Socialist Democracy charged the Romanian journalist with treason, endangering the principles of the Constitution and the national character and indivisibility of the Romanian state. The Justice Department found Gherman not guilty in 1999. Significant changes took place in Romanian Transylvanian-policy and consequently, in minority policy, in 1999. Some of the reasons for the changes were obvious:

1. the DAHR's invitation into the government was due to the country's ambitions for NATO membership;
2. the "Hungarian danger", which manifested itself in the parallel between Kosovo and Transylvania, i.e., if autonomy was possible in Kosovo, then the same could happen in Transylvania, was still used to lessen socio-economic tensions;
3. the government coalition won the election with the help of the Transylvanian votes. Consequently, every party drew aim at winning the Transylvanian voters;
4. the demand for regional politics has become ever stronger. This demand enjoys support among the Romanians living in Moldova, Transylvania and the Banate, along with some moderate support among the intellectuals of the Regat (Bucharest).

The Transylvania issue can be approached from another point of view. Nowadays, Transylvania, as the most Western region of Romania, has become more valuable, for the Romanians also. According to a national survey, conducted by the Cluj Napoca-based Metro Media Transilvania social and market research and communications institut, in August, 74% of those polled wished to live in Transylvania and 46% of them demanded comprehensive autonomy for the region. The survey uncovered that the living standard was the highest in Transylvania – 54% of those polled, while only 6% held that view in Bucharest. Corruption was thought to exist in state and administrative institutes in the Regat by 75%, while it was held by 17-18% in the local administrative bodies in Transylvania and the Partium. It was also no secret - Sabin Gherman was among the first to state – that Transylvania accounted for 65% of the nation's gross domestic product. To put this into context, what was produced in Transylvania was used to keep the counties of the Regat afloat. Therefore, it was not the Transylvanian population who enjoyed the fruits of its own labor. This was Sabin Gherman's main argument and the primary cause of his anger, as well.

It was not only Gherman and his circle who was dissatisfied with the Transylvanian policy of the government. There were politicians also in every Transylvanian party who were of the same opinion. Would it not be better – asked the next question the moderate Hungarian politicians in Transylvania – if after Schengen, a considerable portion of the Romanian population in Transylvania would not think it better to separate from the Regat and to be a citizen of an independent Transylvania, belonging not to the Balkans but to Central-Europe. European way of living was the norm in Transylvania, as that of the Balkans was in the Regat, not only in the past today. According to certain non-official sources, it is not accidental that 10%, that is 750,000 Romanians in Transylvania, would claim themselves as Hungarians on a national census if the Schengen Agreement came into force.

The coming elections, as stated previously, added to the importance of Transylvania. Every party knew that winning the elections was impossible without the Transylvanian votes. Consequently, special attention was paid to the region in every party's election strategy. A columnist of *Curentul* wrote: "The parties see Transylvania as the Eldorado of politics." It is worth mentioning that Iliescu would like to attract the (several?) millions of Gypsies for his party.

The parties already started to count the votes. For example, the Christian-Democratic National Peasant Party expected that 30% of their support would come from Transylvania. However, the parties were very cautious about making promises to Hungarians, as a pro-Hungarian party could not expect too much admiration in Romania. Thus, it was no surprise to hear the contradictory statements of the Romanian Prime Minister. Meeting with the Hungarian Prime Minister, at one of the sessions of the Free University at Unguras (Bálványosváralja), he stated that "there were only some technical obstacles" in the way of the establishment of the State Hungarian University. The following day, he stated in Cluj Napoca (Kolozsvár) that the establishment of the university "was impossible in this legislative period." The law on the restoration of nationalized church properties did not yet meet all what was expected from it. Hungarians held interest in only 50 of the 200 pieces of real estate it covered. It also did not bode well that there was widespread talk that the 50 hectare maximum should be lowered to 10 hectares. (Favorable events took place in reprivatization in December of that year.)

On June 16, 1989, the representatives of the Hungarian Democratic Forum and Romanian exiles signed an agreement in Budapest on Hungarian-Romanian reconciliation and dialogue. Romanian and Hungarian intellectuals planned to hold a commemoration in Romania on the 10th anniversary of the birth of the "Budapest Statement".[500] The so-called draft Cluj Napoca (Kolozsvár) Statement was worked out in preparation for this event. Unfortunately, it accidentally leaked out of the Bucharest office of the Helsinki Committee, or more precisely, when Gabriel Andreescu's briefcase, containing the document, was stolen. The draft envisaged the traditional regional development and administrative autonomy of Transylvania and the Banate as ideal, and that it could be the first step in the expected decentralization in Romania.

The Cluj Napoca (Kolozsvár) Statement must certainly have provided the basis for Adrian Nastase's remark about "the script of Hungarian revisionism." When Nastase returned from Moscow in mid-June of 1999, he stated in an outrage to journalists in Cluj Napoca (Kolozsvár) that, according to an elaborate scenario of the Hungarian revisionists, an attempt to detach Transylvania was going to take

---

[500] The Freedom (Szabadság) covered this topic several times in June, 1999.

place that autumn. Nastase predicted that during that autumn, while Romania would face its most serious economic and political crises since the 1989 revolution, this "policy of maximum tension will be provoked by certain internal forces - abetted by external forces."

During the free summer university seminars at Unguras (Bálványosváralja), where the Prime Ministers of both countries appeared or gave lectures, the European Dragan Foundation reported to the police, for incitement against constitutional order and for conspiracy, the signatories of the Cluj Napoca (Kolozsvár) Statement. Emil Constantinescu also gave voice to his worries stating that, by raising the issue of federation, the Statement endangered the territorial integrity of the Romanian state. By his statement, the President, however, drew the attention, at least of a narrow layer of Romanian intellectuals, that federation and autonomy, or more precisely, the ceding of certain powers of the central government to local administration, which would become reality in the near future in Romania. Gusztáv Molnár called this a process of devolution.

During that summer, Sabin Gherman announced that the Pro-Transilvania Foundation would commence political activities for the completion of this process. The establishment of the Transylvania-Banate League was to serve this purpose. Gherman also spoke about devolution, underlining his point with the examples of Scotland and Wales. He thought it should be important that Transylvanians' taxes should be retained in the region, that Transylvania should have its own governing council to manage the economic and administrative matters of the region, over which the Transylvanian provinces would have exclusive right to make decisions. Fewer and fewer people spoke about the Transylvania-Kosovo parallel, formerly mentioned by the Romanian president and others. Many explain it by the realization of the absurdity of the comparison; to wit, to date the Hungarians in Transylvania have always fought by peaceful means for those aims that made the Albanians of Kosovo, the Irish or the Welsh to take up arms and resort to force - and which resulted in significant gains. The mere mention of the parallels in most Romanian-Hungarian circles was looked at as a provocation.

The 6th DAHR Congress, Miercuera-Ciuc (Csíkszereda), May 15-17, 1999

The DAHR laid out its demand for the internal autonomy of the Hungarian national community in its Statement, issued in Cluj Napoca (Kolozsvár) in November of 1992. The document defined the three levels of self-government - individual, local and territorial autonomy - as necessary and feasible. This was endorsed by the then current leadership. It was based on this document that the Coordinating Council of the Szeklerland announced the program of Territorial Autonomy of the Szeklerland in the spring of 1995. By the time of the 6th Congress, or to be more exact, in the course of adopting the resolutions of the Congress – when the Romanian Parliament had just rejected the bill on the re-establishment of the Hungarian state university in Cluj Napoca (Kolozsvár), with an overwhelming majority – that the border between the so called Moderates and Radicals within the DAHR became clear.

270

The Moderates – actually the entire DAHR leadership, including Béla Markó, György Tokay, Attila Verestóy and Csaba Takács - who narrowed minority rights down to the use of the mother tongue, a definition with which western-European minority groups are no longer satisfied.

The Radicals – László Tokés, Elod Kincses and the members of two of the five platforms: the Fidesz-like platform of the Reform Unification (Reformtömörülés) and the Adam Katona-led Transylvanian Hungarian Initiative, rounded out by the members of the sixth group, the Nation-Building Platform (Nemzetépíto Platform), established in September of that year by Károly Vekov, historian and member of Parliament – thought within an autonomy-based solution. They demanded the transfer of certain state authority to local self-governments on the basis of existing and functioning Western-European models. The two groups differed on dual citizenship, as well. The Radicals, referring to the Israeli, German and Croatian examples, were in support of it. Also at issue was whether the DAHR should be a party or an association representing the common interest.

The Council of Federal Representatives (CFR – Szövetségi Képviselok Tanácsa, the mini-parliament of the DAHR) adopted the agenda of the Congress at its session held in Tirgu Mures (Marosvásárhely) on April 17. The CFR held the following points as the most important ones:[501]

1. Considering the fact that Transylvania is the closes to the Western-European model in Romania, this region plays a key role in the country's NATO integration. Therefore, the CFR recommends that the DAHR should concentrate on a Transylvania-centric policy;
2. The economic portion of the program emphasized:
   ?? the equal opportunity of Hungarian entrepreneurs in Romania;
   ?? the economic and infrastructural development of regions populated by Hungarians;
3. The CFR stated that the Permanent Hungarian Conference (Állandó Magyar Értekezlet) was the designated forum of Hungarian-Hungarian relations;
4. Constraining the authority of the Honorary President, Bishop László Tokés, was also proposed.

The entire Congress bore the imprint of the Tokés-Markó conflict. According to Tokés, a Kosovo-like crisis could be avoided by introducing an autonomy based on internal self-government. He also added that the DAHR leadership had no right to renounce this in return for government positions. Bishop László Tokés, DAHR Honorary President, tabled a 12-point motion to the Congress. The most important points were touched on the review of the DAHR's role in government, the elaboration of a new national strategy, the re-opening of the Hungarian-language state university, the restoration of the Liberty statue in Arad, the modification of the nation-state status of Romania, the organization of a Romanian and Romanian-Hungarian round table conference, enacting the Transylvania-centered program and encouraging the return of Transylvanians living abroad.

---

[501] Freedom (Szabadság). 1999, April.

On the other side of the argument, Béla Markó stated that joining the Romanian government coalition was the right step. As a reminder, the Romanian government and President demonstrated the change in minority policy by including the DAHR in the government. Internal critics blamed the DAHR – proven by documents – for not asking anything in return, i.e., that it missed an opportunity for a bargain when, for example, it could have demand assurance for the re-establishment of the Hungarian-language state university. Markó, however, blamed the other members of the government coalition for the breaking of the promises. For the time being, the DAHR unity held, however, it gives food for thought that Béla Markó was re-elected with 274 votes, while his rival, Elod Kincses, received 157 votes. Romanian circles greatly objected that Béla Markó kept "running to Budapest" to ask for support from the Orbán-government, every time he thought his position was endangered. The Romanian-Hungarian opposition tends to hold this view, as well.

The DAHR radical wing took it as another failure that the party elections, planned for November 13, were postponed. It would have settled the real power relations and the support for each platform. The platforms were designed to represent the various political trends instead of parties because, if they were to be transformed into parties – five to six parties at present – they would not reach the 5% minimum threshold of admission to Parliament. After the DAHR's VI. Congress, the problems splitting the Association into two factions remained. It can be summed up in three points:

1. establishing a national survey (the census of the Hungarian population in Romania);
2. lack of internal elections (key positions were filled by appointment);
3. supporting the three-tiered autonomy.

Unchanged priorities in foreign policy on the eve of the 21st century

Steadiness characterized the foreign policy of the government that described itself as a Christian Democratic and center-right coalition.

1. Urging Euro-Atlantic integration (NATO- and EU-membership);
2. The problem burdened Romanian-Russian relationship;
3. Strengthening the Polish-Ukrainian-Moldavian-Romanian axis, not the least of which was aimed against Hungary and Russia;
4. Maintaining good Romanian-Serbian relations and strengthening Croatian-Romanian relations, also with anti-Hungary aims;
5. Promoting Romania's leading role in the Balkans, meaning stronger ties with Greece, Turkey and Bulgaria;
6. Complex, but not improving, Romania-Hungary relations.

One of the greatest failures of President Emil Constantinescu's American visit in 1997 was being told that, regarding its NATO-membership, Romania will remain on the waiting list for quite a while. Hungary's admission on March 12, 1999, and the outcome of the efforts for solving the Kosovo crisis in its wake, caused a real shock. The spokesman of the Romanian Foreign Ministry expressed his hopes that the principle of "open doors" would result in Romania's admission in the near future.

The lively diplomatic activity in mid-summer of 1997 – when the U.S. Secretary of State, the German Foreign Minister and the Secretary-General of the European Union all spoke in appreciative terms about Romania's attitude during the Kosovo crisis – provided cold comfort for Romania. As Solana put it, Romania got very close to NATO, but not to NATO-membership. President Constantinescu could say with reason that beyond praise and nice words, Romania did not received anything from the NATO countries. In fact, Romania could not expect to gain admission in the second round, either. Chancellor Gerhard Schröder of Germany played an important role in dashing Romania's hopes when, during his visit to Bucharest at the end of September, he stated that the slow-down of the transformation of Romanian economy and society caused disappointment in the Western-European partners.

In 1999, the urging – forcing – of NATO-membership remained a prime task of the Radu Vasile government. In this, complete harmony seemed to develop between President Constantinescu and the government. It also referred to the EU-membership of the country. Right before the railway strike in December, the Romanian Prime Minister briefed Günther Verheugen, EU commissioner in charge of expansion, that he accepted the EU-proposal for the establishment of a committee of Romanian and foreign experts, to be charged with working out a medium-range economic strategy – at a time when the country did not even have a short-term economic plan. The committee included the President of the National Bank of Romania, and the Chairmen of the International Agency for Regional Development and the National Development Agency, who worked in close co-operation with the experts of research institutions and the parties.

The Visegrád Four (the Czech Republic, Hungary, Poland and Slovakia) were invited to the Baltic-Black Sea Co-operation Conference held in Yalta in September of 1999. The host, President Kuchma of the Ukraine, and the guests – including the Hungarian and the Romanian Presidents – expressed their support for a united Europe, although every participant was aware that Romania was far from it. Nevertheless, Hungarian diplomacy raised several times the suggestion that Romania and Bulgaria should be taken off the list of countries with visa requirements to the European Union. This would pave the way of relations between their countries when Hungary joins the EU – some time in 2003-2005.

Croatian and Romanian Defense Ministers discussed their two countries' military cooperation in Zagreb on February 25, 1999. Bucharest, like Zagreb, signed an agreement for the modernization of aircraft with Israel. Under the agreement, Croatian MiG-21s were to be up-dated in Croatia, Israel and Romania. The parties also discussed the possibility of other agreements on the training of servicemen and the exchange of intelligence service information. During the year – in October – French and Romanian defense cooperation was further expanded. Two Romanian MiG-21s and one C-130 Hercules aircraft took part in an exercise on the military airbase of Orleans. The French side stressed that the modernization of Romania's defense system was carried out "in view of the country's joining the NATO in the future." (Several French military-industrial companies signed agreements with the Romanian Aerostar company, manufacturer of civilian and military aircraft. The French-German Eurocopter concern also wanted to take part in Romanian privatization though acquiring the Brasov firm manufacturing the Puma military helicopter.)

From time to time, Romania reminds that one of the reasons for the worsening of Romanian-Russian relations is that Russia has not returned those treasures – 93 tons of gold – which were taken to Russia for safety in 1916 when the German army entered Bucharest. Russia states that the treasure has been lost without a trace. On the other hand, former President Ion Iliescu's friendly relations with Moscow were known world-wide. Moreover, in certain circles he is held to be a KGB agent because he was the first to sign the Treaty with the disintegrating Soviet Union. That is why it caused great surprise when Iliescu published an anti-Russian article in the May issue of *The Washington Post*. In the article, he asked the United States to keep Russian tanks (i.e., the Russian army) away from the Danube and not to offer even a chance for it to return and gain a foothold in the Eastern-European countries. According to Iliescu, it was Moscow's firm intention "to again play an active role in the region."

In early March, during the meeting of the Romanian and Polish Presidents, Constantinescu stressed that his country would feel itself in greater safety if Poland also joined NATO. Figures made public during their press conference indicated that the agreements signed in January of 1997 were working well. Trade relations grew by 19% within a year. Furthermore, The parties also considered the establishment of a joint Romanian-Polish-Croatian peace keeping battalion, and that trilateral relations would be extended to four-sided by the inclusion of the Republic of Moldova. By the strengthening of Romanian-Croatian and Romanian-Polish relations, Romania's overt intent was to distance or sever Hungary from these two traditional allies.

Kosovo and Romania. Romanian-Serbian relations [502]

The eruption of the Kosovo-crisis, whose first phase stretched from February to October of 1996, once again put Romania at a crossroads:
1. Either it keeps out of the war or else it supports Serbia with all its forces, based on the traditional Serb-Romanian friendship, orthodoxy and Russian orientation,
2. or, it agrees with every NATO action and, as it President Emil Constantinescu said at the end of April, "with it paves Romania's road into NATO."

This, however, pre-supposed some sort of active participation, e.g.- opening its air-space, or perhaps allowing arms and troops transportation over its territory or sharing intelligence information. Consequently, Romania's involvement in the latest Balkan war, either on this side or that, was anticipated. This was confirmed by the news that Russian military aircraft flew through Romanian airspace in early April, and another at the end of April that Romania offered the use of its air-space

---

[502] Juhász, József: Once there was a Yugoslavia (Volt egyszer egy Jugoszlávia). Bp., AULA Publisher, 1999.

for NATO. Finally, after contradictory statements from government members, Romania made a decision in favor of Euro-Atlantic integration as opposed to the Russian orientation.

In early April, Foreign Minister Zivadin Jovanovic of Yugoslavia called upon his Romanian colleague, Andrei Plesu, who was, at the time, the chairman of the regional organization, Southeastern European Cooperation, to close Romania's air-space to NATO aircraft and demand to stop the war against Yugoslavia. The spokesman of the Romanian Foreign Ministry called it an unfounded supposition that the Romanian government would open its air-space for NATO attacks against Yugoslavia. It can be added that the Romanian Defense Minister and the army's Chief of Staff confirmed several times that Romania would not send active units to Yugoslavia. This act was widely demanded all over Romania as a result of extreme political agitation. The same can be said of President Constantinescu's statement that Romania was ready to send soldiers to aid Serbia - but later recanted.

The opening of its airspace made the NATO action in Yugoslavia Romania's affair on several levels, among them a weapon in the power struggle. Adrian Nastase harshly criticized the Romanian government's support of the NATO air campaign, as well as a coarse attack on Hungary. "Hungary sensed the blood and scent of carrion. For this reason, if the Yugoslavian situation does not ease soon, it is not inconceivable that tempers will flare in Voivodina." (After the 2000 election, the post-communists formed the government, led by Adrian Nastase.) The Romanian media paid great attention to the reactions of Serbs living in Romania to the current international conflict. The Alliance of Serbs in Romania, the Vatra and a string of student organizations organized a mass solidarity meeting in Timisoara (Temesvár) on April 3, 1998. The signs most often seen read "We don't give up Kosovo!" and "Kosovo today, Transylvania tomorrow!" In addition to anti-Clinton and anti-NATO slogans, many of the speakers emphasized that the DAHR's 7% put the current government into power, a direct consequence of which was Constantinescu's and Radu Vasile's suicidal - pro-Western and anti-Russian - policy against the interests of the Romanian nation.

In mid-March, Ziua published the full text of the statement of the Alliance of Serbs in Romania: "Serbs will fight to the last drop of their blood for their sacred land, Kosovo ... Romanians would do the same if their sacred land was in danger. This is what Romanian politicians should think when they advise the Serbs to let foreign troops occupy their land." And finally, they remind the two nations of their orthodox brotherhood ties.[503]

In Romanian, almost every party and news media connected the settling of the Kosovo situation with the Transylvanian issue, long before the NATO intervention. Former Foreign Minister Teodor Melescanu voiced his opinion that everybody who demanded autonomy for Transylvania was encouraged by Hungarian Premier Viktor Orbán's statement urging "a similar treatment in Voivodina (Vajdaság) as in Kosovo." A statement issued by the Romanian National Unity Party drew the attention of the Romanian government that "the

---

[503] Ziua. 1998, March 16.

275

political and military scenario unfolding in Yugoslavia may soon be repeated in Transylvania."

The Romanian opposition not only rejected Foreign Minister Andrei Plesu's declaration that a partition of Kosovo was a possibility but also the Yugoslavian parliament's decision the Russian-Belarus alliance as being dangerous to Romanian national security. (Yeltsin and Lukashenko signed a military-political agreement on April 2, 1996.) Enlarging the alliance would further isolate Romania, as well as exerting pressure on Romania and influencing its internal political order – meaning a possible turn to the left.

Good relations between Romania and Hungary could only be found in official communiqués. According to them, Romania was pleased with Hungary's NATO membership and expected from it an improvement in its safety. Behind the scenes, Romanian-Hungarian relations were burdened with unchanged and severe problems. Only the opposition dared to voice open criticism or threats.

Shortly after Romanian Premier Radu Vasile's visit to Hungary at the end of February 1999, the state attorney's office of Brasov (Brassó) began criminal proceedings against 19 Hungarian public figures living in Romania. They were charged for their statements on the further development of self-government made at an open political forum held at Cernat (Alsócsernáton) on September 24, 1998. The indictment, handed down shortly before the March 15 celebrations and the Pope's visit to Romania, charged subversive activities against the constitutional order, which carried the possible sentence of 5 to 15 years of imprisonment.

Even moderate Hungarian political circles in Romania compared the case with the show trials and stressed that they were in contradiction with the principles of democracy, the minority legal framework suggested by the European Council and they infringed on section 10 on the freedom of speech in the European Charter of Human Rights. The attorney of Brasov (Brassó), and implicitly the Romanian government, wanted to make the affected parties known that it would be not remain unavenged that Hungary was admitted to NATO and Romania was not.

The Romanian National Unity Party politician Valeriu Tabara refused to recognize the right of national minorities to establish political parties 'on an ethnic basis' - ignoring the basis of his own party. He considered Hungary's NATO membership as fatal for Romania because it reinforced the separatist ambitions of the DAHR and the growing trend of returning nationalized community properties of Hungarians living in Romania. Moreover, Tamara voiced his worries about the intention of the Orbán government – using international terminology – to extend its protective status to the Hungarians living in the neighboring countries. According to him, that clearly constituted intervention in the internal affairs of Romania.

The existence of the Permanent Hungarian Conference (Állandó Magyar Értekezlet) and the Hungarian government subsidy to Hungarian organizations in Romania were also disapproved in Romania. Whereas subsidizing Romanian institutions, and even individuals living beyond the borders, was a part of the Romanian budget for a long time.

Moreover, the Hungarian refusal of Romanian claims concerning the Gozsdu Foundation caused serious diplomatic problems. According to an agreement signed in 1953, both parties abandoned their mutual claims, which for the Hungarian side meant renouncing a significant national asset. In Romania, under the pretext of 'enemy assets,' the properties of the Hungarian state, legal persons and individuals were continuously nationalized between 1945 and 1948. Their value, at the 1945 exchange rate, amounted to over 10 million Swiss gold francs. In spite of the 1953 agreement, applications for returning nationalized properties were delivered to the Hungarian foreign affairs bureaus to the end of the 1960s.[504]

In one of its latest letters, dated November, 1999, the Hungarian government pointed out that if Romania continued to revive its claim to the Gozsdu property, then Hungary would lay claims for a part of its one-time properties. During his talks in Bucharest in the end of July (conducted with his colleague, Plesu, on the opening of new consulates, on an occasion when Premier Radu Vasile did not receive him), Hungarian Foreign Minister János Martonyi stated that Hungarian claims would automatically come be revived, too.

Hungarian Law LXII - the status law - passed in 2001, opened a new but not necessarily positive chapter in Romanian and Hungarian relations.[505] It is another matter that the opposition to the Orbán government also sharply criticized the status law [ed: defining who, living outside the country, is entitled to Hungary's support], which provided various support to Hungarians, living outside Hungary, in the cultural, social and educational areas.[506]

---

[504] Lipcsey, Ildikó: CASBI and the Gozsdu Foundation (A CASBI és a Gozsdu Alapítvány). Transylvanian Hungarians (Erdélyi Magyarság).

[505] Hungarian Minority (Magyar Kisebbség). 2002, issue 1.

[506] Hungarian Minority (Magyar Kisebbség). 2001, issue 10.

Appendix A – The Romanian Intelligence Service

A short history of the State Security Agency, the Securitate[507]
August 30, 1948 to December, 1989

It was not accidental that internal reorganization took place in Romanian Interior agencies in 1924. It was at this time that the Siguranca, and its successor the Securitate, began its activities and continued for 65 years in the role of thought police. The event that prompted is founding was the adoption into its program by the, then still legal, Romanian Communist Party of a Comintern decision to treat the minority question according to the Leninist principle. The autonomy principle extended "to the complete separation of some areas from the Romanian state." The areas specifically named were those which were annex to Romania subsequent to the 1920 Paris Treaty. (Bukovina, Bessarabia, Dobrudja, the Banate and Transylvania.)

It can be stated that the attention of the Siguranca was not focused primarily on breaking up civic demonstrations or keeping an eye on the activities of opposition parties. Rather, it concentrated on effective countermeasures to the minority movements, on attempts at territorial revisionism, on irredentism and external intelligence activities aimed at Romania. It is not difficult to draw a parallel between the previous statement and the RSS report of November 1995 in which irredentism and spy activity from Hungary towards Romania form the central theme.

After Romania became part of the Soviet sphere of interest, several measures were introduced which seriously wounded the nation's dignity by
1.   The Soviet authorities gained key positions in the information gathering and repressive apparatus, and
2.   The most important bodies became subservient to Moscow's general political interests.

This process was generally completed between 1944 and 1948 when the Special Information Service, the Siguranca, the Gendarmerie and policy organizations were filled with Soviet agents.

The Siguranca took part in the arrest of approximately 70,000 Iron Guardists, the liquidation of the anti-Communist nationalist opposition, as well as the deportation to the Soviet Union of about 70,000 Germans (Saxons and Schwabians). Furthermore, it was active in cleansing the government bureaucracy from Iron Guardists, Fascists, democratic and civic elements through the Communist controlled Interior Ministry. It also liquidated, or helped to reorganize, the Royal Intelligence Service, the National Peasant Party's Fact-finding Service, the Romanian Army's II. Directorate, the Special Intelligence Service and the Legionnaire Movement's Information Service.

It was born on August 30, 1948 out of Decree 221 as a part of the Interior Ministry and named Chief Directorate for Civilian Security (Directiunea Generala

---

[507] Troncota: Cristian Troncota: Istoria serviciilor secrete romanesti de la Cuza la Ceausescu. Bucuresti, Editura Ion Cristoiu S.A., 1999.

a Securitatii Poporului). The new organization had the assigned task of "the protection of the democratic relations and security assurance against enemy intrigue, both internal and external, of the Romanian People's Republic." In carrying out their task, only the Securitate had the right to open proceedings against those who endangered the democratic process and the security of the populace. Its jurisdiction extended over the whole country. The authorities must take a stand – said the decree – against reactionary forces because they hamper the industrialization of the country, the socialist transformation of agriculture, create internal tension, are terrorizing certain areas and are creating doubt about the future of the socialist system. In other words, they were an obstacle in the fulfillment of the socialist revolutionary progression. The reasons given were such that with them anyone, at any time, could be charged and proceedings started – with the appropriate consequences – as in any of the so-called People's Republics during the varied lengths of heightened class struggle.

According to the Securitate's "White Book,"[508] Nicolschi Alexandru (born Boris Grumberg of Russian-Jewish extraction) was the second highest person in the organization with Sergiu Nicolau (Sergei Nikolov), Pintilie Gheorghe (Bondarenko Pantelij, Ukrainian) and Vladimir Mazuru (Mazurov) filling high level positions in Romanian information gathering organizations. The Russian advisors of yesterday are today looked on unequivocally as planted agents. Their director between 1944 and 1947 was Dimitrij Gheorghievski Fedicikin, a Balkan expert, followed in the post by Alexander Saharovski between 1949 and 1953. These Soviet – mostly NKVD – officers trained their Romanian colleagues in the tasks of the trade. However, from a Romanian perspective, the transmitted all essential information to Moscow. Furthermore, they recruited agents inside the government apparatus and the Interior Ministry, obviously to inform Moscow, as well as making use of their activities in the Western countries.

The doubling of the trusted Soviet advisors, from the perspective of the organizations and the Soviets, is linked to the new Interior Minister Alexandru Draghici, named to the post in 1952, following Teohari Georgescu. Georgescu, of Jewish descent, was as much Moscow's man as the Romanian born Draghici, who had a serious blot on his file due to having a Hungarian wife. (The Romanians requested his extradition several times from Hungary after 1999.) The creation of two new Directorates (namely the Military Counter-Intelligence Directorate and the Deception Directorate) between 1953 and 1955, independent from the Securitate's Investigative Directorate, is attributed to Draghici. In this era, Soviet advisor Pintilie Gheorghe (Bondarenko), with Deputy Interior Minister rank, held full authority over the Romanian intelligence services.[509]

Secret services have their own methods, organizations and tasks. This was true in the West, as it was in Romania between the two world wars. Contrary to this, the chief task of the Chief Directorate for Civilian Security, similar to the Hungarian State Protective Authority (ÁVH), was the arrest and investigation of

---

[508] Cartea Alba a Securitatii. Bucuresti, Editura Presa Roameasca, 1996.
[509] Raduica, Grigore: Crime in lupta pentru putere. 1966-1968: ancheta cazului Patrascanu. Bucuresti, Ed. Evenimentul Zilei, 1999.

those who threatened the Communist system. The state security agents were recruited from those strata of society who were considered 'nation aliens' and the minimum requirement was that they had elementary schooling. The interrogators were semi-literate and crude, a fact skillfully used by the Soviet advisors. The chief organizer of the show trials, the Securitate, aided the Romanian Communist Party in liquidating the opposing groups. Between 1948 and 9158, the internments, the compulsory assignment of living accommodations and the creation of forced labor camps was among its major assignments. (Those interned were able to move back to their homes after 15-16 years.) Active Romanian resistance, especially the stemming the Romanian consequences to the 1956 Hungarian revolution, brought significant changes. The Securitate came to the conclusion from analyzing the events that its network of informants was inadequate. As an example, for 9,000 students and 700 teachers in Cluj Napoca, it had three informers. Thus, the 1956/14, /54 and /109 decrees announced a Securitate review of the informant network and the recruitment among the students and teachers of new, reliable informers. At the same time, they strengthened the regulations covering national security.

As there was no armed insurrection against the authorities in Romania, as there were in East Germany, Poland, Czechoslovakia and Hungary, as a reward the Soviet Union ended the presence of military and other experts (mainly in the Interior Ministry) in 1958. Thus, a chapter ended in the history of the Securitate. The 'White Book' suggests that, freed from external (meaning Soviet) and internal (cleansing of the officer core, ridding itself of captains of Jewish, Hungarian and other backgrounds) influences, the Securitate became a 'friend of the people.' The editors of the publication of 1995 devote great energy to the creation of an image of the 'good' Securitate officer and non-com.

The years between 1958 and 1968 can be best described at the striving for independence from the Soviet Union. This political direction was begun by Gheorghiu-Dej, carried on by Ceausescu.[510] The Party's three strategic goals – independent foreign policy, the removal of Russian and other external influences, and winning the confidence of the politically condemned – placed great tasks on the Securitate, especially in regards to the RCP's creation of an independent, nationalistic way. It is in regards to this that the current intelligence agency is trying to bolster its popularity by stressing that, even today, is supports the authorities in their national vision.

Popular Romanian opinion held that it was not enough to relieve Bondarenko-Pintilie, Mazurov-Mazuru and Nicolschi-Grumberg of their posts but also deport the Russian women with Romanian husbands, as that was only used as a cover and they were really in the service of the Soviet party and intelligence services. The husbands – used as sacrificial offerings – were Securitate officers or held high rank in the party or in economic organizations. Bucharest rejected in the years 1957 into the 1960's (e.g.- at a secret meeting in Prague between the secret services of the two countries) a suggestion for the creation of a special section in the Securitate whose task would be to spy for the Soviet Union. To prevent the

---

[510] Delatant, Dennis: Ceausescu and the Securitate. C. Hurst & Co. (Publishers) Ltd., 1995.

infiltration of Soviet agents, a special school was established in Romania in 1964. The officers of the Counter-Intelligence Directorate came from its graduates. Using covert methods, they recorded a conversation on December 31, 1963. In it, the first secretary of the Greek high consulate, Kerkinos Euripides, in analyzing Romania's situation said that Hungary wants Transylvania back – a position held by Romanian diplomats today – that Bulgaria wants a part of Dobruja and that the Soviets were looting Romania. According to the Securitate, "Khruschov encouraged the Hungarian leadership on his visits to Budapest (April 1964) to raise the Transylvanian question" and "to demand the return of Transylvania."

According to information from the Romanian secret services, it was once again Khruschov who suggested the idea of a Hungarian-led 'Danube Federation' within the bounds of the Warsaw Pact and COMECON. This would have meant nothing less, according to the report, than the first phase of the annexation of Romania by the Soviet Union.

The period between 1968 and 1978 can be characterized as a conflict between the intelligence services of Romania and the other Warsaw Pact countries. This is usually explained that the latter, especially the Soviet Union, Hungary and Czechoslovakia, opened a 'desperate battle' against Romania and its intelligence services. Without denying the statement, it must be admitted that period ending in 1989, when the cult of the personality peaked, the country's citizens felt not the Securitate's independence efforts but the terror it meted out – for once, the idea 'without regard for minority differences' holds true. It was held in as low esteem as the State Protective Authority (ÁVH) was in Hungary.[511]

As it touched on Hungarian, the Securitate ran an advanced school in Bran (Törcsvár) in the 1970's, named the 'Helga Operation,' where the students were only allowed to converse among themselves in Hungarian about Hungarian history, literature and daily events to allow the graduates to be integrated into Hungarian political and everyday life. It was also in the 1970's that the party and the innermost circle of the Securitate worked out a program to cleanse the country of its minorities.

December, 1989 to November, 1995

The most opposing facts exist in the public's mind regarding the Romanian Intelligence Service. President Ion Iliescu and Virgil Magureanu have added to this dim weaving of images. The events of December and its aftermath are still hotly debated in Romania today. The opposition holds that President Iliescu, and a few members of the former Communist apparatus, manipulated events is such a way that, immediately after the execution of the Ceausescu couple, they could assume power. Many Romanians are convinced that the former Securitate agents created disturbances – by unlawful methods – to create the impression of a mass uprising. They speak of tens of thousands of deaths. During the events, several high ranking officials, with the help of the Securitate, carried out a coup d'état.

---

[511] Pacepa, Ion: Cartea neagra a Securitatii. Buc. Ed. Omega SRL 1999; In umbra Kremlului.

The Romanian media do not give the Romanian Intelligence Service an easy time. They consider it the successor of the once famous, and infamous, Siguranca and from 1948 onwards, the Securitate. The Romanian opposition feels that the Communists simply co-opted or 'took over' the popular uprising to allow the Securitate to take over control already on December 22. They are convinced that the Securitate deployed its terrorist special units against the demonstrators to create chaos and that the KGB had a presence during the events, observing and directing as reported by eyewitnesses. (In Cluj Napoca, Soviet advisers were allegedly observing events from the Citadel.) Among other things, Magureanu denies even the existence of such units.

It is interesting to cast an eye on the RIS's version of events. The RIS addressed the 1989 Romanian revolution in a 163 page report, published in 1994. The report emphasizes the participation of several foreign organizations, i.e., Hungarian, Russian and Yugoslavian, in the events. According to the report, shortly before the December events, Romanian refugees from the Bicske (Hungary) refugee camp were inserted over the border to gather information. Apart from this, agents sent from Hungary were especially active in the Banate who, beside their usual tasks and information gathering, supplied Kossuth Radio and Panorama Television with up-to-date information.

The RIS report stresses the role of several Transylvanian-born Hungarian refugees for their part in organizing the demonstration before the Protestant church on Maria Square in Timisoara (Temesvár). Beginning on December 9, 1989, the report states, cross-border traffic to Yugoslavia grew. On an average, 80 to 100,000 cars arrived in Romania. The columns of Russian plated cars each contained 2-3 men between the ages of 25 and 40. The service mentions by name the then-consul of Yugoslavia in Timisoara (Temesvár), Mirko Atanackovic, as someone who had a hand in the eruption of the revolution and as one who was in close contact with the Hungarian intelligence services. The tone of the report is that in December of 1989, the Romanian government was overthrown as a result of an international conspiracy.

Another report contained a correction, a retraction, regarding the KGB's activities in the December, 1989 events. It seems that Ceausescu had previously gathered the KGB agents in Romania and sent a message to Gorbachev to take them home. Rather, Russian military intelligence had a hand in the matters. According to a report of the Hungarian intelligence service, in December of 1989, there were two opposing groups in the Securitate: one supporting the revolution, the other opposing it. The latter tried to harass the activities of the National Rescue Front Council (Nemzeti Megmentési Front Tanács) by a disinformation campaign. One example, they drove cars festooned with Romanian flags and spread the rumor that the army has abandoned the revolutionaries. As an aside, it must be pointed out that the Securitate favored recruitment from orphanages.

It is a fact the Ceausescu-era Securitate was disbanded on January 3, 1990. There is a great likelihood that the March, 1990 events in Tirgu Mures (Marosvásárhely) were provoked by the old Securitate – says a popular opinion – to justify the creation of a new secret service, which came about in the same month. Official Romanian circles, however, stress that the creation of the RIS was linked to another significant political event, the June, 1990 miners' strike. Around the same time, rumor had it – repeated in government circles – that the 10,000 Hungarian tourists were really 10,000 Hungarian spies, taking advantage of the March 15, 1990 ceremonies and sow dissension in Romania.

Conflicting reports circulated about the staffing of the new intelligence agency. As earlier, when the cadre of the Securitate was mostly made up of the personnel of Siguranca, the RIS was similarly constituted of former Securitate agents. When questioned, different people gave different answers. According to Iliescu, the RIS accepted only 17-18% of Securitate personnel. Magureanu, on the other hand, in a statement made in September of 1993, said in Parliament that that percentage was sixty; in the spring of 1994, he spoke of only 35%. In fact, not too much later, Iliescu trumpeted that – contrary to reality – Romania was the only Communist country, which dissolved its old secret service and created a totally new apparatus.

According to the editor of the opposition paper, Petre Mihai Bancu of the *Romania Libera*, all that happened was a massive reassignment in January of 1990. For example, those serving in Baia Mare (Nagybánya) were relocated to Constanta where they were not known and thus about 80% of the old Securitate were 'saved'. The remaining 20% found positions in the various parties, the opposition, in foreign trade and private firms. Bacanu knew of 1,200 high ranking officers who were active in the extremist Romanian parties. Also to be considered were those who found jobs in the economic sphere, whose good contacts and access to hard currency were paying dividends in selling their knowledge to foreign-owned companies.

While Magureanu claimed that his organization consisted of 6,000 people – and the aggregate of all the other intelligence services another 10,000, according to Bancu the total intelligence community was, in reality, made up of 100,000 people. It must be pointed out that after December of 1989, whole units of the Securitate, under their officers, were transferred to the Interior Ministry. These new recruits received military training, the same as the green collar-patched ones. These units are continuously deployed in the Szeklerland. Therefore, when Romania made statements of observing the international agreements on disarmament, those only apply to the Defense Ministry, but excluded the Gendarmerie attached to the Interior Ministry. Hence, the strength of the armed forces were covertly maintained, in fact, probably increased.

As controversial as the relationship of the governing party (the successor of the National Rescue Front), and the nationalist parties included in it, also the historical opposition parties of Romania – the liberals, the National Peasant Party and the Social-Democrats – and the DHAR towards Magureanu, the opinions of all of the above have equally controversial views of the activities of the intelligence services.

It is no secret to the Romanian opposition what painter Sorin Dumitrescu voiced in Alba Iulia (Gyulafehérvár) in June of 1992: "Do you not see that the Securitate is being privatized in front of your eyes? The minute that ex-colonels and generals become capitalists – they having all the money – thcy will elect the President!" The opposition poet Mircea Dinescu reinforced it in July of 1993, at the Unguras (Bálványos) Summer University by "the nouveau riche Securitate are leading the country." Although people are no longer terrified when talk turns to the intelligence services – and it is worth noting that, with the RIS, there are eight of them – everyone is cognizant of the facts of what the two intellectuals said. The Romanian opposition maintains that the mentality and methods of the Securitate have been retained by the new organizations, amid new parameters. They know first hand that telephone lines are tapped, that mail is opened, that people are observed and that the old activities of the Securitate are present in the institutions and workplaces. "Nothing has changed. It is astounding that only Mr. Magureanu is unaware what is happening around him and spouts angry denials. He denies everything he comes across, even what is blatantly obvious" wrote the erudite Petre Mihai Bacanu in his paper, *Romania Libera.*

Based on the existing files, reminds Bacanu, they can blackmail anyone, as in the past. He draws the conclusion that today's "Securitate" also draws its strength from fear. It was and remains a pillar of the state. In January of 1992, a member of the National Peasant Party raised in Parliament that the Securitate files should be made public, similar to the Stasi files of East Germany. The same idea was raised by Magureanu, but of course not with the same intent. It would be easy to blackmail people in responsible positions with threats of revealing their links to the old, or new, secret services. It was already mentioned that the secret service methods – wiretaps, mail openings – were raised on countless occasions as being the same as before. Petre Roman, as president of the National Security Committee, denied the use of wiretaps; Magureanu was forced to admit it but defended it by saying that it was for information gathering, but that they do not make use of them.[512]

Corneliu Vadim Tudor accused, in his paper, the *Romania Mare,* in December of 1992, the Hungarian Republic's State Security Bureau and the RIS inciting anti-Romanian activities. The RIS termed the accusation as baseless 'panic-mongering.' During the two year debate on the National Security Law, many touchy questions came to light. The European Council-delegates objected that the RIS activities were not subject to parliamentary scrutiny. Furthermore, the draft law's section 4, paragraph 45, makes independent associations, economic companies and specialized societies possible. The RIS could thus be financially independent and impossible to supervise. This, Magureanu naturally denied and stated that it is funded only from the national budget.

The Romanian opposition holds that the National Security Committee has no real power over the RIS, as it places itself above the law and maintains its own army and a virtual financial empire. In the space of a year, to take 1993 as an example, the RIS created 18,000 informational reports. That is 50 each day, of which 2,500 deal with the breaking of a law and in 623 cases notified the investigative branches. In spite of the large numbers, many feel that the RIS should uncover the crimes committed to 1989, as the only criminal named is Draghici who escaped to Hungary. The annual report mentions 75,000 victims but only one criminal. Romanian opposition are quick to point out that the

---

[512] Evenimentul Zilei, 1992, September.

investigation is being held up because the present officer corps of the RIS took part in the reprisals. Magureanu himself admitted that apart from Securitate General Julian Vlad, and about 20-30 high ranking secret service officers, nobody was held responsible. He was only willing to talk about the one-time NKVD agent Nicholski and the former Interior Minister, Alexandru Draghici, whose files were handed over to the judiciary.

In the spring of 1994, a virtual bomb exploded when the *Evenimentul Zilei*[513] began to publish copies of some 'Top Secret' documents dealing with the intelligence networks active at main economic institutions, at customs and finance police departments and at ministries, publicizing the conspiratorially acquired apartments and their owners, and the names of the officers serving with the intelligence branches. Nicolae Ulieru made a statement to the Radio Free Europe that the list made public by the paper was part of a disinformation campaign. When asked, who could be behind this trick, Ulieru replied: "The authors may be the sons of our nation, or they may be foreigners. That is to say, Romania is still in the focus of certain intelligence agencies which were active on the country's (Romania's) soil and in whose interest it is to create turmoil and insecurity in Romanian society." (from his response, it is impossible to know who he was referring: the CIA, KGB or the Hungarian secret service. It can be assumed that he was referring to the secret service of a neighboring country.) Finally, according to his statement, since the activities of the former Securitate are illegal under the current laws, the RIS can not be equated to the Securitate and, in any case, the files of the former informants are no longer available.

The hostility of the Romanian population does not seem to conflict with the fact that the four year National Security Academy has twenty applicants for each opening. As in the Soviet Union, the secret services are seen as a state within a state, whose members are an exceptional caste and membership is a guarantee of advancement in society. Since 1968, the protection of the homeland – of the nation – was extended over all of society, all strata of which was militarized in some fashion, the result of which (and not in last place) was an exaggerated anxiety for country and feeling threatened by strangers, both internal and external. This last can one be explained by the fact that one of the criteria for students, future secret service officers, seeking admission at the academy was that they could not have relatives abroad in Israel, Hungary, Germany, Ukraine, Russia and Bulgaria. In practical terms, it meant that they were not related to Jews, Hungarians, Germans, Ukrainians, Russians, Lipovans or Bulgarians living in Romania. Naturally, it is not a excluding fact if the Romanian applicant has relatives in France or America. Among the requirements are a pleasant appearance, good presence and a height of at least 175 cm. The academy has an average of 200 students. Beginning with the 1995-1995 school year, 14 year-old applicants could begin to acquire their craft the Iasi National Security High School. The compensation of secret service employees was exceptional, too, exceeding that of a university professor.

---

[513] Evenimentul Zilei, 1994, April.

The director of the RIS, Virgil Magureanu reported his organization's activities between October of 1993 and September of 1994 in a 44 page report to parliament. In it, he highlighted the following as dangers to national security:[514]

1. Foreign terrorist organizations;
2. Mafia-type criminal organizations;
3. Extreme right-wing Romanians;
4. The activities of the Romanian left-wing;
5. The separatist actions of Hungarian and Gypsy minority groups;
6. The activities of Hungarian, Ukrainian, Russian, etc. Intelligence services inside Romania; and
7. Economic espionage.

The report makes no mention of the case of István Király, Under-Secretary for Industry, who was arrested in February of 1995 and charged in November of the same year. The gathering of evidence against him were begun in 1994. According to information from those close to him, it was a show trial into which Hungary was dragged as he was charged with economic espionage for Hungary.

In the chapter titled "Counter-Intelligence Activities of the RIS,"[515] Magureanu reports at length that foreign special services have become particularly active under various covers. He considered the secret services of two countries especially dangerous. First, he mentioned a case involving the Moldovan Republic, then went on: "In another instance, the secret service of a neighboring country attempted to recruit an officer of the RIS assigned to a unit in one of the Transylvanian counties. The selection of the officer was through a former (female) informant. The woman settled in a neighboring country after 1990. The offices was under observation, both at home and abroad (using both pictures and videos). While the person was in the capital of that country, two members of the local intelligence service took brutal action against him. He was taken to a motel and pressured to cooperate. Psychological pressure was applied and financial incentives were offered. After the person returned home, they attempted to re-establish contact with him, as was agreed. To protect the officer and prevent the infiltration of the RIS, certain protective steps were taken."

The 1994 report devoted a lengthy chapter to the 'Hungarian threat.' Magureanu stated that "The RIS is in possession of information regarding the agents of some foreign extremist-nationalist organizations who assist anti-constitutional groups. They are in contact with some people here and attempted to influence some ethnic minority communities in Romania. Similar actions are seen more and more in extremist and separatist forms – in the heated nationalist atmosphere. The analysis of the gathered data, using global and intelligence methods, points to the conclusion that at this point – in the internal political arena – they do not threaten the state's basic interests, national sovereignty, unity or territorial integrity."

---

[514] Raport referitor la ideplinirea tributiilor ce reviu, potrivit legii, Serviciului Roman de Informatii, pentru realizarea sigurantei nationale Octombrie 1993 – Septembrie 1994. R. issue. 18/15.10.1994.

[515] Ibid, p. 22.

The report names a few people whose activities are especially damaging: Ádám Katona, the proponent of the Transylvanian Hungarian Initiative and Szeklerland autonomy; József Csapó, signer of a memorandum supporting the national autonomy aspirations of Hungarians living outside Hungary; Sándor Csurkuly, leader of the Tirgu Mures (Marosvásárhely) Free Democratic Alliance of Romas; and Dr. Eva Maria Barki. The report says the following about the Viennese lawyer: "Considerable number of instigations and insulting actions have been confirmed, in which certain leaders of Austrian organizations of the Hungarian diaspora, such as Eva Maria Barki, have spread hatred toward the Romanian people. These people call themselves the protectors of the Hungarian minority in Romania and in this role cover their real intentions in international organizations and are besmirching the country to some Western power brokers, on an international level are damaging Romania's interests."

An international expert in minority law, she held the first anti-Ceausescu press conference in her office; aided Hungarian refugees gain legal refugee status; took up the challenge to free Pál Cseresznyés; alerted the Strasbourg Human Rights Committee to the number of suicides among youths freed from jail. In the fall of 1994, she began a movement called 'Autonomy Now.' On her trips to Transylvania, she asked for autonomy for Hungarians based on the South Tyrol model. She swore on the necessity of the Fundamental Pact (alapszerzodés).

The chief of the Austrian state police handed her, on November 24, 1994, a copy of an RIS decision, dated November 22, 1993, in which a decision was made to liquidate her, along with some others. The Austrian Foreign Ministry called the Romanian ambassador, Petru Fornat, on January 11, 1995, and officially protested the threats made against the lawyer. At the same time, the Austrian ambassador to Bucharest handed over a similar letter. On January 27, 1995, Dr. Eva Maria Barki and László Tokés held a press conference in the Budapest offices of the World Federation of Hungarians (MVSz).

As part of his report to the combined session of the House of Representatives and the Senate, Magureanu touched upon the harmful activities to Romania done by certain embassies, some publications of the Hungarian Scientific Academy and Duna Television. On the latter topic, professor Titus Raveica, president of the Romanian Audio-visual Council, made a statement to the Hungarian Telegraph Bureau (MTI).[516]

Finally, what happened in the near past – and is happening today – in Romania, Emil Hurezen recapped: "In Romania, the red version of Fascism was in power. Romanian Communism was anti-Soviet, with strong Fascist influences. The tensions between anti-Russian feelings and Romanian nationalism, between rationalism and irrationalism, are peculiar characteristics in today's political life, including Iliescu and Magureanu.

RIS report on the period between September 1995 and December 1996[517]

---

[516] Romanian Hungarian Word (Romániai Magyar Szó /RMSZ/). 1995, November 13.
[517] Raport referitor .... 1995-1996. op.cit.

The resignation on April 24 of the Director of the RIS, Virgil Magureanu, was taken by the Greater Romania Party as a success of its making. According to spokesman Ulieru and former president Iliescu, internal and external pressure played an equal part. The *Presse France* referred to a "battle between secret agents."

The RIS flagged the following as dangerous and increasing activities against Romanian national security:

?? Foreign intelligence is motivated by new goals;
?? The interests of the national economy were damaged on several occasions;
?? Terrorism increased on Romanian soil;
?? The anti-constitutional activities of groups, parties and ethic minorities;
?? The growth of religious sects; and
?? The rise of dangerous trends in the state of the population's health.

Anti-Romanian intelligence activities

Persons or organizations in possession of economic, military and political secrets, or confidential information, are of increased interest to foreign intelligence services. In the middle of April, a Romanian citizen was charged with handing over to his employer, for a considerable amount of money, papers from one of the most important national institutions – his place of work – containing national secrets.

Military intelligence is especially interested in the modernization of military technology, nuclear energy and the defensive strategy of the country. Some foreign secret services continue to carry out disinformation, propaganda and anti-propaganda. Their aim is to prevent Romania's integration into NATO, minimize its defensive capabilities and maintain its dependence on certain foreign power. (The report does not name the certain foreign power but the wording makes it clear, it refers to the Russian secret service. It also becomes clear from the text that national secrets have not been defined by law.)

Activities against the interests of the national economy

The foreign economic espionage was directed primarily at the mineral wealth, electrical energy and military technology. The counties most imperiled were Marmatiei (Máramaros), Satu Mare (Szatmár) and Fejér. According to recent reports, a Romanian citizen was unmasked who furnished information to a foreigner about the location of silver and gold ore deposits.

The RIS often comes across instances where people making contract decisions make them against the economic interests of Romania. Investigations in many cases revealed that public servants were bribed. Serious abuses took place in banking and financial matters. Some people, taking advantage of highly placed connections, were able to receive so much credit that, as a result, the economic balance was seriously threatened. Thirteen cases came to the attention of the authorities – in shipping, lumber and machine parts – where the trade transactions were so unfavorable as to cost the country tens of billions of Lei.

The ranks of the Customs and Finance inspectors were rife with corruption. Several bribery cases were uncovered, mostly involving Arab export-import companies. Besides the port of Constanta, three cities near the western border are named: Arad, Timisoara (Temesvár) and Oradea (Nagyvárad). Especially in petrochemical refining did the wholesale selling of assets take on huge proportions. Frequently, products were sold without being delivered, illegal credit advanced, lack of formal bidding or billing for services not delivered. The sale of the Romanian merchant fleet caused tremendous damage to the country. If it continues – the report went on – within ten years, the whole Romanian merchant marine will be privatized.

Factors endangering the health of the population

The report covered this topic for the first time, as well as making special reference to the environment. It pointed out that:
?? The necessary financial basis for health services has shrunk;
?? Pharmaceutical distribution is badly organized;
?? Expensive foreign drugs enjoy advantageous treatment; and
?? There have been serious abuses in the food processing industries in Bucharest, Botosani, Suceavan, Arad and Covasna (Kovászna).

According to official records, at the moment, there are 1,116 tons of illegal wastes within the country. The regions most endangered are Teleorman, Iasi (Jászi) and Arad counties.

Anti-constitutional phenomenon

The report mentions draws attention to three as being the most threatening to the country's national security:
?? Ethnic separatism;
?? Political extremism; and
?? Illegal political activities.

Ethnic separatism

"Today's reality is that social, political and economic circumstances have led to the situation where certain foreign circles have attempted to prevent Romania from becoming a constitutional state and a NATO member. Increasingly evident are incidents which attempt to legitimize the notion of territorial changes.

Information gathered by the RIS seems to suggest that in recent times, certain Romanian and anti-European forces have falsified and consistently misrepresented certain archival documents, in the attempt to create a historical precedent for their territorial revisionist goals. The inroads made by ethnic-based autonomist/separatist concepts are the work of foreign agents.

In the mainly Hungarian populated areas, tremendous propaganda campaign is active with the aim to bring about Hungarian autonomy. The country's territorial integrity and constitutional order is endangered by organizations such as the Transylvanian Hungarian Initiative (Erdélyi Magyar Kezdeményezés) and the Group for Szeklerland's Civil Society (Csoport Székelyföld Civil Társadalmáért). These tendencies have cropped up not only in the one-time Szekler counties but all over Transylvania. These are rounded out by the universities and post-graduate institutions of Oradea (Nagyvárad), Odorheiu-Secuiesc (Székelyudvarhely), Miercuera-Ciuc (Csíkszereda) and Sfântu Gheorghe (Sepsiszentgyörgy), which are funded by foreign organizations, make use of foreign textbooks and teach according to a foreign curriculum."

The report does not state, but is evident, that it means Hungary every time it makes reference to 'foreign.' It is also obvious that creating educational institutions in a mother-tongue are seen as attempts at instigating separatism, including claims to the Bólyai University.

Extremist political movements

The extreme-Right wing, legionnaire movement operated illegally. The movement called 'Michael Archangel's Legion' carried out its traditional activities in nests. The external symbols such as a uniform, the swearing of an oath, marching and a flag all contributed to the stressing of its military nature. To curry favor with the masses, its racist, anti-Semitic and propaganda call for extreme actions increased. It was an especially dangerous step when they decided to amalgamate the nests into families and to choose a party leader, or rather a national leader.

The strongest local organizations exist in Bucharest, Constanta, Kraiovan, Campulung Moldovenesti and two south-Transylvanian towns: Sibiu (Nagyszeben) and Brasov (Brassó), recently making an appearance in Medias (Medgyes).

The extreme-Left wing parties also carry out their activities outside the law. Exploiting the poor living conditions of the population, the mention 'Communist restoration' ever more frequently. Following the decision of the Supreme Court and Attorney-General's Office, some of the leaders of the movement ceased their activities. An exception was the Romanian Communist Party – the Tirgu Jiu dissident group – which maintains offices in most counties of the country. The illegal Communist movement is the strongest in Mehedenti, Gorj and Temes counties.

It seems that the Right is gaining converts – and this is true today – especially among young intellectuals, while the Left is losing ground.

Pseudo-religious sects and Satanism

Under religious cover, several information gathering groups appeared with the aim of intelligence gathering and recruitment. In the South-East of the country – around Constanta and the Turkish populated areas. A hard core group of 30 students and professors came into being. They were successfully influenced by these pseudo-religious persons to reject family, learning, moral obligations and the dehumanization of the person. The judiciary took the necessary steps against them.

Countless organizations parading under the cloak of religion, many banned in countries around the world, were able to recruit adherents among the young, especially in Bucharest. Examples are the "Light and Love" and the "Children of God," or its new name "Family."

The RIS was able to gather data on Satanists from 15 counties of the country. The most threatened towns were Bucharest, Constanta, Arges, Dambovita, Iasi, Prahova, Neamt, Teleorman and Tulcea, the counties of Temes and Huned, as well as Harghita county in Szeklerland. Polls show them to be particularly appealing to Hungarian youths. The Satanist made an unsuccessful attempt during the summer to transfer the center of their operation to Transylvania. The Church of Scientology made its appearance and is building centers (in Cluj Napoca), as well as the sect of the Rev. Moon.

International terrorism

The presence of Islamic fundamentalists and the representatives ethnic separatists presented a continuing threat. In this regard, intelligence operations in the reporting period uncovered the following:

?? 19 foreign terrorists were expelled from the country, who were observing foreign diplomatic bodies;

?? 5 terrorist actions were neutralized; and

?? RIS agents prevented 8 attempts against foreign diplomats.

Arms trade, transportation and trade of nuclear materials, kidnapping and organized crime are all present in Romania. Significant data are available on human smuggling.

It seems that the Italian Mafia is concentrating its efforts on hotels and the entertainment industry. The Russian and Ukrainian Mafia are primarily involved in organized crime (auto theft), drug trafficking, prostitution and terrorism. (There is no mention of the Gypsy Mafia, whereas most recent reports show them active in Colombia and New Zealand and operate highly organized inside the country, similar to the Sicilian Mafia.)

The authorities have information that the several thousand Kurds settled in the country are planning terrorist activities against Turkey and other countries. The authorities questioned several Afghanis, Pakistanis, Kurds, Tamils and Sikhs who took refuge in Romania after the Bosnia-Herzegovina war.

Virgil Magureanu's report made special mention of the fact that since the creation of the RIS, 3,000 officers were relieved of duty. Some were suspended for breaking the oath of office; others for plotting against the service, for imperiling its work, for undermining society's trust in the service, for leaking information.

Changes at the civilian intelligence services

The European Council document handed to Romania in part refers to the undeveloped infrastructure. Also, from an environmental protection point of view, several extremely polluted areas are on record in Romania, not a few of them in Transylvania. These are not only industrial polluted areas but the radiation pollution of the Cernavodã atomic energy plants and the aftermath of the Chernobyl explosion, which left its strongest mark in Bucharest and Cluj Napoca (Kolozsvár).

The government could not overcome such socially harmful phenomena as corruption and the black market. The latter is equivalent to about 30-40% of government revenues. The President made a promise that very soon – with priority – he would introduce a law against corruption and organized crime. Economic uncertainty brings with it social instability, corruption, growth in organized crime and the Mafias, – firstly, the homegrown Roma Mafia – and the appearance of sects, all of which the towns of Transylvania experienced first hand.

According to the EC document, neither the police forces nor the intelligence services were acting according to European standards. Creating the new structures, however, is a relatively long task. For the moment, only the 'beheading' of the former services has taken place, similar to the diplomatic service, where foreign appointments were being handed to well known, previous opposition intellectuals – not career diplomats.

After several months of debate to reach a consensus among the coalition partners, new heads were named to the SRI, SIE and SSI, the military intelligence and counter-intelligence services. In the spring of 1997, Costin Georgescu, President Constantinescu's trusted choice, took over from Virgil Magureanu as head of the RIS. This represented only the preliminary steps in the restructuring of the service.

In the fall of 1997, the head of the RIS, Georgescu, and his party, the Liberal Party, tabled a draft proposal for sweeping amendments to the national security law. A similar proposal was made in 1995 but the then leadership rejected it. The aim of the amendment was to put into place strict supervision of the intelligence services, their observance of the laws and the demilitarization of the services. The proposal suggests the reduction of the intelligence community to six:

?? The Foreign Intelligence Service;
?? National Security Service (Siguranca);
?? Police Security Directorate;
?? Military Intelligence and Counter-intelligence;
?? Anti-terrorist Service; and

?? Protective-Defensive Service.

The draft also contains the following fundamental changes:

1. In the future, the services will be forbidden to carry out economic activities, or be politically active.
2. The Foreign Intelligence Service is charged with uncovering external activities that threaten the security of the state.
3. The National Security Service is empowered to maintain surveillance of persons or organizations who are a threat to national security.
4. The gathered information and data must be forwarded to the Police Security Directorate.
5. Only the police can order arrests.
6. The secret services are only empowered to request the use of such covert methods as wiretaps, mail intercepts, with the concurrence of the judiciary.

The services must make any information regarding national security known to:

?? The National Supreme Defensive Council (Ország Legfelsobb Védelmi Tanács, CSAT in Romanian);
?? The presidents of both Houses; and
?? The President of the Defense Council.

The president of the NSDC is the Prime Minister; its members: the ministers of the Exterior, the Interior, Defense, Justice and the directors of the security services. Its activities are coordinated by the under-secretary responsible for national security affairs; he is the vice president of the NSDC. The under-secretary is a civilian, appointed by the State President, and he compiles the annual report covering the activities of the NSDC.

Costin Georgescu added, during his parliamentary hearing on October 7, 1997 that all candidates to the service receive a six month professional training course after completing university. He stressed that he will retire everyone at age 55, as well as removing anyone who fills any function in a business firm. He went on to say that he will close and reorganize the local operational centers where bureaucracy has blossomed while information gathering withered.

The new management of the RIS was behaving in typical beginner fashion and did not see the big picture, as illustrated by several events:

1. For months, the media prominently features Foreign Minister Adrian Severin's statement that several Romanian party leaders and newspaper editors were paid agents of foreign governments. The services confirmed this but the promised detailed information – the publication of the 'Severin list' – never materialized.
2. In 1995, the RIS named István Király, former Under-Secretary, by name as one against whom there existed serious charges of economic espionage. At the time – wrote the *National* newspaper – the SRI (the predecessor of the RIS) managed to thwart a Hungarian action aimed at cornering a certain Romanian rare-metal reserve. In August of this year, shortly after the law on leasing mines to foreign concessions came into effect, the seven-year sentence given Király for 'leaking information' was increased to 16 years for treason. His plea for clemency is has been on President Constantinescu's desk

for months. The upper echelon of the RIS obviously did not want to get involved in a case inherited from their predecessor.

3. According to defense committee member Senator Corneliu Guse, the RIS is maintaining 'top secret' surveillance of the leaders of the political parties through agents embedded in the organizations. This contradicted the Director's statement whereby the intent is to de-politicize the service.

Contrary to current practice, when the entire RIS report was made public in the media, the December 20 parliamentary report was completely contained. Hardly any of it was leaked to the press. All that is know of it that in the Szeklerland, the service is "master of the situation."

The Securitate-dossiers again before the Romanian Parliament

The Romanian House of Representatives again placed on the agenda on May 11, 1999 the debate on the Bill on the Secret Service, drafted by Titu. The coalition parties were mostly in support of it. The Great Romania Party repeatedly stated that the modification would cause great tension in wide masses of the population.

According to the Bill:

1. every Romanian and foreign citizen had the right to see the Securitate files compiled on him/her;
2. to make copies of it and make notes;
3. to identify the person, agent or collaborator who provided information on him/her to the Securitate;
4. the name of every informant, network and collaborator – except the staff of the diplomatic and consular corps – should be published;
5. the following persons are obliged to confess about their past as informant, collaborator or denouncer and to have their files made public:

- the county's President,
- the members of the Government,
- the members of the Parliament,
- the State Secretaries,
- the presidential advisors,
- the Directors of Ministries,
- the Prefects and Vice-Prefects,
- the senior officials of local administrations,
- the senior officials and officers of the RIS, the SIE (the foreign intelligence service), the Interior Ministry and of the Customs Service,
- the members of the Superior Court (Alkotmánybíróság) and District Attorneys,
- the proprietors and editors of newspapers,
- university professors,
- school principals, and
- the senior members of local artistic life.

The debate of the draft bill was continued on May 26. Despite their promise, nobody represented the RIS. The Advisory Board, formed to examine the

Securitate files, had the right to inspect every piece of paper "except those which contains information threatening national security." To determine those files, a special committee was established, made up of Securitate and RIS collaborators. The Advisory Board was made up of 11 members - including those of the Ministries of Foreign Affairs, National Defense and Internal Affairs - who were authorized to examine materials from other archives. Some MP's – including Ervin Székely of the DAHR – were of the opinion that the Board would be at the mercy of the archives and, despite all efforts and inquiries, would not receive the requested documents.

Several problems came to the limelight in the course of the debate. One of them was that the Act on Archives provided a 50-year secrecy period in certain cases, i.e., the examination, or more precisely, access to some documents was sequestered for that period.

During the fall session of parliament, the 'transparency' law was passed. It equally divided the politicians and public opinion. During the Ceausescu-era, every tenth person was an informant. Those affected felt they had the right to know their denouncers, to whom they owed their discrimination and persecution. Signs abound that the law is receiving resistance because of its shortcomings.

The Frunda report

(The proposal of the Romanian Parliamentary Committee examining of the RIS's activities on behalf of the General Assembly of the Council of Europe)

The EU Parliamentary General Assembly unanimously accepted the proposal, consisting of three chapters, which was drafted by a working group headed by DAHR Senator György Frunda, and which was presented to the General Assembly the spring of 1999.

Chapter One

In connection with the structure of the Romanian intelligence services, it was stated:

a) the intelligence services' scope of authority should only extend to national interests, and nothing should be brought under the umbrella of national interest that fell under the authority of the police;

b) the General Assembly should ban its member states the use of secret services against national minorities, denominational groups and political opposition;

c) intelligence services should by funded only out of the national budget. According to Costin Georgescu, the RIS spent in the first six months all the money granted by parliament for the whole year. Intelligence service spending had to be accountable; all unaccountable sources of funds should be eliminated, as Romanian laws permitted the secret services to pursue independent economic activities; and

d) intelligence services should stop operating as military organizations, as experience so far indicated that autocratic regimes infringed on legality.

Chapter Two

In determining spheres of authority:
a) a decision of the court is required for police surveillance and wiretapping;
b) it should not extend to more than three months;
c) it can be extended after the initial three months;
d) it the suspected person has not commit the crime with which he/she is charged, he/she has to informed that he/she was under intelligence service surveillance; and
e) if the action was arbitrary, he/she has the right to sue the state and demand compensation.

Chapter Three
Control over the intelligence services should be on three levels:
a) government level: a Minister to ensure that the services do not infringe on human rights;
b) parliamentary level: by a committee; and
c) judicial level.

Presently, the activities of the Romanian intelligence services and the Romanian judicial system are, in effect, contradictory with the European Declaration of Human Rights:
1. wiretapping requires court consent, but there is no obligation for report it;
2. wiretapping has no time limit – it happens that some phones are tapped for years; and
3. although Department One of the RIS, in charge of investigating national minorities, mainly Hungarians, was dissolved in 1997, the organization has not completely ended this type of activity.

Finally, the Frunda-report stresses that Romania does not need eight intelligence services. Two, one military and one civil service would perfectly meet the requirements, as similar organizations do in Western democracies.

Parliamentary Report on the Activity of the Romanian Intelligence Service, June 1998 - June 1999

SRI Director Costin Georgescu took the floor in mid-September, at the beginning of the autumn session of the Romanian parliament, and reported on the activities of the service between June 1998 and June 1999

Georgescu put special emphasis on economic problems and social movements in his report. The SRI Director was worried about the drastic fall-back in living standards. In an emotional voice, he stated that 80% of the service personnel had been replaced since 1990. Those who remained from the service of the previous regime were all necessary for their expertise, mainly technical. It was the first time that not one person was specifically named as endangering Romania's national safety. Consequently, the RIS Director denied that the service shadowed Corneliu Vadim Tudor, President of the Great Romania Party.

On the other hand, Daniela Buruiana, representative of the Great Romania Party and member of the National Security Committee (CSDC), objected that Costin Georgescu failed to mention "Hungarian irredentism in Transylvania" in his report. The final text of the report, which was presented to both houses of the Parliament in December, included Buruiana's objections, and thus, both apparent oversights were addressed.

The RIS admitted that they infringed on several occasion on the Act on State Secrets in the economic sphere. It was found in numerous cases that the representatives of certain companies made, and were still making, use of illegal methods during the privatization processes. The reason it could transpire was that Romanian national economic life was best described as a series of 'leaks.' The report then emphasizes that, in order to take measures to prevent it, counter-intelligence methods should be used, including the dissemination of false information.

A special chapter of the report dealt with the embezzlement of public funds and assets, and corruption. Furthermore, it stated that some "responsible persons" made every effort to thwart certain large scale investments in Romania, for example, in the energy sector, merchant shipping and ship building.

The RIS could not escape the conclusion that significant forces hampered the process of the country's integration into the Western-European structure. They are supported by external forces who, by their effective propaganda, discouraged Romanian official at the time of certain NATO actions and when talks on EU-admission began.

In the reported period, the Georgescu led organization could ascertain that certain forces made every effort to put out rumors abroad that Romania's financial and banking system were unstable, the country as unreliable.

It was also found that local, so called guardian-protection (orzo-védo) companies infringed on human rights more and more frequently. They use illegal means – wiretapping, covert surveillance – in order to threaten and blackmail citizens.

The smuggling alcohol, tobacco and coffee caused a US$250 million loss to the state in the reporting period, read the report, based on information gathered by the service.

The spread of extremist organizations was alarming. At the time of the report there were 51 extremist organizations operating in Romania: 28 on the extreme Right, Iron Guard-like groups, 12 of which openly advocate violence and murder as means of political struggle. Trotskyites made attempts to infiltrate the trade unions – their support presumed to come from abroad. The number of Satanic groups had increased to 450 in the country.

The number of anti-Kurd organizations also increased since the arrest of Abdullah Öcalan. Foreign terrorist organizations, like Hamas, Al-Fatah and Militant Islamic Group (Fegyveres Iszlám Csoport) continued to be active in Romania, generally under the cover of commercial enterprises.

The report confirmed the statement of former, and dismissed, Foreign Minister Adrian Severin - see the "Severin list" - that some senior officials of the Ministry of Foreign Affairs and leading newspaper editors regularly forwarded, and continue to forward, information on Romania to certain foreign intelligence services.

From the perspective of Hungary, it deserves attention that the RIS report stated "...during the Kosovo crisis, certain external groups, assisted by internal forces, openly pursued autonomist-separatist propaganda. Some radical groups, along with foreign intelligence services, intended to activate certain extreme groups, organized on ethnic and denominational grounds, in various parts of the country," meaning that they wanted to transform Romania on an ethnic basis. The RIS received 700 tips on the issue.

Concurrently with the presentation of Costin Georgescu's report, weekly *Romania Mare* published, in a series of articles, another intelligence service report on the extension of Hungarian capital in the Szeklerland, publishing the names of local Hungarians who took part in the process. The Great Romania Party's conclusion, based on the secret service report, was that Hungarian capital, and indirectly Hungary, could only be kept away from Romania by the use of tanks.

Forecasts for 2000 indicate that Romania will be the only former Communist country where further economic decline can be expected. Even the possibility of hunger strikes are probable.

Romania, therefore, has to choose not only between East and West in foreign policy, but also between the one-man, autocratic regime and democracy. At the moment, the latter seems to be losing.

Appendix B - Sabin Gherman article

I am fed-up with Romania!
by Sabin Gherman (Romanian journalist)

I am fed-up with John Doe, with the smart-arseness and with the Gypsy-like behaviour that are associated to this country name, Romania. I talk to several politicians who hold the power and all of them tell me that "we have no chance whatsoever"(*Transl. note: to join modern Europe*). I read in the newspapers and find that the government took care to give more funds to Bucharest than to the entire Transylvania, from the '98 revenue. I drive the car South and East and I notice the difference: there are better highways there, funds are always pumped in there. I wait in line at the revenue office, at the state-owned bank, at anything state-owned and tips are given everywhere. Bribes. Payola. Turkish habits, which one cannot do without.

So what? I don't want to emigrate, just because nothing has been done in ten years. I'm just fed-up with Romania. With its synonyms. With its heroisms taken out of any historical context. Other nations show their pride in Michelangelo or Da Vinci, whereas I'm shown the letter of Neacsu from Cimpulung (*Transl.note: the first document written in Romanian, dated 1521 and sent by Neacsu to the Saxon mayor of Brassó, Transylvania, with reference to Turkish war ship movements on the Danube*). What a fantastic achievement, this delation! (*Transl, note: a quotation from Ion Luca Caragiale*) If I regret anything at all now, at 30 years old, it is that I was born here, that I am among those who had been taught in school that this people, - "the beoble" (*Transl. note: another quotation from Ion Luca Caragiale*), Gentlemen, was in a permanent erection in front of history. What people? We, who hadn't shown virility at least once, we, who were packing up in times of invasion and ran for our lives to the forests, we, who were fainting in the halls where history was being decided (*Transl. note: reference to the Romanian Foreign minister's faint, when he heard the Vienna decision in 1940, returning Northern Transylvania to Hungary*), we, who nowadays scream for a piece of bread and don't know what more tricks to invent.

Here we are, bum-patched, elbow-ripped, we enter history as if a filthy pub in the neighbourhood. Between two burps and a swearing, the people (*the beoble, gentlemen!*), talk fiercely about Posada (*Transl. note: the pass where King Karoly Robert of Hungary lost the battle in 1330 after being attacked from the back*), about Michael The Brave (Mihai Viteazul, prince of Walachia, or Muntenia, who conquered Transylvania and Moldavia at about 1600), about "Long live and prosper Moldavia, Transylvania and Muntenia!" (*Transl.note: historical provinces of the nowadays Romania*). And yet another victorious burp. I'm fed-up with being ashamed of myself. That's why I tell my Western friends that I am from Transylvania. *Altra paese. Other country. L'autre pays.* I'm fed-up with being told by all non-Transylvanians that here, in Transylvania, I have troubles with Hungarians. That, weren't they... That hunger is the mother of wisdom. That federalisation is the most terrible danger watching me, stalking on me around the corner of the tower of flats along to the mugger whom I pay taxes for. That I ought to tighten the belt, as if Nastratine's donkey (*Transl.note: reference to folk stories about Nastratine Hodja*). In the name of the "unity" and "prosperity" of the Rrromanian kin. Yet I, who have been waiting for 10 years for a real unity, the unity of Transylvanian parliament members for Transylvania, the civic campaign to save the few that is left.

Yet I, praying each evening to finally come to an end with László Tokés, with his ethnical aberrations against everyone. (*Transl.note: ironical reference to the Hungarian Reformed bishop, the frequent target of Romanian nationalists' attacks*). Yet, in vain. So far. Some people carried out the Unification [of Transylvania with Romania] in 1918. Other people put their hopes in a Swiss-type confederation, together with Hungary, Czechia, and Austria. And still others, as *Ioan Slavici*, said that the unification of Transylvania with Romania is hogwash, and were jailed. Now we can see its outcome. Sobriety, elegance, and discipline - features of Transylvania - were invaded by johndoeisms, by ordinary Balkan habits, by the civilisation of the pumpkin seeds. It was Romania's chance to unite with Transylvania, to learn something from its organisation, from its systems of values. It did not happen so; Romania swallowed Transylvania - this is why nowadays one can slide every three yards on the saliva spat on the great boulevards. It is not myself who says this, but someone equal to God, *Cioran* (*Transl.note: Romanian born Emil Cioran (1911-1995), active in France as a writer*). Many will throw in their two cents to argue the aforesaid. But: how many of you didn't go to Bucharest with your filled bag, with the famous wovenbag, stuffed with bottles of hard drink? And you didn't bring it to your friends, but to chief executive officers, to ministries, to high places behind closed doors. And if, naive as you are, you didn't carry those bags, how many times weren't you warned that one enters Bucharest with one's head, since your hands are busy with "luggages". Bucharest, this place where the phthisic genius kisses the billionaire illiterate, taught all the country that "one is given". "Meat is given", "Eggs are given". One is given. Mollusk attitude.

One has no rights here, only conventionalities. Here one eats pumpkin seeds, one uses to talk like: "*there is many*", and people generally are born, spawn, and die. They haven't learned anything from Hungarians, they haven't learned anything from Austrians, they haven't learned anything from Germans. Too early they switched from "forktion" (*Transl.note: a quotation from Vasile alecsandri; an ironical reference to snobs, who, having no good French skills, thought enough adding the -tion suffix to the Romanian word furculita=fork, to get its foreign version*) to "*Romanian brigades pierce through Carpathians!*" (*Transl. note: the marching song of the royal Romanian army when in 1916, after two years of neutrality, attacked the Hungarian held Transylvania, but withdrawn soon, after 3 weeks, because of military failure*). Maybe this is why the bravest "defenders" of Transylvania were born beyond the Carpathians. Maybe this is why Europe ends somewhere near Brasov(*Hungarian: Brassó*). There's where Transylvania ends as well. Since, besides language and poor highways we have nothing in common.

We will have to wake up. To admit that what happens now is a comedy. But one in which your children ask you for a chocolate, and you just raise your shoulders. In which, tremblingly, you always look for a recommendation for anything. In which you whisper round corners about the villas of policemen, or of parliament members. A world doomed to borrowing from one salary to the next one. We will have to see that it can be otherwise. That we are different. That all the evil comes from Bucharest, from the luxury palaces, where politicians dispute the bone without any shame at all. We will have to see that it's not Hungarians, or Germans, or people of Burundi those who are our enemies, but ourselves, who live from one day to the next one, doomed to steal and swear around corners. We have nothing what to tell each other anymore, we have been doing this for 75 years (*Transl. note: since 1918 when Transylvania was united with Romania*) and we are 75 times poorer now. Otherwise, have nice days - I'm fed-up with Romania, I want my Transylvania!

(Sept. 16, 1998)

Torkig vagyok Romániával!
Írta: Sabin Gherman (román újságíró)

Torkig vagyok Miticával (*kb. Öcsike, vagy uramöcsém*), az ügyeskedéssel és cigánykodással, ami a Románia országnévhez hozzátapad. Különbozo, hatalmon lévo politikusokkal beszélgetek, és mind azt mondják nekem: "már nincs semmi esélyünk". Olvasom az újságban, hogy a kormánynak volt gondja arra, hogy a '98-as költségvetésbol nagyobb összeget adjon Bukarestnek, mint egész Erdélynek. Utazom a gépkocsival délen és keleten és látom a különbséget, ott jobbak az utak, mindig új beruházásokat eszközölnek. Sorban állok az adóhivatalnál, a CEC-nél (*megj: az OTP megfeleloje*), bárminél, ami az Államé és mindenütt kenopénzt adnak. Csubukot, borravalót. Török szokások, ami nélkül nem megy.

És akkor? Én nem akarok kivándorolni csak azért, mert tíz éve nem tesznek semmit. Mindössze, torkig vagyok Romániával. A szinonimáival. A hosködéseivel, amelyeknek semmi közük a történelemhez. Mások Michelangelóval vagy Da Vincivel dicsekszenek, miközben nekem a campulungi Neacsu levelét mutogatják (*megj.: az elso román nyelvemlék 1522-bol, amelyben Neacsu, a havasalföldi Campulung polgármestere török csapatmozgásokról értesíti a brassói városi tanácsot*). A besúgás képzeletet felülmúló megvalósítása!...

Ha valamit most, harmincéves koromban sajnálok, az az, hogy itt születtem, hogy egyike vagyok azoknak, akik azt tanulták az iskolában, hogy ez a nép, "a néb" (boborul), uraim, szüntelen erekcióban állt a történelemmel szemben. Melyik nép? Mi, akik még legalább egyszer sem tanúsítottunk férfiasságot, mi, akik a népvándorlások idején szedtük a sátorfánkat és az erdokbe futottunk, mi, akik elájultunk azokban a szalonokban, ahol a történelemrol döntöttck (*megj.: utalás arra, hogy, amikor 1940-ben meghozták a bécsi döntést, az akkori román külügyminiszter elájult*), mi, akik egy darab kenyérért szarakodunk és akik nem tudjuk, még milyen huncutságot találjunk ki.

Ezek vagyunk, foltos ülepuek, rongyos könyökuek; úgy lépünk be a történelembe, mint egy mocskos külvárosi csehóba. Két böffentés és egy káromkodás közölt, a nép - a néb, uraim! - magát kihúzva szónokol Posadáról (*megj.: itt vesztett csatát Károly Róbert visszavonuló csapata 1330-ban, egy*

301

hegyszorosban, az ot orvul megtámadó románok ellen), Vitéz Mihályról (*Mihai Viteazul havaselvi, majd erdélyi és moldvai uralkodó 1600 körül*), arról, hogy "éljen és virágozzék Moldva, Erdély és Havasalföld". És ismét egy gyoztes böffentés. Torkig vagyok azzal, hogy szégyelljem magam. Éppen ezért nyugati barátaimnak azt mondom, hogy Erdélybol való vagyok. Más országból. Altra paese. Other country. L'autre pays.

Torkig vagyok azzal, hogy az összes nem-erdélyi azt mondja: itt Erdélyben gondjaim vannak a magyarokkal. Mert ha ok nem lennének... Hogy az éhség a tudás anyja... Hogy a föderalizálás lenne a legnagyobb veszély, ami rám leselkedik a tömbház sarka mögül, mint egy tyúktolvaj, akiért fizetem az adót. Hogy kötelezoen muszáj meghúznom a nadrágszíjamat, mint Nastratin szamara (*megj.: irodalmi hasonlat*). A román nép "egysége", "felvirágzása" nevében. Én pedig tíz éve várom a valódi egységet, az erdélyi honatyák egységét Erdélyért, a civil offenzívát ama kevés megmentéséért, ami még megmaradt. És én, aki minden este azért imádkozom, hogy legyen már vége Tokés Lászlónak, a mindenki ellen irányuló etnikai aberrációival együtt. És mindhiába. Egyelore. Néhány ember megvalósította az 1918-as Egyesítést. Mások svájci típusú, Magyarországgal, Csehországgal és Ausztriával való konföderációban reménykedtek. Megint mások, mint Slavici (*megj.: Ioan Slavici erdélyi író*), azt mondták, hogy Erdély egyesülése Romániával disznóság, és börtönbe kerültek. Most látni, mi lett belole.

A komolyságot, eleganciát és fegyelmet, amelyek Erdély jellemzoi, elárasztotta a "miticaság" (megj.: kb. kisöcsémezés), az ordináré balkániság, a tökmag-civilizáció. Romániának esélye volt arra, hogy Erdéllyel egyesüljön, hogy megtanuljon valamit annak szervezettségébol, értékrendszerébol. Nem így történt: Románia elnyelte Erdélyt - épp ezért a nagy sugárutakon az ember három méterenként elcsúszik a flegmákon. Nem én mondom, hanem az, aki egyenlo az Istennel, Cioran (*megj.: Emil Cioran - román író, újságíró*). Sokan szöknek majd az égig, hogy cáfolják a fentebb mondottakat. De: hányan nem mentetek Bukarestbe tele szatyorral, a híres-neves raffia szatyorral, amelyben pálinkásüvegek szorongtak? És nem barátaitoknak vittétek, hanem igazgatóknak, a minisztériumokba, a vasalt ajtajú magas portákra... És, ha együgyu módon nem vittétek azokat a szatyrokat, hányszor figyelmeztettek rá, hogy Bukarestben fejjel kell ajtót nyitni, mert kezeidet lehúzzák a "csomagok". Bukarest, ez az a hely, ahol a tébécés zseni az analfabéta milliárdossal puszilózik, megtanította az egész országot, hogy valamit "osztanak". "Húst osztanak", "Tojást osztanak". Osztanak. Puhatestuek magatartása. Itt nincsenek jogok, csak hajlongások. Itt tökmagot esznek, és úgy beszélnek, hogy "sokan van", és az utca népe úgy általában megszületik, szaporodik és meghal.

Nem tanultak semmit a magyaroktól, nem tanultak semmit az osztrákoktól, nem tanultak semmit a németektol. Túl hamar tértek át a furculitionról (*megj.: utalás azokra a sznobokra, akik nem ismerik a román villa - furculita - szó angol vagy francia megfelelojét, és azt gondolják, elég, ha a román fonévhez csak hozzáadják a -tion végzodést*) a "Román zászlóaljak, törjetek át a Kárpatokon"-ra (*megj.: Treceti batalioane romane Carpatii - az addig semleges román királyi hadsereg 1916-ban ezt a katonai indulót dalolva tört be Erdélybe, de az elszenvedett vereségek után, alig 3 hét múlva vissza kellett vonulnia*). Meglehet, ezért is van az, hogy Erdély legvitézebb "védelmezoi" a Kárpátokon túl születtek. Lehet ezért is ér véget Európa valahol Brassó mellett. Ott ér véget Erdély is. Mivel a nyelvet és a rossz utakat leszámítva, nincs semmi, ami bennünk közös lenne. Fel kell ébrednünk. Be kell ismernünk, hogy ami most történik, az egy komédia. Méghozzá olyan, amelyben a gyermekek csokoládét kérnek, te meg vállvonogatással válaszolsz. Amelyben állandóan reszketve keresel protekciót, támogatót, mindenre. Amelyben az utcasarkon pusmogsz a rendorök és a honatyák villáiról. Egy olyan világ, amely arra van ítélve, hogy egyik fizetéstol a másikig kölcsönbol éljen. Rá kell döbbenünk, hogy lehet ez másként is. Hogy mások vagyunk. Hogy minden igazán rossz Bukarestbol jön, a luxuspalotákból, amelyekben a politikusok szégyentelenül marakodnak a koncon. Be kell látnunk, hogy nem a magyarok, a németek vagy a burundiak az ellenségeink, hanem mi magunk, akik egyik napról a másikra élünk, akik arra vagyunk ítélve, hogy lopjunk és szitkozódjunk az utcasarkon. Nincs mit egymásnak mondanunk; 75 év alatt elmondtunk mindent, és 75-ször szegényebbek vagyunk. Amúgy, további kellemes napokat - torkig vagyok Romániával, Erdélyemet akarom.

(Sept. 16, 1998)

APPENDIX C – Adrian Severin Article

ADRIAN SEVERIN: TRANSYLVANIA – ROMANIAN PADANIA?

[Padania: a northern Italian region striving to gain its autonomy.-*Editor*]

"If I want a good glass of beer, and want to have good service, I won't go to Bãile Felix (Félixfürdo), but rather cross the border and stop at one of the pubs along the highway to Budapest" said to me a Romanian of Oradea (Nagyvárad), recently. [For those not in the know, let me clarify that Bãile Felix is a splendid little place, 10 minute drive from Oradea.] On another occasion, a Tirgu Mures (Marosvásárhely) Romanian said that if he has very little time, but wanted to feel like a real gentleman in a European city, he runs up to Budapest, drinks a coffee while admiring the marvelous flow of the Danube, and then he returns. The road to the border is the worst part of the trip. From then on, everything is perfect. "Why don't you go to Bucharest?" I ask him. "If I take a look at the roads that take me to Bucharest, it is easier to travel to Budapest than to Bucharest and there everything is nice and tidy and the people are more civilized," was the reply. I can not escape the connection of the fragments of these two completely real conversations with those relatively heated debates I conducted with some Romanians of Cluj Napoca (Kolozsvár), who were lamenting that "the invasion by Moldavian Romanians a few of year ago has ruined the atmosphere of our city." In addition, they state that those from Bucharest, "those from the Regat," in general do not understand Transylvania. The conclusion is that Transylvania should be left alone to manage its own affairs, without mixing with, and interference from, the uncivilized gate-crashers coming from beyond the Carpathians, who have not really been invited here, at all. Similar vehement thoughts were shared by Romanians of Sibiu (Nagyszeben), not to mention those from Timisoara (Temesvár). [It is possibly interesting and indicative that I have never heard Romanians of Iasi or Botosani or Vaslui speaking about the "invasion of the Transylvanians." The Bukovinians never miss an opportunity to stress that they are not Moldavians, just like the Szeklers (Székelys) of Harghita (Hargita) and Covasna (Kovászna) always state that they are not Hungarians. Once some villagers in the vicinity of Suceava (Szucsáva) sternly lectured me that they had such traditions and laws – like the cadastral land-register – which were handed down from the period of Empress Maria Theresa and Emperor Joseph II, and they did could understand why the rulers of Bucharest did not respect and observe them.]

For various reasons, the Banate (Bánát) and Dobrudja are the most cosmopolitan regions of Romania. The ideal of autonomy and European and NATO integration first took hold there, as evident from the election results, especially the votes of the young, and the results of parties open to international relations prove it. It is not accidental that Euro-regionalism and maintaining friendly relations with Western regions and settlements are the most active in the counties of Temes, Caras-Severin (Karán-Szeverin) and Arad and that they are, consequently, the most developed. The Romanians of the Banate explain with evident conviction and pride that they are different from the other Romanians, because they have a more developed community consciousness and civilization, as well as are more experienced in inter-ethnic coexistence for a longer time - and that this is exactly what they expect from European integration. That is exactly why they are do not at all like that their march into Europe is hindered by the "Balkan" and "Levanter" (Middle Eastern) attitude of the "Regatians," the "Wallachians," and the "Bucharesters." All conversations ended with the conclusion those in the Banate, like the Transylvanians, if they had to choose between Europe and Bucharest, would choose the former.

In 1992, when the question of establishing the Independent Civic Party (Független Polgári Párt – FPP) and the division of state assets among the five regional parts, it became evident that the number of small- and medium-sized companies was higher in the Banate and Transylvania, while the money-losing industrial giants were to be found mainly in Moldova, Muntenia and Oltenia. This is why it is not surprising that economic dynamism and entrepreneurial spirit is more developed in the Banate and Transylvania where, as a consequence, privatization progressed quicker. At the same time, in the old Regat, losing ones roots and sinking into the lower classes is becoming wide spread, leading to statism (ed: reliance on the state), protectionism and conservatism, as well as a fear of strangers and rapid change.

It is also well known when those in the Banate and in Transylvanians calculate the value of their Lei, they take the German Mark as the basis for evaluation, while those from the Regat (the Muntenians, Oltenians, Moldavians and Dobrudjans) use the American dollar. This phenomenon, too, indicates a divided Romania, existing in both European and Transatlantic spheres, divided from the point of view of its citizens. Germany and America are the two countries where Romanians turn with their hopes.

Engaging into conversation with simple people while traveling in the Banate and Transylvania, one thing becomes obvious: as Schengen is approaching the borders of our country, so is the fear growing among Romanians that free travel to Europe, or at least to Vienna, where their parents could travel without passport will be taken away from them because of "the Balkan attitude of the Regaters." It is interesting to listen to some citizens of Timisoara (Temesvár) asserting what an important waterway the Bega canal would be, but only if Romania, Hungary and Serbia were treated as one economic-administrative unit. The experience of Romanians in Bihar, Marmatiei (Máramaros) and Beszterce-Naszód is fascinating, namely that the taxes paid to Bucharest, the yield of their labor, does not return but enriches the lazy, the corruptible and swindlers of the South. The recent plan to move the center of methane gas production from Medias (Medgyes) to Bucharest – real or not – caused a virtual uprising in Transylvania, where people feared that they are working for others' profit, wealth and development, even if those others are Romanians, too.

In these thoughts, gestures and inner turmoils, I discover the same worries, discontent and reasons that characterize the relations between Northern and Southern Italians. The process that has gradually led from the seemingly harmless comment, "the Milanese work so the Romans can sleep and the Neapolitans can singing," to the movement demanding the separation and independence of Padania (the region of the Pad River in its narrower sense, the Northern region of Italy, in its broader sense).

And similar to Italy, although the South is not satisfied with the attitude of the North, no one really wants separation in Romania. Let's not be unfair with our Moldavians, either. They made genuine contributions to the glory of Romanian history, Romanian culture, and the development of Romanian economy. And what did they get in return? Detestation and backwardness. Since the unification of the principalities (a little less than a century and a half ago) the Moldavians have been feeling that they were deceived. The Moldavians are sentimental, tradition-bound, honest and legitimist. They do not reject change, but the elements of change pile up at a faster pace than they could adopt; they do resist development in general, but they prefer deliberate progress to development by leaps. It they keep their distance with the West, it is only because they have never maintained contact with it. None of the European arterial roads cross Moldova, and the region is not in contact with any country that esposes Western European standards. Therefore, through immense investments in the infrastructure and the realization of the planned Warsaw-Bucharest highway (running from Gdansk in the North on the Baltic Sea through Lvov (Lemberg), Chernovci (Csernovic), Suceava (Szucsáva), Iasi (Jászváros), and down to Alexandropol on the Aegean Sea in the South), the spirit of the European community could slowly seep into Moldova, too. If it does not happen, the differences between the cosmopolitan enthusiasm of the Transylvanians and the historical cautiousness of the Moldavians will continue to grow, bringing unfortunate consequences. At this moment, it is hard to handle the establishment of the "Moldavians' Party", although its presence is quite moderate in public life, because it forecasts the prospect of another separation.

What will remain of Romania's unity under these circumstances? Let us put it straight: national unification has not been completed yet, it is merely on its way to realization. At the same time, certain centrifugal forces are endangering it, which are embedded in the very basis of Romanian society and fed by the very diversity of its structure. Totalitarianism made an attempt to make the Romanian society consistent and to unify all Romanians, living in all the historic regions within the borders. Democracy brought the differences to the surface, again. By themselves, they are not harmful. The wide cultural and civilizational gap does not cause inconvenience, the feeling of being deceived, nor do they inspire hopes, desires and diverging attitudes. The political elite praises in vain the ideal of a unified state if it does rest on the feelings, interests and conviction of the people, which are determined by economic, social and cultural reality. It seems that the Romanian governments following the totalitarian regime consider national unity as a fact, and they neglect the differences in development of the Romanian communities living in the various historic regions of the country. That is why a real Romanian national policy is missing, the aim of which will be the establishment of the fundamental harmony of the Romanian nation and the assurance of the uniform character on a given path, which includes the decentralization of public administration and local autonomy. Not the foreigners, nor the ethnic minorities raise the issue of national unity but the Romanians themselves. They do it not because they are not good patriots but because they are governed badly.

Adrian Severin: Ardealul, o Padania romaneascã? (Erdély – Román Padánia?), *Ziua,* August 18, 1998.
(Translated from Romanian by Ildikó Lipcsey.)

Biographical endnotes

Ady, Endre (1877-1919): Hungarian poet, publicist. Outstanding personality of 20th century Hungarian literature. Contributor to the *Debreceni Lapok, Nagyváradi Napló, Budapesti Napló, Holnap* and *Nyugat* publications. His lyric works on contemporary social issues and love poems are unique in Hungarian literature.

Andropov, Jurij Vladimirovics (1914-1984): Soviet politician. From 1951-1953, he worked in the Communist Party's central organization. From July, 1953, held the position of counsellor in the Soviet embassy in Budapest and between July, 1954 and March, 1957 was the ambassador to Hungary. He was the Secretary of the Central Committee (1961-1967 and in 1982) and head of the KGB (1967-1982), a member of the Politbureau (from 1973), Secretary General of the Central Committee (1982-84), and finally the President of the Party Presidium (1983-84).

Antonescu, Ion (1882-1946): Romanian fieldmarshal, right-wing politician. Took part in the occupation of Hungary in 1919. Between the wars, he was a military attaché in several western countries. Prime minister 1940-1944, national leader 1941-1944. The Romanian Holocaust is attributed to him. He crushed the Iron Guard when they turned against him; joined in the anti-Soviet war side. His government was ended by an armed uprising on August 23, 1944. Executed in 1946 as a war criminal.

Antonescu, Mihai (1904-1946): Romanian journalist, university professor, politician. Between 1940 and 1944, Minister of Propaganda and Foreign Affairs. Executed by a decree of the People's Court.

Apponyi, Albert count (1846-1933): conservative Hungarian politician. Member of the Hungarian Academy of Science. Leader of the moderate parliamentary opposition. President of the Independence and '48 Kossuth Parties (Függetlenségi és a '48-as Kossuth Párt). He led the Hungarian delegation to the peace talks in 1919. Strives for revisions of the terms of the peace pact in the Peoples Alliance. His daughter, Gerardine, became the wife of the Albanian king, Zog.

Apostol, Gheorghe (1913-): Romanian left-wing politician. Charged with Communist activities in 1937. From 1945, a member of the Central Committee of the Romanian Workers Party /RMP/, 1948-1965 a member of the Party Committee /PB/, First Secretary (1954-1955), First Vice-President of the Council of Ministers (1961-1967) and President of the Central Council of Unions from 1968. In 1969, he was removed from the Central Committee. Diplomat in Latin America (1969-1988). Signatory of the letter of the 'Six' in 1989.

Apró, Antal (1913-1994): Hungarian Communist politician. Member of the Hungarian Communist Party /MKP/, Hungarian Workers Party /MDP/ Executive /VB/ and Party /PB/ Committees, Hungarian Socialist Workers Party /MSZMP/ Central /KB/ and Party /PB/ Committees. From 1976, president of the Hungarian-Soviet Frienship Society.

Auer, Pál (1885-1978): Hungarian politician, diplomat, lawyer. Representative in the Independence and '48 Kossuth Parties (Függetlenségi és a '48-as Kossuth Párt), later in the Independent Small Landholders Party. After the Second World

War, takes part in the work of the Hungarian peace delegation. A supporter of limited border revisions. Subsequently, emigrates to the West.

Averescu, Alexandru (1859-1938): Romanian fieldmarshal, politician. Expert military theoretician. Took part in the Second Balkan War and World War I. Military attaché in Berlin. Founder of the People's League Party.

Bajcsy-Zsilinszky, Endre (1886-1944): Hungarian politician. Leader of the National Radical Party. Executed during the Second World War, by the ultra right-wing Arrow Cross Party, for his anti-German behaviour. In his books, he searches for Hungary's place in European political life.

Balcescu, Nicolae (1819-1852): leader of the 1848 revolt in Muntenia /Havasalföld/. After its crushing, he flees to Transylvania. On July 14, 1848 he and Lajos Kossuth signed the Romanian-Hungarian reconciliation draft.

Balogh, Edgár /Kessler/ (1906-1996): Romanian-Hungarian public figure, writer. Schooled in Bratislava and Prague. Founded the leftist Sickle /Sarló/ movement in 1931. Deported from Czechoslovakia in 1935. Joined the leftist Hungarian movement in Romania. Published the *Illumination /Világosság/* daily paper in Cluj Napoca /Kolozsvár/. Vice president of the Hungarian Peoples Alliance. Arrested in 1949, rehabilitated in 1956. Teacher at the Babes-Bolyai University, assistant editor-in-chief of *Our Times /Korunk/*. Editor of the Romanian Hungarian Literary Encyclopedia.

Bánffy, Miklós count (1873-1950): Transylvanian politician, Foreign Minister, writer. Commissioner of the Opera House and the National Theater. Returned to Transylvania in 1925. Organized theatrical and literary life. His works appeared under the *nom de plume* of Kisbán Miklós.

Bányai, László /Baumgarten/ (1907-1981): Romanian-Hungarian publicist, historian. Dean of the Bolyai Scientific University, 1952-1956; Deputy Minister of Education, 1956-1957.

Bárdossy, László (1890-1946): Hungarian diplomat, politician. Foreign Minister and Prime Minister, 1941-1942. Declares war on the Soviet Union, on June 27, 1941 without Parliamentary approval. Executed as a war criminal, having been found guily by the People's Court.

Beke, György (1927-): Romanian-Hungarian writer, journalist. His sociographic writings portray the reality of today's Hungarians in Romania. Resident of Hungary since 1990. For a time, he was an official of the Transylvanian Alliance. Recipient of several literary awards.

Benes, Eduard (1884-1948): Czechoslovak politician. In 1918, together with Masaryk, the leader of the anti-Austrian Czech émigrés. One of the leaders of the Paris Peace Talks, Foreign Minister (1918-1935), Prime Minister (1921-1922). One of the founders of the Little Entente. After the dissolution of Czechoslovakia, the leader of the London émigré group (1940-1945).

Beniuc, Mihai (1907-1988): Romanian poet, psychologist of Transylvanian origin. Between 1949 and 1965, leading officeholder in the Romanian Writers Guild, its president 1956-1957. Member of the Romanian Scientific Academy, professor of the University of Bucharest. Visited Hungary on numerous occasions.

Bethlen, Gábor (1580-1629): Prince of Transylvania. Joining the Thirty Years War against the Habsburgs, he reached as far as the walls of Vienna. Allied himself with the Protestant rulers of western Europe. His aim: the re-unification of the Kingdom of Hungary. Under his rule, Transylvania stabilizes and lives its „Golden Age".

Bethlen, István   count (1874-1946): Transylvanian-born Hungarian politician. Prime Minister (1921-1931) under who Hungary's economic and foreign affairs were consolidated. During the Second World War, leader of the anglophone oriented movement. Interned in the Soviet Union where he died.

Birladeanu, Alexandru (1911-): left-wing Romanian economist, politician. Fills high government and party offices between 1948 and 1968. Belonged to the parties opposing Ceausescu. Member of the Romanian Scientific Academy. In 1990, President of the Romanian Senate.

Bitay, Árpád (1896-1937): Transylvanian-Hungarian teacher, literary historian. Councillor to the Hungarian Bureau of the Minorities Ministry of the Iorga government. Member of several literary associations, contributor to publications. Member of the Alba Iulia /Gyulafehérvár/ diocese council.

Bodnaras, Emil (1907-1976): member of the Romanian Communist Party from 1934. Jailed from 1934-1944 on charges of espionage for the Soviet Union. Led the armed uprising in August, 1944. Between 1945 and 1965, member of the Central Committee /KB/ and the Party Committee /PB/. Minister of Defence (1947-1956), oversaw the Romanian secret services, member of the Executive Committee /VB/. In 1967, member of the Romanian Communist Party's Praesidium, President (1965-1967) of the Ministers' Council.

Boldizsár, Iván (1912-1988): Hungarian writer, publicist, public figure. Writes pamphlet about the fate of Hungarians in Czechoslovakia, 1946. Under-Secretary of Foreign Affairs, 1947-1951. In 1960, president of the national Peace Council. National award (1975). Edited the *New Hungarian Quarterly*.

Borbély, Imre (1948-): Romanian-Hungarian chemical engineer, politician. Takes part in the 1989 uprising in Timisoara /Temesvár/, formulator of the Temesoara Manifesto's 8th point which condemned persons who took part in the Communist regime. Parliamentary representative in the Romanian Hungarian Democrats Alliance /RMDSZ/, active in inter-parliamentary affairs. In 2002, President of the Carpathian Basin Region of the Hungarians' World Alliance /MVSZ/.

Borila, Petre /Iordan Dragan Rusev/ (1906-1973): Romanian left-wing politician. Member of the Romanian Communist Party's Central Committee from 1924, fights in the International Brigade in Spain. Emigrates to Moscow and returns to Romania as the military commander of the Tudor Vladimirescu division. Between 1948 and 1969, again a member of the Central Committee /KB/; 1952 to 1965 of the Party Committee /PB/; 1965 to 1969 of the Executive Committee /VB/. Vice President of the Ministers' Council.

Bratianu, Ion C.C. (1864-1927): Romanian politician. From 1908, the president of the Liberal Party, Prime Minister on several occasions between 1909 and 1927. In 1919, initiates contact with the Soviet Republic of Hungarian /Tanácsköztársaság/. Founding member of the Little Entente.

Brtatianu, Vintila (1867-1930): Romanian politician. Minister of Defence and Finance. Founder of the National Liberal Party; Prime Minister from 1927-1928.

Briand, Aristide (1862-1932): French politician. Foreign Minister and Prime Minister on several occasions between 1915 and 1931. Founding member of the League of Nations.

Brucan, Silviu (1916-): Romanian left-wing political theorist, diplomat. His academic writings analyze the errors of existing socialism. Belonged to the parties opposing Ceausescu.

Buracu, Octavian: Transylvanian-Romanian writer. Leading proponent of Romanian-Hungarian reconciliation. Died in the mid-90's.

Bugnariu, Teodor (1909-?): Transylvanian-Romanian politician. Collaborator of the Romanian Communist Party's Provincial Committee in Cluj Napoca, 1945. Professor at the Cluj Napoca and Bucharest universities.

Ceausescu, Nicolae (1918-1989): Romanian Communist politician. Party member since 1933. Fills several party functions, among them the responsibility for the Romanian armed forces. 1965, First Secretary of the Romanian Communist Party; 1965-1969, Secretary-General of the Central Committee; 1969-1989, Secretary-General of the Romanian Communist Party. 1967-1974, President of the National Council; 1974-1989, President of the Romanian Socialist Republic. Executed in December, 1989.

Chisinevsci, Josif /Roitman/ (1905-1963): Communist party member from 1928. Released, along with Teohari Georgescu, after August 23, 1944, from the Karánsebes jail. From 1948, fills party post for agit-prop. Until 1957, Deputy President of the Ministerial Council.

Chivu, Stoica (1908-1975): Romanian railway worker, Communist politician. Romanian Communist Party member from 1931. PV. Executive Committee /VB/ member. 1965-1969, member of the Permanent Praeasidium; 1950-1955, Deputy Prime Minister; 1955-1961, President of the Ministers' Council. From 1969, President of the Revisionist Committee /Reviziós Bizottság/.

Ciorbea, Victor (1954-): Transylvanian-Romanian jurist, union leader, Prime Minister.

Codreanu, Corneliu Zelea (1899-1938): extreme right-wing racist Romanian politician. Founder of the Archangel Michael Legion (from 1930 called the Iron Guard). Jailed on charges of treason and shot while allegedly attempting to escape.

Constantinescu, Emil (1939-): Romanian lawyer, geologist, politician. President of the Democratic Convention; 1996-2000, President of Romania.

Constantinescu, Miron (1917-1974): Romanian politician, historian, sociologist. Arrested in 1940 for spreading Communist propaganda among students. 1945-1959, member of the Romanian Communist Party's Executive Committee, responsible for minority affairs. 1948, Party Committee member; 1952-1954, Secretary of the Central Committee; 1949-1955, President of the National Planning Board. The Central Committee, in its meeting of June 28 to July 3, 1957, stripped him of Party membership.

Coposu, Corneliu (1916-2000): Transylvanian-Romanian politician, close collaborator of Iuliu Maniu. 1936-1947, one of the leaders of the National Agrarian Party. In 1947, condemned for 14 years.

Csapó, József (1938-): Romanian-Hungarian agricultural engineer, politician. 1990-1992, parliamentary representative of the RMDSZ; 1992, senator. Composes a plan for Romanian-Hungarian communal autonomy.

Csögör, Lajos (1904-): Romanian-Hungarian doctor. Took part in the populist and left-wing movements. After 1945, Deputy Sheriff of Kolozs County, active in organizing the Bolyai University. 1945-1956, jailed during the period of the show trials. After his rehabilitation, to 1967, a doctor in Tirgu Mures /Marosvásárhely/ and Dean of the Hungarian Phamacology University. Parliamentary representative on several occasions. Resides in Hungary since the '80s.

Cuza, Alexandru Ion (1820-1873): Romanian army officer, politician. In 1859, Prince of Moldova and Muntenia /Havasalföld/ and instrumental in creating Romania in 1862. Due to his liberal reforms and for freeing the serf, exiled by the large landholders.

Csáky, István   count (1894-1941): Hungarian diplomat, Foreign Minister. Follower of German and Italian direction in foreign policy. Signatory, on behalf of Hungary, of the Anti-Comintern Pact and the Tripartite Pact. Worked on the preparation of the Second Vienna Resolution.

Csehi, Gyula (1910-1976): Romanian-Hungarian aesthetician, critic. Became familiar with the left-wing movement during his student days in France. For this, he was later branded as a Trocky-ite. Teaches in Cluj Napoca, 1947-1952 and Nagyenyed, 1952-1954. University professor in Cluj Napoca from 1957. In the years 1956 and 1957, a collaborator of *Our Path /Utunk/* publication.

Csurka, István (1934-): Hungarian writer, dramatist, politician. One of the leaders of the Hungarian Democratic Forum /MDF/. Expelled in 1991. Starts the Hungarian Truth and Life Party /Magyar Igazság és Élet Párt - MIÉP/. Editor-in-chief of the *Hungarian Forum* weekly. Representative of Hungarian radicalism.

Daicovici, Constantin (1898-1973): Transylvanian-Romanian historian, archeologist. Elected member to the Romanian Scientific Academy in 1955. Professor of the Cluj Napoca University. In 1959, Dean of the amalgamated Cluj Napoca University. Proponent of the theory of the Dacian-Roman continuity. Recipient of the 1968 Herder award.

Deák, Ferenc (1803-1876): liberal Hungarian politician. Member of the Hungarian Scientific Academy. A leader of the reform movement of the 1830's. Subsequent to the 1848-1849 revolt and fight for freedom, espouses political passivity and supporter of the Compromise (1867) with the Habsburg monarchy.

Demeter, Béla (1910-1952): Romanian-Hungarian journalist, editor. Active with the *Transylvanian Youth, Eastern News and Transylvanian Farmer /Erdélyi Fiatalok, a keleti Újság, az Erdélyi Gazda/* publications. Transylvanian-Hungarian village life and Romania's economy occupies his studies. Took active part in political life. Leader in the Transylvanian Hungarian Economic Association. Organizer of the anti-German resistance in Cluj Napoca. Provides recommendations to the Hungarian Peace delegation, for which he was sentenced and executed by Romania.

Demeter, János (1908-1988): Romanian-Hungarian lawyer, university professor, writer. In 1945, Deputy Mayor of Cluj Napoca, a leader in the Hungarian People's Alliance /MNSZ/. Jailed in 1949 on trumped-up charges, rehabilitated in 1956.

1956, Dean of the Bolyai University; 1969-1979, Chancellor of the Babes-Bolyai University. President of the Hungarian National Workers Council of Cluj Napoca.

Dobai, István (1924-): Transylvanian-Hungarian lawyer, lay leader in the Reformed Protestant Church. Broached the Transylvanian question in 1956. Arrested in 1957 and sentenced in the 'UN memorandum' case.

Domokos, Géza (1928-): Romanian-Hungarian writer, editor, politician. Graduate of Moscow's Maxim Gorki College. Editor of several papers. 1969-1984, alternate member of the Romanian Communist Party's Central Committee; 1969-1990, director of Kriterion Publishing; 1989-1992, one of the founders of, and representative for, the Romanian Hungarian Democratic Alliance /RMDSZ/.

Dragomir, Silviu (1888-1962): Transylvanian-Romanian historian, professor at Cluj Napoca University. Member of the Romanian Scientific Academy. Minister.

Duca, Ion Gheorghe (1879-1933): Romanian Liberal Party politician, party president, journalist. Minister on several occasions; Prime Minister, November to December, 1933. Assassinated by the Romanian extreme right-wing.

Draghici, Alexandru (1913-1993): Roman railway worker. Secret Communist, sentenced to 9 years in 1936 in the Craiova case. From 1944, secretary of the capital's party organization. State's attorney at the People's Court. 1951, Deputy Interior Minister; 1952-1965, Interior Minister; 1965-1968, Secretary of the Central Committee. In 1968, was called to account and expelled from the party. Emigrated to Hungary in 1991.

Entz, Géza (1949-): Hungarian art historian. Founding member of the Hungarian Democratic Forum /MDF/, 1987. 1990-1992, Under-Secretary for political affairs in the Prime Minister's Office; 1992-1994, President of the Office for Hungarians Across the Border; 1998, Deputy President of the National Board for Historical Preservation.

Eötvös, József (1813-1871): Hungarian politician, writer, publicist. Member of the Hungarian Scientific Academy. Representative of the reform generation. Lived in exile, in Munich, from 1849 to 1853. His accomplishment was the introduction of universal and compulsory public education.

Erdei, Ferenc (1910-1971): Hungarian sociographer, agrarian politician. A leader of the National Agrarian Party; from 1945, its Vice President, from 1947, its General-Secretary. 1944-45, Interior Minister; 1948-1949, Minister of State; from 1949, holds the post of Minister of Agriculture and Justice. Deputy Prime Minister from Nov. 15, 1955 to Nov. 2, 1956. Arrested in Tököl by Soviet security forces as part of the Hungarian truce delegation. From 1957, Director of the Agricultural Economic Research Institute.

Fazekas, János (1926-): Romanian-Hungarian politician. From 1945, Romanian Communist party member. Initially, a functionary in the Young Workers movement. 1954 onwards, Central Committee member; from 1956, one of the five person Secretariat; 1965-1981, on the Executive Committee. Member of the Political Sciencees Academy. Having lost the favour of Ceausescu regime, he devoted himself to minorities – European aminorities and the Hungarian minority.

Féja, Géza (1900-1978): Hungarian writer, sociographer, poet. Joined the folk/village research movement. (*Stormy corner /Viharsarok/*, 1937). In the circle of popular writers, theoretician of the *Reply* /Válasz/ journal. One of the composers of the March Front's program, espouser of the 'third way'. After 1945, retires from literary life; publishes regulary after 1957.

Ferencz József I. (Habsburg) (1830-1916): Emperor of Austria from 1848. Allied with the Russians, puts down the Hungarian revolution of 1848-49, which was followed by harsh retributions. His losses in the Italian and German question forced him to open a dialogue, followed by reconciliation, with the Hungarians in 1867. King of Hungary from 1867. Rejected the possibility of the Austro-Hungarian dualist monarchy becoming a federalist state.

Földes, László (1922-1973):Romanian-Hungarian literary critic, editor. Degree in psychology-philosophy from the Bolyai Science University. Later teaching assistant there; teaches esthetics at the Arts and Music College. 1950-1956, editor-in-chief of the National Literary and Arts Publishing's Cluj Napoca office; 1956-1958, editor-in-chief of *Our Path /Utunk/*. Due to the criticism of his contemporaries, he is sidelined. From 1970, assistant to the editor-in-chief of *Week /Hét/*.

Frunda, Görgy (1951-): Romanian-Hungarian lawyer, politician. 1990-1992, parliamentary representative of the Romanian Hungarian Democratic Alliance /RMDSZ/; 1992-1996, Senator of the Romanian Parliament. Nominated for the presidency of the RMDSZ in 1996.

Funar, Gheorghe (1949-): Transylvanian-Romanian economist, politician. Deputy president of the Vatra Romaneasca, a nationalist organization; representative in the Romanian National Unity Party /Román Nemzeti Egységpárt/; Lord Mayor of Cluj Napoca.

Für, Lajos (1930-): Hungarian historian, politician. Took part in the events of 1956. 1980-1987, science secretary of the Agricultural Museum; 1988-1990, teaches at the Eötvös Lóránd University of Liberal Arts and Sciences /ELTE/. Founding member of the Hungarian Democratic Forum /MDF/. 1990-1994, Minister of Defence. His area of research: Hungary's human losses during the Second World War.

Gaál, Gábor (1901-1954): Hungarian editor, literary critic, leftist thinker. Due to his role in the Hungarian Republic /Tanácsköztársaság/, he is forced to emigrate, first to Vienna, then Cluj Napoca. Editor of *Our Time /Korunk/* between 1926 and 1940. Proponent of 'Romanianism' as opposed to 'Transylvanianism'.Editor-in-chief of *Our Path /Utunk/* from 1946, professor at the Bolyai University. President of the Romanian Hungarian Writers Guild. Expelled from the Party in 1950.

Gafencu, Grigore (1892-1957): Romanian lawyer, diplomat, politician. One of the founders of the National Agrarian Party. 1938-1949, Foreign Minister; 1940-1941, ambassador to Russia; in 1941, to Switzerland. Tried to maintain Romania's neutrality and later was one of those who prepared Romania's early exit from the war. Recipient of several international diplomatic awards.

Gavra, Ioan: contemporary Romanian politician. One of the founders of the Romanian National Unity Party.

Georgescu, Costin: liberal Romanian politician. 1997-2000, chief of the Romanian Intelligence Servive /RHSZ/.

Georgescu, Teohari /Burhah Tescovici/ (1908-1976): Communist party member since 1929. 1944-1945, Under-Secretary of the Interior; 1945-1952, Minister of the Interior and member of the Politbureau's Secretariat. Arrested and expelled from the Party in 1952 for right-wing leanings. After Stalin's death, he became the director of a factory in the printing trade.

Gero, Erno (1898-1980): Hungarian Communist politician. Active in the western European movement on the instructions of the Comintern. From 1944, holds various positions in the Hungarian Communist Party, then a member in the Hungarian Workers Party's Central Board /MDP KV/ and Political Commission /PB/; 1951-1953, Secretary of the Central Board. At the same time, holds various ministerial positions of Transportation, Finance and Secretary of State; 1953-1954, Minister of the Interior. Until July 30, 1956 Deputy Prime Minister; between July 18 and October 25, first Secretary of the Central Board. Emigrated to the Soviet Union where he remained until 1960. Expelled from the Party in 1962.

Gherea, Constantin Dobrogeanu /Katz, Salamon/ (1855-1920): Ukrainian-born theoretician of the Romanian Social Democratic movement. His best known work: The New Serfs in Romania. His son, Alexandru, was a victim of Stalinist cleansing.

Gheorghiu-Dej, Gheorghe (1901-1965): Romanian railway worker, party leader. Arrested in the 1933 Grivita strike. The subsequent national and Party leaders arose from the Communist members incarcerated in the Karánsebes jail and the circle around Gheorghiu-Dej. Fóris István was expelled from the Party ohis instructions on April 1, 1944. From 1945, Secretary-General of the Romanian Communist Party; from December 1947, First Assistant of the Council of Ministers; 1952-1954, President of the Council of Ministers; 1960-1965, President of the National Council.

Goga, Octavian (1881-1938): Transylvanian-Romanian politician, writer, poet. Minister, on several occasions, between 1918 and 1937; 1937-1938, Prime Minister. Leader of the National Christian Party. Sympathetic to Italian and German fascism. Translated Hungarian literature.

Goldis, Vasile (1862-1934): Transylvanian-Hungarian politician. The Transylvanian-Hungarian Governing Council sends him to the Bucharest government as member. Took part in public educational affairs.

Goma, Paul (1935-): Bessarabian-born Romanian writer. Arrested for his solidarity with the 1956 Hungarian Revolution. Emigrated in 1977 for his anti-Communist beliefs. Published novels in Paris, dealing with his age and a biography of his prison years.

Groza, Petre (1884-1958): Transylvanian-born Romanian politician. Schooled in Budapest. Urged the unification of the Romanian territories. Looked after Transylvanian affairs in the Avarescu government, later President of the Plow Front /Frontul Plugarilor/. Dec. 6, 1944-March 1945, Deputy President of the Council of Ministers; 1945-1952, Prime Minister; 1952-1958, President of the Greater National Assembly.

Cs. Gyimesi, Éva (1945-): Romanian-Hungarian linguist, literary historian. Professor of the Hungarian Faculty at Babes-Bolyai University. Honorary doctor of the Szeged University. 1994-1995, educational president of the Romanian Hungarian Democratic Alliance /RMDSZ/. Supporter of multicultural university education, in opposition to those demanding an independent Hungarian national university.

Gyöngyösi, János (1893-1951): Hungarian politician, journalist. Member of the Independent Small Landholders Party; 1947-1948, its Secretary-General. 1944-1947, as Foreign Minister, leader of the deputation to the Moscow truce talks and the Paris Peace Conference; 1947-1951, President of the Central Mint.

Hatieganu, Emil (1878-1959): Transylvanian-Romanian politician, lawyer. Minister of the National Agrarian Party. Secretary of State in the Groza government. Jailed on political grounds, 1948-1951.

Horn, Gyula (1932-): Hungarian politician, economist. Educated in the Soviet Union. 1983-1989, heads the foreign affairs department of the Hungarian Socialist Workers Party's /MSZMP/ Central Committee, Under-Secretary of Foreign Affairs, and Foreign Minister; 1994-1998, Prime Minister.

Horthy, Miklós (1868-1957): Hungarian admiral. Minister of Defence in the 1919 Szeged government, from 1920, Hungary's Regent and governor. His aim was to revise the terms of the Trianon Treaty. Abdicates after the October 15, 1944 unsuccessful attempt to withdraw from the war. Emigrated to Portugal.

Huszár, Sándor (1929-): Romanian-Hungarian writer, editor, literary translator. Received his degree at the Bolyai University. Editor of *Our Path /Utunk/*. 1959-1964, director of the Cluj Napoca National Hungarian Theatre; from 1970, editor-in-chief of the national weekly *The Week /A Hét/*. Resides in Hungary.

Iliescu, Ion (1930-): Romanian engineer, politician. Educated in the Soviet Union. Filled various party positions. In disfavour due to opposition to the Ceausescu party. 1989-1990, president of the National Deliverance Front's council; 1990-1996 and 2000 to this writing, President of Romania. President of Romania's Social Democratic Party.

Illyés, Gyula (1902-1983): Hungarian writer, agrarian-based politician. After the fall of the 1919 Hungarian Republic, emigrates to Paris (1921-1926). On his return, publishes his first volume and joins the circle of popular writers. (People of the Puszta, 1936, Hungarians, 1938) Attends the 1934 Writers' Congress in Moscow. Kossuth awards for literature (1948, 1953, 1970). In October, 1956 active in the re-organization of the National Agrarian Party, member of the directorate of the Petofi Party. In his dramatic works, he addresses the dramatic changes of the nation's fortunes.

Iorga, Nicolae (1871-1940): Romanian historian, politician. From 1910, leader of the National Democratic Party; 1931-1932, Prime Minister. Left a body of written works: reference works, monographs, articles, literary works. His contemporary historians criticised him for his Dacian-Romanian continuity theories. Murdered by the extreme right-wing Iron Guard.

Ivasiuc, Alexandru (1933-1977): Romanian writer. In his writings, critical of the dictatorial system. Died in the earthquake of Bucharest.

Jakab, Sándor: Romanian-Hungarian left-wing politician, economic expert. Parliamentary representative in the Hungarian People's Alliance /MNSZ/. Sentenced in the case of Vasile Luca /Luka László/.

Jar, Alexandru (1911-): Romanian writer. After 1944, leading figure in the Romanian Writers Union and Party secretary. Represents Socialist realism. After the XXth. Congress of the Soviet Communist Party, criticizes Stalinism in Romania. The Party condemned him and was forced to express self-criticism and retract.

Jászi, Oszkár (1875-1957): Hungarian sociologist, expert in the issue of nationalities. Hungarian proponent of bourgeois radicalism. Opposes the attempted Communist takeover during the 1919 Hungarian Republic. Resides in the USA from 1925. In 1949, turns anti-Communist.

Jordáky, Lajos (1913-1974): Romanian-Hungarian sociologist, historian. From 1931, member of the Socialist Youth Alliance; 1934, joins the Social Democratic Party. Takes part in the resistance movement during the Second World War. Supporter of an independent Transylvania. 1945-1947 and 1955-1957, professor at the Bolyai University. From 1957, scientific researcher of the Romanian Scientific Academy's Cluj Napoca branch.

Kacsó, Sándor (1901-1984): Romanian-Hungarian writer, publicist, editor. Between the wars, belongs to the circle of Transylvanian writers; a leader in the Transylvanian freemasons. 1927-1940, works for the *Brasov Pages* /Brassói Lapok/; from 1940, editor of the *Transylvanian Farmer* /Erdélyi Gazda/ in southern Transylvania; 1945-1946, editor-in-chief of the *People of the Villages* /Falvak Népe/. Between 1947 and 1951, president of the Hungarian People's Alliance /MNSZ/. Works for the National Literary and Art Publisher's Cluj Napoca branch, its director from 1956 to 1968.

Kádár, János (1912-1989): Hungarian Communist politician. Between 1946 and 1951, Deputy Secretary-General of the Hungarian Communist Party /MKP/ and its successor, the Hungarian Workers Party /MDP/, Executive Committee and Party Committee member. 1948-1950, Minister of the Interior. Arrested in 1951 and sentenced to life imprisonment. Freed in 1954 and readmitted to the Party Committee, becomes Secretary of the Executive Committee. First Secretary of the Hungarian Workers Party from October 25, 1956; president of the Praesidium from October 28. Secretary of State in the Nagy government, President, from November 4 until 1958, of the Hungarian Revolutionary Workers and Agrarian government. 1961-1965, Prime Minister; 1956-1985, First Secretary of the Hungarian Socialist Workers Party /MSZMP/; 1985-1988, its Secretary-General, then president.

Kállai, Gyula (1910-): Hungarian Communist politician, journalist. Party member since 1931. Foreign Minister and Deputy Minister of Education. Central Board member of the Hungarian Communist Party and its successor, the Hungarian Workers Party. After 1956, Central Committee and Party Committee member of the Hungarian Socialist Workers Party. 1957-1989, president of the Patriotic National Front; 1965-1967, Prime Minister.

Kányádi, Sándor (1929-): Romanian-Hungarian poet. Student at the Tirgu Mures Szentgyörgyi István Dramatic Arts Institute and the Bolyai University. Completes his education, in 1954, at the Bolyai Scientific University's Hungarian linguistics and literature faculty. Discovered by Páskándi Géza in 1950. Co-worker of the *Literary Almanac* /Irodalmi Almanach/, *Our Path* /Utunk/, *Working Woman* /Dolgozó No/ and finally, the *Ray of Sunshine* /Napsugár/ publications, from where he retires in 1990. In 1987, quits the Romanian Writers Union. Holder of the Déry, Kossuth and Herder literary awards.

Károly II. (Hohenzollern) (1893-1953): King of Romania between 1930 and 1940. In 1938, suspends the Constitution and introduces a royal dictatorship. Emigrates when overthrown by the 1940 coup d'etat of Ion Antonescu.

Károlyi, Mihály count (1875-1855): Hungarian politician. 1901-1916, member of the Liberal and Independence Parties; in 1916, founder of the Indepondence and '48 Party. October, 1918, Prime Minister; January, 1919, President of the Hungarian Republic. Hands power to the Communists in March, 1919. Emigrates to the West. 1947-1949, Hungarian ambassador to France. As a result of the show trial of Rajk, terminates relations with the Communists.

Katona, Ádám (1935-): Romanian-Hungarian cultural historian, historian, politician. Leader of the Romanian Hungarian Democratic Alliance's Szekler domain /Székelyföld/ political group and the Transylvanian-Hungarian Initiative's Christian-National platform.

Kemény, János (1903-1971): Romanian-Hungarian writer, editor, literature and theater organizer. Transylvanian multicultural literature was presented, from 1926 onwards, at his country estate in Marosvécse. 1941-1944, president of the Kemény Zsigmond, and later, of the Transylvanian Literary Society, director-general of the Cluj Napoca Hungarian National Theater. 1945-1952, dramaturg at the Tirgu Mures Szekler Theater; 1954-1958, librarian of the Szentgyörgyi István Dramatic Arts Institute.

Király, Károly (1930-): Romanian-Hungarian economist, politician. 1968-1972, Party secretary for Kovászna county and National Deputy President of the MNDT. In opposition to Ceausescu from 1973. 1990-1992, member of the Romanian Hungarian democratic Alliance, Vice President of the Senate. President of the 'For the Szekler Village Foundation'.

Kós, Károly (1883-1977): Romanian-Hungarian architect, painter, graphic artist, writer, politician. Founder of the Transylvanian National Party and the Transylvanian Fine Arts Guild (1924-1944). After 1945, enters political life in the Hungarian National Alliance and is also president of the Transylvanian Hungarian Economic Union.

Kossuth, Lajos (1802-1894): liberal Hungarian politician, statesman. One of the leaders of the 1848-1849 Revolution and Fight for Freedom. He pronounced the deposition of the Habsburg monarchy in Hungary. After the failure of the Revolution, emigrates to the West. Garners great acclaim in America. Drafts a plan for a Central European confederation.

Kurkó, Gyárfás 1909-1983): Romanian-Hungarian politician, writer. 1945-1947, President of the Hungarian People's Alliance /MNSZ/, an organization for the protection of Hungarian interests; 1947, representative in the Romanian Parliament. Sentenced and jailed in 1949, the period of show trials. Freed in 1964, rehabilitated in 1968. Became insane during incarceration.

Lakatos, István (1904-2000): Romanian-Hungarian typographer/printer, politician. 1944-1947, Vice President of the Cluj Napoca branch of Social Democratic Party's Executive Committee and president of its National Hungarian Committee. Proponent of an autonomous Transylvania. Arrested in 1949 and sentenced to 25 years of hard labour in the 1951 'Memorandum' case. Freed in 1964 after an amnesty. Worked on his memoirs.

Laval, Pierre (1883-1945): French politician. Prime Minister and Foreign Minister.

Litvinov, Makszim Makszimovics /Max Wallach/ (1876-1951): Soviet politician. People's Commissar for Foreign Affairs; 1941-1943, Ambassador to the United States. Central Committee member of the Soviet Communist Party.

Luca, Vasile /Luka László/ (1898-1960): Romanian-Hungarian Party worker. In 1919, takes part in the activities of the Hungarian Republic. Arrested in 1924 by the Romanian secret service and allegedly recruited. 1933-1938, arrested again for spreading Communist propaganda. Flees to the Soviet Union, returning in 1944. 1945-1952, member of the Secretariat of the Romanian Communist Party's Central and Party Committees; 1947-1952, Minister of Finance. Arrested in 1952 and sentenced to death, which was commuted to life in prison.

Lupas, Ion (1880-1967): Transylvanian-Romanian historian, professor of theology, Minister. Taught at the Cluj Napoca University.

Lukács, György (1885-1971): Hungarian philosopher. An émigré between the wars for his actions in 1919. After his return, a university professor, the Party's leading ideologist after 1949. Education Minister, from Oct. 27 to Nov. 2, 1956, in the government of Imre Nagy. As a member of the group taking refuge in the Yugoslavian Embassy, he is taken to Romania, returning home in April, 1957. From 1958, the Party, which never readmitted him, reckoned him to be a chief proponent of revisionism.

Madách, Imre (1823-1864): Hungarian dramatist. Pricipal work: The Tragedy of Man, a drama in 15 scenes, in which he searches for the reasons of human existence within the framework of the biblical story of original sin. Member of the Hungarian Scientific Academy.

Magureanu, Virgil /Asztalos Imre/ (1941-): teacher at the Bucharest Political Academy. Officer of the Romanian Secret Service from 1972. 1990-1997, leader of the Romanian Intelligence Service.

Manescu, Corneliu (1916-2000): Romanian diplomat. 1961-1982, Foreign Minister, ambassador to Hungary and France; 1967-1968, President of the XXII. session of the UN. Senator in the Romanian Parliament in 1990 and 1992.

Maniu, Iuliu (1873-1953): Transylvanian-Romanian politician. Parliamentary representative from Hungary in the Austro-Hungarian Monarchy; leader of the National Agrarian Party between the wars; 1928, Prime Minister. The Communist regime sentenced him, in 1947, to a lengthy term during the period of the show trials. Died in the Máramarossziget jail - the jail of the politicians.

Markó, Béla (1951-): writer, editor, politician. Member of the Romanian Writers Union. From 1990, politician and president in the Romanian Hungarian Democratic Alliance.

Márton, Áron (1896-1980): Roman Catholic Bishop, Transylvanian-born of Szekler descent. In the '30s, chaplain at Cluj Napoca University and editor of the *Transylvanian School /Erdélyi Iskola/* publication. 1938-1980, Bishop of Alba Iulia /Gyulafehérvár/. Raised his voice against the early deportations, after 1948, about the nationalization of the religious schools. During the Paris Peace Talks, spoke out against the decesions made regarding Transylvania without consultation of the Hungarian people. 1949-1955, spends hard years in various Romanian prisons; 1956-1967, lives under house arrest in Alba Iulia.

Maurer, Ion Gheorghe (1902-): Romanian politician, diplomat. 1957-1958, Foreign Minister; 1958-1961, president of the Grand National Council's Praesidium; 1961-1974, Prime Minister. Member of the Romanian Communist Party's Central and Executive Committees.

Melescanu, Teoodor (1941-): Romanian lawyer, politician and foreign expert. Represents Romania at the UN in 1966. 1991 onward, Under-Secretary of Foreign Affairs, then Foreign Minister.

Méliusz, József (1909-1995): Romanian-Hungarian writer, poet, editor. His works retain both socialist and middle class values. Sentenced in 1949, the time of the Romanian-Hungarian show trials; freed in 1955. His memoirs are significant source material for the study of the era.

Mihály I. (Hohenzollern) (1921-): King of Romania from 1927 to 1930, and again from 1940 to 1947. Offers no opposition to the government's policies sympathetic to Germany but takes part in the early cessation of the armed conflict. Stripped of the throne in 1947, lives in exile. After 1990, makes several attempts to return to Romania. Recently, the government returned several of his estates.

Mikó, Imre (1911-1977): Romanian-Hungarian politician, writer. His public activities were begun between the wars. A member of both the Hungarian and Romanian parliaments (after the Second Vienna Resolution). After his incarceration in the Soviet Union, earns his living as a manual labourer, then as the director of the Cluj Napoca branch of Kriterion Publishing.

Mocsáry, Lajos (1826-1916): liberal Hungarian politician. Expert on the topic of nationalities. Opposes the Reconciliation of 1867 and the policy of hungarification. One of the founders of the Independence Party.

Moghioros, Alexandru /Mogyoros Sándor/ (1911-1969): Romanian-Hungarian Communist politician. Arrested in the '40s for his politics. 1948-1968, member of the Central and Party Committees; 1954-1957, First Deputy President of the Council of Ministers; 1957-1965, Deputy Minister of the Council.

Moldovan: official at the Romanian embassy in Budapest.

Nagy, István (1904-1977): Romanian-Hungarian writer of the workers. Vilified on several occasions for his leftist views. 1950-1952, Rector of Bolyai University; 1952, admitted to the Romanian Scientific Academy. Worked in the Romanian Writes Union in 1956; from 1956, director of *Our Path* /Utunk/.

Nagy, Imre (1896-1958): Hungarian Communist politician. During his Moscow stay, agricultural expert. 1945, Minister of Agriculture; 1946, Minister of the Interior; 1950, Minister of Provisioning, then of Harvesting; 1952; deputy Prime Minister; July 4, 1953 to April 18, 1955, Prime Minister. November 1944 to April 1955, as well as October 24 to 30, 1956, member of the Hungarian Communist Party and its successor, the Hungarian Workers Party's Central Committee. 1945-1949, 1951-1955 and October 24 to 30, 1956 member of the Party Committee and the Party Praesidium. Prime Minister from October 24 to November 4, 1956 and member of the Hungarian Socialist Workers Party's first Executive Committee.

On November 4, receives asylum at the Yugoslavian embassy and is transported to Romania. Arrested in April, 1957 and executed in July, 1958.

Németh, László (1901-1975): Hungarian writer, doctor. Outstanding figure in the field of 20th century Hungarian prose and drama. Sole writer of the *Witness* /Tanu/ journal. Ideologically represents the 'Third Way'. Better known essays: The Revolution of Quality /A Minoség Forradalma/ and In Minority /Kisebbségben/. 1945-1950, teacher in Hódmezovásárhely; after 1950, makes a living from translating. Writes social and historical dramas; his novels have unique, headstrong female central characters. Awarded the Kossuth literary prize (19156).

Pacepa, Ion: General of the Securitate. Defected to the West

Pándi, Pál /Kardos/ (1926-1987): Hungarian literary historian, critic. Professor of the Eötvös Lóránd University of Liberal Arts and Sciences /ELTE/, member of the Hungarian Scientific Academy. Researcher of 19th and 20th century hungarian literature, the Reform Age and the works of the poet, Petofi.

Pascu, Stefan (1914-): Transylvanian-Romanian historian. Before the second World War, a member of Maniu's Party. Researcher of the history of the Middle ages in Transylvania. Supporter of the theory of the Dacian-Roman continuity. Historical advisor to Ceausescu. From 1962, professor at the Babes-Bolyai University in Cluj Napoca, then its Rector.

Patrubány, Miklós (1952-): Romanian-Hungarian politician, electrical engineer. 1990-1992, member of the governing council of the Romanian Hungarian Democratic Alliance; 1992-1996, Deputy President of the World Federation of Hungarians /MVSZ/; 2000 to present, its President. President of the Transylvanian branch of the MVSZ.

Patrascanu, Lucretiu (1900-1954): Romanian lawyer, sociologist, Communist politician of intellectual background. Joins the Social Democratic Party in 1919; a founder of the Romanian Communist Party. Harshly censured in 1930 for factional behaviour. Leader of the Red Aid Legal Defence Office. 1933-1934, represents the Romanian Party in the Comintern. During preparations for the armed uprising in 1944, he maintained liaison between the leftist parties and the others. 1944, Minister without portfolio; from 1946, Minister of Justice. Opponent of Gheorghiu-Dej inside the Party. Central and Party Committee member. Arrested in 1948 on trumped up charges and executed in 1954.

Páskándi, Géza (1933-1995): Romanian-Hungarian poet, writer, essayist, dramatist. His historical dramas are outstanding. Discovered at the age of 16 by Majtényi Erik. Student at the Bolyai University; journalist in Bucharest.. Arrested in the spring of 1957, freed in 1963. Manual labourer, then editor at the Cluj Napoca branch of Kriterion Publisher. Moved to Hungary in 1974. His dramas were also staged abroad. Winner of the Kossuth and Széchenyi literary awards.

Pauker, Ana /Robinsohn Hannah/ (1893-1960): wife of Marcel Pauker, executed in the Moscow show trials. Carries on activities abroad at the order of the Comintern. Sentenced in the Craiova case in 1936. Emigrates to the Soviet Union in 1940. Organizes various Romanian divisions there. Returns to Romania in 1944. Member of the Romanian Communist Party's Central Committee. 1947-1957, Foreign Minister; 1952, arrested on charges of right-wing deviationism.

Pirvulescu, Constantin (1895-1992): Romanian leftist politician. Member of the Romanian Communist Party from 1921, in the Central Committee from 1929. Emigrates to the Soviet Union. A conflict develops between himself and Fóris István, who leads the Party secretariat. 1945-1961, president of the Screening Committee. Expelled from the Party in 1961 for factional behaviour. In 1979, at the Party's XII. Congress he raises his voice against Ceausescu's cult of personality. Signatory to the 'Letter of the Six'.

Plesu, Andrei (1950-): Romanian art historian, politician. Minister of Culture in the Roman government. 1997-1999, Foreign Minister.

Pop Cicio, Stefan (1865-?): Transylvanian-Romanian politician, lawyer. One of the leaders of the National Agrarian Party. The Governing Council sends him to the Romanian government in 1920.

Radesu, Nicolae: Romanian general. 1944-1945, President of the Council of Ministers.

Rákóczi, Ferenc II. (1676-1735): ruling Prince of Transylvania. Leader of 1703-1711 freedom fight against the Habsburg Monarchy. After the failure of the uprising, emigrated to Poland, France and, finally, Turkey.

Rákosi, Mátyás (1892-1971): Hungarian Communist politician. In 1919, People's Commissar, commander of the Red Guard. 1921-1924, secretary of the Comintern's executive Committee. For his Communist activities, he is jailed in Hungary from 1925 to 1940 when he is handed over to the Soviet Union. From 1945, Secretary-General of the Hungarian Communist Party and its successor, the Hungarian Workers Party; 1945-1952, Secretary of State, Deputy Prime Minister; 1952-1953, Prime Minister.1953 to July 1956, First Secretary and Party Committee member. Relieved of his office in July 1956, emigrated to the Soviet Union in August. Expelled from the Party in 1962.

Rautu, Leonte /Lev Oigenstein/ (1910-1993): Romanian Communist. After the fall of Bessarabia, emigrates to the Soviet Union and becomes the editor-in-chief of Moscow's Romanian language radio programs. From 1944, responsible for the agit-prop activities in the Romanian Communist Party. After 1965, secretary of the Central Committee and member of the Political Executive Committee; 1969-1971, Deputy President of the Council of Ministers; after 1971, rector of the „Stefan Gheorghiu" Political Academy.

Robotos, Imre: Romanian-Hungarian leftist journalist, writer. In 1956, editor-in-chief of the paper *Forward* /Elore/. Lost favor due to his Jewish background. Lived in Hungary since the end of the '80s.

Roman, Petre (1946-): Romanian engineer, university professor, politician, son of Valter Roman. 1971-1974, student in France. Prime Minister after the May 20, 1990 elections in Romania until September 1991. Later Foreign Minister.

Roman, Walter /Neulander Erno/ (1913-1984): Romanian Communist politician of Hungarian descent. Educated at the technical university of Brno, where he becomes active in the Communist movement. Took part in the Spanish Civil War. Emigrates to France, then the Soviet Union. In the '40s, Chief of Staff of the Romanian Army. Central Committee member. Visited Hungary on several occasions. In Romania, he interrogated Imre Nagy with Mogyorós Sándor and Vass Gizella. From 1964, the director of the Political Publisher.

Sabin, Gherman: contemporary Transylvanian-Romanian poet, television editor, politician. Adherent of public administrative autonomy for Transylvania, leader in the Pro-Transylvania Foundation and the Transylvanian- Bánát League. Published a pamphlet in 1998, „I've had Enough of Romania".

Sanatescu, Constantin: Romanian general. In 1944, President of the Council of Ministers.

Stirbey, Barbu: romanian politician, diplomat.

Stoica, Ghivu (1908-1975): Romanian Communist politician. One of the organizers of the Grivica strike. From 1945, Central Committee member in the Romanian Communist Party; 1948-1952, Minister of Industry; 1952-1955, First Vice President of the Council of Ministers; 1955-1961, its President; 1965-1967, President of the National Council.

Stoica, Gheorghe /Moscu Kohn/ (1900-1976): takes part in the founding meeting of the Romanian Communist Party as a representative of the Social Democratic Party. A member of the International Brigade in Spain. First Secretary of the Bucharest and area Party Committee, then, between 1965-1976, member of the Council of Ministers; 1974-1976, member of the Romanian Communist Party's Central and Executive Committees.

Süto, András (1927-): Romanian-Hungarian dramatist. Hungarian drama's eminent personality alongside Páskándi Géza. The relationship of power and freedom, and personal responsibility, recur in these works. His works, such as A Horse Trader's Palm Sunday, Star on the Pyre, Cain and Abel, Marriage in Sosan, Advent on the Hargita were mounted on stages in Europe. Recipient of several literary awards, such as the Kossuth award. Lost sight of one eye during the March 1990 storming of the Romanian Hungarian Democratic Alliance head office.

Szabédi, László /Székely/ (1907-1959): Romanian-Hungarian poet, linguistic esthete. From 1947, professor at the Bolyai University. Conducted research into linguistics and poetry metrics. Commmitted suicide in protest of the merging of the Cluj Napoca Romanian and Hungarian universities.

Szocs, Géza (1953-): writer, editor, politician. Member of the Romanian Writers Union. Author of the *Counterpoints /Ellenpontok/* , Romania's first Hungarian samizdat paper. Emigrated to the West in 1986. Co-worker of Radio Free Europe. 1990-1991, Secretary-General of the Romanian Hungarian Democratic Alliance; 1991-1993, its Vice President. Director of the Transylvanian Diary Book and Journal Publishing. Editor-in-chief of the *Transylvanian Diary /Erdélyi Napló/*.

Takács, Lajos (1908-1981): Romanian-Hungarian nationality politician, jurist. Began his political activities in southern Transylvania in 1944. In the national leadership of the Hungarian Popular Alliance, headed the Hungarian block in Partiament in the late '40s. 1947, Under-Secretary for Minorities; 1956-1957, rector of the Bolyai University; after 1971, one of the leaders of the Hungarian Nationality Workers Council. Protested in a 1977 memorandum against romania's ethnic policies.

Tamási, Áron (1897-1966): writer of Szekler descent. Became well known with his Abel trilogy and Crested Ones. Organizer of literary life between the wars. Leaves for Hungary. September, 1956 elected to the leadership of the Hungarian

Writers Union; October, joined the leading body of the Petofi Party. Kossuth literary award (1954).

Tatarescu, Gheorghe (1886-1957): Romanian politician. 1931-1934, Secretary-General of the National Liberal Party; 1934-1937 and 1939-1940, Prime Minister; 1945-1947, Foreign Minister. Jailed from 1950 to 1955 for political reasons.

Teleki, Béla count (1888-1979): Transylvanian-Hungarian politician. President of the Transylvanian Hungarian Farmers Union /EMGE/. Represented the returned Northern Transylvania in the Hungarian Parliament, 1940-1944, as president of the Transylvanian Party. Supported the fall, 1994 attempt led by Admiral Horthy to withdraw from the war. Helps prevent anti-Romanian atrocities as a member of the council governing a coalition constituted Transylvania. The entering Romanians arrested him in 1944. After regaining his freedom, emigrated to the USA.

Teleki, Pál count (1879-1941): Transylvanian-Hungarian politician. Member of the Hungarian Scientific Academy. 1919-1921, Foreign Minister abd Prime Minister. 1927, creates the Revisionist League. 1936-1937, Minister of Religions and Education; 1939-1941, Prime Minister. In 1939, reorganizes the governing party into the Hungarian Life Party. Follows a neutral, anti-Soviet and anti-German foreign policy. In 1941, signs a Permanent Friendship Pact with Yugoslavia. Hitler forced him to rescind it, which drove him to suicide.

Tokés, László (1952-): Transylvanian-Hungarian pastor, Reformed Protestant bishop. Takes part, in 1983, in the editing of the *Counterpoints* samizdat publication. 1984-1986, removed from his pastoral position for political reasons. Has pivotal role in the collapse of the Romanian Communist regime. Honorary president of the Romanian Hungarian Democratic Alliance. Recipient of several international (American, Finnish, Dutch, Hungarian) awards and honours; holds honorary doctorates from several universities.

Tradieu, André (1878-1945): French politician. Prime Minister on several occasions. Takes part in the Paris Peace Conference, assisting Clemenceau.

Tiso, Jozef (1887-1947): Slovak right-wing politician, Roman Catholic priest. 1938-1945, president of the Slovak People's Party; 1938-1939 and again in 1939-1945, Prime Minister of the newly independent, Greman created and supported, Slovak nation. Later, its President. Executed for war crimes.

Tisza, István count (1861-1918): conservative Hungarian politician. Member of the Hungarian Scientific Academy. Adherent of the '67 principles (reconciliation of 1867). 1903-1905 and 1913-1917, Prime Minister. Falls victim to political assassination.

Titulescu, Nicolae: Roman politician, diplomat.

Tudor, Corneliu Vadim: writer. President of the Greater Romanian Party.

Vaida-Voevod, Alexandru (1871-?): Transylvanian-Romanian politician. Parliamentary representative. Interior Minister during the Maniu government.

Vasile, Radu: ex-Prime Minister. Secretary-General of the Christian Democratic National Agrarian Party.

Várhegyi, István (1932-): Romanian-Hungarian sociologist, historian. Arrested in 1956 as leader of the student union at Bolyai University. Left the country in the mid-70s to Germany where he taught in university. Currently lives in Hungary. Visiting professor at several foreign universities.

Verdet, Ilie (1925-): Communist politician. From 1945, member of the Romanian Communist Party's Central and Executive Committees. Leader of the Socialist Work Party, successor to the RCP.

Vescan, Teofil: Transylvanian-Romanian teacher, politician. Active in public life in Cluj Napoca in the '40s.

Visinszkij, Andrej Januárjevics (1883-1954): Soviet lawyer, diplomat. 1935-1939, chief Soviet public prosecutor during the Stalin ordered show trials; 1939-1944, Deputy President of the Council of People's Commissars, then of the Council of Ministers; 1944-1953, Deputy Foreign Minister, then Foreign Minister. Head of the Inter-Allied Control Committee in Romania.

Visoianu, Constantin: Romanian politician. 1944-45: Foreign Minister.

Vita, Sándor: Transylvanian-Hungarian publicist, sociologist. Active in the Transylvanian Hungarian Farmers Union /EMGE/, Transylvanian Hungarian Economic Union, and *Credit*.

Vladescu-Racoasa, Gheorghe: Romanian politician. 1944-1946, Minister of Minority Affairs.

Zilahy, Lajos (1891-1974): Hungarian writer. Member of the Hungarian Scientific Academy. His writings between the wars deal with fundamental questions of Hungarian society. Several of his novels were made into films. Emigrates to the USA in 1947.

Geographic place names

Alsócsernáton	Cernat
Arad	Arad
Balázsfalva	Blaj
Barót	Baraolt
Bálványosváralja	Unguras
Bánffyhunyad	Huedin
Brassó	Brasov
Csernovic	Chernovci
Csíkszentdomokos	Sindominic
Csíkszereda	Miercuera-Ciuc
Déva	Deva
Egeres	Aghiresu
Erdoszentgyörgy	Sîngeorgiu de Padure
Földvár	Feldioara
Gyergyószentmiklós	Gheorgheni
Györgyfalva	Gheorghieni
Gyulafehérvár	Alba Iulia
Hargita	Harghita
Havasalföld	Muntenia
Hídvég	Haghig
Jászváros	Iasi
Kajántó	Chinteni
Kalotaszeg	Calatei
Karán	Caras
Kézdivásárhely	Tirgu Secuiesc
Kolozs/vár/	Cluj /Napoca/
Kovászna	Covasna
Kohalom	Rupea
Magyarlóna	Luna de Sus
Maros	Mures
Maroshévíz	Toplita
Marosvásárhely	Tirgu Mures
Máramarossziget	Sighetu-Marmatiei
Medgyes	Medias
Nagybánya	Baia Mare
Nagyenyed	Aiud
Nagykároly	Carei
Nagyszalonta	Salonta
Nagyszeben	Sibiu
Nagyvárad	Oradea
Nyárád	Nirajului
Regát	Regat, Trans-Carpathia
Régen	Reghin
Segesvár	Sighisoara

Sepsiszentgyörgy	Sfântu Gheorghe
Szatmár	Satu Mare
Szatmárnémeti	Satu Mare
Szárazajta	Aita-seacá
Szászfenes	Floresti
Szászváros	Orastie
Székelyföld	Szeklerland (Terra Siculorum)
Székelykeresztúr	Cristuru-Secuiesc
Székelyudvarhely	Odorheiu-Secuiesc
Szinaja	Sinaia
Szucsáva	Suceava
Temesvár	Timisoara
Torockó	Rimetea
Törcsvár	Bran
Túrócszentmárton	Martin
Vajdahunyad	Hunedoara
Válaszút	Rascruci
Zilah	Zalau
Zsil	Jiu

Bibliography

A nemzetiségi kérdés demokratikus megoldása a Román Népköztársaságban. (Bukarest, Román Intézet a külföldi kapcsolatok ápolására, 1949)
A nemzetiségi politika három éve a demokratikus Romániában. (Bukarest, 1948)
A romániai, csehszlovákiai, jugoszláviai kisebbség sorsa a Népszövetség elott. 1930-1937. (Budapest, Államtudományi Intézet, kézirat, 1938)
A Szekuritate fehér könyve. In: *Romania Libera,* 1994, Aprilie.
Apostol, Stan: *Iuliu Maniu. Nationaliism si democratie. Biografia unui mare roman.*
Aradi, Nóra: *A Liga Culturala és az erdély román nemzeti törekvések.* (Budapest, Sárközy Kiadó, 1939)
Ádám, Magda: *Egy amerikai terve Közép-Európára. 1918-ban.* In: *História,* 1987, 4 nr.
Bajcsy-Zsilinszky, Endre: *Helyünk és sorsunk Európában.* (Budapest, 1941)
Bajcsy-Zsilinszky, Endre: *Transylvania. Past and Future.* (Geneva, 1944)
Balogh, Arthur - Szego, Imre: *Románia új alkotmánya.* (Kolozsvár, Concordia Kiadó, 1923)
Balogh, Arthur: *A székely vallási és iskolai önkormányzat.* (Cluj/Kolozsvár, Minerva, 1932)
Balogh, Edgár: *Férfimunka. Emlékirat 1945-1955.* (Budapest, Magveto Kiadó, 1986)
Balogh, Sándor: *A népi demokratikus Magyarország külpolitikája. 1945-1947. A fegyverszünettol a békeszerzodésig.* (Budapest, Kossuth Kiadó, 1982)
Bán, D. András /szerk., bev. írta/: *Pax Britannica. Brit külügyi iratok a második világháború utáni Kelet-Közép-Európáról, 1942-42.* (Budapest, 1996)
Bánffy, Miklós: *Emlékirat.* (Budapest, Károli Gáspár Református Egyetem, Ráday Levéltár, kézirat)
Bíró Sándor: *Kisebbségben és többségben. /Románok és magyarok 1867-1940/.* (Bern, Európai Protestáns Magyar Egyetem, 1989)
Bitoleanu, Ion: *Din istoria Romaniei moderne. 1922-1926.* (Bucuresti, 1981)
Bodor, Pál: *A hisztéria szükségállapota. Kellemetlen kézikönyv Romániáról.* (Budapest, Szabad Tér Kiadó, 1990)
Bokor, Péter: *Végjáték a Duna felett. Interjú egy filmsorozathoz.* (Budapest, MTV-Minerva-Kossuth Kiadó, 1982)
Boldizsár, Iván: *Megbunhödte már e nép.* (Budapest, Új Magyarország Kiadó, 1946)
Borbély, Zsolt Attila: *Erdélyi Magyarság 2002. 50 nr.*
Borsi, Kálmán Béla: *Együtt vagy külön utakon. A Kossuth-emigráció és a román nemzeti törekvések kapcsolatának története.* (Budapest, Magveto Kiadó, 1984)
Bulla, Béla – Mendel, Tibor – Kocsis, Károly: *A Kárpát-mdence földrajza.* (Budapest, Lucidus Kiadó, 1999)
Calafeteanu, Ion: *Diplomatia romaneasca in sud-estul Europei. 1938-1940.* (Bucuresti, Editura politica, 1980)

Campeanu, Pavel: *Ceausescu, anii numaratorii inverse.* (Bucuresti, Polirom, 2002)

Campus, Eliza: *Din politica externa a Romaniei. 1928-1940.* (Bucuresti, Editura Militara, 1980)

Cartea Alba a Securitatii. (Bucuresti, Editura Presa Roameasca, 1996)

Ceausescu, Ilie – Constantiniu, Florin – Ionescu, M.E.: *Kétszáz nappal korábban. Románia szerepe a második világháború megrövidítésében.* (Bukarest, Kriterion, 1986)

Ceausescu, Nicolae: *Románia a szocializmus építése kiteljesedésének útján. Jelentés, beszédek, cikkek.* (Bukarest, Politikai Kiadó)

Ciato, Ludovic: *Problema minoritara in Romania-Mare.* (Cluj, Tip. Lyceum, 1924)

Costantiniu, Florin: *Istoria Romaniei.* (1845)

Cornea, Toma: *A kisebbségi kérdés. Politikai tanulmány.* (Cluj/Kolozsvár, Studium Kiadó, 1928)

Dávid, Gyula: *1956 Erdélyben és ami utána következett.* In: *Korunk,* 1996, 10 nr.

Dávid, Zoltán: *Népszámlálási adatok a Kárpát-medencében.*

Delatant, Dennis: *Ceausescu and the securitate.* (C. Hurst & Co. (Publishers) Ltd., 1995)

Demeter, János: *Századunk sodrában.* (Bukarest, Kriterion, 1975)

Dezbateri parlamentare. Deputariilor. (Bucuresti)

Dezbateri parlamentare. Senatul. (Bucuresti)

Dobrogeanu-Gherea, Constantin: *Neoiobagia.* (Bucuresti, 1910)

Enciclopedia romane. (1904)

Enescu, Ion: *Politica externa a Romaniei in perioada 1944-1947.* (Bucuresti, 1979)

Epoca Nicolae Ceausescu. Cronologie istorica. (Bucuresti Ed. Stiintifica si enciclopedica, 1988)

Erdély története. (Budapest, Akadémiai kiadó, 1987)

Erdélyi Magyar Évkönyv. 1918-1929. (Kolozsvár, Juventus Kiadó, 1930)

Fazekas, János: *Egy romániai magyar politikus és a kor melyben élt.* (Zrinyi Kiadó, 1990, kézirat)

Finta, Ella: *Szilágysomlyó.* In: *Erdélyi Magyarság,* 1996, 4 nr.

Florescu, Mihai: *Cucerirea puterii revolutionar-democratic la 6 Martie 1945 catre masele populare in frunte cu P.C.R..* In: *Anale de istorie,* 1982, 2 nr.

Fodor, Sándor: *Diverzio Kolozsváron.* In: *Erdélyi Magyarság,* 1992, 12 nr.

Frannck, Nicolette: *La Roumanie dans l'engrenage. Comment le Royaume est devenu republique populaire. /1944-1947/.* (Paris, Ed. Révesier Séqueia, 1977)

Frunza, Victor: *Istoria partidului Comunist Roman.* (Nord, 1984)

Fülöp, Mihály – Sipos, Péter: *Magyarország külpolitikája a XX. Században.* (Budapest, Aula, 1998)

Gabanyi, Anelli Ute: *Partei und Literatur in Rumaniei seit 1945.* (München, R. Oldenbourg Verlag, 1975)

Gál, Mária: *Haláltáborok itthon.* In: *Erdélyi Napló,* 1997, Május 20.

Gáti, Charles: *Magyarország a Kreml árnyékában.* (Budapest, Századvég Kiadó, 1990)

Gheorghiu-Dej, Gheorghe: *Válogatott cikkek és beszédek.* (Bukarest, 1951)

Gosztonyi, Péter: *Endkampf an der Donau.* (Wien, 1969)

Gosztonyi, Péter: *Magyarország a második világháborúban.* (München, HERP, 1984)

Gyarmati, György: *Békében együttmuködni az egész Duna-völgye javára. Föderációs tervek 1945 után.* In: *Alföld,* 1985, 4 nr.

Gyárfás, Elemér: *Az elso kísérlet: az Averescu-paktum elozményei, megkötésének indokai, szövegek módosításai, következményei, felbomlása és tanúsága.* In: *Magyar Kisebbség,* 1937, 2-3 nr.

Habsburg, Otto: *Jalta és ami utána következett. Válogatott cikkek, tanulmányok.* (München, Újváry „GRIFF" kiadó, 1978)

Halmos, Déncs: *Nemzetközi szerzodések.* (Budapest, 1983)

Hévizi, Józsa: *Autonómia-típusok Magyarországon és Európában.* (Budapest, Püski Kiadó, 2001)

Hóry, András: *A kuliszák mögött. A második világháború elozményei, ami és ahogy a valóságban történt.* (Wien, 1965)

Hunya, Gábor: *Románia – szélsoséges eset.* (A MTA Világgazdasági Kutató Intézet Tudományos Tájékoztató Szolgálatának Közleménye, 1987, Augusztus)

Iorga, Nicolae: *Cinci ani de restauratie.* (Valenii-de-Munte, 1932)

Jancsó, Benedek: *A Román Parasztpárt.* In: *Magyar Szemle,* 1928, Május-Június.

Jászi, Oszkár: *A Habsburg Monarchia felbomlása.* (Budapest, Gondolat Kiadó, 1983)

Jordáky, Lajos: *A Román Nemzeti Párt megalakulása.* (Budapest, Akadémiai Kiadó, 1974).

Jordáky, Lajos: *Napló.* In: *Medvetánc,* 1992, 3 nr.

Juhász, József: *Volt egyszer egy Jugoszlávia.* (Budapest, Aula Kiadó, 1999)

Karácsonyi forradalom. Riportkönyv Romániáról. (Népszabadság Villám könyvek, 1989)

Katona Szabó, István: *A nagy reménységek kora.* (Budapest, Magveto Kiadó, 1990)

Katus, László: *Magyarok, nemzetiségek a népszámlálás tükrében. 1850-1910.* In: *História,* 1982, 4-5 nr.

Katus, László: *Erdély népei 1910-ben.* In: *História,* 1986, 2 nr.

Kelemen, Sándor: *Az erdélyi helyzet.* (Budapesti Magyar Parasztszövetség kiadása, 1946)

Kincses, Elod: *Marosvásárhely fekete márciusa.* (Budapest, Püski Kiadó, 1990)

Kosáry Domokos: *Az oláhok beözönlése.* In: *Magyar Szemle,* 1940. Október.

Kós, Károly – Pál, Árpád – Zágoni, István: *Kiáltó szó.* (Kolozsvár, 1920)

Lahav, Yehuda: *Soviet policy and the Transyvanian Question (1940-1946).* (Hebrew University of Jerusalem. The Soviet and east European Research Centre, research paper No. 27. Jerusalem, July 1, 1977)

Lipcsey, Ildikó: *Erdély 1918-1920.* (Kézirat)

Lipcsey, Ildikó: *133 nap. Budapest elso román megszállása.* (Budapest, kézirat)

Lipcsey, Ildikó: *Magyar-román kapcsolatok 1956-1957.* (Kézirat)

Lipcsey, Ildikó: *A CASBI és a Gojdu Alapítvány.* In: *Erdélyi Magyarság.*

Lipcsey, Ildikó: *Egy békésebb jövo jegyében.* In: *História,* 1982, 2 nr.

Lipcsey, Ildikó: *Petru Groza emlékezete.* In: *Életünk,* 1985, 2 nr.

Lipcsey, Ildikó: *Egy sorsforduló nap krónikája. 1944. Augusztus 23, szerda.* In: *Világtörténet,* 1985, 2 nr.

Lipcsey, Ildikó: *A Maniu gárdisták.* In: *Kritika,* 1989, 10 nr.

Lipcsey, Ildikó: *Észak-Erdély szovjet katonai közigazgatás alatt. 1944. november 15-1945. mácius 13.* In: *História,* 1989.

Lipcsey, Ildikó. *A Magyar Népi Szövetség az önfeladás útján. 1944-1953.* (Budapest, Possum Kiadó, 1998)

Lipcsey, Ildikó: *Adalékok a magyar-román lülkapcsolatok történetéhez 1945-1955.* In: *Külpolitika,* 1999, 3-4 nr.

Lipcsey, Ildikó: *A CASBI. (A magyar vagyonok államosítása Romániában 1945 után.)* (Budapest, Possum Kiadó, 2001)

Livezeanu, Vasile: *Transformarile revolutionare premise ale proclamarii Republicii Populare Romane.* In: *Studii,* 1964, 4 nr.

Magyar történeti kronológia. (Budapest, Akadémiai Kiadó, 1982)

Marcou, Lilly: *Une enfance stalinienne.* (Paris, Presses Universitaires de France, 1982)

Marea Adunare nationala. (Bucuresti, Editura Academiei, 1972)

Mikó, Imre: *A székely közületi önkormányzat.* In: *Magyar Kisebbség,* 1934, Július-Augusztus.

Mikó, Imre: *A romániai magyar kisebbség panaszai a Nemzetek Szövetsége elott.* In: *Hitel,* 1936, 3 nr.

Mikó, Imre: *A kisebbségi statutum.* In: *Hitel,* 1938, Május.

Mikó, Imre: *Huszonkét év. Az erdélyi magyarság politikai története, 1918. december 1-tol 1940. augusztus 30-ig.* (Budapest, Studium, 1941)

Mester, Miklós: *Az autonóm Erdély és a román nemzeti törekvések az 1863-64 évi nagyszebeni országgyulésen.* (Budapest, 1936)

Móricz, Miklós: *Az erdélyi föld sorsa.* (Budapest, Erdélyi Férfiak Egyesülete, 1932)

Musat, Mircea – Popisteanu, C. – Constantiniu, Florin – Dobrineascu, V.: *Dictatul fascist de la Viena – expresie a politicii de forta repudiata de istorie.* In: *Magazin istoric,* 1987, 6 nr.

Nagy, Zoltán Mihály: *Kolozsvár az észak-erdélyi szovjet katonai közigazgatás idoszakában.* In: *Kolozsvár 1000 éve,* Kolozsvár, 2001.

Ormos, Mária: *Franciaország és a keleti biztonság. 1931-1936.* (Budapest, Akadémiai Kiadó, 1969)

Ormos, Mária: *Padovától Trianonig. 1818-1920.* (Budapest, Kossuth Kiadó, 1983)

Paál, Árpád: *Törvénytervezet a székely közületek közmuvelodési önkormányzatához.* (Kolozsvár, 1932)

Pacepa, Ion: *Cartea neagra a Securitatii.* (Bucuresti, Editura Omega SRL, 1999)

Papp, József: *Az erdélyi székelyek vallási és tanügyi önkormányzat.* (Lugos, 1931)

Pop, Adrian: *A temesvári és a bukaresti diákok tiltakozása.* In: *Korunk,* 1996, 10 nr.

Popisteanu, Cristian: *Bucuresti, 6 martie 1945. Orale 19.* In: *Magazin istoric,* Bucuresti, 1975, 3 nr.

Popisteanu, Cristian: *Cronologie politico-diplomatice romaneasca. 1944-1947.* (Bucuresti Editura Pol., 1976)

Porter, Ivor: *Operatiunea „autonomus."* (Bucuresti, Humanitas, 1991)

Radescu, Nicolae: *Sowjetische Bajonette.* (Paris, Comite International Paix et Liberte)

Raduica, Grigore: *Crime in lupta pentru putere. 1966-1968: ancheta cazului Patrascanu.* (Bucuresti, Editura Evenimentul Zilei, 1999)

Raffay, Erno: *Erdély 1918-1919-ben.* (Szeged, JATE Kiadó, 1988)

Ratiu, Ion: *Romania de astazi. Comunism sau independenta?* (Bucuresti, Condor, 1990)

Ránki, György: *Gazdaság és külpolitika.* (Budapest, Magveto Kiadó, 1981)

Rehák, László: *A kisebbségek Jugoszláviában.* (Novi Sad / Újvidék, Forum Kiadó, 1967)

Reuben, L. – Markham, H.: *Le Roumanie sous le joug soviétique.* (Paris, Colman-Lévy, 1949)

Roesler, Robert: *A dákóromán kontinuitásról.* (Romanische Studien, 1871)

Romanescu, Gheorghe – Longhin, Leonida: *Cronica participarii armatei la rasboul anihitlerist.* (Bucuresti, Editura Militara, 1971)

Román eszmetörténet. 1866-1945. (Budapest, Aetas, Századvég Kiadó, 1994)

Romsics, Ignác /szerk., bev. írta/: *Amerikai béketervek a háború utáni Magyarországról. Az Egyesült Államok Külügymisztériumának titkos iratai. 1942-44.* (Gödöllo, 1992)

Scurtu, Ioan: *Din viata politica Romaniei, 1926-1947.* (Bucurest, Editura Stiintifica si Enciclopedica, 1983)

Serbulescu, Andrei: *Monarhia de drept dialectic. A doua versiune a memoriilor lui Belu Silber.* (Bucuresti, Humanitas, 1991)

Sfetcu, Paul: *13 ani in anticamera lui Gheorghiu-Dej.* (Bucuresti, Editura Fundatiei Culturale Romane, 2000)

Sin-Giorgiu, Ion: *Problema minoritara in Romania.* (Bucuresti, Editura, independenta, 1932)

Sitariu, Mihaela: *Rezistenta anticomunista. Timisoara 1956.* (Bucuresti, Editura Sophia, 1998)

Szalay, Jeromos: *Vértanú püspök vértanú népe. Márton Áron.* (Detroit, 1958)

Szász, Zoltán: *A Tisza-féle magyar-román paktumtárgyalások 1910-1914.* In: *Magyar-Román filológiai tanulmányok.* (Eötvös Lóránd Tudomány Egyetem, Román tanszék, 1984)

Szász, Zoltán: *Román egyesületek a magyar államban. 1867-1918.* In: *História,* 1993, 2 nr.

Szász, Zsombor: *A román politikai élet útja.* In: *Magyar Szemle,* 1930, Augusztus 28.

Szász, Zsombor: *A román politikai élet.* In: *Magyar Szemle,* 1931, Július.

Szász, Zsombor: *A második parasztpárti kormány.* In: *Magyar Szemle,* 1934, Március.

Szász, Zsombor: *Numerus Valachicus.* In: *Magyar Szemle,* 1935, Május.

Szász, Zsombor: *Alkotmányrevizió Romániában.* In: *Magyar Szemle,* 1935, Október.

Szász, Zsombor: *Az új román állam.* In: *Magyar Szemle,* 1938, Április.

Szász, Zsombor: *Az új alkotmány és a kisebbségek.* In: *Magyar Kisebbség,* 1938, Május.

Szentimrei, Krisztina: *„ Bal" és „ Jobb" az erdélyi magyar politikában.* In: *Erdélyi Magyarság,* 1998, 34 nr.

Stanescu, Flori – Zamfirescu, Dragos: *Ocupatie sovietica in Romania. Documente. 1944-1946.* (Bucuresti Editura Vremea, 1998)

Strategii si politici electorale in alegerile parlamentare din 19 noiembrie 1946. Selectia documentelor, sturdiu introductiv, argument si note de Virgiliu Tarau, Ioan Marius Bucur. (Cluj-Napoca, Centrul de Studii Transilvane, Fundatia Culturala Romana, 1998)

Takács, Ferenc: *Kései gyertyagyújtás.* In: *Erdélyi Magyarság,* 1992, 4 nr.

Takács, Ferenc László: *A román kormányzat magyarság politikája. 1989. December 22 - 1996. Szeptember 17.* (Budapest, Határon Túli Magyarok Hivatala, kézirat)

Tamás, Lajos: *Romains, Romans et Roumains dans l' histoire de la Dacie Trajane.* (Budapest, 1936)

Tofik, Iszlamov: *Erdély a szovjet külpolitikában a második világháború alatt.* In: *Múltunk,* 1994, 1-2 nr.

Tófalvi, Zoltán: *Erdély 56-os mártirjai.* (Kézirat)

Tófalvi, Zoltán: *40 éve végeztek ki 12 erdélyi 56-ost.* In: *Erdélyi Magyarság,* 1998, 4 nr.

Tornya, Gyula: *A népkisebbségi törvény tervezete.* (Cluj/Kolozsvár, Lyceum Nyomda, 1928)

Tóth, László: *A Román Szocialista Küztársaság állami, gazdasági és politikai rendszere jogi szabályozásának politológiai szempontú elemzése.* (Budapest, 1980-1981. Kandidátusi értekezés)

Tóth, Sándor: *Jelentés Erdélybol.* (Párizsi Magyar Füzetek, 1987)

Tokés, László: *Temesvár ostroma. 1989.* (Budapest, Hungamer Kft., 1990)

Troncota, Cristian: *Istoria serviccilor secrete romanesti de la Cuza la Ceausescu.* (Bucuresti, Editura Ion Cristoiu S.A., 1999)

Tugoi, Pavel: *Istoria si limba in vremea lui Gheorghiu-Dej. Memorile unui fost sef de cabinet de Sectie a C.C. al PCR.* (Bucuresti, Editura Ion Cristoiu S.A., 1999)

Tusa, Gábor: *A székely vallási és tanügyi autonómia.* (Kolozsvár, Miverva, 1930)

Udrea, Traian: *Preliminarile semnarii conventiei de armistitiu intre Romania su Batiunile Unite.* In: *Revista de istorie,* Bucuresti, 1987, 8 nr.

Vaida-Voevod, Alexandru: *Chemarea catre tara.* (Bucuresti, 1935)

Vékony, Gábor: *Dákok, rómaiak, románok.* (Budapest, Akadémiai Kiadó, 1989)

Viorel, Tilea: *Románia diplomáciai muködése 1919 november-1920 március.* (Lugos, Magyar Kisebbség, 1926)

1956. Explozia. Perceptii romane, iugoslave si sovietice asupra evenimentelor din Polonia si Ungaria. Editie intocmita de Corenliu Mihai Lungu, Mihai retegan. Postfata de Florin Constantiniu. (Bucuresti, Editura Univers Enciclopedic, 1996)

9317